# The Canterbury Preacher's Companion 2010

# The Canterbury Preacher's Companion 2010

*Sermons for Sundays, Holy Days,*
*Festivals and Special Occasions*
*Year C*

## Michael Counsell

CANTERBURY
PRESS
Norwich

© Canterbury Press 2009

First published in 2008 by the Canterbury Press Norwich
Editorial office
13–17 Long Lane,
London, EC1A 9PN, UK

Canterbury Press is an imprint of Hymns Ancient and
Modern Ltd (a registered charity)
St Mary's Works, St Mary's Plain,
Norwich, NR3 3BH, UK

www.scm-canterburypress.co.uk

British Library Cataloguing in Publication data

A catalogue record for this book is available
from the British Library

Scripture quotations are mainly drawn from the New Revised
Standard Version Bible © 1989 by the Division of Christian
Education of the National Council of Churches of Christ in
the USA

Readings are from *Common Worship: Services and Prayers
for the Church of England*, which is copyright © The
Archbishops' Council 2000: extracts and
edited extracts are used by permission.
Readings for days not covered by that book are from
*Exciting Holiness*, second edition 2003, edited by Brother
Tristam, copyright © European Province of the Society of
Saint Francis, 1997, 1999, 2003, published by Canterbury
Press, Norwich; see www.excitingholiness.org

ISBN 978-1-85311-958-3

Typeset by Regent Typesetting, London
Printed in the UK by
CPI William Clowes Beccles NR34 7TL

# LIST OF ADVERTISERS

# Contents

Preface                                                      xvii

How to Choose Hymns                                          xviii

SUNDAYS

Unless otherwise stated, the readings and the verse numbers
of the psalms are taken from *Common Worship: Services and
Prayers for the Church of England* (Church House Publishing,
2000), with revisions, and are for Year C.

2009
Nov. 29   First Sunday of Advent, Year C, The Year of Luke
          *Principal Service: Rev. 6:2 Four horsemen*          1
          *Second Service: Joel 3:14 The valley of decision*   4

Dec. 6    Second Sunday of Advent
          *Principal Service: Luke 1:79*
          *The way of peace*                                   6
          *Second Service: Luke 1:14–15*
          *St Nicholas, the children's friend*                 9

Dec. 13   Third Sunday of Advent
          *Principal Service: Zeph. 3:19 AIDS*                 11
          *Second Service: Luke 1:78–79 Benedictus*            13

Dec. 20   Fourth Sunday of Advent
          *Principal Service: Luke 1:53*
          *Filling the hungry*                                 16
          *Second Service: Matt. 1:23 Who was Jesus?*          18

**Dec. 25**  **Christmas Day**
*Set I: Ps. 96:1 New-found happiness*          21
*Set II: Luke 2:8 People like us*              24
*Set III: John 1:14 Truly human*              26
*Second Service: Isa. 65:17 Recreation*        29

**Dec. 27**  **First Sunday of Christmas**
(St John the Evangelist)
*Principal Service: Col. 3:16*
  *The word of Christ*                         31
*St John the Evangelist: John 21:25*
  *Too many books*                             34

2010
**Jan. 3**  **Second Sunday of Christmas** (or Epiphany)
*Principal Service: Eph. 1:7–8 Redemption*     36
*Second Service: 1 John 4:11*
  *A virtuous circle*                          38

**Jan. 10**  **The Baptism of Christ** (First Sunday of
  Epiphany)
*Principal Service: Luke 3:15*
  *Filled with expectation*                    41
*Second Service: Ps. 46:10 Contemplation*      43

**Jan. 17**  **Second Sunday of Epiphany**
*Principal Service: John 2:11 Signs*           46
*Second Service: Eph. 4:14–16 Truthfulness*    48

**Jan. 24**  **Third Sunday of Epiphany**
(Week of Prayer for Christian Unity)
*Principal Service: Luke 2:14 Clearly displayed*  51
*Second Service: Num. 9:15 Transcendence*      53

**Jan. 31**  **Fourth Sunday of Epiphany** (or Candlemas)
*Principal Service: Ezek. 44:4*
  *His glory is his love*                      56
*Second Service: Acts 7:48 Why go to church?*  58

Feb. 7      Second Sunday before Lent
            *Principal Service: Gen. 2:8*
              *The Garden of Eden*                        60
            *Second Service: Matt. 6:30*
              *Learning from nature*                      63

Feb. 14     Sunday next before Lent
            *Principal Service: Luke 9:28*
              *Mountain-top experiences*                  66
            *Second Service: John 12:32*
              *When I am lifted up*                       68

Feb. 17     Ash Wednesday
            *Isa. 58:6 Miserable Lent or happy Lent?*     71

Feb. 21     First Sunday of Lent
            *Principal Service: Luke 4:1–2 Lead us not*   74
            *Second Service: Luke 18:9 Contempt*          77

Feb. 28     Second Sunday of Lent
            *Principal Service: Luke 13:34 Deliver us*    79
            *Second Service: Luke 14:31–32*
              *A Pyrrhic victory*                         82

Mar. 7      Third Sunday of Lent
            *Principal Service: Luke 13:1–2*
              *Suffering and sin*                         84
            *Second Service: John 1:29 The Lamb of God*   87

Mar. 14     Fourth Sunday of Lent
            (or Mothering Sunday)
            *Principal Service: Luke 15:18–19 Forgive us* 90
            *Mothering Sunday: Col. 3:12 Party clothes*   93

Mar. 21     Fifth Sunday of Lent
            *Principal Service: John 12:2 God's will*     96
            *Second Service: Luke 22:1–2*
              *The Passover Plot*                         98

Mar. 28    Palm Sunday
           *Principal Service: Luke 22:42 Gethsemane*    101
           *Second Service: Ps. 69:10 Passion*           103

Mar.       First Three Days in Holy Week
29–31      *Heb. 9.22 Blood*                             106

Apr. 1     Maundy Thursday
           *1 Cor. 11:23–24*
           *A sacrament to meet all needs*               108

Apr. 2     Good Friday
           *Isa. 53:5 Rigoletto*                         110

Apr. 3–4   Easter Vigil
           *Luke 24:5 Why seek the living among the*
           *dead?*                                       113

Apr. 4     Easter Day
           *Principal Service: Ps. 118:17 New life*      115
           *Second Service:*
               *John 20:27 The leap of faith*            118

Apr. 11    Second Sunday of Easter
           *Principal Service: John 20:29 Secularism*    120
           *Second Service: Luke 24:35 Odessa*           122

Apr. 18    Third Sunday of Easter
           *Principal Service: John 21:11*
               *153 fish*                                125
           *Second Service: Isa. 38:19 I nearly died*    127

Apr. 25    Fourth Sunday of Easter
           (St Mark the Evangelist)
           *Principal Service: John 10:30*
               *One, holy, catholic, apostolic*          130
           *St Mark the Evangelist: Mark 13:13*
               *Staying-power*                           132

| | | |
|---|---|---|
| May 2 | **Fifth Sunday of Easter** | |
| | *Principal Service: John 13:34–35* | |
| | *Love and acceptance* | 134 |
| | *Second Service: Mark 16:3–4* | |
| | *Who moved the stone?* | 137 |
| | | |
| May 9 | **Sixth Sunday of Easter** (Rogation Sunday) | |
| | *Principal Service: John 5:6* | |
| | *Do you want to change?* | 139 |
| | *Second Service: Zeph. 3:15* | |
| | *God is in your midst* | 142 |
| | | |
| May 13 | **Ascension Day** | |
| | *Matt. 28:20 The unseen presence* | 144 |
| | | |
| May 16 | **Seventh Sunday of Easter** | |
| | (Sunday after Ascension Day) | |
| | *Principal Service: John 17:20–21* | |
| | *That the world may believe* | 146 |
| | *Second Service: Eph. 4:12–13 Maturity* | 148 |
| | | |
| May 23 | **Day of Pentecost** (Whit Sunday) | |
| | *Principal Service: Acts 2:1–4* | |
| | *First-fruits of God's harvest* | 151 |
| | *Second Service: Ex. 33:11* | |
| | *God speaks face to face* | 153 |
| | | |
| May 30 | **Trinity Sunday** | |
| | *Principal Service: John 16:13–15* | |
| | *Faith transcends knowledge* | 156 |
| | *Second Service: Ps. 29:1 Give unto the Lord* | 158 |
| | | |
| June 6 | **First Sunday after Trinity** (Proper 5) | |
| | *Principal Service: Luke 7:15–16* | |
| | *Jesus and Elijah* | 161 |
| | *Second Service: Gen. 9:1 Ecology* | 163 |
| | | |
| June 13 | **Second Sunday after Trinity** (Proper 6) | |
| | *Principal Service: Gal. 2:16 Galatians* | 166 |
| | *Second Service: Mark 4:33–34 Stories* | 168 |

ix

| June 20 | **Third Sunday after Trinity** (Proper 7) | |
| | *Principal Service: Luke 8:29* | |
| | *Facing our inner demons* | 171 |
| | *Second Service: Gen. 24:15 Rebecca* | 173 |
| | | |
| June 27 | **Fourth Sunday after Trinity** (Proper 8) | |
| | *Principal Service: Gal. 5:22–23* | |
| | *Fruit of the Spirit* | 176 |
| | *Second Service: Mark 6:1–5 Vulnerability* | 178 |
| | | |
| July 4 | **Fifth Sunday after Trinity** (Proper 9) | |
| | *Principal Service: Gal. 6:14 Boasting* | 181 |
| | *Second Service: Mark 6:17 The Herod Mob* | 183 |
| | | |
| July 11 | **Sixth Sunday after Trinity** (Proper 10) | |
| | *Principal Service: Col. 1:7* | |
| | *Every-member ministry* | 187 |
| | *Second Service: Ps. 77:11 Memory* | 189 |
| | | |
| July 18 | **Seventh Sunday after Trinity** (Proper 11) | |
| | *Principal Service: Luke 10:38–39* | |
| | *Human biodiversity* | 191 |
| | *Second Service: Gen. 41:15–16* | |
| | *Any dream will do* | 194 |
| | | |
| July 25 | **Eighth Sunday after Trinity** (Proper 12) | |
| | (St James the Apostle) | |
| | *Principal Service: Luke 11:9–10 How to pray* | 196 |
| | *St James the Apostle: Acts 12:1–2 Compostella* | 199 |
| | | |
| Aug. 1 | **Ninth Sunday after Trinity** (Proper 13) | |
| | *Principal Service: Luke 12:20 Generosity* | 201 |
| | *Second Service: Gen. 50:9–11* | |
| | *A splendid funeral* | 203 |
| | | |
| Aug. 8 | **Tenth Sunday after Trinity** (Proper 14) | |
| | *Principal Service: Heb. 11:8* | |
| | *Faith is the compass* | 206 |
| | *Second Service: Isa. 11:10* | |
| | *An ensign for the nations* | 208 |

Aug. 15    Eleventh Sunday after Trinity (Proper 15)
           (The Blessed Virgin Mary)
           *Principal Service: Luke 12:51 Dividing families* 210
           *The Blessed Virgin Mary: Gal. 4:4–5*
             *Honouring mothers*                            213

Aug. 22    Twelfth Sunday after Trinity (Proper 16)
           *Principal Service: Heb. 12:22, 24 The mediator* 215
           *Second Service: Isa. 30:21 The sat-nav*         218

Aug. 29    Thirteenth Sunday after Trinity (Proper 17)
           *Principal Service: Luke 14:11*
             *Humble goodness*                              220
           *Second Service: John 3:29 The Best Man*         222

Sept. 5    Fourteenth Sunday after Trinity (Proper 18)
           *Principal Service: Philemon 15–16*
             *Slavery today*                                225
           *Second Service: John 5:39–40*
             *Search the Scriptures*                        227

Sept. 12   Fifteenth Sunday after Trinity (Proper 19)
           *Principal Service: Luke 15:3–4*
             *God the storyteller*                          230
           *Second Service: John 6:63*
             *You can't reason with them*                   232

Sept. 19   Sixteenth Sunday after Trinity (Proper 20)
           *Principal Service: 1 Tim. 2:1–2*
             *Politics and prayer*                          234
           *Second Service: Ezra 1:2 Ezra*                  237

Sept. 26   Seventeenth Sunday after Trinity (Proper 21)
           *Principal Service: Luke 16:31 Afterlife*        239
           *Second Service: John 8:32*
             *The truth will make you free*                 241

Oct. 3     Eighteenth Sunday after Trinity (Proper 22)
           *Principal Service: Luke 17:6*
             *Believe and you'll achieve*                   244
           *Second Service: John 9:7*
             *The pool which means 'sent'*                  246

Oct. 10    Nineteenth Sunday after Trinity (Proper 23)
           *Principal Service: Luke 17:14 Lepers*         248
           *Second Service: John 15:14 Aelred*           251

Oct. 17    Twentieth Sunday after Trinity (Proper 24)
           (Eve of St Luke the Evangelist)
           *Principal Service: 2 Tim. 3:15–16*
              *The Word of God*                          253
           *Second service: Neh. 8:18, 17*
              *Rejoicing in the law*                     256

Oct. 24    Last Sunday after Trinity (Proper 25)
           *Principal Service: 2 Tim. 4:7–8*
              *I finished the race*                      258
           *Second Service: Matt. 22:42 David's Son*     260

Oct. 31    All Saints' Sunday
           *Principal Service: Eph. 1:17–18 Whatever*
              *next?*                                    263

Oct. 31    Fourth Sunday before Advent
           *Principal Service: Isa. 1:18 Sins as scarlet*  265

Nov. 7     Third Sunday before Advent
           *Principal Service:*
              *Luke 20:38 Contemporary language*         267
           *Second Service:*
              *Rom. 8:39 The love of God in Christ*       270

Nov. 14    Second Sunday before Advent
           (Remembrance Sunday)
           *Principal Service: Ps. 98:1 The power of music*  272
           *Remembrance Sunday: Micah 4:3*
              *Does religion cause wars?*                275

Nov. 21    Christ the King
           *Principal Service: Luke 23:42*
              *When you are king*                        277
           *Second Service: 1 Sam. 8:18*
              *Charles, King and Martyr*                 280

xii

## SERMONS FOR SAINTS' DAYS AND
## SPECIAL OCCASIONS

Readings are from *Common Worship*, or from *Exciting Holiness* by Brother Tristam SSF, second edition, Canterbury Press, 2003.

**2009**

**Dec. 26**    St Stephen, Deacon, First Martyr
              *Acts 7:56 Reality*                                        284

**Dec. 27**    St John, Apostle and Evangelist (see First
              Sunday of Christmas, p. 34)                               286

**Dec. 28**    Holy Innocents
              *Jer. 31:15 When children die*                           286

**2010**

**Jan. 1**     Naming and Circumcision of Jesus
              *Luke 2:21 Hallowed be thy name*                         289

**Jan. 6**     Epiphany
              *Ps. 72:11 Kings bow down*                               291

**Jan.**       Week of Prayer for Christian Unity
**18–25**      *John 17:20 That they may be one*                       294

**Jan. 25**    Conversion of St Paul
              *Acts 9:18 Paul's priorities*                            296

**Feb. 2**     Presentation of Christ in the Temple
              (**Candlemas**, *or may be observed on
              Sunday Jan. 31) Ps. 24:7 Open the gates*                 298

**Mar. 1**     St David, Bishop of Menevia, Patron of Wales
              *Ps. 16:5 The Celtic Fringe*                             301

**Mar. 17**    St Patrick, Bishop, Missionary, Patron of
              Ireland
              *Matt. 10:16 Without loss of life*                       303

| | | |
|---|---|---|
| Mar. 19 | St Joseph of Nazareth<br>*Matt. 1:19 Cuckolded?* | 306 |
| Mar. 25 | Annunciation of Our Lord to the Blessed<br>Virgin Mary<br>*Luke 1:37 Nothing's impossible* | 308 |
| Apr. 23 | St George, Martyr, Patron of England<br>*Rev. 12:7 Myths and heroes* | 310 |
| Apr. 25 | St Mark the Evangelist (see Fourth<br>Sunday of Easter p. 132) | 312 |
| May 1 | SS Philip and James, Apostles<br>*John 14:8–9 No indispensable man* | 313 |
| May 14 | St Matthias the Apostle<br>*Acts 1:16–18 Suicide* | 315 |
| May 31 | Visit of the Blessed Virgin Mary to<br>Elizabeth<br>*Zeph. 3:14 The Music Makers* | 319 |
| June 3 | Day of Thanksgiving for the Institution<br>of Holy Communion (Corpus Christi)<br>*John 6:54 The banknote* | 322 |
| June 11 | St Barnabas the Apostle<br>*John 15:12–13 Barnabas the martyr* | 324 |
| June 24 | The Birth of John the Baptist<br>*Luke 1:76–77 Death row* | 327 |
| June 29 | SS Peter and Paul, Apostles<br>*Matt. 16:17–18 Institutions* | 329 |
| July 3 | St Thomas the Apostle<br>*John 20:25 The limits of science* | 331 |

| July 22 | St Mary Magdalene | |
| | *John 20:16 God knows you by name* | 334 |
| July 25 | St James the Apostle (see Eighth Sunday after Trinity, p. 199) | 336 |
| Aug. 6 | The Transfiguration of Our Lord | |
| | *Daniel 7:13 The Son of Man* | 336 |
| Aug. 15 | The Blessed Virgin Mary (see Eleventh Sunday after Trinity, p. 213) | 338 |
| Aug. 24 | St Bartholomew the Apostle | |
| | *Luke 22:29–30 A God with a mission* | 338 |
| Sept. 14 | Holy Cross Day | |
| | *Ps. 22:27 Empress Helena* | 341 |
| Sept. 21 | St Matthew, Apostle and Evangelist | |
| | *Ps. 119:72 Riches* | 343 |
| Sept. 29 | St Michael and All Angels | |
| | *Ps. 103:20 Heavenly worship* | 345 |
| Oct. 18 | St Luke the Evangelist | |
| | *Isa. 35:4 Do not fear!* | 347 |
| Oct. 28 | SS Simon and Jude, Apostles | |
| | *Acts 1:13 Zealot terrorists* | 350 |
| Nov. 1 | All Saints' Day | |
| | *Matt. 5:1–3 Beatitudes* | 352 |
| Nov. 2 | Commemoration of the Faithful Departed (All Souls' Day) | |
| | *John 5:25 Unchanging love* | 354 |
| Nov. 8 | Saints and Martyrs of (our own nation) | |
| | *Rev. 19:6–7 My native land* | 357 |

Nov. 30   **St Andrew the Apostle**
          *Matt. 4:18 Galilee*                          359

          **Sermon for Harvest Festival**
          *Ps. 100:4 Ethical eating*                     362

          **Sermon for a Wedding**
          *Mark 10:6–9 The wedding ring*                 364

          **Sermon for a Baptism or Christening**
          *2 Cor. 3:18 We are being transformed*         366

          **Sermon for a Funeral or Memorial
          Service**
          *John 11:35 How to grieve*                     369

*Scripture Index*                                        372
*Subject Index*                                          374
*Author Index*                                           378

# Caris

## a glossy lifestyle mag for girls aged 12-16

*Caris* features a fun mix of fashion, beauty, health, real-life stories, competitions, music, interviews, reviews, quizzes and advice PLUS campaigns, global issues, faith-based pages and much more! *Caris* is produced by Christians for Christian girls AND their non-Christian mates.

### Free copies!
If you have never seen *Caris* simply send for a free sample. See more about us at **www.carismag.co.uk**

### Discounts
Don't miss the next issue! Youth groups, churches, drop-in centres, schools workers and youth organisations can group order from just £1 per copy (incl p&p). Group subscription form also available online. Please quote CA10PC_1

*Make friends. Have fun. Feel good. Find passion. Be strong. Celebrate. Be inspired. Get creative. Enjoy life. Have hope. Be kind. Love God. Campaign. Make a difference.*

**www.carismag.co.uk**

# Preface

Preparing sermons can be an exhausting business. If you have little experience of preaching, reading one of these sermons aloud may carry you through until you gain the confidence to prepare your own. If your week has been so crowded that you have had no time to prepare a sermon of your own – and preparing a good sermon takes several hours – you may wish to read one of these to solve the emergency. If you have been preaching on the same text for years, and cannot think of anything fresh to say about it, this book may give you an idea for a new approach to a familiar subject. Then you can either rewrite it in your own words, or make notes from it and preach from notes; or prepare a completely new sermon but borrowing some of my jokes and illustrations. Sometimes you may even bang the table after reading one of my sermons, shouting 'I don't agree with that at all!' Then I shall have helped you by firing you up to preach a brilliant sermon, presenting the opposite point of view! In any of these ways, I hope this book may prove to be a useful tool for preachers.

But if you are someone who sits in the congregation and listens to sermons, and would like them to be more helpful, why not give a copy of this book to the preacher as a present, tactfully saying that you have enjoyed the sermons you have heard already, and you hope this book might give some helpful new ideas? Preachers cannot give a stimulating sermon if they are discouraged and bored. The listeners should give a word of encouragement from time to time, so that the preacher knows that somebody is listening, and the work which has been put into sermon preparation has been worth it.

*Michael Counsell*

# How to Choose Hymns

Singing hymns during a church service should be an enjoyable experience for everybody, whether they are very musical or only slightly so (whatever they say, nobody is completely unmusical). If they come away from a service frustrated because they didn't like any of the hymns which were chosen, the blame may lie with whoever's task it was to choose the hymns to be sung at that service, but it is far more likely to be the fault of the grumbler, who is unprepared to work at learning new hymns, or exploring unfamiliar types of music. We should remember that there are other people present who may have completely different tastes from ours, and they, too, need to be helped to enjoy the service. Nobody can please all of the people all of the time. Whatever that strange phrase in the Bible, 'the sacrifice of praise', meant when it was first written, it is a very good description of a modern worshipper who gives up demanding to have their own way all the time, and is willing to sing something they don't really enjoy for the sake of others. Remember, there are some who have been singing the same few hymns for years, and are thoroughly bored by them, so most congregations need to be slowly introduced to a wider selection.

The tunes used for the hymns, and the styles of music used in church, are vexed questions, though a lot of argument could be avoided if worshippers would not selfishly demand what *they* like, ignoring what may be inspiring for others. But with words, as with tunes, it is important to retain a core repertoire of familiar hymns, without repeating them too frequently, and introduce less familiar or new material, perhaps no more than one new hymn at any service, and that not every week. Yet the new material should be repeated quite soon after its first introduction, so that the congregation may become familiar with it. Soon they will begin to describe as 'the good old familiar hymns' words and music which have only been introduced quite recently!

*The Canterbury Preacher's Companion* lists four suggested hymns, in alphabetical order, after each sermon. They have been carefully chosen to relate to the subject of the sermon. This is the only place I know of where you can find such a close correlation between the words of the hymns and the topic that is preached on. Worshippers often comment on how the words of a particular hymn have helped them understand the sermon, or reinforced its message, by their appropriateness – or vice versa. But the caveat above applies here: no more than one set of unfamiliar words or music at any one service.

So the basis of the choice will be to find a wider selection based on the season and on all the readings set for that service. Most hymn books have an index of hymns listed by their relevance to particular themes or to certain passages of Scripture, or both, and this is probably the first place to go when you know what the Bible readings are going to be. *Common Praise* is the only hymn book I know of so far which lists suggested hymns for the Principal Service for each Sunday, according to the readings in the Common Worship lectionary of the Church of England. Common Worship is based on, but is not identical with, the *Revised Common Lectionary*. The RCL is the selection of Bible Readings used in the Roman Catholic Missal, the Book of Common Prayer of the American Episcopal Church and some other parts of the Anglican Communion, and in many Lutheran and Methodist churches. The Church of England made a number of modifications; notably Sundays following Pentecost Sunday, which have Collects and Post-Communion Prayers according to the number of Sundays after Trinity, but readings according to the days of the month, called 'Proper 4' and so on; whereas the RCL lists the Sundays of the Year in Ordinary Time. There are also differences in the Sundays following Candlemas and All Saints respectively. Both lectionaries have a three-year cycle of readings, with Gospel readings mostly from Matthew in Year A, Mark in Year B, and Luke in Year C at the Principal Service. *The Canterbury Preacher's Companion* lists and is based on the Common Worship lectionary, but the Scripture index at the end of this book could help anyone who is preaching on readings chosen on any other basis.

Canterbury Press published in 2007–2008 two books which are invaluable for those who choose hymns. The first was a Revised Expanded Edition of *Sing God's Glory*. This lists a wide selection of hymns based on all the readings of the Common Worship lectionary at the Principal Service on Sundays, Principal Feasts and Holy

Days, and special occasions, with reference to more than fourteen different hymn books. With the help of this, it is easy to choose a selection of hymns that will illuminate the readings for any particular service, whatever hymnal or hymnals are used at your church. The other book which will also be invaluable is called *Sunday by Sunday* and does the same thing for the readings at the Second Service on each Sunday, together with suggested choral music, songs for children and organ voluntaries.

But when it comes to choosing hymns for saints' days, whether they are celebrated on a weekday or a Sunday, there is no alternative, so far as I know, to *The Canterbury Preacher's Companion*. There are very few hymns written especially for a particular saint's day. But for each of what Common Worship calls the Festivals, plus the Patron Saints of the British Isles, you will find here after the sermon, four suggested hymns appropriate to the day. They are not the same year after year, so if you save your copies of this book each year, you will soon have a selection of suitable hymns to choose from.

Canterbury Press publishes hymn books in the well-known *New English Hymnal, Hymns Ancient and Modern, Common Praise* and *Irish Presbyterian Hymn Book* series. In addition in 2008 they published *Hymns of Glory, Songs of Praise*, which is *The Church Hymnary* edition 4 for general use. See www.canterburypress.co.uk

It can be inspiring to use hymns from a variety of sources; but remember, if you want to photocopy copyright material, or use it on a projector, you need to get a licence from Christian Copyright Licensing (Europe) Ltd. See www.ccli.co.uk.

I admit that I am one of those who came to church music first, and was led by that to an encounter with God in Christ. So I believe that choosing hymns is important. I also find it hugely enjoyable.

# Could you be vicar of this parish?

The RAF needs full-time and part-time Chaplains to take the church to where it's needed most. As an RAF Chaplain you'll be responsible for all our personnel, regardless of rank or religious background. Your personal sacrifice may be considerable as you move with troops and air-crew, providing vital support in areas of conflict, including on the front line. Your non-operational duties will be equally important as you bring spiritual succour to personnel at our RAF bases. And as well as offering counsel, mediation and advice, you will fulfil more traditional roles, holding weekly services and officiating at weddings, christenings and funerals. If you're ready for a challenging, highly rewarding position, contact us now. A whole new congregation awaits you.

Text CHAPLAIN followed by your email address to 88RAF (88723)
rafcareers.com

The Royal Air Force values every individual's unique contribution, irrespective of race, ethnic origin, religion, gender, sexual orientation or social background. Usual network charges apply.

# YEAR C, the Year of Luke

*(Year C begins on Advent Sunday in 2009, 2012, 2015, etc.)*

---

**ADVENT**

*Advent, consisting of the four Sundays leading up to Christmas, is a penitential season. Altar frontals and vestments are therefore purple (except that the Third Sunday in Advent may be rose), and there is an air of solemnity in the services. 'Glory to God in the highest' is often omitted. 'Advent' means 'coming'; there is a sense of eager expectancy looking forward to the coming of Christ into the world at Christmas, but singing Christmas carols during Advent – except in carol services – robs us of the chance to enjoy some splendid Advent music, and could bring a sense of anticlimax when Christmas comes. We also celebrate the coming of Jesus into our lives daily, at our death, and at the end of the world. Traditional themes for sermons on the four Sundays are Death, Judgement, Heaven and Hell. Candles can be lit, mounted on an Advent wreath, one on the first Sunday, two on the second, and so on, leading up to five on Christmas Eve.*

---

## First Sunday of Advent   29 November 2009
### *Principal Service*   **Four Horsemen**

Jer. 33:14–16 A King is promised; Ps. 25:1–9 Waiting for God; 1 Thess. 3:9–13 Prayer to be blameless at the coming of Christ; Luke 21:25–36 The coming of Christ

> *'I looked, and there was a white horse! Its rider had a bow; a crown was given to him, and he came out conquering and to conquer.' Revelation 6:2*

I

## Four horsemen of the Apocalypse

In the sixth chapter of the book of Revelation there's a description of four men riding on different coloured horses; they symbolize God's judgement. Another name for the book of Revelation is 'The Apocalypse', so these figures are often called the Four Horsemen of the Apocalypse. Don't confuse the word with Acropolis, which is the name of a hill in Athens. In the early twentieth century the British Ambassador's wife in Athens was a somewhat frightening person, with three equally awesome friends who made up a four at bridge with her. They were known to the rest of the community as the Four Horsewomen of the Acropolis!

## Justice

The message of the last book in the Bible is that God is a God of justice, and ultimately justice will triumph, either in time or eternity. Now, if you're a victim of injustice, that's good news. One day all wrongs will be righted, and faithfulness to God will be rewarded. If, on the other hand, you're a perpetrator of injustice, the message of God's judgement is very bad news for you. It tells you that sooner or later you'll be punished for all the harm that you've caused other people. But the people of the world aren't divided into good and bad people like cowboys in black and white hats. All of us are a complete mixture. Basically good-natured and well-meaning, we often do selfish things which harm other people, often without realizing what we've done. The Bible reminds us that we can't just shrug this off; we've got to take responsibility for our own actions. This is the teaching of the season of Advent: Advent means 'coming', and we think about Jesus coming into the world at Bethlehem, and coming to each one of us as our judge.

## Symbols

So what do the four horsemen represent? Basically, they're symbols for some of the ways in which God's judgement comes to us. The usual interpretation goes like this:

- The first horseman rides on a white horse. In several other places in the Revelation, Jesus is described as riding a white horse; so the first horseman represents Christ.
- The second rider's on a red horse, and represents war: 'its rider

2

was permitted to take peace from the earth, so that people would slaughter one another.'
- The third horseman, on a black horse, represents famine: 'I heard ... a voice ... saying, "A quart of wheat for a day's pay, and three quarts of barley for a day's pay".'
- The fourth horseman rides a pale horse. It represents pestilence and epidemic disease.

I want to talk about each of these on the Sundays of Advent this year.

## Modern parallels

Although the words are old-fashioned, the problems they refer to are very contemporary: people ignoring Jesus; a world torn apart by warfare; starvation in the Third World, or due to global warming; and epidemic diseases like AIDS. The media are full of these things, and burying our heads in the sand's no way to deal with the threat.

## Judgement

But dare we speak of AIDS, climate change and terrorism as God's judgement on a wicked world? Surely to talk of a God who causes innocent people to suffer and die because other people have sinned, isn't the way Jesus described his loving heavenly Father! These things aren't caused by an arbitrary god throwing down thunderbolts; they're caused by human beings behaving in a sinful, selfish way. Everybody shares a little of the guilt, because we do nothing about carbon emissions, or promoting fair trade and a more equal distribution of wealth. We judge ourselves, and punish ourselves. But the mother who's been given a blood transfusion infected by the HIV virus isn't being punished by God; she's suffering for other people's selfishness.

## Forgiveness

War, disease and hunger, three of the horsemen of the Apocalypse, are the result of our misuse of the freedom that God has granted us. Jesus said, 'This is the judgement, that the light has come into the world, and people loved darkness rather than light because their deeds were evil.' It's good that we have four Sundays in Advent to remind us of our corporate responsibility. But we have with us Jesus, the rider on the white horse, who'll help us to conquer the evil in the world, if we let him, and bring us all to live with him in eternity, if we repent.

### All-age worship

*Draw the four horsemen. What can you do to overcome AIDS, terrorism and climate change?*

### Suggested hymns

*Judge eternal, throned in splendour; O come, O come Emmanuel; O Lord, the clouds are gathering; Sleepers wake.*

## First Sunday of Advent
### *Second Service*   The Valley of Decision
Ps. 9 The Lord judges the world; Joel 3:9–21 The Valley of Decision; Rev. 14:13—15:4 Blessed are the dead; *Gospel at Holy Communion*: John 3:1–17 Nicodemus

> *'Multitudes, multitudes, in the valley of decision! For the day of the LORD is near in the valley of decision.' Joel 3:14*

### Locusts

Huge swarms of locusts, a type of grasshopper, still sweep across Africa today, darkening the sky in their millions, and eating every form of plant life in the space of a few hours. The people starve in the areas where this happens. They are rightly called 'a plague of locusts', as many people die when a swarm has landed, and the country will take years to recover economically.

### Joel

Plagues of locusts descended on the land of Judah, not once, but two years running, at the time the book of Joel was written. The prophet describes it graphically: 'Before them the land is like the garden of Eden, but after them a desolate wilderness, and nothing escapes them.' Joel calls the people to repent, and promises that if they do, God will restore their prosperity. But at the same time, Judah was being invaded by foreign armies, and Joel compares the troops devastating the population to the locusts who'd passed that way shortly before:

What are you to me, O Tyre and Sidon, and all the regions of Philistia? . . . For you have taken my silver and my gold, and have carried my rich treasures into your temples. You have sold the people of Judah and Jerusalem to the Greeks, removing them far from their own border.

So God promises to judge the foreign nations, and restore Judah's prosperity: 'Let the nations rouse themselves, and come up to the valley of Jehoshaphat; for there I will sit to judge all the neighboring nations.'

## Jehoshaphat

Jehoshaphat was one of the kings of Judah, who gave his name to one of the valleys south of Jerusalem, either the Kidron Valley or the Valley of Hinnom. But the name means 'The Lord judges', and it's used here to symbolize God's eternal judgement on the world. The prophet promises that God will pronounce a guilty verdict on all warmongers, and those who use violent means to get their own way in the world, who descend on the ordinary people like a plague of locusts. For a while, the people will suffer, but then God will restore the prosperity of the land, and pour on them the Holy Spirit. But God will only remove the oppressors if the people repent: 'Blow the trumpet in Zion; sanctify a fast; call a solemn assembly; gather the people.' The Old Testament hasn't got as far yet as the promise of Jesus, that everybody can be forgiven if they truly repent. But Joel makes it quite clear that genuine repentance is essential. There can be no indecisive hovering; there must be a clear decision that you're on the Lord's side. 'Multitudes, multitudes, in the valley of decision,' says Joel. 'For the day of the LORD is near in the valley of decision.'

## The valley of decision

Sadly, when things are going well, many people forget about God altogether. It's only when disaster, plague or loss happens to us that we realize the importance of turning back to the Lord. Have you

5

made up your mind which side you're on? There can be no neutrals in the struggle between good and evil.

- Maybe you gave your life to the Lord many years ago, but love has gone cold. Then you need to decide all over again that obeying Jesus is the most important thing in your life.
- Maybe you haven't quite made up your mind about the claims of Christ yet. You can't go on for ever being a 'Don't know' in the great opinion poll of life, or one day you may find it's too late. If you haven't put Jesus in charge of your life yet, then now's the time. Get down on your knees now and say silently, 'Jesus, I want you to forgive my sin, take charge of my life, and help me to live it to your glory.' Then come up and tell me after the service that that's what you've done.
- Maybe you suspect preachers of putting too much emotional pressure on people to decide before they've thought through what they're doing. But even a provisional conversion or a partial conversion's better than nothing; you can always renew and deepen your commitment later.

Are you one of the multitudes in the valley of decision? If so, decide now, or renew the promises you made earlier, or at least decide to study carefully what Jesus is asking of you, and talk to somebody in the coming week about what conversion means. 'For the day of the LORD is near in the valley of decision.'

### Suggested hymns

*All for Jesus, all for Jesus; I want to walk with Jesus Christ; O Jesus, I have promised; Who is on the Lord's side?*

## Second Sunday of Advent   6 December
### *Principal Service*   The Way of Peace
Bar. 5 God will lead his people with joy; *or* Mal. 3:1–4 A messenger to prepare the way; *Canticle*: Luke 1:68–79 Benedictus; Phil. 1:3–11 Overflowing love; Luke 3:1–6 John the Baptist

*'To guide our feet into the way of peace.' Luke 1:79*

## The way of peace

Zechariah sang the song we call the Benedictus when his son John the Baptist was born. John prepared for the coming of Jesus, and Zechariah rejoiced that God would now 'guide our feet into the way of peace'. Yet peace on earth seems even more unattainable now than it was then. Did God fail to guide us correctly, or did we fail to follow his guidance? Revelation chapter 6 describes 'the Four Horsemen of the Apocalypse', and I want to talk about each of them on the Sundays of Advent. The second is described as 'Another horse, bright red; its rider was permitted to take peace from the earth, so that people would slaughter one another; and he was given a great sword.'

Tragically, the weapons that people use to slaughter each other now are much deadlier than those used in Bible days. Suicide bombers are weapons against which there's no defence. Their object is to die, so shooting them doesn't defeat them. Excellent intelligence services may be able to anticipate the bombers and arrest them before they set their bombs off. Yet we all live in fear that sooner or later a terrorist will slip through the net. Which, of course, is just what terrorists want: their object is not just to kill a number of innocent civilians: they chiefly want the whole population to live in an atmosphere of terror – that's why we call them terrorists. So how does God guide us into the way of peace in the post-9/11 world?

## Swords into ploughshares

Terrorism needs to be discussed in church. Wars are caused by sin, and Jesus is involved with us in a battle against evil and sin. So Christians should use whatever wisdom God has given us to bring wars to an end. We must beat swords into ploughshares.

## The war on terror

The problem with the war on terror is that it has no clear target. Every other war starts with an enemy army; you know roughly where they are, and you go to the front line and defeat them. The only way to deal with terrorists is to work out what their motives are, and remove the motivation. High on that list is the desire for revenge for the wrongs that they perceive have been committed by us and our allies against them and their people. Terrorists hope that by reducing us to a quaking fear, they'll force us to withdraw from the land which, as they see it, we have illegally occupied. They're certainly wrong about that, but we'll never defeat terrorists unless we understand what they want.

## Popular support

There's nothing new in terrorist tactics. The first terrorists were the Jewish Zealots, who, around the time of Jesus, would go up to the Roman soldiers in the crowd and stab them with a dagger concealed in their clothes. Amazingly, a former Zealot was one of the twelve apostles. The Zealots succeeded because there was a sympathetic crowd to hide among. Terrorists only stop when they lose the support of the 'moderates' among their people. The only way to defeat them is to ask why the crowd supports them.

## Grievances

As soon as you say that, someone howls that you're condoning what the terrorists do. On the contrary, nothing can justify the taking of innocent life. But the terrorists would soon be handed over by the moderates if they had nothing to grumble about. So we should ask, 'What have we and our allies done to the nations from which the terrorists come?' At the very least, we have a much higher standard of living than most of the ordinary people in those nations, and we've done almost nothing about sharing out our wealth more fairly. Loving our neighbours includes caring for those who live in other nations.

## Loving our enemies

Jesus did in fact guide our feet into the way of peace, when he told us to love our enemies. It's easy to say, but we haven't yet learnt to do it. It doesn't mean condoning violence, but it does include removing the perceived grievances which make even moderates support terrorists. Only so will the red horseman of war cease trampling over the earth.

### All-age worship

*Draw a poster about making swords into ploughshares, headed 'Love Your Enemies'.*

## Suggested hymns

*And did those feet?; God is working his purpose out; Lord of Lords and King eternal; Peace, perfect peace.*

# Second Sunday of Advent
## *Second Service*   St Nicholas, the Children's Friend
Ps. 75 I will judge [76 To save the oppressed]; Isa. 40:1–11
Comfort my people; Luke 1:1–25 John's birth foretold

> *'You will have joy and gladness, and many will rejoice at his birth, for he will be great in the sight of the Lord.' Luke 1:14–15*

### The tomb of St Nicholas

Demre is on the West Mediterranean coast of Turkey. In ancient times it was named Myra, from the myrrh spice traded there; it was the port where most of the grain boats from Egypt called after their voyage across the open sea, to take advantage of the shelter of the Greek islands for the rest of their journey to Rome. No visit to Myra is complete without seeing, in a church protected by an ugly iron roof near the centre of Demre, the tomb of Saint Nicholas, who was Bishop of Myra in the fourth century AD. Because Myra was an important port, he became the patron saint of sailors, and the tomb's empty because most of his bones were stolen by Italian seamen from Bari. In Myra, three girls in one poor family couldn't get married because they couldn't afford the dowry. They were about to be sold as slaves instead when, one night, Bishop Nicholas secretly threw three bags of gold into their house for the dowry money. This story gave rise to the three gold balls of the pawnbroker's sign, and the European custom of giving presents to children on St Nicholas' day, December 6. The story of St Nicholas and the presents was developed by Clement Clarke Moore in his poem *'Twas the night before Christmas*, published anonymously in the Troy Sentinel in New York in 1823. He chose the Dutch form of the name and called him Santa Claus; a road sign outside Demre reads 'Father Christmas 1, Myra 3'. But historically, the original Santa Claus was a compassionate Christian bishop, with a special affection for children.

## The children's festival

As we prepare for Christmas, we're reminded constantly that this is the children's festival. It celebrates the birth of baby Jesus in Bethlehem, and the magi brought him gifts. The origins of the modern celebration are in the story of Bishop Nicholas, who gave gifts to children. For adults, it can easily degenerate into an orgy of self-indulgence, unless they try to concentrate their efforts into making some child or children happy. There's only one thing more beautiful than the expression of expectation on the face of children as they unwrap long-hoped-for presents, and that's the expression of awe and wonder on the face a child looking at a Christmas crib, and hearing for the first time the story of the birth of the child who came to earth to love us. Advent serves a useful purpose in arousing a sense of joyful expectation in all of us. You may think that some children are over-indulged today with over-expensive presents, but anything which helps them to learn and grow brings them a blessing, and sets them an example of the virtue of generosity from an early age.

## Jesus and the children

It's right that we should concentrate on the children. Not only are they the Church of tomorrow, they're important members of the Church today, in their own right. Some Christians try to exclude them from our church services, because they're a distraction. But Jesus would have none of that. Jesus has no message for any one of us, unless it's for all of us, including the children. Parents used to bring their small children to Jesus, for him to bless them, and his disciples tried to protect him and whoosh them away, so that he could concentrate on more important people. But Jesus gave the disciples a good telling-off for their prejudice. 'Let the little children come to me,' he said, 'don't try and stop them; for it's to such as these that the kingdom of God belongs.' Children are important citizens of God's realm, in their own right. 'Jesus loves the little children,' we used to sing, 'all the children of the world.' So did St Nicholas; so should we, for Jesus's sake.

## *Suggested hymns*

*Away in a manger; It is a thing most wonderful; Lully, lulla; Once in royal David's city.*

## Third Sunday of Advent   13 December
*Principal Service*   **AIDS**

Zeph. 3:14–20 God in your midst; *Canticle*: Isa. 12:2–6 Great
in your midst; *or* Ps. 14:4–10 Justice; Phil. 4:4–7 Rejoice in the
Lord; Luke 3:7–18 John the Baptist's witness

*'I will save the lame and gather the outcast, and I will change their
shame into praise and renown in all the earth.' Zephaniah 3:19*

### Statistics

About 40 million people around the world now carry the HIV virus,
which leads to AIDS; the number increases by nearly 5 million a
year, or one every eight seconds. Over 3 million people die of AIDS
each year, about half of them women and children. More than half
of the people infected with HIV live in sub-Saharan Africa. Probably between 40,000 and 120,000 people in Britain have the virus.

### Why discuss AIDS?

AIDS is one of the cruellest killers of the modern age, and its sufferers deserve our deepest compassion. But why should we mention
AIDS in a sermon? To do so means using the word S E X, which
many people think shouldn't be pronounced in church. But to
ignore AIDS would be ignoring our Lord's command to love our
neighbours – burying our heads in the sand makes us complicit in
the slaughter. The book of Revelation describes a rider on a pale-
green horse, killing by means of pestilence, an old word for epidemic
disease. AIDS is the epidemic galloping across the earth today.

### What is AIDS?

The HIV virus doesn't kill people; it attacks their immune system,
the body's natural defence against disease; when that's gone, the
patient has AIDS, and is vulnerable to every infection. HIV can only
be passed on by exchange of body fluids from an infected person to
another. A small proportion are drug addicts using infected needles;
in a few tragic cases, infected blood transfusions are the source. The
vast majority are infected by sexual intercourse. It scarcely matters
how or with whom this takes place, but those who have multiple
partners are the most likely to catch it.

## Prevention and cure

Condoms cut the infection rate, but even so, a quarter of those whose partners are HIV-positive, and who always use so-called 'safe sex', nevertheless become infected. The virus was first recognized in the USA among homosexuals. Now the vast majority in Africa and around the world are heterosexual users of prostitutes, and their partners and children. If a mother's infected when she gives birth, her child will usually die of AIDS within a few years. No cure for AIDS or the HIV virus has yet been discovered, though retro-viral drugs delay the onset of AIDS. Heart-breaking photos show children in an African orphanage, both of whose parents have died of AIDS, and who only have a short life-expectancy themselves.

## How to stop it spreading?

So is there anything we can do to stop AIDS spreading? Providing free condoms would help, but only slightly, because in Africa many people's homes are far away from suppliers, and the patterns of family life make it hard to use them. The only way is to change people's way of life away from multiple partners. Women become prostitutes because that's the only way to avoid starvation. Men use them because the mobility of labour takes them far from their families. Gay people are discouraged from forming faithful partnerships by their rejection from mainstream society. People are prevented from forming deep and lasting relationships by the economic and social patterns which we've all played a part in setting up.

## A punishment?

This isn't helped when Christians describe AIDS as a punishment sent by God. What sort of God would cause an orphan child to die to punish his or her dead parents? Some Christians describe God surrendering his omnipotence when he creates a world independent of him, and human beings with free will. The cross shows us that even if God can't prevent our suffering, he shares it with us.

## What can Christians do?

So what can we, as Christians, do about AIDS?

- We can support medical workers who care for AIDS sufferers, and we can provide affordable drugs.

- We can teach people that the Bible condemns people who are forced into an irregular way of life, far less than the people who judge and reject them.
- We can challenge those Christians who totally reject contraception, faithful but irregular partnerships, and gay people. By their words they conceal the God of universal love behind a mask of condemnation.
- We can offer genuine friendship and support to neighbours with HIV and AIDS.
- We can encourage others to form deep, lasting and unselfish partnerships, whatever their orientation.
- Finally, we can pray for the outcast people of our society.

God says, 'I will save the lame and gather the outcast, and I will change their shame into praise and renown in all the earth.'

### All-age worship

*Find out about AIDS orphanages in Africa.*

### Suggested hymns

*From thee all skill and science flow; God of mercy, God of grace; Immortal love, for ever full; The King is among us.*

## Third Sunday of Advent
### Second Service   Benedictus
Ps. 50:1–6 Our God comes [62 Wait for God in silence]; Isa. 35 Here is your God; Luke 1:57–66 The birth of the Baptist [67–80 Benedictus]

> 'By the tender mercy of our God, the dawn from on high will break upon us, to give light to those who sit in darkness and in the shadow of death, to guide our feet into the way of peace.' Luke 1:78–79

### Is it time to wake up yet?

I wonder how many children will burst into their parents' bedroom at some unearthly hour on Christmas morning and bounce all over

13

them, knocking all the breath out of them, and with it any chance of ever getting back to sleep? 'Is it time to wake up yet?' chime the children. 'No it isn't,' growl the grown-ups. 'It's only about – goodness – four o'clock. Go back to sleep.' And of course they won't, any more than their parents will, because Christmas Day morning is so eagerly awaited. Ah, the price of parenthood!

## The dawn

This eagerness for morning was known to all the biblical writers. The Psalmist sang:

> My soul waits for the Lord,
> more than the night watch for the morning,
> more than the night watch for the morning.

If you were a sentry on the city walls, you waited for 'the roseate hues of early dawn' to tell you that your period on duty was coming to an end. If you were a nomad in the desert, you watched for the 'morning star', the planet Venus which is so bright that it can still be seen when the sun's growing light has made all dimmer stars invisible. 'Now ends our waiting, now we can travel, now life begins afresh.' According to St Luke, Zechariah, the father of John the Baptist, looked forward to the birth of the Messiah like that: 'By the tender mercy of our God,' he sang,

> the dawn from on high will break upon us,
> to give light to those who sit in darkness and in the shadow of death,
> to guide our feet into the way of peace.

## The Benedictus

These words come in a great poem which Zechariah sang after the birth of his son, John the Baptist. You remember? He'd been struck dumb for having doubted the angel's promise, and after he named his newborn offspring 'John' his power of speech was returned to him, and he came out with these words:

> Blessed be the Lord the God of Israel,
> who has come to his people and set them free.

When sung at Morning Prayer this remarkable hymn is called 'the Benedictus', from the first word of the old Latin translation. There are many theories about who else might have written it, which needn't concern us. If the old priest Zechariah did compose it, he'd had nine months without talking, to polish his poetry.

## The dawn of a new age

The Benedictus has as much to say about Jesus, the 'mighty Saviour, born of the house of his servant David', as it has about his cousin John, who 'will go before the Lord to prepare his way'. The birth of the Messiah was awaited by the prophets of the Old Testament even more eagerly than Christmas Day morning is longed for by children today. That's because it really did bring in the dawn of a new age. Until that first Christmas, God had been a distant judge, and to avoid offending God you had to obey a complicated set of rules. Now, God's as close to us as the baby in the manger, and all we need to do is respond to God's love by loving him in return. Before the birth of Jesus, death was something to be dreaded; now, death is the gateway to eternal life. The poet Richard Crashaw calls the baby Jesus the 'young dawn of our eternal day!' He wrote:

> Gloomy night embrac'd the place
> Where the Noble Infant lay;
> The Babe look'd up and show'd his face,
> In spite of darkness, it was day.
> It was thy day, Sweet! and did rise
> Not from the east, but from thine eyes . . .
> We saw thee in thy balmy nest,
> Young dawn of our eternal day!
> We saw thine eyes break from their east
> And chase the trembling shades away.

Everything's changed because Christmas has dawned. We've begun a new life; a life which never ends, but leads on into eternity. Knowing that, who wouldn't be eager for Christmas Day to dawn?

## *Suggested hymns*

*In a world where people walk in darkness; O come, O come Emmanuel; The people that in darkness sat; Wake, O wake! With tidings thrilling ('Sleepers wake' or other translations of 'Wachet auf!').*

## Fourth Sunday of Advent  20 December
*Principal Service*   **Filling the Hungry**

Micah 5:2–5a A leader from Bethlehem; *Canticle*: Magnificat
Luke 1:46–55; *or* Ps. 80:1–8 Come with salvation; Heb. 10:5–10
When Christ came into the world; Luke 1:39–45 [46–55] Mary
visits Elizabeth

> '[God] has filled the hungry with good things, and sent the rich
> away empty.' Luke 1:53

### What's Christmas about?

In 1984 Bob Geldof's Band Aid sang 'Do they know it's Christmas?' He showed film of starving people in the developing nations,
and brought home to many people for the first time the obscenity of
celebrating Christmas by huge expenditure on food and drink and
so on, while millions in the Third World lack the basic necessities
for keeping themselves alive. This jolts us with the realization that
celebrating Christmas isn't about extravagant self-indulgence: it's
about Jesus and the message which he brought of love for all our
neighbours.

### Social justice

Certainly the birth of the Redeemer brings us personal happiness
and the joy of knowing that God loves us. But Jesus's mother Mary
reminded us, when she sang the song we call the Magnificat, that
it's also about social justice: '[God] has filled the hungry with good
things, and sent the rich away empty.' Christmas is *principally*
about what we can do to right the world's inequalities by feeding
the hungry.

### Starvation

You've heard the statistics many times, though by now these figures
may be out of date:

- In the Asian, African and Latin American countries, well over
  500 million people are living in what the World Bank has called
  'absolute poverty'.
- Every year 15 million children die of hunger, or one every two
  seconds.

16

- Those deaths could be prevented for what the world spends on its military in two days.
- The World Health Organization estimates that one-third of the world is well fed, one-third is under-fed, and one-third is starving.

Unless your conscience has been numbed by compassion fatigue, we can't escape concern for our needy world at Christmas time. The irony is that, up until recently, the food was there to feed everybody, it just wasn't being distributed fairly.

## Global warming

But in recent years a new cause for starvation has emerged, and that's global warming. Nomadic people in East Africa move with their cattle to find land where rain has fallen. But in the last 30–40 years droughts have become more frequent, and there's been virtually no rain there since 1999. The Sahara isn't the only desert to spread, destroying land which up till now's supported life. At the same time temperatures have been rising slowly but inexorably all over the world. This could be a natural periodic variation, but that seems unlikely. Many people believe it's caused by the increasing amounts of oxygen released in the atmosphere from fires, cars, generators and aeroplanes, and by cutting down forests.

## Gambling with the future

We can't yet prove whether global warming's natural or caused by human activity. If it's because of carbon emissions, then doing nothing about it will result in the deaths of millions by the spread of deserts and the rise of sea levels. Millions more will try to flee the nations we've destroyed and settle in our own lands where there's plenty, and we shan't be able to keep them out. If there are two options, one of which – doing nothing – will destroy millions of lives, and the other – reducing emissions – will cause a little inconvenience, there's really no choice. It's our children's future we're gambling with.

## Big reforms and small gestures

The main causes of pollution are the smoky chimneys of newly industrialized countries, and air travel. There's little you and I can do about that, though we could vote for politicians who will. But small gestures like using energy-efficient light bulbs, and cycling to work, at least show the world that we take the problem seriously – that we're willing to make sacrifices for the sake of our grandchildren.

## Ignoring Christmas

Worldwide famine's predicted in the book of Revelation:

> I looked, and there was a black horse! Its rider held a pair of scales in his hand, and I heard . . . a voice . . . saying, 'A quart of wheat for a day's pay, and three quarts of barley for a day's pay.'

But Mary promised that the birth of her son Jesus would lead his followers into abolishing famine: '[God] has filled the hungry with good things, and sent the rich away empty.' This Christmas, think about it, and make up your mind to do your bit towards filling the hungry with good things.

### All-age worship

*Make posters about world hunger and global warming.*

### Suggested hymns

*From heaven you came; Hark, the glad sound; Tell out, my soul; Thou who wast rich beyond all splendour.*

## Fourth Sunday of Advent
### Second Service    Who was Jesus?

Ps. 123 As a maid looks to her mistress [131 My soul is like a weaned child]; Isa. 10:33—11:10 A shoot from the stump of Jesse; Matt. 1:18–25 Joseph and the angel

> *'"Look, the virgin shall conceive and bear a son, and they shall name him Emmanuel", which means, "God is with us."' Matthew 1:23*

## Arundel

We're about to celebrate the birth of Jesus of Nazareth, but who was he? In the lovely town of Arundel, on the south coast of England, stands Arundel Castle, the home of the Roman Catholic Dukes of Norfolk. The chapel is half inside and half outside the walls; the inside bit's used by Roman Catholics, and the outside half is Church of England. But there's another Roman Catholic church in Arundel, the Cathedral. In the Cathedral's leaflet rack there's a paper which makes a very good answer to the question I've just asked: who was Jesus? The black and white leaflet is simply headed: 'Welcome to Arundel Cathedral – please find a seat and read this.' I'll paraphrase what it says: this is the gist of the welcome they give to their visitors.

## Life

Jesus Christ was born in Bethlehem, an obscure village south of Jerusalem, in the Middle East. For about thirty years he was known as the carpenter's son, and lived in Nazareth earning his living by carpentry and house-building. He shared the life of an ordinary home. Then he spent the next three years travelling around, healing sick and troubled people, welcoming the outcast, and teaching anyone who'd listen to him, in the villages and in the open air near the Lake of Galilee. He gathered together twelve ordinary men to help him. He had no money. He had no university degree. He never wrote a book. He commanded no army, and he had no political power. He never travelled more than two hundred miles in any direction. He was executed by the Roman authorities when he was in his early thirties, in Jerusalem. Yet over a thousand million people, all across the world, regard this man, Jesus Christ, as God-Among-Us.

## Teaching

The paragraph you've just heard, I've put into my own words. Knowing that the original's a leaflet distributed in a Roman Catholic Cathedral, you'll be surprised that there's no doctrine or dogma, no stress on the Virgin Birth. Nothing that a non-Christian or agnostic would have any problem with except that last word, God-Among-Us. The leaflet continues with a description of Jesus's teaching which is simply factual, based on the Gospels. Jesus taught by what he said, what he was and what he did, it says. He taught us to trust God, regarding him as a loving, merciful father; and to talk to him in prayer, in all our difficulties, trusting God to give us the help we need. Jesus taught us that God regards us as his precious, beloved children, and gives us his Spirit so that we can treat each other with love, understanding, respect and forgiveness. He taught us to thank God for all he's given us, and be sensitive to other people's needs, especially people who are sick in mind or body, lonely or upset. Jesus taught us that God has put us on earth to test us and train us for a fuller life with God in eternity.

## Resurrection

So far I've paraphrased what the people of Arundel Cathedral have written in their welcome leaflet, and I hope they'll forgive me for that. Let me end by quoting four sentences exactly as they're printed:

> Towards the end of his earthly life, Jesus endured cruelty, suffering and death. God raised him from the dead to demonstrate to all people for all time that Goodness will triumph over Evil, Justice over Injustice, Love over Hate, Life over Death. Without the Resurrection of Christ, there would have been no Christian Church, and this Cathedral would never have been built.

## Emmanuel

End of quotation. What better description could you ask of who Jesus was, and why we celebrate his birth at Christmas? Jesus is the reason for the season. Christmas brings great happiness, even to unbelievers. But you can only receive the depth of joy in the Christmas Spirit when you accept that Jesus was, and is, God-Among-Us. Or as the angel explained it to Joseph, Jesus is Emmanuel – 'with us is God'. That's why we can wish each other a truly happy Christmas.

### Suggested hymns

*Be still, my soul; Hills of the North, rejoice; Immanuel, O Immanuel; O come, O come Emmanuel.*

## CHRISTMAS, EPIPHANY AND CANDLEMAS

*Christmas is magical – a season of joy. The churches are brightly decorated, vestments and hangings are gold, if possible, on Christmas Day and white on the Sundays following. On 6 January we celebrate the Epiphany, which means the revelation or revealing of who Jesus really is. We read about the visit of the Wise Men, who were the first non-Jews to recognize Jesus as 'King, and God, and Sacrifice'. The following Sundays have readings about other occasions when Jesus was 'manifest': when the Father spoke at his Baptism, when he 'revealed his glory' at the wedding in Cana, when he proclaimed his programme in Nazareth, when Nathanael recognized him as Son of God, and when he called the first disciples and sent them out as 'fishers' to reveal him to all races. The Epiphany season reminds us, therefore, that God calls us, too, to spread the Good News. Then on 2 February comes 'The Presentation of Christ in the Temple', when old Simeon recognized Jesus as the Messiah, and sang of him as 'a Light to lighten the Gentiles'. This day, therefore, is also called 'Candlemas', and candle ceremonies are held in some churches. Simeon also predicted that a sword would pierce Mary's heart, looking onward to the crucifixion; so Candlemas is a watershed between the Sundays following Christmas and those leading up to Holy Week, and is often celebrated on the Sunday falling between 28 January and 3 February. From then until Ash Wednesday there are a number of 'Sundays before Lent'.*

## Christmas Day   25 December

*Any of the following sets of readings may be used on the evening of Christmas Eve and on Christmas Day. Set III should be used at some service during the celebration.*

### Set I   New-found Happiness

Isa. 9:2–7 A child is born; Ps. 96 Tell of his salvation; Titus 2:11–14 Salvation has come; Luke 2:1–14 [15–20] The birth and the shepherds

*'Sing to the LORD a new song.' Psalm 96:1 (Common Worship)*

## Carols

Christmas wouldn't be Christmas without the singing of carols. Even musicians who have to perform at several different carol services during the season, and who inevitably become a bit jaded, often find the words or music of some familiar carol taking on new life as it suddenly strikes an emotional chord. But the word 'carol' originally meant a dance; it's thought to be derived from the word for the flute player who accompanied the 'chorus', who danced and sang during the ancient Greek dramas. The medieval round dance soon developed, however, into a song, usually to words concerning the birth of Christ. The 'Boar's Head Carol', printed in 1521, was sung as the traditional dish was carried in on Christmas Day at Queen's College, Oxford. In France they were called 'Noëls', from the word *natal* meaning birthday.

## Folk-music

Like most folk music, the early carols were passed on by word of mouth, and many of them weren't written down until the nineteenth or twentieth centuries. To be honest, some of the village 'waits', who sang unaccompanied melodies from house to house, may have been more enthusiastic than musical! But many of the ancient carols were harmonized by the folk-music collectors. The Service of Nine Lessons and Carols, sung at King's College, Cambridge, every Christmas Eve since 1918, and broadcast by the BBC since the early 1930s, introduced some splendid choral arrangements. Many fine new carols have also been composed in recent years, and have become favourites in churches and on radio stations across the world.

## A new song

The growing popularity of the Christmas carol tradition comes from a welling-up of happiness in human hearts. The Christmas message, that God loves us so much that he sent his Son to be born as a baby in Bethlehem, and laid in a manger, is an overwhelmingly joyful one. This joy finds its natural outpouring in song. Of course, the birth in the stable's only the beginning of the story of God's love. Jesus proclaimed the same message in his teaching, and demonstrated it by a life of compassionate care and healing. But the pastoral idyll of the shepherds, the wise men, the angels and the star, focuses our minds on the beauty of the story, and its meaning for you and me. In the book of Psalms, in the Bible, we find many times the phrase, 'Sing to the Lord a new song.' Music's a spontaneous reaction to the realization that we're loved by God.

## New music

Mind you, not everybody likes new music. They forget that many of what they call the 'old favourites' go back less than a hundred years. There's a story of a woman who wrote to her vicar that 'In over sixty years that I've been attending this church, you've been singing the same totally unfamiliar new hymns every year.' You'd think by now she'd have taken the trouble to learn them! A church council was disturbed by the amount of modern music which the new organist, whom they'd recently appointed, was introducing into their old traditional services. They wrote to him in these words:

> Complaints have been made to the Council that you now accompany the hymns with surprising variations and irrelevant ornaments which obliterate the melody and confuse the congregation. If you desire to introduce a theme against the melody, you must go on with it, and not immediately fly off to another.

The year was 1706, and the name of the organist was Johann Sebastian Bach!

## New-found happiness

Our response to God's love, at least since the Psalms were written, has been to 'Sing to the Lord a new song', to express our joy. The depth of the love of God, revealed by the Christmas story, brings us new-found happiness. Inevitably, we want to put this new joy into music. Even to those who can only produce a croak, turning our enthusiasm into singing at Christmas time comes as naturally as it does to the blackbird, which sings because it can't help it. Whether it's a folk song from the fifteenth century, a choral arrangement, or a new composition, everyone must sing at Christmas. Praise the Lord for Christmas, and sing a new song because of our new-found happiness!

### All-age worship

*Write a new carol, telling the Christmas story or telling God how happy it makes you. It will be even better if you can make the lines rhyme, and fit it to a well-known tune.*

### Suggested carols

*Away in a manger; Hark, the herald angels sing; It came upon the midnight clear; Sing to God new songs of worship.*

## Christmas Day   25 December
### Set II   People Like Us

Isa. 62:6–12 Prepare a way; Ps. 97 God comes to rescue his people; Titus 3:4–7 Salvation by grace; Luke 2:[1–7] 8–20 Shepherds go to Bethlehem

> *'In that region there were shepherds living in the fields, keeping watch over their flock by night.' Luke 2:8*

### Reread the Gospel story

Anyone who's watched a nativity play knows that shepherds always wear a tea-towel on their heads and a dressing-gown over their shoulders! Some things get imported into the Christmas story which aren't there in the Bible. Yet it's a good idea to try and see the narrative through childish eyes, free from preconceptions and sup-positions. Pick up your Bible sometime today, and read again the first two chapters of Matthew and the first two chapters of Luke, as though you were reading them for the first time. The first thing that strikes you is that they're quite different, with hardly any overlap. Matthew was writing for Greek-speaking Jews, so he concentrates on the fulfilment of the Scriptures, which they knew so well. Luke wrote for non-Jewish Greeks, and sets the story in the framework of the Roman Empire.

### Follow your star

Yet it's Matthew who tells the story of the first non-Jews to worship Jesus: the wise men from Persia. They had seen his star in the east, and come to worship him. In the words familiar in songs from the shows and popular psychology, they learnt that everyone must follow their star. We each have a destiny to fulfil; each of us will be presented with opportunities to do something significant and good, and when it comes we must grab it, and do what God wants us to. The star led the wise men to Bethlehem, where each offered his distinctive gift to the Christ-child. Each of us has some unique gift which we alone can offer to God in building his kingdom.

## Warned in a dream

Herod told the wise men to return to him, so that he too could worship the new-born king. They recognized his hypocrisy, and refused to fall into his trap. Warned against Herod in a dream, they returned home another way. Our dreams are as important as our destiny, sometimes more so. Martin Luther King had a dream of America free from racial prejudice, and gave his life to make his dream come true. Following our dream may mean giving up the approval of political leaders, and turning our back on posh connections, the nice pension, the smart lifestyle, the perks and the celebrity. But the wise men took home their self-respect and their integrity, and their memories of the time when God came to earth and lay in a manger.

## Worldly power

Herod, however, represents the temptations of worldly power. The scorching reality of power is that it can brook no rivals. A new king must be killed, because otherwise he would bring death to the old king. But sometimes we have to surrender our earthly power in order to do what's right and moral. Novelty means death to the old ideas. We resist new ideas, because they disturb our comfortable prejudices. But new ideas represent new life; we can massacre it in its infancy if we choose, like Herod, or we can welcome novelty and let it transform us, as the wise men did.

## Shepherds don't count

Now we come to the shepherds. St Luke's story begins with the census, when everybody had to go to their birthplace to be counted. Yet shepherds have to follow their flocks to wherever there's grass for them to graze. They can't abandon them, even for a government order. So while everyone else was being counted, the shepherds were *dis*-counted. You couldn't say it more clearly if you tried: shepherds don't count. A lot of people don't count in the calculations of politicians: the eccentric, the awkward, the excluded and the underclass. But they count where God's concerned. Jesus isn't just for the rich and powerful, though he has a message for them too. Jesus came to earth for the ordinary folk like you and me; and ordinary working shepherds, those who don't count, were among the first to see that God is, at heart, an ordinary person just like us.

## Reason or dreams?

Christmas reminds us that truth isn't only found in scientific reasoning; truth's there too in stories about stars and the poetry of dreams. Often we pay far too much attention to reason, and fail to follow the vision of an ideal world of love, brought to us by this ancient narrative. Look at the Christmas story again, through the wondering eyes of children kneeling before the crib at their first ever nativity play. Then follow your star, and live out your dream.

### *All-age worship*

*Prepare a short nativity play, putting into your own words what the wise men and shepherds were feeling.*

### *Suggested carols*

*See him lying in a bed of straw; Unto us a child is born; Where is this stupendous stranger?; While shepherds watched.*

## Christmas Day   25 December
### *Set III*   Truly Human

Isa. 52:7–10 The messenger of peace; Ps. 98 God's victory; Heb. 1:1–4 [5–12] God speaks through a Son; John 1:1–14 The Word became flesh

*'And the Word became flesh and lived among us.' John 1:14*

## The king who loved a peasant girl

Once upon a time – that's to warn you that what follows is a fictional tale, not gospel truth. Though it's related to gospel truth, as you'll see. So I'd better start again. Once upon a time, there was a king who fell in love – with a peasant girl! Despite her humble station in life, this girl was beautiful and charming, and the king wanted nothing more than to be with her for ever. Yet there was an obvious snag. If he went to her in all his royal panoply, in his ermine cloak and his crown, one of two things would happen. When he proposed to the girl, either she'd be so alarmed at the thought that she'd have to behave as a queen that she'd turn him down. Or else she'd say yes because she thought it was her duty to obey her monarch, and that wasn't the sort of relationship he wanted; he wanted her free consent to his proposal, and her willing choice to return his love with a willing heart. Nobody can be terrified into love. If, on the other hand, he dressed up as a peasant when he went to call on her, and pretended to be one, she might well fall in love with him and agree to marry him. But then, when she discovered the trick he'd played on her, she'd say she agreed to marry him under false pretences, and she could never love a liar. Poor king! What could he do? There was only one solution. If living in love together for the rest of their lives was more important to him than anything else, then he had to actually *become* a peasant himself, to marry her. It was the only way, and he took it. He abdicated as king, resigned his throne to his younger brother, married the humble maiden, and they loved each other until they died. Aah!

## A parable

It's not an original story. It was first told over 150 years ago by the great Danish philosopher Søren Kierkegaard. And though it's only fiction, he used it to explain the truth of the Gospels. The story helps us to understand the meaning of Christmas. Because if what the Gospels say is true, then what happened in the stable in Bethlehem's almost too big to grasp with our little human minds. Certainly we could never understand it without the help of a story like that of the king and the peasant girl, which is a sort of parable.

## God loves you

The first idea you have to get your head around is the concept that God loves you. But that's ridiculous, you say. God! Loves little me! Don't be absurd! How could the great creator of the universe be interested in an insignificant worm on an obscure planet? ... Of course, that's exactly what God knew you'd say. And yet this fantastic fact is true: God is love, through and through, and he loves the human race. He created us to return his love and live with him in eternity, for ever and ever. But how can he make us realize that? How can God tell us that he loves us?

## God's dilemma

God's dilemma was exactly like that of the mighty king who loved the humble peasant girl. If God suddenly appeared on a cloud in all his glory, we'd all shrivel up with fear and shame, and we'd be too terrified to return his love. If God commanded us to love him, what we'd give him wouldn't be love but grudging obedience. Yet if God came down to earth and pretended to be human, like some of the Greek gods did in the ancient legends, we should be unconvinced. 'It's all right for him,' we'd say; 'he doesn't know what it's really like to be in pain, and not sure where your next meal's coming from. I can't love a God who dresses up as a human being.'

## Incarnation

If the king wanted the peasant girl to love him, the only way was to become a peasant. If God wants human beings to love him, then the only way for God to win our love is to become a human being. And *that's* what Christmas is all about. St John's Gospel proclaims that 'the Word was God . . . and the Word became flesh.' If that doesn't make the hairs on the back of your neck tingle at the sheer incredible wonder of how much God loves you, then you must have a heart of stone. Happy Christmas!

### All-age worship

*Draw a strip-cartoon of the king who loved the peasant girl, using think-bubbles.*

### Suggested carols

*Behold, the great Creator makes; I cannot tell why he, whom angels worship; Meekness and majesty; O come, all ye faithful.*

# Christmas Day
## Second Service  Recreation
Morning Ps. 110 This day of your birth, 117 Steadfast love;
Evening Ps. 8 Out of the mouths of babes; Isa. 65:17–25 A new
creation; Phil. 2:5–11 Jesus emptied himself; *or* Luke 2:1–20 *(if
it has not been used at the Principal Service of the day)*

> *'I am about to create new heavens and a new earth; the former
> things shall not be remembered or come to mind.' Isaiah 65:17*

## Recreation

Christmas Day's a holiday. Holidays are a time for recreation.
Some lucky people are able to go away at Christmas time, skiing
or snow-boarding. Those with family responsibilities may take the
children out for a romp in the open air. Knowing that there'll be a
good deal of eating and drinking on Christmas Day, some people
go for a good brisk walk to keep themselves fit. In Australia, of
course, those who want to can swim or go surfing on Christmas
Day. All these are forms of recreation. Look at that word; if you
split it in two you realize that it means re-creation, or making
ourselves afresh. Those who have any leisure time like to use it in
physical or mental activity to refresh their jaded minds and bodies.
However fresh we were at the beginning of the week, by the time it
comes to the weekend, we need some activity which will restore us
to something like our ideal condition for enjoying life. Much more,
when the holidays come.

## Recreating the human race

We've been looking at individuals. Isn't there a sense, also, in which
the whole human race needs a holiday? Our life together as a community's far from ideal. We're loaded down with memories of events
that have hurt us in the past, and guilt for times when we've hurt
other people. If only we could start over afresh as a species, and do
things right this time! Who knows whether there ever was an ideal
time, a golden age when everybody was innocent? Is the Garden of
Eden history, or is it a story to remind us that even if we start life
as innocent children, as soon as we have a choice, we throw that
innocence away, start disobeying God and attacking each other? If
only we could get back to the way the creation was meant to be!

Well, the Bible tells us that God has done just that. God's recreated the human race – he did it on Christmas Day.

## Isaiah

Listen to what God promises in the book of Isaiah, remembering that this is picture language, and Jerusalem stands for the people who believe in Jesus:

> For I am about to create new heavens and a new earth; the former things shall not be remembered or come to mind. But be glad and rejoice forever in what I am creating; for I am about to create Jerusalem as a joy, and its people as a delight . . . Before they call I will answer, while they are yet speaking I will hear. The wolf and the lamb shall feed together, the lion shall eat straw like the ox . . . They shall not hurt or destroy on all my holy mountain, says the LORD.

This gives us the ideal. I've yet to see a wolf and a lamb feeding together, so the prophecy's only partially fulfilled so far. But the suggestion is that, once God's remade the human race as it ought to be, we shall begin putting right whatever's wrong in the rest of the natural world as well.

## The ideal

God began the process of re-creating the human race on the first Christmas Day, when Jesus was born. Jesus shows us what human beings were intended to be. He's the ideal – when we believe in him, God can set about remaking us as we were meant to be. Now that's very interesting. Maybe we've been going around with an idealized picture of what it means to be human. Jesus was really human – he wasn't pretending. So being human means needing food and drink, and recreation. Being human means sharing in the cultural life of a particular nation. Being human means having to learn from the bottom upwards. Being human means being tempted, being angry, knowing grief, being abused and feeling pain. Those are inevitable parts of human experience. But if Jesus is the ideal, then being human doesn't inevitably mean disobeying God and hurting other people. Jesus was without sin, and that's the pattern according to which God's trying to remake us.

## Recreation

So enjoy your recreation at Christmas time, whatever form it takes. And remember while you're trying to restore fitness to your mind and body, God is trying to re-create your soul. God's plan is to give you a spiritual makeover, so that you become more like an ideal human being – in other words, more like Jesus. God's plan is to create a new heaven and a new earth; he started out at the first Christmas, and the area where he's at work now is in your soul.

### Suggested carols

*Christians, awake; Hark, the herald angels sing; It came upon the midnight clear; Joy to the world.*

## First Sunday of Christmas
(St John the Evangelist)   **27 December**
*Principal Service*   **The Word of Christ**
1 Sam. 2:18–20, 26 Giving children to God; Ps. 148 Young and old together; Col. 3:12–17 The Word of Christ; Luke 2:41–52 The child Jesus in the Temple

> *'Let the word of Christ dwell in you richly; teach and admonish one another in all wisdom; and with gratitude in your hearts sing psalms, hymns, and spiritual songs to God.' Colossians 3:16*

### My Fair Lady

'Words, words, I get words all day long,' complains Eliza Doolittle in *My Fair Lady*. Professor Higgins, who's training her to speak 'properly', is, after all, a linguist, so his passion is for words. But Eliza knows that words are no use if they don't lead to action.

### Words or the Word?

In the time of Jesus, the Scribes respected the Hebrew Scriptures as the words which God had spoken to their ancestors. They themselves wrote thousands of words explaining and interpreting the Scriptures. Jesus, when he visited the Jerusalem Temple at the age of twelve, asked them questions about God's words. The Son of

God had become so completely human that he had to question the experts about the words of God. He respected the words in the Scriptures as inspired by God, but later, he queried the experts' way of interpreting them. What use were all these words, he demanded, if they don't lead to loving actions towards others? We call the Bible the Word of God. But that's not quite accurate. Most Christians hold that the words of Scripture *contain* the word of God, and you have to sift through all those words to find the overall message of God's saving love.

## My word is my bond

The idea of the word of God shining through the words of the Bible's a very powerful one. It drives us to search the Scriptures, believing that God has something to say to us. The word of God was what created the universe, 'when God spoke and it was done'. God said that his word always resulted in action: 'My word will not return to me empty,' he said. When God spoke a promise, then he will always keep his promises: 'My word is my bond,' as we say. The first Christians recognized that in the birth of the baby in Bethlehem, God's promise was coming true. In a stroke of insight and perception, St John's Gospel tells us that Jesus actually was the Word of God. The whole message of God's love for his children is contained in the life, death and resurrection of Jesus. The Word became flesh, and dwelt among us.

## The word of Christ

That means that the words that Jesus spoke are a direct communication from God to us. We'd be mad not to study them and learn them by heart, for in the words of Jesus, he tells us of God's forgiveness for our past, God's love for us in the present, and how God wants us to live in the future. But once again, it's easy to get so bogged down in words that we can't see the wood for the trees, and lose sight of the central message. So St Paul tells us to 'Let the word of Christ dwell in you richly.' The word, he says, not the words. At the core of all those words that Jesus spoke is the word of Christ, which must make its home in our hearts as Jesus made his home in our world.

## Colossians

St Paul was writings to the Christians in Colossae, a small town in the valley of the River Lycus in what we now call Turkey. It had lost its former importance, and the Christians there felt isolated. So the apostle encouraged them to delve into the Bible so deeply that its central message of love would dwell in their hearts, and with it they could support each other. Christians are supposed to teach each other; nobody's too old to learn. They're to instruct each other, helping each other to understand how God wants us to behave. Next, the Colossians must 'with gratitude in your hearts sing psalms, hymns, and spiritual songs to God'. A congregation should be joyful, singing as they go about their work, encouraging each other by singing together, like an army singing to keep their spirits up as they march.

## Using our words to support others

That surely shows us the right use of words. Not for nit-picking analysis of texts, but to encourage other Christians. Are your words used to criticize others, or to build up their self-confidence? Is ours a supportive congregation, where the word of Christ dwells richly in our hearts, and results in loving action, as we encourage each other by singing together as we progress in Christian understanding?

### All-age worship

*Make up a song or learn a hymn to encourage each other that God's pleased with what you're doing.*

### Suggested hymns

*Lord, thy word abideth; Love came down at Christmas; Thou didst leave thy throne; Thou whose almighty word.*

## St John, Apostle and Evangelist   27 December
(or may be transferred to 28 December)
### Too Many Books
Ex. 33:7–11a The tent of meeting; Ps. 117 Praise God, all
nations; 1 John 1 The word of life; John 21:19b–25 The Beloved
Disciple

> *'But there are also many other things that Jesus did; if every one
> of them were written down, I suppose that the world itself could
> not contain the books that would be written.' John 21:25*

### Too many books

By law, every book and periodical published in the United Kingdom has to be deposited at the British Library. At present it holds
around 150 million items, about 25 million of which are books;
they add some 3 million new items every year. Any aspiring writer
who's tried to find a publisher for their precious manuscript knows
that far more books are written than ever make it to the bookshops.
As the author of the biblical book called Ecclesiastes wrote, 'Of
making many books there is no end, and much study is a weariness
of the flesh.' Yet St John, at the end of his Gospel, writes:

> There are also many other things that Jesus did; if every one of
> them were written down, I suppose that the world itself could not
> contain the books that would be written.

That's a playful way of putting it, but its an exaggeration. A word-
for-word description of what Jesus said and did on even one day
would fill a book, and he lived for some 33 years, so that's over
12,000 books. But if you included the different interpretations that
various people have put upon the words of Jesus, in every language
in the world, you could probably fill the British Library with books
about Jesus.

### Gospels

Which makes it surprising that there are only four Gospels in our
New Testament. It took the Church several hundred years to come
to a final decision on which books were or were not to be included
in the Bible, but anyone who's tried to read the alternatives can

have no doubt that the Church made the right decision by including Matthew, Mark, Luke and John, and no others. For there were others; we call them the Apocryphal Gospels. Some of them report fantastic miracles from the childhood of Jesus and the Virgin Mary, and are clearly legendary. Some impart teachings, quite different from the mainstream doctrine of the Church, and teach that only those who have been initiated into this secret knowledge can be saved. Some of the early Gospels which were rejected have not survived, but from quotations in other writers it seems that they may have included different versions of the sayings of Jesus found in our Bibles. The most interesting is the *Gospel of Thomas*, which was rediscovered in the twentieth century. It's a collection of sayings of Jesus, over half of them already in our four Gospels, but Thomas's are often in a simpler and therefore possibly earlier version. The other sayings emphasize the unity of the human race, and the need to look for the kingdom of God within us. It could well contain some early independent traditions passed down by word of mouth, but it also claims to be imparting secret knowledge, which sounds suspicious. We can be sure that the four Gospels in the New Testament are basically accurate in their description of the historical Jesus and his teaching. And what a remarkable description that is!

## Invented?

Matthew, Mark, Luke and John report the story that's familiar, of the preacher and healer from Nazareth, who proclaimed a father-like God who loves us, and is eager to forgive us our sins and give us eternal life. Jesus preached of love, and demonstrated in his own life what love means. The loving Father-God that he described was so like Jesus himself, that people began to refer to Jesus as the Son of God. Then Jesus was crucified, and rose on the third day. But how do we know that the gospel story wasn't invented by the writers? The American historian Will Durant wrote:

> That a few simple men should in one generation have invented so powerful and appealing a personality, so lofty an ethic, and so inspiring a vision of human brotherhood, would be a miracle far more incredible than any recorded in the Gospels.

So thank God especially for St John, whom we celebrate today, and who wrote down an account of what Jesus said and did, and added his own interpretation, the fruit of a lifetime of meditation. The fourth Gospel's resonated in the minds of wise people all around the world as being a true understanding of what Jesus meant then, and what he means for us now.

## Suggested hymns

*Be thou my vision; Disposer supreme, and Judge of the earth; O come, all ye faithful; Thou, whose almighty word.*

# Second Sunday of Christmas
(or Epiphany; see p. 291)   **3 January 2010**
*Principal Service*   **Redemption**
Jer. 31:7–14 God will send salvation; Ps. 147:13–21 God's Word brings peace; *or* Ecclus. 24:1–12 God's Wisdom comes to earth; *Canticle*: Wisd. 10:15–21 Salvation; Eph. 1:3–14 God's plan to gather everything in Christ; John 1:[1–9] 10–18 God gave grace through Jesus

> *'In him we have redemption through his blood, the forgiveness of our trespasses, according to the riches of his grace that he lavished on us.' Ephesians 1:7–8*

## John Profumo

John Profumo was British Foreign Secretary from 1959 to 1960, and Secretary of State for War from 1960 to 1963. He had an affair with Christine Keeler, who was at the same time involved with a Russian diplomat. There was no evidence that any state secrets had been passed on by this route, but most people considered he had been unwise to lay himself open to such an accusation. Yet he denied the affair when questioned about it in Parliament. In 1963 he resigned, not so much because of what he had done, but because he had misled the House of Commons. He then wanted to do something to make up to his wife for being unfaithful, and to the nation for having lied and risked a breach of security. He devoted the remaining 40 years of his life to social and charitable work, helping the needy in East London. By the time he died, everyone agreed that he had more than redeemed himself for whatever sins he had committed.

## Redeeming the past

In those words, people described how he'd paid off any debt he owed to society. Redeeming oneself's a term we use for good deeds which compensate for some harm that we've done. In the morning hymn 'Awake my soul, and with the sun', Bishop Ken began the second verse with the advice:

Redeem thy mis-spent time that's past,
and live this day as if thy last.

It's certainly a strong motive for trying to live a good life, if you want to make up for the harm you've done to others in the past, as John Profumo did. But it's not enough. Nobody can fully balance, by doing good, the hurt they've caused to others.

## Calculation

I doubt whether Profumo made this mistake, but many people who talk about 'making up for what I've done wrong' seem to think that you can add up right and wrong like a balance sheet. But how can you calculate how many good deeds are needed to atone for one bad deed? The harm that evil actions do consists largely in the hurt they cause to personal relationships, and there's no way of measuring that. It's good to do something kind for somebody you've harmed, to show that you're sorry and want to restore the relationship; but there's no way you can pay for the damage you've done. In particular, every selfish or cruel thing you do wounds the loving heart of God. To heal that injury requires a far greater gesture than we can make for ourselves; Jesus has to make it for us.

## Ephesians

So we claim Jesus as our Redeemer, and rely on the redemption Jesus has achieved by sacrificing his life for the sins of the whole world. St Paul writes: 'In him we have redemption through his blood, the forgiveness of our trespasses, according to the riches of his grace that he lavished on us.' Jesus came to earth and was born at Christmas time to do something we couldn't do for ourselves: he came to redeem us from the effects of our misdeeds, the broken relationships, the betrayed trust, and above all the harm done to the relationship of intimate love with God our Father.

## Grace

That relationship's essential to us, because when it's broken, we're incapable of receiving the blessings God longs to pour on us. In particular he wants to give us his grace, the strength we need if we're to do any good deeds at all. That way even the most notorious offender can be readmitted to full membership in society. Then the good things we do can be taken up into the great redeeming action of Jesus on the cross, and made a part of his sacrifice.

## Freeing slaves

Originally the word 'redeem' meant to buy something back, and it was used for buying freedom for a slave. A slave couldn't own money, so he or she couldn't buy their own liberty; they had to be bought by some god and then set free. Yes, it was a legal fiction, but the first Christians, many of whom were slaves, realized immediately that redemption from the effects of all their sins was something only Jesus could do for them. Thank God that Jesus was born to be our Redeemer, and bring liberty to us who were slaves to sin and death.

### All-age worship

*Support a charity that helps the homeless at Christmas.*

### Suggested hymns

*Awake my soul, and with the sun; Come, thou Redeemer of the earth; See, amid the winter's snow; There is a Redeemer.*

## Second Sunday of Christmas
### Second Service    A Virtuous Circle
Ps. 135 Greater than the idols; 1 Sam. 1:20–28 Hannah gives Samuel; 1 John 4:7–16 Love is from God; *Gospel at Holy Communion*: Matt. 2:13–23 Escape to Egypt

> *'Beloved, since God loved us so much, we also ought to love one another.' 1 John 4:11*

38

## Yobs

Periodically the newspapers and the television draw our attention to the incidence of antisocial behaviour among teenage boys and young men. In a word, yobs. They'll point out that these young people mostly come from deprived backgrounds, and that boys from single-parent families have no role model to imitate, showing them how adult males are supposed to behave. This is probably an oversimplification; it's a question of individual choice, whether or not to behave badly.

## As I am loved

But the truth behind the statistics is that it's very hard for anyone to give love if they've never received it. If adults have no time to listen to young people, if youngsters grow up believing that nobody loves them, then they'll have no example of love to imitate, and then they won't know how to behave lovingly or even considerately towards other people. In a familiar phrase, we can all say, 'As I am loved, so will I love.' We learn to love through the experience of receiving love from others.

## A virtuous circle

So the wheel of love goes round and round. We are loved, so we love others, and they in their turn learn to give love. We use the expression 'a vicious circle' to describe what happens when one sin leads to another and so on, spiralling down into misery. The circle of love is the very opposite, where virtue in one leads to virtue in others – perhaps we should call it a 'virtuous circle'.

## God is love

That's why the letters of St John, in the New Testament, seem to go round in circles. The schoolchild was wrong who said that 'an epistle is the wife of an apostle'! Epistle is simply an old word for a letter. The first letter of John's all about love. This is how the argument goes round and round; I've selected verses which refer to love:

> See what love the Father has given us, that we should be called children of God . . . For this is the message you have heard from

the beginning, that we should love one another ... Whoever does not love abides in death ... We know love by this, that [Jesus] laid down his life for us – and we ought to lay down our lives for one another ... Little children, let us love, not in word or speech, but in truth and action ... Beloved, let us love one another, because love is from God; everyone who loves is born of God and knows God. Whoever does not love does not know God, for God is love.

## Love flowing from and to God

And so the virtuous circle turns and turns. It's no use trying to put it into a rational order, for this isn't logic, it's poetry and mysticism. Perhaps you could draw what John's saying in one of those flow-charts, beloved of managers of organizations and those who design industrial processes. Love flows from God the Father, the source of love, to Jesus the Son of God, causing Jesus to sacrifice himself from love for us. Love then flows from Jesus to those who believe, causing them to love Jesus in return, and thus our love flows back to God our Father. As we are loved, so will we love. Because we're loved by God, we want to do something practical to show God our gratitude. But God doesn't need us to give him anything; there are no presents you can give to the God who has everything. There are only two ways we can show our love for God: by worshipping him, and by loving our neighbours for his sake. Because we're loved by God, we love our fellow Christians, and even our neighbours who don't yet know of the love of God. They're all children of God, and God loves them. If God finds our neighbours lovable, how can we resist loving them? So the love of God flows through us into them. Then our neighbours are astonished at the experience of being loved by us, and want to know where this love comes from. So we tell them our love comes from Jesus, and they learn to love Jesus too, and through Jesus to love God his Father. God is love, and God flows into all those who know of his love, and love him in return, and love their neighbours for his sake. So God is all in all. If only all the world could know about this circle of love, and be drawn into it!

## *Suggested hymns*

*God is love, and where true love is; God is love, his the care; God is love, let heav'n adore him; Love came down at Christmas.*

# The Baptism of Christ

(First Sunday of Epiphany)   **10 January**

*Principal Service*   **Filled with Expectation**

Isa. 43:1–7 When you pass through the waters; Ps. 29 The voice
of the Lord is over the waters; Acts 8:14–17 Baptism and the
Holy Spirit; Luke 3:15–17, 21–22 The Baptism of Jesus

*'The people were filled with expectation.' Luke 3:15*

## Cynics

'Blessed is the man who expects nothing,' wrote the cynical poet
Alexander Pope, 'for he shall never be disappointed!' The cynic's
right; if you expect the worst in life, the results are seldom worse
than you expected. But then your pessimistic attitude to life may
prevent you from gaining the good things that might have been
yours if you'd been more open. People avoid a pessimist; as Ella
Wheeler Wilcox wrote:

> Laugh, and the world laughs with you:
> Weep, and you weep alone;
> For the sad old earth must borrow its mirth,
> It has troubles enough of its own.

### Messianic expectation

When Jesus was baptized in the River Jordan, the Jewish people
were on tip-toes with eager expectation. Their ancient Scriptures
promised them a Messiah, a new king, descended from the great
King David, who'd liberate them from the occupying Roman power
and give them their independence. The predictions of the Messiah
were couched in poetic language, and some took this literally, expecting that there'd be a magical end to hunger, sickness and death
when the Messiah came. Even those who accepted that the words
might be symbolic had an inner feeling that they were standing at
a turning point in history, one of those watersheds which mark
the end of the old era and the emergence of a new world order
in which everything's different. When John preached a baptism of
repentance for the remission of sins, the crowds flocked to him,
wondering whether this was to prepare them for the new age. So,

As the people were filled with expectation, and all were questioning in their hearts concerning John, whether he might be the Messiah, John answered all of them by saying, 'I baptize you with water; but one who is more powerful than I is coming; I am not worthy to untie the thong of his sandals. He will baptize you with the Holy Spirit and fire.'

The people now began to wonder whether Jesus was going to be the Messiah. But they were still fixated on the idea that he'd be a military Messiah who'd drive out the hated Romans.

## The better way

Yet it was better that the people should be on tip-toes, than that they should have been cynical. The voice from heaven said to Jesus at his Baptism, 'You are my Son, the Beloved; with you I am well pleased.' After a brief retreat into the desert to sort his ideas out, Jesus started attracting followers, and right up until Palm Sunday the crowds heard him gladly. They wouldn't have been open to receive his teaching, if they hadn't been full of eager expectation that something new was about to happen. Hope's a great blessing; it's better than hopelessness.

## Hope

Samuel Johnson was a bit of a curmudgeon, and when one of his friends married again soon after the death of his first wife, with whom he'd been very unhappy, Dr Johnson described it as 'the triumph of hope over experience'. Hope needs to triumph. The optimist will often be disappointed, but sometimes optimists know a joy which the pessimists never experience because they aren't looking for it. Hope's a reasonable attitude, when it's founded on a firm faith in God, who wishes us well, and will bring us through all our trials to the bliss of heaven at the last.

## Filled with expectation

The Jewish people didn't get the type of Messiah they were expecting. But those who were willing to follow Jesus down unexpected paths received blessings better than they'd hoped for. There's a message in that for us. If you expect great things from God, often the outcome of your efforts on his behalf will be greater than you'd dared to dream. But if you expect nothing, then that's precisely what you'll get. When you come to church on a Sunday, are you 'filled with expectation'? The music and the sermon may not be perfect, but there's always something you can learn and enjoy, if you come with an open mind and a hopeful heart – if you come with faith that God wants to meet you in his house each week – if you're willing to listen to what he's telling you to do. But if you turn to prayer expecting to be disappointed, inevitably you will be, and it won't be God's fault, it'll be yours.

### All-age worship

*List the times in your life when you were 'full of expectation'. Was what happened better or worse than you expected? Did you remember to pray?*

### Suggested hymns

*All my hope on God is founded; Christ, when for us you were baptized; O worship the Lord in the beauty of holiness; When Jesus came to Jordan.*

# The Baptism of Christ
## Second Service   Contemplation
Ps. 46 There is a river, 47 Clap your hands; Isa. 55:1–11 Come to the waters; Rom. 6:1–11 Baptized into Christ; *Gospel at Holy Communion*: Mark 1:4–11 The baptism of Jesus

'Be still, and know that I am God!' Psalm 46:10

### Happy together

A parish priest noticed that a poor man came into his church and sat there for several hours, quite still, but with a smile on his face. The priest asked the old man what he did when he came into church. 'Well,' the countryman replied, 'I looks at God and God looks at me, and we're happy together.' This story's been told about the Curé d'Ars in France and about George Herbert in England, but the name of the priest doesn't really matter. The old man had summed up briefly what Christians mean by contemplative prayer, prayer without words.

43

## Progress in prayer

Contemplation's the final stage of prayer, though some people, like the old farmer, seem to slip into it with no effort at all. But for most of us, progress in prayer is hard work. Childlike simplicity in prayer is acceptable to God, but it's sad to see a Christian who's made no progress beyond the sort of prayers they were saying at their mother's knee. Most people start with written prayers, taken from a book of prayers or a manual on prayer. They continue by memorizing prayers and poetry and repeating them by heart. Then, slowly, we learn to pray in our own words, perhaps with a list of people and subjects we want to pray for open in front of us. St Teresa of Avila wanted to pray naturally, but she could never think of the words to say. In frustration she wrote down what she wanted to say, and always added, 'Please Lord, help me to pray spontaneously and naturally.' One day her carriage went off the road and threw her into a muddy ditch. As she crawled out she said angrily, 'Lord, it's no wonder you have so few friends, when you treat the ones you have so badly!' Then she realized her prayer had been answered!

## Meditation

Next comes what's called, in the centuries-old, but much neglected, Christian teaching on prayer, the art of meditation. This is thinking about God in a systematic and structured way. St Francis de Sales and St Ignatius Loyola are among those who have written advice on how to meditate. Eastern religions and organizations like the Transcendental Meditation movement teach something which they call meditation but is in fact more like Christian contemplation. We can learn a lot about the technique of relaxation from the Eastern religions. Remember, however, that, for the most part, they want to be absorbed into a great nothingness, whereas Christians want a relationship with a personal God.

## Contemplation

Contemplation is wordless silence focused on God, when the mind is relaxed and stops the effort to reason. Usually Christians only begin contemplative prayer after training themselves in other types of prayer, but there should be times in every Christian's life when we hear our Lord's call to 'Be still, and know that I am God!' It begins with

- the *'purgative way'*, which is the stage in which we try to be cleansed from sin and distraction and everything that hinders us from the vision of God. The second stage is
- the *'illuminative way'*, in which the soul is cleansed from attachment to the pleasures of the five senses; sometimes it's called the *'dark night of the senses'*. It may lead into
- the *'dark night of the soul'*, a term invented by St John of the Cross, to describe the stage when we learn to dispense with even the awareness of the presence of God. Sometimes simple depression is described as the dark night of the soul, but that could distract people from seeking treatment for a medical condition. God gives us comforts in prayer when we begin, but we should be flattered that he considers us to be able to manage now without the cosy feelings with which we started. Contemplation eventually leads to
- the *'unitive way'*, the *'vision of God'* or *'beatific vision'*, and the *'mystical union'* of the soul with God, by a bond of love which we couldn't attain without God's help.

## Resting

But please don't be put off by these technical terms. In this noisy world we often need help to become quiet, such as repeating the Jesus prayer, 'Jesus, mercy', in time with your breathing, perhaps using rosary beads. But the thing towards which we're aiming is very simple: it's just learning to rest in God's love, free from distractions and worries. In fact, to 'be still and know that I am God'. Remember the old farmer: 'I looks at God, and God looks at me, and we're happy together.'

## *Suggested hymns*

*Be still and know that I am God; Be still, for the presence of the Lord; Dear Lord and Father of mankind; Let me have my way among you.*

## Second Sunday of Epiphany  17 January
*Principal Service*  **Signs**

Isa. 62:1–5 Nations shall see your salvation; Ps. 36:5–10 All peoples; 1 Cor. 12:1–11 Many gifts, one Spirit; John 2:1–11 The wedding at Cana

> *'Jesus did this, the first of his signs, in Cana of Galilee, and revealed his glory; and his disciples believed in him.' John 2:11*

### Customs

The customs officer who was examining the priest's luggage asked him, 'What's in this bottle?' 'Holy water,' answered the priest. The customs man took the stopper out and sniffed the contents, then said, 'It smells more like whisky to me.' The priest exclaimed, 'Praise the Lord! Another miracle!'

### Miracles

Christians believe that Jesus turned water into wine, so why not whisky? Well, first, because that would be a misuse of his miraculous powers. The miracle at Cana of Galilee may have been to save the families of the bride and groom from embarrassment when the wine ran out; but to enable a priest to bypass the customs regulations sounds more like putting God to the test, a temptation which Jesus had already resisted. But, second, turning water into wine was something Jesus did to teach his disciples something. The Gospel says, 'Jesus did this, the first of his signs, in Cana of Galilee, and revealed his glory; and his disciples believed in him.' The word 'miracle' means things to wonder at, things to admire. St John calls the miracles 'signs', signboards or finger posts, arrows pointing us towards God. Jesus performed miracles to point out that God the Father was at work in the life and activity of Jesus. Like those signs on the road that used to say, 'Men at work', the miracles point us to God at work.

### Predictions

So the meaning of the miracles was more important than the method by which they were performed. The signs were full of symbolism. The disciples were able to recognize the activity of God in

46

this particular sign, because they knew their Old Testament well. The Hebrew Scriptures looked forward to a time when God would intervene in history, to establish his kingdom. Jesus wanted his disciples to recognize that through his life, death and resurrection, the kingdom of God was breaking into the present time. One of the commonest metaphors the Jews used to describe the kingdom of God was to say, it's like a wedding. The prophet Isaiah cried out:

> Your Creator 'is your husband, the LORD of hosts is his name . . . for the LORD has called you like a wife forsaken and grieved in spirit . . . with everlasting love I will have compassion on you, says the LORD, your Redeemer.'

## A wedding banquet

When the Son of God came into the world as its king, it was as though he was marrying the people that he loves – you and me. And that's something to celebrate. Isaiah also said:

> On this mountain the LORD of hosts will make for all peoples a feast of rich food, a feast of well-aged wines, of rich food filled with marrow, of well-aged wines strained clear.

What a party it is, when Jesus comes to us; like the best wedding reception you've ever been invited to. The prophet Amos said:

> The time is surely coming, says the LORD, when . . . the mountains shall drip sweet wine, and all the hills shall flow with it. I will restore the fortunes of my people Israel . . . and they shall rebuild the ruined cities and inhabit them; they shall plant vineyards and drink their wine.

Jesus created an enormous quantity of wine at the wedding, to show that our generous Creator has come to bring us eternal joy, like a non-stop wedding reception. EMA.

## New wine

Jesus compared his teaching to new wine, bubbling and fermenting until the old brittle wineskins can contain it no longer, or they'd burst under the strain. New wine needs new wineskins, he said. That's because old-fashioned religion, which goes no further than

47

laying down rules and regulations for everybody to obey, can't cope with the vigorous liberating love that Jesus brought. This metaphor doesn't mean that Jesus was encouraging lawlessness and immorality, any more than he encouraged drunkenness. But his religion's based on love; anything which isn't loving and liberating can't call itself the religion of Jesus.

## 'The water blushed'

The English poet Richard Crashaw put it beautifully: 'The conscious water saw its God, and blushed.' He compares the water at Cana of Galilee to a modest nymph, who's been caught bathing naked, and blushes till she looks like wine. Poetry's the only way to talk about miracles; describing them scientifically gets you nowhere. The miracle was a sign, to point us to Jesus, and help us to recognize who he is.

### All-age worship

*Shine a light on some glasses of water. Then put red cellophane® in front of the light.*

### Suggested hymns

*At Cana's wedding, long ago; Come, my way, my truth, my life; Sing of the bride and sing of the groom; Songs of thankfulness and praise.*

## Second Sunday of Epiphany
### *Second Service*   Truthfulness
Ps. 96 Tell of his salvation; 1 Sam. 3:1–20 The boy Samuel; Eph. 4:1–16 Unity in the Body of Christ; *Gospel at Holy Communion*: John 1:29–42 The first disciples

> 'Speaking the truth in love, we must grow up in every way into him who is the head, into Christ, from whom the whole body, joined and knit together by every ligament with which it is equipped, as each part is working properly, promotes the body's growth in building itself up in love.' Ephesians 4:14–16

## Napoleon

An inventor brought to Napoleon Bonaparte what he claimed was some bullet-proof armour which he had developed. The French leader called for a loaded pistol and told the inventor to put on his armour and stand at the other end of the room. When the inventor refused, Napoleon asked why he should believe him, when he didn't even believe in his own product. Trust is a reward which can only be won by truthfulness.

## Ephesians

St Paul advised the church in Ephesus to tell the truth in love. If you want to be believed, it's best always to tell the truth. Lies come from the devil, said Jesus. People start telling little white lies, then have to tell other lies to cover up their earlier falsehood, and before they know what's happened, they've dug themselves deeper and deeper into a hole. It's easy to become entrapped in a web of deceit, from which there's no escape. The commandment against bearing false witness was formulated in the context of the law court; telling lies in court makes achieving justice impossible.

## In love

But notice the important qualification that Paul adds: you should always tell the truth, but you should tell the truth in love. Many people are brutally truthful: they proclaim their opinion of others with no thought about the hurt this will cause. Before saying anything about somebody else you should ask, is it true? Is it kind? Is it necessary? If the answer to any one of these is no, say nothing at all. Saying unkind things under the excuse of telling the truth, the whole truth, and nothing but the truth, is no justification for crass insensitivity. When recommended to tell the pure and simple truth, a character in Oscar Wilde's play *The Importance of Being Earnest* replies, 'The truth is rarely pure, and never simple.'

## Confidences

You should never reveal confidences, even if they're true. The lawyers who mustn't reveal their clients' business affairs or their guilt; the doctors who must keep their patients' medical details to themselves at all costs unless they have permission to reveal them to a colleague; the priest who mustn't break the seal of the confessional by revealing what's been told in private by a penitent, even at the cost of going to prison for contempt of court – they all know this. No charges of contempt have been levelled at these professionals, though there have sometimes been attempts at forcing journalists to reveal their sources. But nobody will tell you anything in confidence if they believe you're going to go straight out and blab about it to your neighbours.

## Reticence

There are other circumstances when the only moral course is to be reticent. A past head of the British Civil Service was pilloried for using the expression 'economical with the truth'. But it's an old moral principle. Economy is a Greek word for housekeeping, and just as a good housekeeper only gives out as much food and other supplies as are actually needed at the moment, so someone in full possession of the facts has a moral duty only to reveal as much as will be helpful at any one time. Truth must always be withheld if that's the lesser of two evils.

## Medical problems

The thorniest problem is the question whether to tell someone they're dying. For a start, you can never be 100 per cent certain whether somebody's going to die or not. Some patients want to know the probability of their recovery, so that they can make their peace with their family, their friends, their enemies and their God, and then fight hard to stay alive, but without feeling that they are unprepared if death creeps up on them. Yet those patients who don't want to face up to the inevitability that we all die sometime, always find a way of changing the subject, so that the conversation never comes round to the issue of mortality.

## I am the truth

Jesus said, 'I am the truth.' We honour Jesus when we speak the truth. But we must always look to see whether absolute truthfulness is kind and loving. Just as an avalanche can be set off in the mountains by an unwise noise, so a whole succession of hurtful consequences can be caused by just one injudicious remark. We should never tell lies, and always speak the truth in love.

*Forth in the peace of Christ we go; Thou art the way, by thee alone; True-hearted, whole-hearted; We pray thee, heavenly Father.*

## Third Sunday of Epiphany   24 January

*See also 'Week of Prayer for Christian Unity', p. 294.*

**Principal Service   Clearly Displayed**

Neh. 8:1–3, 5–6, 8–10 Joy in the Commandments; Ps. 19 The heavens declare the glory of God; 1 Cor. 12:12–31a The unity of Christ's body the Church; Luke 4:14–21 Jesus reads the Scriptures at Nazareth

*'A report about [Jesus] spread through all the surrounding country.' Luke 2:14*

### Cellophane®

Shops like to wrap their wares in cellophane, so that they can be clearly displayed. There are many forms of wrapping, but the advantage that cellophane, and the very similar cling film, have over all the rest is that you can see through them. 'What you see is what you get.' When you buy pork wrapped in transparent wrapping, you're not 'buying a pig in a poke'. There's no deception. Cellophane's a registered trade mark; the word's a combination of 'cellulose', which is what it's made of, and the Greek word for 'to see'. Which brings me to the period of the year that we're now enjoying. The time between Christmas and Candlemas is known as the season of Epiphany. Can you hear the connection between the words 'Epi-*phan*-y' and 'Cello-*phane*'? They're both derived from the same word for 'to see'; they both mean 'clearly displayed'.

### Epiphany readings

The readings for this time of year are chosen so that the glory of Jesus can be seen with the utmost clarity. First we have the story of the wise men from the East coming to worship the baby in Bethlehem. They weren't Jews, but they recognized that Jesus was the Saviour of all the world, and that in the humility of that tiny child, the love of God for all the world was clearly displayed. Next come the readings about the baptism of Christ, when the voice of God from heaven was clearly heard proclaiming, 'You are my Son, the Beloved; with you I am well pleased.' A week later we had the story of the wedding at Cana, where Jesus turned water into wine. The story ends with the words, 'Jesus did this, the first of his signs, in Cana of Galilee, and revealed his glory; and his disciples believed in him.' The glory of Jesus was clearly seen. Then, in different years we have readings from the Gospels telling how the love of God was clearly seen through the wrapping of the things Jesus did.

## Manifest

The hymn, 'Songs of thankfulness and praise', by Christopher Wordsworth, lists the ways that Jesus was 'manifest'. We mainly talk these days about 'the manifest', the paper on which cargo in a ship or passengers on an aeroplane are listed. Not long ago, however, 'manifest' meant 'clearly displayed'. The hymn sings of how Jesus was manifested to the wise men, at the baptism and at the wedding feast. It continues:

> Manifest in making whole
> palsied limbs and fainting soul;
> manifest in valiant fight,
> quelling all the devil's might;
> manifest in gracious will,
> ever bringing good from ill . . .

## Clearly seen in us

Then the hymn prays that we may imitate Jesus, so that God's love may be seen in our lives. Today we read how Jesus clearly proclaimed the love of God in the synagogue in Nazareth, setting free those who are captives to the guilt of sin and the fear of death. 'A report about him spread through all the surrounding country. He began to teach in their synagogues and was praised by everyone.' It was the ordinary people who spread the good news, when they reported excitedly to their friends what Jesus had said and what he'd done for them. God's love must be passed on to others, in our words and by our lives. You and I are the cellophane wrapping, through which the love of God can be clearly seen.

## Regular churchgoing

How can we possibly do this? Well, notice a little phrase in the reading, where it says, 'When [Jesus] came to Nazareth, where he had been brought up, he went to the synagogue on the sabbath day, as was his custom.' The synagogue's the Jewish equivalent of the local church. In church and synagogue, the love of God is read in the Scriptures and proclaimed in the sermon. Inspired by the joy of knowing that God loves you, you can go out and share that love with others in your words and deeds. People often say, 'You don't have to be a regular churchgoer to be a Christian.' They're right: you don't *have to*, there's no compulsion. But you *need to*. If Jesus needed to go to the synagogue every week, 'as was his custom', I'm sure you and I need it even more than he did. So that the love of God can be clearly seen, by us and through us.

### All-age worship

*Write on a piece of wood, 'God's love'. Wrap it in cellophane or cling film, and write on the wrapping, 'Clearly seen, by us and through us'.*

### Suggested hymns

*God's Spirit is [deep] in my heart; Songs of thankfulness and praise; The people that in darkness sat; Will you come and follow me?*

## Third Sunday of Epiphany
### Second Service   Transcendence

Ps. 33 The greatness and goodness of God; Num. 9:15–23 The cloud of God's presence; 1 Cor. 7:17–24 The life that the Lord has assigned; *Gospel at Holy Communion*: Mark 1:21–28 Authority over an unclean spirit

> 'On the day the tabernacle was set up, the cloud covered the tabernacle, the tent of the covenant; and from evening until morning it was over the tabernacle, having the appearance of fire.' Numbers 9:15

## Existence

Atheists busily deny the existence of God. But first, they should decide what they mean by the word 'God'. If they mean an old man sitting on a cloud, of course that sort of god doesn't exist. If they mean some sort of celestial meddler who's always interfering with the laws of nature, that sort of god doesn't exist either. If they mean a tribal god, who wants his people to kill and to pillage as they seize other people's lands from them, that's not the god I worship. Or if they're talking about a severe judge waiting to pounce on and punish anyone who breaks any detail of his pettifogging regulations, that sort of god is dead, thank God. The sort of god the atheists deny is one that no Christian would want to worship, either. Our God is far greater than any form of words could possibly describe. In the awesome presence of that sort of God, 'existence' isn't an appropriate word to use. Things exist, people exist, lower animals exist. But God isn't an object, he isn't a human being, far less a lower animal. God is higher than anything else, and everything else in the whole creation exists because of God.

## Transcendence

So if we can't say that God exists, in that sense, how are we to talk about God? We shall have to use words like 'transcendence', which means 'climbing beyond'; God climbs beyond any description we can make. King James the First once said of the preacher John Donne, 'Dr Donne's verses are like the peace of God, they pass all understanding!' But if we could understand God, he wouldn't be God any longer, he'd be something smaller than our minds. But how can you worship a God like that?

## Shekinah

The Old Testament resorts to the use of picture language. 'God's like this, God's like that.' Of course God isn't *actually* those things, but they're useful ideas to compare God with. In the book of Numbers, God's compared to a fiery cloud. The cloud's described as covering the tent the Israelites had built to worship him in; and in their journey through the wilderness, they only broke camp and moved on when the cloud moved ahead of them. It's a good metaphor, because it reminds us that God's a concept you can't get a grip of. Like some sermons! But it's only a metaphor; God isn't a cloud, really. A theologian was once accused of worshipping nothing but a sort of Scotch mist; too insubstantial to offer any sort of challenge or invitation.

## Immanence

So we must always balance our recognition of God's transcendence by reminding ourselves of his immanence. God's everywhere, God's presence pervades the whole universe. God's not remote, far off and uncaring, but available to hear our prayers at all times. Without a sense of the immanence of God, religion becomes a theoretical, comfortless and impersonal affair. Yet if we swing too far the other way, our religion remains merely cosy and domestic, without that sense of awe and wonder which challenges us to change our ways and become more like God. The challenge to the Christian is to hold the immanence and transcendence of God together in creative tension in our minds. God is ultimately unknowable, yet God wants to be known.

## Incarnation

That's why the incarnation of Jesus, the Son of God, is so precious a gift. In Jesus, we see God in human form. He can be our friend, companion and guide. Jesus tells us that God is like a Good Shepherd, or like the Father of the prodigal son. God isn't actually those things, but they're parables which give us a handle on thinking about the character of God. Jesus gave God a body, because he revealed God's nature in terms we could grasp. We still fall down in awe before the God who's like a fiery cloud; but that God has come close to us, and we can chat to him as a child talks with his father. 'Existence' is still too small a term to use of such a God; but we can know him (or her!) as our friend through Jesus.

### Suggested hymns

*Be still, for the presence of the Lord; Immortal, invisible, God only wise; Lead me, O thou great Redeemer; My God, how wonderful thou art.*

# Fourth Sunday of Epiphany

(or Candlemas; see p. 298)

31 January

*Principal Service*   **His Glory is His Love**

Ezek. 43:27—44:4 The glory of the Lord filled the Temple; Ps. 48 The greatness of God; 1 Cor. 13:1–13 Love; Luke 2:22–40 The presentation of Christ in the Temple

> *'I looked, and lo! the glory of the LORD filled the temple of the LORD.' Ezekiel 44:4*

## A mother's love

One of the most beautiful sights in the world is a mother with her newborn baby. She places her arms around her child in a protective way. She looks proudly down, as though having a baby is the cleverest thing in the world – and, of course, she's right. She smiles with delight, since hers is the most beautiful baby there's ever been. And her smile offers her love, with the promise that she will feed and protect her child, and meet its every need for as long as she can. Provided the babe's been fed and winded, and had a nappy change, the expression on the child's face is one of supreme contentment and confidence. It knows that it's loved, and in its babyish way it returns its mother's love with its whole being. The two together are a glorious sight. Their glory is their love.

## Simeon

The old priest Simeon must have seen something of this glory when the Virgin Mary carried the baby Jesus into the Temple. He was righteous and devout, the Gospel tells us, 'looking forward to the consolation of Israel'. He waited hopefully for the day when God would keep his promise, by rewarding his people for all they'd suffered in recent years. Some believed this would be when God sent a great king, the Messiah, to drive out the occupying Roman army and give self-rule back to Israel. Others thought it would be a supernatural event, with the Son of Man descending on the clouds, bringing an end to history, and ruling with God's people in glory. Probably Simeon, like many others, believed and hoped strongly that God would keep his promise, but wasn't at all sure what form the fulfilment would take. Perhaps he'd just been reading the

Scriptures, and found the verse in which Ezekiel, seeing a vision of the days to come, writes, 'I looked, and lo! the glory of the LORD filled the temple of the LORD.' This had happened before, when King Solomon consecrated the first Temple in Jerusalem, and when Moses dedicated the tent in the desert which was the predecessor of the Temple. God himself had come into the Temple, and made it holy by his glorious presence. So what should Simeon expect to see when God brought the promised 'consolation of Israel'? Would glory take the form of a bright light, smoke, fire, an earthquake, or what?

## Insight

Then Simeon saw an everyday sight: a mother walked into the Temple with her newborn baby. It wasn't the glory that the old priest had been expecting! Yet we're told that 'the Holy Spirit rested on him'. The Holy Spirit gave Simeon insight – the ability to find the unexpected in the everyday, and to recognize the glory of God in a young mother with her newborn baby. So he sang the Nunc Dimittis – 'for mine eyes have seen thy salvation . . . the glory of thy people Israel.'

## The glory of love

He was right, too. There's no more beautiful sight than a mother with her newborn baby; and there's no greater glory than the glory of love. The bright light which filled the Temple in days of old was to teach Moses and Solomon that God was present there, and ready to listen. But the expression of love on the faces of baby Jesus and his mother Mary was to show old Simeon that God's present wherever there's love. In the words of the old Maundy Thursday hymn, 'Ubi caritas', 'God is love, and where true love is, God himself is there.' The glory of God's not in a military campaign, nor is it only in supernatural events; glory lies around us every single day.

## The glory of God

Will you allow the Holy Spirit to open *your* eyes to the glory of God? Today, in the beauty of nature, and in the love of the family? Will you talk to God, and enjoy his presence, in this church which is his Spirit-filled temple; but also in every situation where God's at work creating love? Will you try, today, to find the unexpected in the everyday, and to recognize the glory of God in every parent and child? For God's glory is his love: the love that's willing to humble himself and become a child, so you may be able to speak to God without fear, confident that God loves you, and his presence is about you everywhere.

### All-age worship

*Make a collage of pictures of mothers with children. Write underneath, 'God loves us like this'.*

### Suggested hymns

*Angels from the realms of glory; Faithful vigil ended; God is love, and where true love is; Hail to the Lord who comes.*

## Fourth Sunday of Epiphany
### Second Service    Why Go to Church?
Ps. 34 O taste and see; 1 Chron. 29:6–19 Giving to the Lord; Acts 7:44–50 God does not dwell in temples; *Gospel at Holy Communion*: John 4:19–29a True worship

> 'The Most High does not dwell in houses made with human hands.' Acts 7:48

### 'We don't need churches'

Your hearty neighbour sees you setting out for church, and asks where you're going. 'I don't need to go to church,' he boasts. 'You can talk to God anywhere.' Then he spends the day in the shopping mall or on the golf course, and never thinks of God for even half a second. The trouble is, he's right, you know. You *can* talk to God anywhere. So why do we have church buildings, and go to them Sunday by Sunday?

### A dilemma

We're caught up here on the horns of a dilemma. It's an argument in which both sides are partially right, and partially wrong. You find both arguments summarized in the readings at this service.

In the Old Testament, King David rejoices in the generosity of his people, who'd given large sums so that a beautiful Temple could be built in Jerusalem. What blessings did King David expect this Temple to bring?

- First, it would be a symbol of national unity. Like the national flag which is carried into battle, the Temple would give the people of differing opinions a common cause to fight for.
- Second, the Temple would remind them of God's presence among them. All believers know that God's everywhere, but it's very easy to forget his presence unless you have a visual aid to remind you.
- Next, the Temple would be a focus for prayer. Jesus told us to go into our own room and pray in private, but what if you haven't got a room of your own? What if the distractions of family life prevent you having more than a few minutes of quiet at a time? A holy building provides somewhere quiet, where the architecture reminds you that God's listening.
- Then, the regular routine of prayer and sacrifice in the Temple reminded the people that we owe everything to God, and must offer nothing less than everything to God in return.
- Linked with this, there was a teaching ministry, often carried out by Scribes discussing the Scriptures with small groups under the porticoes which surrounded the Temple courtyard. This helped the people to discover the will of God and to follow it.

## Dangers of the Temple

You could add other reasons to this list why it's vital to a community to have a place of worship in their midst. Yet there are equally powerful arguments, put forward in the same Scriptures, why loyalty to the Temple was very dangerous. Some people thought God would defend them, however much they sinned, crying out that his protection was guaranteed because 'This is the Temple of the LORD, the Temple of the LORD, the Temple of the LORD!' The prophets reminded the people that 'God requires mercy, and not sacrifice'. At the time of Jesus, several pious groups, including the authors of the Dead Sea Scrolls, rejected the powerful priestly hierarchy of the Temple. The High Priests crucified Jesus because he attacked the money-changers in the Temple – after all, this was the source of their income. Then, in our New Testament reading today, St Stephen launches a frontal attack on the Temple, arguing that 'The Most High does not dwell in houses made with human hands.'

## Why go to church?

We all need to listen to both sides of this debate, then ask ourselves the challenging question, why *do* we go to church? Beware of the dangers of thinking that your church is a sort of magic charm, conveying immunity from suffering even on those who have only a nodding acquaintance with its services. Don't consider that because you go regularly to church, that guarantees you a seat in heaven – those are offered free to anyone who has faith in God and shows love in their lives. And you can, and must, pray wherever you are, in the countryside or at your place of work. But just imagine what would happen if there was no church here, or if you stopped attending the services. You might go on saying your prayers for a while, but without the encouragement of others you'd soon lose heart. You might go on trying to be good, until it appeared to be in your own interest to be selfish, for it's only belief in God's love for us that inspires us to be loving to the unlovely. And who'd teach our children to love God and love their neighbours, if the parables of Jesus were no longer regularly read? Yes, churchgoing brings a great temptation towards hypocrisy; but there's no alternative, if faith, hope and love are to survive for more than a generation – it all depends on you, the faithful few.

### Suggested hymns

*Christ is our corner-stone; Jesus, where'er thy people meet; The Church's one foundation; We love the place, O God.*

# Second Sunday before Lent   7 February
*Principal Service*   **The Garden of Eden**
Gen. 2:4b–9, 15–25 Creation; Ps. 65 Creation, harvest; Rev. 4 The living creatures cry 'Holy!'; Luke 8:22–25 Stilling the storm

> 'The LORD God planted a garden in Eden, in the east; and there he put the man whom he had formed.' Genesis 2:8

## Several accounts of creation

There are two accounts of creation in the book of Genesis. In the first chapter, the plants and trees are created on the third so-called 'day', the fish and the birds on the fifth 'day', and the animals and the human race, men and women together, are created on the sixth day. In the second chapter of Genesis, the same story's told with no mention of the timescale. The man is created first; then God formed the Garden of Eden and filled it with plants. The man is told to look after the plants and the animals. Eventually God creates a woman to be a companion for the man, and they live happily together in the garden, naked and unashamed. There are other accounts of creation in the books of Job, Isaiah, and in the Psalms, which are different again.

## The feminist version

More recently, another version of the Garden of Eden story's been told. That's the feminist version. According to this, God created Eve first, then decided she needed a man to do the heavy work. 'There's only one condition,' said God to the woman: 'you have to let him believe that he was here first!'

## General Gordon

If you look in the *Journal of the Palestine Exploration Society* during the nineteenth century, you'll find a paper there written by General Gordon, the hero of Khartoum. In this he seriously suggests that the Seychelles Islands, where he'd served as a young engineer officer, was the actual site of the Garden of Eden. To prove this he has to suggest that the rivers Jordan, Tigris and Euphrates all once flowed from south to north, instead of the other way as they do now. It just shows the tangles you get into when you take the Bible literally. It's much better to regard the different accounts of creation as poems by different authors, each aiming to give not a historical and scientific account, but an insight into why the world's as it is.

## How the world was meant to be

There's no evidence that there ever was an earthly paradise. The life of the ordinary human being's been 'nasty, brutish and short', ever since the human race evolved. But the Garden of Eden's a very stimulating poetic image. We shouldn't abandon the idea altogether; neither should we allow scientific arguments to distract us from the poetic truth. The biblical account of paradise is a description of what the earth's meant to become. It's a story of a world where human beings live in harmony with their own bodies, with their environment, with each other and with God. That world has never existed yet, but that's the goal towards which we're meant to strive. We're intended to struggle with chaos, and create peace from it, as God did in the beginning, and as Jesus did during the storm.

## Our bodies

We're meant to progress towards harmony with our own bodies. The man and the woman were 'naked, and . . . not ashamed'; they accepted their human nature, with all its vulnerability; they accepted their sexuality with all its delights. We should aim to live in such a way that our bodies remain healthy and strong.

## The environment

Then we're meant to live in harmony with our environment. Only recently have we begun to realize how much harm the human race is doing to our climate, and the animals and plants which are essential for our own survival. God wants us to change our ways, so that we can restore the harmony of the planet.

## Each other

Men and women are meant to live in harmony with each other. There've been many setbacks and disappointments on the road to universal peace, but we're still meant to aim for a world where individuals can live at peace with each other.

## Harmony with God

The only way to bring about this ideal situation's by learning to live in harmony with God. Willingly following his guidance and obeying his commandments, we shall learn to live peacefully with other nations and with the world around us.

## You can restore harmony

It's up to you. The Garden of Eden may never have existed. But it can come into being if you work with God to bring it about. We must work towards that day, as we sang at Christmas,

> when, with the ever-circling years,
> comes round the age of gold;
> when peace shall over all the earth
> its ancient splendours fling . . .

Then earth really will be paradise, if we want it to be.

### All-age worship

*Write a prayer, asking God to make the world more perfect.*

### Suggested hymns

*All creatures of our God and king; It came upon the midnight clear; Let us, with a gladsome mind; Morning has broken.*

# Second Sunday before Lent
## Second Service    Learning from Nature

Ps. 147 Laws of nature, laws of God; Gen. 1:1—2:3 The creation; Matt. 6:25–34 Do not work for the food which perishes

> 'If God so clothes the grass of the field, which is alive today and tomorrow is thrown into the oven, will he not much more clothe you – you of little faith?' Matthew 6:30

### God's care for nature

Jesus was a nature-lover. He pointed to the birds and flowers around him. The colourful anemones carpeted every field. 'Look at them', he exhorted his hearers. 'Have you ever seen anything like it? I tell you, even when King Solomon was wearing his royal robes, he wasn't decorated as splendidly as these fields are.' Jesus told them that God our Father loves the world of nature which he's created, and cares for it. So why do you worry about getting enough money to wear smart and beautiful clothes, he asked. 'How little faith you have! If God cares for the short-lived grass, and decorates it with royal beauty, surely he'll look after you. Work for God's kingdom, not for greater and greater earthly wealth. Learn a lesson from the wildflowers.'

## How do you know God loves you?

We can learn lessons from nature today. Just as you can tell the character of an artist by looking at the pictures he or she paints, so you can learn about God by looking at the world he created. How do children know their parents love them? Surely, because of the things they've done for them. So we can learn of God's love by looking at the world he's made for us. Like Jesus, I'm taking the metaphor of God as Father, because we traditionally use masculine pronouns when talking about God, and because it's too clumsy to keep repeating 'he or she'; but God's parental love for us is like mother-love also.

## 'Red in tooth and claw'

The world of nature reveals a God who cares for his creatures. Transcendent beauty surrounds us by day and night. Yet there are things about the natural creation which strike us as ugly and unpleasant. Many carnivorous beasts devour other animals with vicious cruelty. Nature is, as Tennyson said, 'red in tooth and claw'. Yet it's a mistake to assume that the lesser animals can suffer as we do. They have no ability to reflect on their own life and death, and death is essential in nature to ensure enough room for the next generation. So the existence of the food chain doesn't reveal a cruel God, only one who makes every living creature dependent on all the rest.

## Created by a scientist

We learn from the natural world that God's a scientist, an artist and a lover. The intricacy with which even the tiniest creatures are formed shows a creative skill as yet unmatched by any micro-biologist. The way that everything fits together and works together argues a designer with great skill and foresight. A scientist was going for a walk, and came across a wall in an unexpected place. 'I don't know what the purpose of that wall is,' he remarked to his friend, 'but I'm quite sure it has a purpose, otherwise it wouldn't have been built. And I'm even more certain that it didn't build itself!' So studying the complicated and efficient world of nature reveals to us that it had a designer of far higher intelligence than our own.

## Created by an artist

We learn from the natural world that God's an artist. A chimpanzee can splash paint about, but the result isn't a work of art. Yet a sensitive person can look at a sunset and marvel. Can such beauty come about by a chance arrangement of light and atoms? Could we ourselves appreciate its splendour, if we weren't made by a creator, who himself enjoys the beauty of creation?

## Created by a lover

We also learn from the natural world that God's a lover. Truly great art can only be created by an artist who loves her materials. A truly efficient machine can only be designed by a craftsman who loves his tools, and loves the fruits of his labours. If God's a scientist and an artist, then he too must love working with recalcitrant but malleable materials. The human heart can sometimes be as difficult to carve into shape as the hardest granite; but when God succeeds in forming it into an organ that beats with love, he must utter a shout of triumph, that his endeavours have come out as he intended. And how he must love us, when we're fully formed as loving human beings, but also when we're imperfect, while he's still struggling with us. 'Look at the wild birds', cries Jesus. 'Look at the flowers of the field. Don't they reveal to you a God of fatherly love?' Amen to that, say I. And if you've an ounce of human feeling in you, I think you must agree with Jesus too.

### Suggested hymns

*Fairest Lord Jesus; Lord of beauty, thine the splendour; The spacious firmament on high; Thou, whose almighty word.*

## Sunday next before Lent  14 February
*Principal Service*  **Mountain-top Experiences**

Ex. 34:29–35 Moses' face is shining; Ps. 99 God spoke in the cloud; 2 Cor. 3:12—4:2 The Spirit unveils God's truth; Luke 9:28–36 The transfiguration [37–43a The epileptic boy]

> *'About eight days after these sayings Jesus took with him Peter and John and James, and went up on the mountain to pray.' Luke 9:28*

### Mountain climbing

The Mother Superior in *The Sound of Music* advises Maria to 'climb every mountain', meaning that we should face with courage every challenge that confronts us. But because the story's set among the mountains of the Austrian Tyrol, many people think there's a second layer of meaning. Have you ever climbed a mountain? Or at least reached the top of a fairly high hill, on foot, in a car or by a mountain railway? The hills really are alive with the sound of music, not only the birdsong and the buzzing of the insects among the wildflowers, but the music in your heart as you rejoice at the grandeur of the view and the splendour of the scenery. The splendour of what God's created can be seen, and the puny size of our best efforts in comparison. Yet this impression of the material world forces on us a realization that materialism isn't everything. We understand that beauty, truth and love, which can't be studied by scientific methods, are equally important.

### Mountain-top experiences

I call this sort of insight a 'mountain-top experience'. It can come upon us unexpectedly anywhere, not only in a hilly landscape. On the coast or at sea, in the countryside, a wood or forest, or from the window of an aeroplane, we often catch a glimpse of the awesome loveliness of nature. At a concert or at the ballet, we experience a form of beauty which no words can describe. In the theatre, or reading a book, we grasp a new truth about human life which comes upon us like a revelation. Religious people will call these spiritual experiences, maintaining that at such times we gain an insight into the creative power of God.

## Transfiguration

So it was on a mountain top that his disciples had a vision of who Jesus really was, and the meaning of his ministry. In St Luke's Gospel we read that 'About eight days after these sayings Jesus took with him Peter and John and James, and went up on the mountain to pray.' Explaining in words what he was up to could only take them so far; to lead them into a deeper understanding, Jesus had to give them an experience of prayer. In the silence, with no distractions from the noise and bustle of daily life, they could concentrate on God. In the purer air of the hills they felt able to approach God's holy presence. They couldn't explain what happened in prose, so they used the symbolic language of poetry to explain their vision. The traditional site of the transfiguration is on Mount Tabor, which rises steeply out of the Valley of Jezreel, where so many major battles had taken place. They must have felt that the whole history of the Middle East was spread out before them. But Luke calls it '*the* mountain', which sounds like a reference to Mount Sinai, where God appeared to Moses and gave him the Ten Commandments. Moses and Elijah appeared with Jesus, and spoke of the salvation he was about to accomplish by his death and resurrection, like the salvation of the Israelites at the Exodus from Egypt.

## The voice of God

On Mount Sinai God spoke to Moses out of the cloud. So when the disciples heard a voice speaking to them out of the cloud on the mountain top, they realized it was the voice of God himself. God said, 'This is my Son, my Chosen; listen to him!' So the disciples gained insight into the true nature of their friend Jesus: he isn't just a wonderful human being, they realized – he's the Son of God.

## Down to earth

When the vision was ended, Jesus led them down again from the mountain to the plain. There a man grabbed hold of them and de-manded that they heal his epileptic son. They must have felt they'd come to earth with a bump. But that's the way it is with mountain-top experiences. God gives us these very special times of joy in our lives for a purpose. They're meant to prepare us and strengthen us for the challenges that follow. You can't just lie back and enjoy your vision of beauty. Can our 'mountain-top experiences' – even those which occur in a theatre, a concert hall or a library – inspire and strengthen us to show practical love to our neighbours when we come back down to earth?

## *All-age worship*

*Tell the story of any occasion when you felt moved by beauty, or especially close to God.*

## *Suggested hymns*

*Christ is the world's true light; Lord, the light of your love is shining; 'Tis good, Lord, to be here; Where cross the crowded ways of life.*

# Sunday Next before Lent
*Second Service*   **When I am Lifted Up**
Ps. 89:1–18 The wonders of God; Ex. 3:1–6 The burning bush; John 12:27–36a Glorify your name

> *'And I, when I am lifted up from the earth, will draw all people to myself.' John 12:32*

## St Valentine

Who's the best-known unknown saint in the Calendar? St Christopher and St George could both compete for that title; practically nothing's known about either of them apart from unreliable legend. But surely the saint whose commemoration falls today, St Valentine, must be the most popular saint about whom absolutely nothing is known at all. There was a church dedicated to St Valentine on the Flaminian Way outside Rome, probably commemorating a Roman priest who was martyred there in the third century. There was also a Bishop of Terni, some 50 miles north of Rome, whose bones were returned there after he was martyred in Rome. Legends are told about these two martyrs, and it's possible that they were one and the same person. But nothing's known for certain about St Valentine.

## St Valentine's Day

Yet Valentine's Day's one of the most widely observed saints' days, because of the tradition that this is the day when the birds begin to choose a mate. Therefore, for over a century, people have been sending each other Valentine's cards, and celebrating courtship and love on this day. Perhaps this custom goes back to the Roman festival of Lupercalia, which fell at this time. Chaucer and Shakespeare both wrote about the legend of the birds, and poor Ophelia offered to be Hamlet's Valentine.

## Courtship

But surely it's good to set aside a day to celebrate human love and courtship? When somebody falls in love, the first thing they have to do is to draw the attention of their chosen one to themselves. Then they have to say something, or do something, to show that they love the one on whom they've set their hearts. Every type of love has these three aspects, choosing, wooing and proving; even God's love for us.

## All people

When Jesus entered Jerusalem, and he alone knew that he would soon be crucified, some Greek people were brought to meet him. Up till now he'd concentrated on attracting Jews to follow him; now he was beginning an appeal to the whole world. 'The hour has come,' he said. 'When I am lifted up from the earth, [I] will draw all people to myself.' All people. Not just Jews, but Greeks too, and barbarians and pagans, and even British people, who were regarded as the worst sort of savages. He was going to begin his courtship of them too. Like every other lover, he would choose them, woo them, and prove his love for them.

## Lifted up

So why did Jesus choose those strange words, 'lifted up from the earth'? What did he mean? Two things, I think, at least. First, he was talking about his crucifixion. He was nailed to the cross, and then the wooden structure was lifted up, with Jesus on it. Then everybody would see him. He was drawing the world's attention to his love. He was saying to you, and me, and everybody else, 'I have chosen you to be my beloved, and I want you to know it.' This reminds us of Moses lifting up the bronze serpent, so that all who looked at it were healed of their snake bites. If there's a cross or a crucifix on your church, in your home or round your neck, it's not there just for decoration: it's part of Jesus's advertising campaign. It's like the kiss that's written on the Valentine, which says 'I love you'. It's all a part of God's courtship of the human race. God woos us all with his love, and a few, all too few, respond by loving God in return.

## Proving

If any of you claim to be in love, and forget to do something on Valentine's day to prove it, your beloved won't believe the sincerity of your love. Jesus gave his life to prove how much he loves us. Nobody has greater love than this, to lay down their life for the ones they love. So Jesus was lifted up on the cross, because nothing less would do.

## Drawing

The other layer of meaning to those words refers to Ascension Day. Jesus was lifted up to heaven, so that he might draw all people to himself. He wants everyone to live with him in eternity; and the only way he has of pulling us up to heaven with him is with the cords of love. That's what he chose us for; that's why he died; so that he could draw us after him into the land of eternal love. 'When I am lifted up from the earth, [I] will draw all people to myself', he said. All people; including me; including you.

## Suggested hymns

*As now the sun's declining rays; Hallelujah, my Father, for giving us your Son; Lift high the cross; Sing, my tongue, the glorious battle.*

## LENT

*Lent is observed in the forty days before Easter. The figure forty is based on the forty days that Jesus fasted in the wilderness after his Baptism, before he began his ministry. It is calculated either by omitting the Sundays, when the Lenten discipline is relaxed, or by finishing on Palm Sunday. In the early Church, candidates for baptism at Easter prepared for it by forty days of learning and fasting, and soon the rest of the congregation wanted to join with them. Instead of going without food, today Christians 'give up something for Lent'. This is good training in self-control, but mustn't lead to self-righteousness. More important is to train oneself to do something good in Lent: to read the Bible, spend more time in prayer, attend extra services or a study group, or do something to help others. Like Advent, Lent is a penitential season, so altar frontals and vestments are purple, or unbleached linen representing sackcloth (except that the Fourth Sunday in Lent may be rose), and 'Glory to God in the highest' is often omitted. It is good to examine our lives, accept responsibility for our sins, and confess them to God. Sermons in Lent are often linked together on a common theme; a series on the Sermon on the Mount or the Ten Commandments can help with self-examination, or sermons on aspects of Christian living can lead to practical action. There are some fine Lenten hymns, but they can be too gloomy unless mixed with others on lighter but relevant themes.*

## Ash Wednesday   17 February
### Miserable Lent or Happy Lent?

Joel 2:1–2, 12–17 Rend your hearts; *or* Isa. 58:1–12 Care for the needy; Ps. 51:1–18 Cleanse me from my sin; 2 Cor. 5:20b—6:10 Suffering of an apostle; Matt. 6:1–6, 16–21 Secret fasting; *or* John 8:1–11 Adultery and forgiveness

*'Is not this the fast that I choose: to loose the bonds of injustice, to undo the thongs of the yoke, to let the oppressed go free, and to break every yoke?' Isaiah 58:6*

## Miserable or happy?

Do you want a miserable Lent or a happy Lent? Recently the Church of England published a booklet with lighthearted suggestions for acts of kindness that Christians could do in Lent. A newspaper article solemnly protested that this was lowering the standards of the past, when everybody had to give up chocolate or other forms of pleasure for Lent. Not at all; if you want to give up things, nobody's stopping you. Maybe you really need to diet, or to conquer some addiction; if so, Lent can be very useful as it gives you a target to do it before Easter. But that isn't what Lent's *really* about. You have a choice: are you going to give up things for Lent, or take on good things that you ought to do? Giving up, or taking on – the choice is yours. Miserable Lent, or happy Lent, whichever you prefer.

## It's easy to be miserable

It's easy to be miserable. You can have a miserable Lent by concentrating on your own faults. God knows, for each of us there are plenty of them, and they need to be repented of. But that should only take a minute or two when you say your daily prayers, then God forgives them and you can forget them. But maybe you've already had your attention drawn to all your faults by other family members. If you share a house with a wife or husband, or what we call these days 'a significant other', they probably tell you every day what's wrong with you. If you're at work, you've been criticized for your faults on a regular basis. If you're in authority, they've been under public scrutiny. Daily self-examination is scarcely necessary in those circumstances; all you have to do is take responsibility for your actions, accept God's forgiveness, and go on your way rejoicing.

## Jesus

And there's one significant other who shares your life with you, who's more significant than all of the rest, and that's Jesus. He knows all your faults, and he's dying to forgive them. But if you ignore his offer of forgiveness, and concentrate on yourself all through Lent, you won't make yourself a better person, and you'll finish up in a wooden box at the end, the same as the rest of us. So it's easy to have a thoroughly miserable Lent.

## Happy Lent

If you want a happy Lent, however, stop focusing on yourself. Forget the harm you've done in the past, once it's forgiven, and think of your potential for doing good in the future. Tear up the book of pettifogging rules, and follow the guidance of the Holy Spirit, as God shows you the joyful way of goodness. If there are bad things you should give up, well, give them up. Then spend Lent taking on new things you can do for God.

## Prayer

For instance, take on board a more positive approach to prayer. Make up your mind that you'll say the Lord's Prayer at least once every day until Easter. But don't just recite it parrot-fashion; say it slowly and think what the words mean. You're never alone when you say the Lord's Prayer, because while you're praying the words 'Our Father', two billion of your Christian brothers and sisters are saying it with you, a third of the world's population.

## Acts of kindness

My second suggestion for positive things you can do for Lent is to find new little acts of kindness to do for others. Listen again to what Isaiah says:

> Is not this the fast that I choose: to loose the bonds of injustice, to undo the thongs of the yoke, to let the oppressed go free, and to break every yoke? Is it not to share your bread with the hungry, and bring the homeless poor into your house; when you see the naked, to cover them, and not to hide yourself from your own kin?

Yes, it'll involve a degree of self-sacrifice, but let it be joyful, not grudging. With prayer and kindness, you can have a very happy Lent, if you choose to. You can follow Jesus for the next forty days on his way to the cross, and on to your own personal happy Easter when you die.

*Come, let us to the Lord our God; Dear Lord and Father of mankind; Father of heaven, whose love profound; Sing to God new songs of worship (or Joyful, joyful we adore thee, www.cyberhymnal. org/htm/j/o/joyful.htm).*

## First Sunday of Lent   21 February
*Principal Service*   **Lead us not**
Deut. 26:1–11 First-fruits; Ps. 91:1–2, 9–16 God's providence; Rom. 10:8b–13 Faith, salvation and unity; Luke 4:1–13 The temptation of Jesus

> *'Jesus, full of the Holy Spirit, returned from the Jordan and was led by the Spirit in the wilderness, where for forty days he was tempted by the devil.' Luke 4:1–2*

### The Sirens

The Sirens, in Greek myth, were imagined as beautiful women. In Homer's *Odyssey*, they lived on an island in the narrow straits between Italy and Sicily, and sang a beautiful song to tempt sailors to destruction on the rock of Scylla or in the whirlpool of Charybdis. Odysseus stopped the ears of his crew with wax, so that they couldn't hear the tempting music, and had himself lashed to the mast. When the Argonauts, however, sailed that way, they had with them Orpheus with his lyre, and he played even more beautiful music than the song the Sirens sang. The Siren voices of temptation come to us every day, and we need to decide in advance how we're going to resist them.

### Occasions of sin

In the old Prayer Book, temptation was said to come from the world, the flesh and the devil.

- The world's made up of people; when other people tempt you to wickedness, they may suggest there's nothing wrong in it, and everybody does it. Then you yield because you don't want to be different. Many good people have gone astray by getting into bad company; the only defence is to be on your guard against such people, and either avoid meeting them, or at least resolve that you won't give in to their blandishments.

- When you relax in a warm swimming pool, your flesh feels good; but if you stay there all day, you won't get any work done. So the temptations of the flesh are when you're tempted to use pleasures, which are good in the right place, to excess and at inappropriate times.
- When you're tempted to use the devil's methods to do something you believe to be good, you know where that temptation's coming from.

All these situations in which we're tempted are known as occasions of sin, and we have a Christian duty to avoid them. It's no use saying the Lord's Prayer every day and asking God not to lead you into temptation if you keep leading yourself into tempting situations.

## Jesus in the wilderness

Yet when Jesus was tempted, it was the Holy Spirit who led him out into the wilderness, to reflect on how he was going to win the people to follow him. He was tempted by the world, the flesh and the devil:

- the world, when he was offered authority over all the kingdoms of the world;
- the flesh, when his natural desire for food tempted him to turn stones into bread;
- and the devil, who tried to tempt him to throw himself from the pinnacle of the Temple.

Jesus was tempted all through his ministry to use wrong means to achieve good ends. He was tempted to feed the crowds, force them, or fascinate them.

- The poor people were always hungry; he could have started a social programme to provide them with food; but then they'd have forgotten his spiritual message.
- Or he could have raised an army and forced people to follow him; but God wants willing obedience, not grudging acceptance. -
- Or he could have performed miracles and won a reputation as a

75

wonder-worker. But followers who are dazzled by the supernatural are like seed sown in shallow ground; when the excitement wears off, they wither away.

The Bible tells us that Jesus was 'tempted in all things just as we are'. The temptations of the world, the flesh and the devil were with him every day. It was only in the garden of Gethsemane that he finally, and with great difficulty, resisted them all, and accepted the only true way to win the world for God his Father: the way of the cross.

## Just say no

There's nothing wrong with being tempted; temptation comes to all of us, and it even came to Jesus. What's wrong is yielding to temptation. Avoid occasions of sin whenever you can. But sometimes temptation's unavoidable, and the only strategy is to be ready for it. We train ourselves in Lent to resist little temptations, so that we're fit to say a firm 'No' to the big ones when they attack us later. Like Jesus, we can only overcome temptation by remembering that the joys of heaven are deeper and more lasting than the transitory pleasures offered to us by the Siren voices.

## *All-age worship*

*Draw posters illustrating temptations that come from the world (other people); the flesh (pleasures used wrongly); and the devil (using wrong ways in an attempt to do good).*

## *Suggested hymns*

*Be thou my guardian and my guide; Forty days and forty nights; O Jesus, I have promised; What a friend we have in Jesus.*

# First Sunday of Lent

*Second Service*   **Contempt**

Ps. 119:73–88 Let those who fear you turn to me; Jonah 3
Nineveh converted; Luke 18:9–14 Pharisee and publican

> '[Jesus] told this parable to some who trusted in themselves that
> they were righteous and regarded others with contempt.' Luke
> 18:9

### Circus strongman

The strongman in a circus squeezed all the juice out of a lemon and
challenged anyone in the audience to get any more out. A weedy-
looking man came forth and squeezed out another glassful of juice.
The astonished strongman said, 'You must be in a job where you
use the strength of your hands a lot, to be able to get more out of
something that's already been squeezed dry!' 'Not really,' said the
other. 'I'm an inspector of taxes.'

### Contempt

Jesus told a story of a tax-collector, and a Pharisee who despised
him. When you have no respect for someone, you regard them
with scorn, you hold them in contempt. Yet while respect has to be
earned, contempt's nearly always undeserved. You can't get a clear
view of anyone's worth by looking down your nose at them. To
treat another person with contempt is the worst form of pride.

### Tax-collector and Pharisee

Pride was a sin of which the Pharisee in the story was guilty. He
paraded his virtues before God, to show how much better a person he was than, he said scornfully, 'this tax-collector'. But God
didn't see it as a competition. God alone knows all the mitigating
circumstances of our actions, so God judges each of us mercifully
and understandingly. The Pharisee was trying to prove to God that
he was a superior individual. You can't pray when you're feeling
supercilious; so the Pharisee, as St Luke puts it, was praying 'with
himself'. Jesus told this parable for people like that – as the Gospel
says, 'to some who trusted in themselves that they were righteous,
and regarded others with contempt'.

## Pride

Here's a true story: a traveller made a journey by train from Scotland to England and back. On his way south it was a gloomy day; he passed a whitewashed cottage in the Yorkshire moors and thought how white it looked against the grey landscape. But on the way back it had snowed, and against the white snow the little cottage looked drab and dirty. It all depends on your standard of comparison. We can usually find some other human being to compare ourselves with, who's worse than ourselves. But that's the wrong yardstick to measure ourselves by. What we should contrast our own lives with, is the perfect life of Jesus; compared with him, none of us has anything to boast about.

## Pharisees today

Sadly, there are 'pharisees' in the Christian Church today. Some Christians hold all others in contempt, and turn to God, like Little Jack Horner, only to say, 'What a good boy am I.' Narrow-minded people who say, 'Only *my* truth is true; only *my* way of life is righteous.' Now it's good to have rigorous standards in what we believe, and to set ourselves the highest targets in morality. But we've no right to impose them on others; that's between them and God. The Pharisee had no idea how difficult it was to be an honest tax-collector in those days, so he had no sympathy with the tax-man's struggle to control his desires and rise above his surroundings. Jesus warned us that the worst sin of all is that of judging others; we must leave judgement to God. Judging others is far more offensive to God than the sexual mores which the modern pharisees take it upon themselves to condemn. Some people, claiming to be Christians, complain that 'We can't have, in *our* church, people with this or that lifestyle – we can only share fellowship with those who believe in God in exactly the same way that we do – we must exclude those who don't come up to our required standards, to keep our church pure.' People who say that are a menace. Such exclusive views create a church that God can't work with.

## God's tolerance

Fortunately we've a God who's not at all narrow-minded. Jesus was often found enjoying parties with tax-collectors and sinners. He offered them unconditional forgiveness, and their response was to become more loving in their dealings with their neighbours. Jesus said that the sinners would enter the kingdom of God before the self-righteous Pharisees. He said that we judge ourselves when we reject the pure light of God's love, and prefer to remain in the darkness of complacency. God's loving tolerance embraces everyone, even those who are despised by their neighbours. The only important sins are causing hurt to other people and being too proud to accept God's love. Love is all that matters. God writes nobody off as beneath his concern; God treats nobody with contempt. Neither should we.

### Suggested hymns

*Come, my soul, thy suit prepare; O! O! O! How good is the Lord; There's a wideness in God's mercy / Souls of men; When I survey the wondrous cross.*

## Second Sunday of Lent  28 February
*Principal Service*  **Deliver us**
Gen. 15:1–12, 17–18 God's promise to Abraham; Ps. 27 Faith and providence; Phil. 3:17—4:1 Citizens of heaven; Luke 13:31–35 Jesus's lament over the city

> *'How often have I desired to gather your children together as a hen gathers her brood under her wings!' Luke 13:34*

### Fire in the farmyard

In the days before chickens were raised by battery-farming, they used to wander around the farmyard, pecking at the grains of wheat that had fallen from the sheaves as they were brought in. Often a hen would be followed by a brood of chicks that she'd hatched, devotedly showing them how to feed themselves. At night she'd call the chicks to snuggle for warmth under the feathers of her outstretched wings. After the wheat had been threshed, the straw was stacked in a barn for later use. Because of the natural processes of decay, it rapidly became hot, and the farmer's deepest fear was that a barn might catch fire. There's at least one recorded instance when, after one such disastrous blaze, the dead body of a hen was found among the ashes, burnt and scarcely recognizable, and then from underneath her charred wings would creep out her brood of chicks. They were alive because she'd sheltered them, but she delivered them from death at the cost of her own life.

## Foxes and sun

During the early stages of her offspring's infancy, like any other mother creature, a mother hen's devotion's concentrated on protecting them. She'll find them somewhere safe to roost, out of reach of marauding foxes. In the baking heat of the eastern summers, she'll save them from being scorched by spreading her wings over them. Four times in the book of Psalms, God's called upon to hide us under the shadow of his wings. We talk a lot about the fatherhood of God, but in these images God's compared to the most devoted of mothers.

## Jesus rejected

These must have been the images in the mind of Jesus, too, when some Pharisees warned him to flee the wrath of King Herod Antipas, who ruled over Galilee, and Jesus described Herod as 'that fox!' The king was as unpopular as the Roman overlords who'd put him in power. Movements of rebellion were bubbling, but Jesus offered to deliver the people from the clampdown which would inevitably follow any uprising, by showing them a more spiritual meaning of the words, 'kingdom of God'. But the people were only interested in political power, and rejected Jesus when they saw he wouldn't give it them. Jesus knew that his final appeal must be made in the capital city of Jerusalem, and that if it failed it would cost him his life. So, continuing with the same set of metaphors, he cried out:

'Jerusalem, Jerusalem, the city that kills the prophets and stones those who are sent to it! How often have I desired to gather your children together as a hen gathers her brood under her wings, and you were not willing!'

## In danger

By these words he implied his oneness with the God whom the Psalmist described as hiding us under the shadow of his wings; and he described the danger of destruction facing the people of the city he loved. But we too are in danger, and call out daily to God, 'Deliver us from evil.' The perils that confront us are more insidious than those that faced the people of Jerusalem; we're in danger of the death of the soul which comes from losing our faith. Prolonged pain could lead us to doubt God's care for us. Failure in our ambitions, shame at losing our self-respect, economic collapse, family problems; all these frighten us into rejecting the only Saviour who can truly deliver us. We've called out to him, and God seems to have rejected our cry.

## Succeeding by failing

But like the people of Jerusalem, we've been looking for a material answer to our prayers; Jesus points us to find deliverance in the spiritual strength that God gives us to cope with our problems. Sometimes we have to fail in order to triumph over compromise; and as Jesus showed us, sometimes our death is the supreme victory which crowns a life of sacrificing ourselves for those we love. Jesus will deliver us from eternal death by gathering us under the shadow of his wings, even at the cost of his own life. But this longed-for salvation's only possible if we're willing to shelter under his protection; and that means conforming our lives to his example. Jesus cries out to *you*: 'How often have I desired to gather you under my wings and deliver you, and you were not willing!' Are you willing, now, this Lent, to live a more unselfish life, accepting the deliverance from solitary fear which he offers?

### All-age worship

*Draw the hen sheltering her chicks under her wings.*

### Suggested hymns

*All my hope on God is founded; A safe stronghold; Come, O thou traveller unknown; There's a wideness in God's mercy / Souls of men.*

## Second Sunday of Lent
### Second Service   A Pyrrhic Victory
Ps. 135 Praise for God's goodness; Jer. 22:1–9, 13–17 Sin in
Jerusalem; Luke 14:27–33 Counting the cost

> 'What king, going out to wage war against another king, will not
> sit down first and consider whether he is able?' Luke 14:31–32

### Pyrrhus

Pyrrhus was King of Epirus in Greece, and a cousin of Alexander
the Great. He led a Greek army, winning several battles against
Rome, but was never able to gain power over them. At the Battle of
Asculum in 279 BC he routed the Romans, but all his best soldiers
were killed. He turned to his generals and is supposed to have said
ironically, 'One more victory like that and we're done for!' Ever
since, the phrase, 'a Pyrrhic victory', has been used to describe some
action which appears to be successful in the short term, but is disastrous in the long run.

### Just war

Among the conditions that St Thomas Aquinas drew up, before
a war can be called a Just War, there are two which would have
been helpful to Pyrrhus. One is that you must be clear about what
you want to achieve by fighting. Another is that you must be likely
to achieve those aims, not only in the short term but in the long
run also. These rules are important to Christians too, in fighting
on behalf of God against evil in the world. It's important to join
in the struggle on behalf of the kingdom of God, but only if we're
absolutely clear what we're trying to achieve; and to be absolutely
certain that we've a strong probability of lasting success in the long
term. Otherwise we may enjoy a merely Pyrrhic victory – losing,
eventually, because we haven't planned with foresight.

### Counting the cost

Jesus told a story about two kings going to war against each other:

> 'What king,' asked Jesus, 'going out to wage war against another
> king, will not sit down first and consider whether he is able with

ten thousand to oppose the one who comes against him with twenty thousand? If he cannot, then, while the other is still far away, he sends a delegation and asks for the terms of peace.'

Like most parables, this story asks a question: what king would do such a thing? To which the obvious answer is: only a very stupid king. Then Jesus asks us to apply it to ourselves. Have we counted the cost of discipleship? Have we calculated what demands being a Christian will make upon us? Have we made sure we have sufficient resources within ourselves to finish the course?

## What we're up against

In other words, have we planned ahead, with a reasonable understanding of what we shall be up against? There are many obstacles, which, if we haven't prepared ourselves to meet them, could easily prevent us achieving what we intend. Let's take, as examples, slovenly thinking, laziness, mockery, suffering, death, and stinginess.

## Slovenly thinking

Slovenly thinking is when we haven't worked out carefully enough what the aims of Christianity are, and find ourselves fighting the wrong enemy. If you're attacking, on behalf of Jesus, ideas about freedom, tolerance and love, you can be pretty sure you've chosen the wrong target.

## Laziness

Laziness is when it becomes too much trouble to struggle for righteousness. We all get exhausted from time to time, and need times of recreation. You must expect that; but make up your mind that when you've caught your breath, you'll return to the fray refreshed.

## Mockery

The favourite weapon that our enemies use against us is mockery, from the atheist who argues that faith in God is an irrational delusion, to your so-called friends who tell you that being a Christian is so-o-o old-fashioned. Then 'always be ready to make your defence to anyone who demands from you an accounting for the hope that is in you', as St Peter puts it.

## Suffering

Fourth, we must expect to suffer. Suffering comes to most of us sometimes. Your Lenten fast's meant to prepare you, by small acts of self-denial, to keep the faith even when the going's tough.

## Death

Death comes to us all. We don't like to think about it when we're young and fit, but it's wise to make up your mind you won't be scared into losing faith in Jesus, just when you need him most.

## Stinginess

Finally, the cost of discipleship is generosity with your time, your love and your money; stinginess makes you want to hold some back. Jesus said, 'None of you can become my disciple if you do not give up all your possessions.' Give everything to God; you'll be amazed at how much he lends back to you.

## Long-term thinking

Slovenly thinking, laziness, mockery, suffering, death, and stinginess are the weapons your enemy will use against you. Be ready for them; otherwise your triumphs may turn out to be merely Pyrrhic victories.

### *Suggested hymns*

*O Jesus, I have promised; Take my life, and let it be; Take up your cross, the Saviour said; Will you come and follow me?*

## Third Sunday of Lent   7 March
*Principal Service*   **Suffering and Sin**
Isa. 55:1–9 A call to conversion; Ps. 63:1–9 Faith and providence; 1 Cor. 10:1–13 Temptation; Luke 13:1–9 The parable of the fig tree

> *'Some [people] told [Jesus] about the Galileans whose blood Pilate had mingled with their sacrifices. He asked them, "Do you think*

84

*that because these Galileans suffered in this way they were worse sinners than all other Galileans?"' Luke 13:1–2*

## Pontius Pilate

Pontius Pilate was an infuriating Governor, and kept angering the Jewish people. The Roman legions carried a carving of an eagle on a tall pole, like a flag. Pilate gave orders for these standards to be set up in the Temple in Jerusalem; but of course they were graven images, and the Jews were deeply offended. He had a new pipeline built to bring extra drinking water into Jerusalem; a praiseworthy project, except that he took the money to pay for it out of the Temple treasury, which the Jews had raised through their tithes for religious purposes. The people were angry and restless, and Pilate gave orders for his soldiers to mingle with the crowds, disguised by cloaks, and then fall on the troublemakers and club them to death. If this happened in the Temple itself, and the blood of the Galilean victims fell onto the dead animals which they'd just sacrificed, it was sacrilege. Maybe the new water supply was brought into the city near the Pool of Siloam, and the tower in the wall there collapsed as a result of the construction work, and some people demonstrating against the misappropriation of Temple funds were killed. So some people told Jesus about these incidents, to see whether he'd become as furious as they were. Jesus's answer was in two parts. First he spoke about suffering and sin; and then he spoke about the kingdom of God. I'll take these two points in reverse order.

## The kingdom of God

Mentioning these incidents was intended to provoke Jesus into raising an armed revolt against the Romans. Yet even if he only uttered a few hasty words critical of Pilate, there'd be a crackdown. Then Jesus would be killed, as they wanted. But Jesus said that unless they repented, his questioners would die in the same way as the Galileans they'd quoted. In other words, if they saw the kingdom of God as a political movement to seize power from the Romans, then the Romans would punish them and destroy Jerusalem. Jesus taught us in the Lord's Prayer to ask for God's kingdom to come 'on earth, as it is in heaven'. So it must be a spiritual kingdom, not a political one. Using politics, you may possibly improve the life of the nation; but the only way to change human nature is by leading people back to God. If we pray that God's will be done, that means that we'll obey God as our king, and the kingdom of God will have started to invade our lives.

## Suffering and sin

Now, going back to the first point that Jesus raised: he asked them, 'Do you think that because these Galileans suffered in this way they were worse sinners than all other Galileans?' In other words, is there a connection between suffering and sin? Many people say yes; if you're suffering, it must be a punishment for something. That's what Job's comforters told him. But it isn't true: good people often suffer horribly, whereas evil people get off scot-free. And the Bible tells us all have sinned, and come short of the example of Jesus's love. If that's true, nobody can ask, 'What have I done to deserve this?' All of us would suffer a great deal more than we do, if we were paid what we deserve. No, God's created a wonderful world for us to live in, where most things work to our advantage; but God's generously allowed the world to continue most of the time without his direct intervention, and sometimes things don't happen as God planned. This way, God's deliberately limited his power by giving us freedom. But love's only possible where there's freedom; if God made it impossible for us to suffer, he'd have to make it impossible for us to love.

## Repent

So Jesus told his hearers to repent. All of them: those who thought they were good as well as those who knew they were bad; those who suffered, as well as those who were in fine fettle. We all need to turn back to God, and build his spiritual kingdom on earth, by doing his will as obediently as the angels in heaven. The more we do that, although suffering won't disappear overnight, life on earth will become more and more 'as it is in heaven'.

### All-age worship

*Dress as nurses and patients: the nurses must treat all patients equally, like God does.*

### Suggested hymns

*Faithful Shepherd, feed me; God moves in a mysterious way; O for a closer walk with God; Through the night of doubt and sorrow.*

# Third Sunday of Lent
## Second Service   The Lamb of God

Ps. 12 No longer any godly, 13 How long?; Gen. 28:10–19a
Jacob's ladder; John 1:35–51 The call of Nathanael

> '[John the Baptist] saw Jesus coming toward him and declared,
> "Here is the Lamb of God who takes away the sin of the world!"'
> John 1:29 [Not in today's readings]

## The Lamb of God

John the Baptist described his cousin, Jesus, as 'the Lamb of God'.
The book of Revelation refers no less than 28 times to Jesus as
'the Lamb'; the lamb and flag became a common symbol for the
resurrection in Christian art, and the 'Agnus Dei' is regularly sung
in our services: 'Lamb of God, you take away the sin of the world,
have mercy on us.'

## Sacrifice

The idea of a lamb conjures up two images in our minds. We think
of a fluffy, gentle, gambolling young creature; but also we remember
that lambs were often used in sacrifice. At Passover time, the blood
of the lamb was painted onto the doorposts, so that the angel of
death would pass over the homes of the Israelites, and they would
be saved. Sacrifices were used as a sign of the people's penitence,
and God's forgiveness. There's no forgiveness without sacrifice; yet
even if we were to surrender our own lives for others, that wouldn't
be a big enough offering to pay off the debt we owe to God for all
our sins. So the lamb takes the place of the worshipper, and the
lamb's death represents the worshippers' offering of their own lives
to God. John the Baptist said that Jesus is 'the Lamb of God, who
takes away the sin of the world'. In life, Jesus was gentle as a lamb;
but when he died he offered to his Father the most perfect life of
goodness there's ever been. That sacrifice of steady, powerful love is
more than enough to pay off the debt for all the sins ever committed
in the world.

## William Blake

William Blake, best known as the author of 'Jerusalem', also wrote a poem called 'The Lamb'. 'Little Lamb, who made thee?' it begins. A small child questions a baby lamb about their creator, who was once a child and was known as 'the Lamb'. So the poet reveals the gentle innocence of the child Jesus, and also the gentle tenderness of God the Father. But this poem is one of a set which William Blake called *Songs of Innocence*. He also wrote a parallel set of poems called *Songs of Experience*. Soon we learn that the world is not such a simple and gentle place after all. Can we reconcile these two opposite views of human nature, and of God? The poem in the second set which mirrors 'The Lamb' is called 'The Tyger'. I'm sure you know it: 'Tyger! Tyger! burning bright/ In the forests of the night,/ What immortal hand or eye/ Could frame thy fearful symmetry?' Here's another question about the character of the creator. What sort of God could create a tiger, with all its sinewy strength and awesome power? Surely, only a Creator who is himself of awe-inspiring majesty. The Creator has those two sides to his character, and we must try to hold these two ideas together in our minds in creative tension: tender strength, and the steely power of weakness. Then we should show these two apparently opposite aspects in the way we treat other people, firmly but at the same time with gentleness. Listen to the two poems again and think: Jesus *was* like that; God *is* like that, and I *should be* like that:

## The Lamb

Little Lamb, who made thee?
Dost thou know who made thee?
Gave thee life, and bid thee feed
By the stream and o'er the mead;
Gave thee clothing of delight,
Softest clothing, wooly, bright;
Gave thee such a tender voice,
Making all the vales rejoice . . .

Little Lamb, I'll tell thee . . .
He is callèd by thy name,
For he calls himself a Lamb.
He is meek, and he is mild,
He became a little child:

I a child, and thou a lamb,
We are callèd by his name . . .

## The Tiger

Tiger! Tiger! burning bright
In the forests of the night,
What immortal hand or eye
Could frame thy fearful symmetry?

In what distant deeps or skies
Burnt the fire of thine eyes?
On what wings dare he aspire?
What the hand dare seize the fire?

And what shoulder, and what art,
Could twist the sinews of thy heart?
And when thy heart began to beat,
What dread hand? and what dread feet?

What the hammer? what the chain?
In what furnace was thy brain?
What the anvil? what dread grasp
Dare its deadly terrors clasp?

When the stars threw down their spears,
And water'd heaven with their tears,
Did he smile his work to see?
Did he who made the Lamb make thee? . . .

## *Suggested hymns*

*Gentle Jesus, meek and mild; Lord of beauty, thine the splendour;*
*Loving Shepherd of thy sheep; The spacious firmament on high.*

## MOTHERING SUNDAY

*In the USA, Canada and Australia, Mother's Day is celebrated on the second Sunday in May; Mothering Sunday is celebrated in the UK on the Fourth Sunday in Lent. 'Mid-Lent Sunday' is a time for relaxing the Lenten fast. In days gone by, people would gather flowers as they walked home to visit their mothers. Or maybe Mothering Sunday is called after the custom of visiting the 'Mother Church' of the diocese, the cathedral, on this day. Instead of a sermon for the Second Service, this book provides a special sermon for Mothering Sunday. If there is a special service, young people can make flowers into posies, or draw pictures of flowers on greetings cards. These can be blessed with words such as the following, then given out at the Peace, or at the end of the service. Then those present can give them to their mothers, saying 'Thank you, mother, for all you have done for me', or put them in a suitable place, in memory of her.*

*O God, bless these flowers, bless us, and bless our mothers. May the flowers remind us how much our mothers have done for us; may they remind our mothers that we love them; and may they remind us all that God cares for us better than any mother ever could. **Amen.***

## Fourth Sunday of Lent    14 March

(For Mothering Sunday, see the Second Service. If the Principal Service readings have been displaced by Mothering Sunday provisions, they may be used for the Second Service.)

*Principal Service*    **Forgive Us**

Joshua 5:9–12 Eating the Passover in Canaan; Ps. 32 Repentance; 2 Cor. 5:16–21 Forgiveness and reconciliation; Luke 15:1–3, 11b–32 The prodigal son

*'Father, I have sinned against heaven and before you; I am no longer worthy to be called your son.' Luke 15:18–19*

## The prodigal son

Television programmes studying abstract ideas like science and history only work well if they tell a story. Similarly, Jesus didn't preach about faith or morality; he told parables, and left us to make up our own minds. The parable of the prodigal son contains profound truths about relationships between parents and children, and between humans and God. But it does this by telling a simple story: a son went off with half his father's wealth and frittered it away. He decided to go home and say sorry, but instead of punishing him, his father came out to meet him and threw a party.

## The forgiving father

The father's a remarkable person. He'd have been quite entitled to fly into a towering rage and punish his wastrel son. Instead he forgave him. Why? The only reason that we can imagine is that he really loved his son. If he'd punished the lad, justice might have been done, but their relationship would have been angry and resentful. By his astonishing act of forgiveness, father and son started a new relationship of love and trust. First the son had to accept some responsibility for what he'd done. He said, 'Father, I've sinned against heaven and before you.' He only dared expect grudging acceptance as a labourer on wages; but his dad's astonishingly generous forgiveness startled him into genuine repentance and devoted love.

## Desmond Tutu

That's the nature of forgiveness. Yet nobody'll listen if you preach at them. So Jesus told it as a story, for people to draw their own conclusions. At the end of the Apartheid struggles in South Africa, Archbishop Desmond Tutu found a society deeply riven by mutual antipathy and hatred. Yet he knew it was no use calling people who had been deeply wounded to forgive each other, because they had the wrong idea of what forgiveness means. He wrote:

> Forgiveness does not mean condoning what has been done. It means taking what has happened and not minimizing it; drawing out the sting in the memory that threatens to poison our entire existence.

So he formed the Truth and Reconciliation Commission. No one was asked to forgive. Simply to tell the truth about what happened;

how somebody'd died. Often it was the first time the relatives had heard the full story; sometimes that was all that they needed. But in other cases people on both sides didn't want to waste the rest of their lives consumed by resentment. Some victims offered forgiveness, and it was not accepted. Some perpetrators of violence asked for pardon, but were told the victims weren't able to forgive – yet. All agreed, however, that to have faced each other honestly was better than hiding the truth.

## The Forgiveness Project

Based on Archbishop Tutu's experience, an international movement called The Forgiveness Project was formed in 2004. They've toured a tremendously successful photographic exhibition, 'The F Word', containing photos of victims and perpetrators of violence from many parts the world, with text telling in their own words what happened when they met. Sometimes mutual forgiveness was exchanged; in other cases that was neither appropriate nor possible. But often both participants started a new way of life, offering themselves to projects designed to bring reparation and reconciliation to all those who'd suffered. Sir Anthony Berry was an MP killed in the Brighton Bombing in 1984. In November 2000, his daughter Jo met Pat Magee, the former Irish Republican activist responsible for her father's death. Pat was released under the Good Friday Agreement in 1999, and since then has been actively involved in peace work. Jo Berry says, 'I'm beginning to realize that no matter which side of the conflict you're on, had we all lived each others' lives, we could all have done what the other did.'

## The price of peace

The Forgiveness Project is a non-religious organization; yet its work mirrors exactly the teaching of Jesus. Forgiveness isn't condoning evil; it's reaching out to achieve reconciliation, so that both sides can start to rebuild. Forgiveness *can't be accepted* until you accept responsibility for what you've done. Yet *offering forgiveness* can sometimes shock a hardened offender into genuine remorse.

## Have you got what it takes?

This is a challenge to us all. Have you got what it takes to achieve reconciliation, to give and receive forgiveness? And when you've grappled with that question, move on to ask how we can possibly pray, 'Forgive us as we forgive others'? What does the parable of the prodigal son tell us about the character of God our Father, and our relationship with him?

### All-age worship

*Gather more information from* www.theforgivenessproject.com.

### Suggested hymns

*Amazing grace; Forgive our sins as we forgive; I cannot tell why he whom angels worship; On a hill far away.*

## Mothering Sunday   14 March
### Party Clothes
(This is the second set of readings for Mothering Sunday from Common Worship.)
1 Sam. 1:20–28 His mother offers Samuel to the Lord; Ps. 127:1–4 Children a gift from the Lord; Col. 3:12–17 Love and care; John 19:25b–27 Mary is your mother

> *'As God's chosen ones, holy and beloved, clothe yourselves with compassion, kindness, humility, meekness, and patience.' Colossians 3:12*

### Party clothes

Do you put on your best clothes to go to a party? Here's a question for you: who do you dress up for? For whose benefit? Do you doll yourself up for your own benefit, because it makes you feel good when you're proud of your appearance? Or is it to impress the friends and strangers you expect to meet at the party? Do you sometimes dress smartly to please your own family? Does it occur to you that your mother, father, husband or wife will be so proud of you when they see that you've taken trouble over how you look? Probably there's a bit of each of these motives behind the care you take over your appearance.

## Looking good

You want to please your family, yet it's not really what you're wearing that impresses them most. Try to *look* good, if you can; but they'll really only be proud of you if you *are* good. When God chose David to be king, he passed over several brothers who were handsomer than he, because, the Bible says, 'God looks not on the outside, but on the inside of a person.'

## Inner clothing

So however smartly we dress on the outside, what God sees is something much more important: God sees what one of our favourite hymns calls our 'inner clothing'. Usually our family, too, is sharp enough to see through any public display we make, and recognize that our character's what counts. In our New Testament reading today, St Paul listed a few of the spiritual gifts which make up what we could call our 'spiritual clothes':

As God's chosen ones, holy and beloved, clothe yourselves with compassion, kindness, humility, meekness, and patience. Bear with one another and, if anyone has a complaint against another, forgive each other; just as the Lord has forgiven you, so you also must forgive. Above all, clothe yourselves with love, which binds everything together in perfect harmony.

## Our Mothering Sunday gift

We call the fourth Sunday in Lent, Mothering Sunday. It's a day for each of us to think about our mum, whether she's here or somewhere else, whether she's with us on earth or alive with Jesus in heaven. It's a day for saying thank you to Mum for all she's done for us, by giving her a card, or a bunch of flowers; by praying for her; and by doing something special to please her. She'll be happy if we give her a present, or dress up to please her. But she'll be even more pleased if we put on our best spiritual clothes.

## Virtues

So let's list again the virtues St Paul says go to make up our inner clothing:

- *Clothe yourselves with compassion*, he begins. Compassion means 'feeling with' somebody; if you understand what they're feeling, you can treat them compassionately.
- *Kindness* is gentleness; we like others to be kind to us, so we must treat them in the same way.
- *Humility*'s the opposite of pride; if you're humble you'll treat even unimportant people with respect.
- *Meekness* is rather an off-putting word: it really means having a soft and mild disposition, and willingly doing what you're asked; it's a good character to develop on Mothering Sunday.
- *Patience* with God, with other people, and with yourself, is not being in a hurry, but waiting for things to develop in God's good time.
- *Bear with one another*, writes St Paul, *and, if anyone has a complaint against another, forgive each other; just as the Lord has forgiven you, so you also must forgive.* It's fatal if family members nurse a grudge against each other; we've all done wrong things, so we must be tolerant of the mistakes of others.
- *Above all*, St Paul finishes, *clothe yourselves with love, which binds everything together in perfect harmony.* Fine clothes are no use if they're falling off you; you need a belt to hold them together. Fine deeds are useless unless they're done from a motive of love. We owe everything to the love that our mothers showed us when we were children; today we must show love to mothers and other family members, and everyone else we meet. Then we shall not only *look* good for Mothering Sunday; we'll *be* good too.

### All-age worship

*Cut out a doll in paper or card, and garments with fold-over tabs, which can be hung from the doll. Label each garment with one of the virtues listed above.*

### Suggested hymns

*Come down, O love divine; Father, I place into your hands; For the beauty of the earth; Lord of the home, your only Son.*

# Fifth Sunday of Lent   21 March
*Principal Service*   **God's Will**

Isa. 43:16–21 Salvation; Ps. 126 Salvation and joy; Phil. 3:4b–14
Perseverance; John 12:1–8 Mary and Martha

*'Martha served.'* John 12:2

## Monica

Monica was the mother of a very wild young man. She went to her
local bishop in tears, asking him what she could do to make her son
a Christian. 'Just pray,' replied the bishop; 'pray that God's will be
done.' 'But how do I know what God's will is,' pleaded Monica.
'You don't,' replied the bishop, 'but how can God will that the
child of such tears should be lost?' So Monica went on praying, and
years later her son did become a Christian, St Augustine of Hippo,
one of the greatest Christian teachers ever. St Augustine himself
said that his conversion was thanks to his mother's prayers. We
don't know what God's will is, exactly; but we do know that God
is love, so whatever he wants for his children must be for the best.

## *Inshallah*

It used to be the custom to announce a forthcoming meeting, adding
the letters DV, which stand for *Deo volente*, Latin words meaning
'God willing'. This recognized that whatever plans we make, they
may not happen unless God wishes them to. Muslims also often
add the word *inshallah*, meaning 'If it's God's will', when talking
about their intentions. Then if everything goes pear-shaped, they
may shrug it off, saying *Kismet*, a Turkish word for fate. But that
suggests that God's a cruel God, who wills us to suffer. Or else he's
a powerless God, who can't prevent the impersonal tread of fate
from shaping our lives. No, the only thing which can stop God's
will being done is when human beings refuse to pray. God wanted
to bless St Augustine, and Monica's prayers helped God to win
him over. But both of them were powerless until Augustine himself
began to pray, and submitted his will to God's will. That's what we
mean when we ask in the Lord's Prayer, 'Thy will be done'. It's not
a cringing submission to the cruel hand of fate. On the contrary,
the words express a firm conviction that God wills the very best in
life for us, and a determination to co-operate with God in any way
he wants us to.

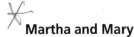
## Martha and Mary

We heard in the Gospel reading today how Jesus visited the home of two sisters, Martha and Mary, and their brother Lazarus. St John's Gospel says that 'Martha served', probably meaning that she brought the food to the table. She thought she knew that Jesus wanted her to do this for him. But we should be careful of thinking that we know for certain what God wants us to do; the will of God's much more complex than we realize. Mary was listening to Jesus while he talked about God, and loved him so much that she poured a jar of precious perfume over his feet. She served Jesus in a different way from Martha, and she did it gladly out of love. You can't do more than that; pray to God to show you what his will for you is, and then do it heartily to the best of your ability. It may be that God willed Martha to do one thing, and willed Mary to do another; we can never assume that we know what God's will is for somebody else. And God's will for us may change from day to day. God's long-term strategy is to bring us to eternal life with him in heaven; but on the way towards that ultimate goal, he may want us to do different things, according to the stage we've reached in carrying out his will.

## Gethsemane

So we must always be ready for anything. In the garden of Gethsemane, Jesus prayed that the cup of suffering might be taken away from him. 'Abba, Father,' he said, 'for you all things are possible; remove this cup from me; yet, not what I want, but what you want.' And, 'My Father, if this cannot pass unless I drink it, your will be done.' Even Jesus, when he was on earth, didn't claim to know for sure what God wanted him to do. But he trusted that whatever it was, it would be for the best. We too, when we pray 'Thy will be done', can't be sure what to expect – we must be ready for anything. But like Monica and Augustine, Martha and Mary, we can be sure that God wants to bless us, and we can co-operate with God with all our strength, doing what we believe to be his will for us at the moment, serving our King in building his kingdom on earth, until he's ready to take us to his kingdom in heaven.

### *All-age worship*

*Write a page of 'Orders of the Day, from God to me'.*

97

*According to thy gracious word; Lord, teach us how to pray aright; O thou, who at thy Eucharist didst pray; Son of God, eternal Saviour.*

## Fifth Sunday of Lent
### Second Service   The Passover Plot
Ps. 35 You deliver the weak; 2 Chron. 35:1–6, 10–16 Josiah's Passover; Luke 22:1–13 Preparing for Passover

> *'Now the festival of Unleavened Bread, which is called the Pass-over, was near. The chief priests and the scribes were looking for a way to put Jesus to death, for they were afraid of the people.'*
> *Luke 22:1–2*

### Chambord

The Chateau de Chambord is one of the most elaborate of the sixteenth-century castles in the Loire Valley. The French court used to assemble on the flat terrace on top of the roof. It's cluttered with towers, cupolas, domes, chimneys, dormers and slate roofs with geometric shapes. It's been described as looking like an over-crowded chessboard. It's almost as if it was designed to provide as many nooks as possible for secret meetings, to plot adultery or assassinations. Woe betide the courtier who miscounted and hid behind the wrong chimney: he'd have found himself caught up in the wrong plot!

### Secrets

There was a plot to kill Jesus, which was hatched in secret meetings. The chief priests met among themselves, because Jesus was threatening their claim to rule the Jews through the Temple, and their secret pact with the Roman authorities to keep the people docile. Judas Iscariot gave way to temptation because he made his plans secretly, instead of discussing them with others. He met secretly with the priests, to formulate a plan to arrest Jesus secretly, thus avoiding a riot. Jesus was condemned by a secret meeting of the council, assembling by night, which was illegal; the Pharisees were afraid that Jesus would take away their power as the sole interpreters of the law. They arranged secretly with the crowd that they should shout for Barabbas to be released instead of Jesus. Pilate was afraid of truth, because he was afraid that if his pact with the priests became known, the secret of what a bad Governor he was would come to the ears of the Emperor in Rome. As Jesus said:

This is the judgement, that the light has come into the world, and people loved darkness rather than light because their deeds were evil. For all who do evil hate the light and do not come to the light, so that their deeds may not be exposed.

As a film title once put it, there's nothing so destructive to the life of a family as *Secrets and Lies*; the same could be said of any secret plotting by politicians or church people.

## The Passover plot

All this plotting took place at Passover time. Hugh Schonfield published a book called *The Passover Plot*. Approaching the story of the crucifixion from the Jewish point of view, he gathered the evidence concerning the Jewish hope for a military Messiah, and concluded that Jesus was crucified because of a failed plot in which he would seize political power. While we may not agree with its conclusions, the book's a reminder that the crucifixion was part of the will of God for the salvation of the world, and not just a result of the secret machinations of the Jewish and Roman authorities.

## Passover

At Passover each year, Jewish families used to kill a lamb and eat its flesh with unleavened bread, to remind them of the last meal their ancestors ate together in Egypt before God saved them from slavery. They thought of the lamb as a sacrifice, and when they painted its blood on the doorposts in a T-shaped cross, the angel of death would know to 'pass over' their home, and spare them from the death of the firstborn which was striking the Egyptians. They were 'saved by the blood of the Lamb'. Christians can eat bread and drink wine, not only at Passover or Easter time but all the year round. Jesus said 'This is my body, this is my blood'. St Paul wrote, 'Christ, our Passover Lamb, is sacrificed for us', and John the Baptist hailed Jesus as 'the Lamb of God who takes away the sin of the world'.

## Failed plots and successful planning

Secret plotting's seldom successful. What Pilate and the priests plotted to do came to naught, yet through their conspiracies God's plan succeeded. Pilate was dismissed a few years later when his brutality came to light; the priesthood came to an end when the people eventually rose in rebellion against Rome – the very thing the priests had been trying to prevent – and Jerusalem was destroyed in AD 70. Yet through the sacrificial death of Jesus at Passover time, people from many nations came to believe that the God of the Jews loves all people and wishes to forgive their sins. 'Behold the Lamb of God, who takes away the sin of the world.' The Passover plots to destroy Jesus may have failed, but the successful planning of God brought us salvation.

### Suggested hymns

*Just as I am, without one plea; O for a closer walk with God; The Church of God a kingdom is; There is a Redeemer.*

---

### HOLY WEEK

*The final week of Jesus's life on earth is celebrated from Palm Sunday to Easter Eve. Long readings of the Passion Narrative are set at all the services. Palm Sunday is often marked with a procession of palms; Maundy Thursday by the washing of feet, Good Friday by the veneration of the cross, and Easter Eve by a vigil with the lighting of the new fire. An informal Passover supper to commemorate the Last Supper can be held on any day but is especially suitable for Maundy Thursday. A series of sermons on the Passion, or on the seven words of Christ from the cross, can be preached throughout Holy Week, or to mark the Three Hours on Good Friday. Most of the sermons provided in this book for specific days in Holy Week could be used on other days instead.*

# Palm Sunday   28 March
## *Principal Service*   Gethsemane

Isa. 50:4–9a I gave my back to the smiters; Ps. 31:9–16
Assurance in suffering; Phil. 2:5–11 Jesus's obedience unto
death; Luke 22:14—23:56 The Last Supper to the burial *or* Luke
23:1–49 The trial before Pilate to death on the cross

> *'Father, if you are willing, remove this cup from me; yet, not my*
> *will but yours be done.' Luke 22:42*

## Sticking to principles

A king who's conquered a city's expected to ride into it on horseback, to claim it as his. Jesus wouldn't do that; he'd no interest in military conquest. So he rode a donkey, a visual symbol that he knew a better way to bring God's kingdom than by fighting. Jesus is the Son of God, so he could have forced people to obey him if he'd wanted to. But forced obedience, without love, isn't true obedience. Jesus was too humble to claim the privileges of divinity. So he rode on a humble donkey, and the people welcomed him. But it was a touch-and-go situation – the cheering crowd could easily turn nasty, when they discovered he wasn't going to lead a revolt. He overturned the tables of the money-changers, showing that money can't bring about the kingdom of God. Then he was daily in the Temple, teaching the people that the only way to victory is the way of love. That means sticking to your principles, and, if necessary, submitting to whatever your enemies do to you, rather than use violence to resist them.

## Gethsemane

Then Jesus ate a last supper with his friends, warning them to expect the worst. Leading them down to an olive grove called Gethsemane, he asked them to leave him alone while he wrestled with his conscience. It wasn't an easy struggle; he was sweating buckets before he finished. Like most moral questions, it wasn't an easy dilemma to resolve. There were no black-and-white certainties. Don't forget, Jesus was human, and he'd deliberately put aside the knowledge of the future which could have been his as the Son of God. He'd chosen to become one of us, and just like us he hoped for the best and feared the worst. He really didn't know what to do for the best. That's the cost of being human.

## Choices

The problem was this. Should he face up to his enemies and resist them when they came for him? Or should he run away and hide? Or should he submit, and let them do their worst?

- To resist would bring the whole nation to arms, and start a revolution. Then the might of the Roman army would fall on its rebel province. People would be killed; there'd be orphans and widows. If Jesus eventually became a victorious king, it would be at such a cost that he'd be further than ever from persuading people to live by love.
- Secondly, should Jesus then have run away? No, that would have been useless. No one could say the provocative things he'd said about those in power, and get away with it for long; they'd find him eventually. It would only postpone the evil day. Besides, who'd believe a preacher of universal love and non-violence, if he wasn't prepared to put it into practice and face the consequences?
- So only the third choice was open to him: to submit to certain death without putting up any resistance. That way, a few people might see that the only way to victory's the way of love and self-sacrifice. If those believed him, and tried to live their own lives on the same principles, then a movement might just possibly grow and spread across the world; though it seems impossible that it can ever be very large, considering what demands it makes. For Jesus was human; he didn't know for sure that this way would work. And he didn't want to die – nobody does. 'Drinking the cup' seems to have been a common expression; Jesus asked his disciples whether they could drink the cup that he'd drink; as we'd say, 'taking your medicine'. So Jesus prayed in an agony of fear that he might suffer one of the most painful deaths ever invented. He wasn't play-acting. Eventually, after a long struggle, he won through, and accepted that 'not my will, but yours, be done'.

## Holy Week

If you'll follow the events of this Holy Week alongside Jesus, re-membering that he's human, and tempted as we are, then on Friday you'll find out the consequences of his choice. But not until next Sunday will you know whether the way of self-sacrifice was right for him. If so, it must be the right way for you and me to live victoriously too.

### All-age worship

*Look at El Greco's picture of Jesus in Gethsemane: <http://commons.wikimedia.org/wiki/Image:El_Greco_019.jpg>. Can you think of people wrestling with difficult decisions today who would be helped by knowing that Jesus understands?*

### Suggested hymns

*According to thy gracious word; From heaven you came; My God, I love thee – not because; Ride on, ride on in majesty.*

## Palm Sunday
### Second Service    Passion

Ps. 69:1–20 Zeal for your house consumes me; Isa. 5:1–7 The Song of the Vineyard; Luke 20:9–19 The parable of the wicked tenants

> *'Zeal for your house has eaten me up.' Psalm 69:10 (Common Worship)*

### Could do worse

In St John's Gospel, when Jesus had turned the traders out of the Temple, his disciples remembered the verse from the Psalms which reads, 'Zeal for your house has eaten me up.' Jesus was passionately concerned that the Jerusalem Temple should be used only for what it was meant for; he was consumed by emotion, and that zeal would be the death of him. Many people are suspicious of strong emotions, because they can be dangerous. A story's told about the vicar of a parish of taciturn people, who was disappointed that they expressed no thanks, praise or sorrow when he left. He was surprised, then, to be invited back to preach a year later, and found they were all over him with affection. He pointed out the change, and asked them what had caused it. 'Well, you see,' replied one, 'when *you* were our vicar we said to each other, "I suppose we could do worse." And now we have. So we realize you weren't so bad after all.'

## Passionate

There's nothing in the Bible, however, to suggest that there's anything wrong with feeling strong emotions, or expressing what we feel. We lose the richness of life when we repress all our feelings. Yes, sharing our emotions in inappropriate ways and at inappropriate moments can be inconsiderate and even manipulative. But, rightly used, emotions can drive us to take action over what we feel passionate about. Zeal is Christ-like.

## Passiontide

So it's entirely right that we should call this season 'Passiontide', and talk about the Passion of Christ. Jesus was passionate, in his love for God and the Temple of God, and in his love for his friends. Jesus loves you passionately – never forget that. And, as he said, there is no greater love than this: to lay down your life for your friends. When you look at the cross, say to yourself, 'That's how much Jesus loves me.' Lewis Carroll prepared something humorous in one of his books about the Passion flower, because he thought it took its name from sloppy romantic feelings. Then he crossed it out when someone pointed out to him that the plant symbolizes the Passion of Christ, with

- the leaves representing the spear;
- the stamens the hammers, and five of them for the five wounds;
- the spiralling tendrils for the whips;
- the central column representing the pillar;
- the three pistils are the three nails;
- the purple crown is the crown of thorns.

So the Passion flower's a reminder of the suffering of Jesus on the cross. Our word 'passion' comes from the Latin word for suffering; and *com*-passion is *suffering with* somebody.

## William Blake

The eighteenth century was possibly the time in Britain most marked by the repression of public emotion. It was the Age of Reason, when everything was supposed to be thought out by cold logic. The poet William Blake protested against this, crying that only passionate conviction would change the world. This is probably the meaning of the sexual imagery in his much misunderstood poem, 'Jerusalem':

> Bring me my bow of burning gold!
> Bring me my arrows of desire!
> Bring me my spear! O clouds, unfold!
> Bring me my chariot of fire!

## Zeal

'Zeal for your house has eaten me up', sang the Psalmist. Jesus was zealous in putting all his energy into achieving what he believed to be right, no matter what it might cost him. We, his followers, are called to be equally zealous in the search for loving and just standards in the way the world is run, among our friends and colleagues, and in our own family. It may not destroy our lives, but it will certainly destroy our cosy refusal to get involved in defending those in need.

## The way of the cross

The way of the cross, then, is to follow Jesus in his passionate love for other people, and his passionate devotion to his Father. Passionate faith must be tempered by reason, but not strangled by it. Passionate faith's not the same as extremism and bigotry; it should be passionately concerned for liberty and tolerance; but it's not to be identified with lazy refusal to be committed to anything. Being a passionate Christian can sometimes mean suffering patiently and long for those you love, as parents do, as Jesus did on the cross. If we're to follow Jesus, this week, in his passion and suffering, we must show passionate compassion for those who suffer, and absorb their suffering as Jesus absorbs ours. I wish you a profoundly moving Passiontide.

### Suggested hymns

*All glory, laud and honour; And didst thou travel light, dear Lord?; Drop, drop slow tears; When I survey the wondrous cross.*

## First Three Days in Holy Week   29–31 March
## Blood

(Following are the Monday readings but this sermon may be used on any day this week.)

Isa. 42:1–9 The servant brings salvation; Ps. 36:5–11 Defend me against the wicked; Heb. 9:11–15 The sacrifice of the new covenant; John 12:1–11 Mary anoints Jesus for his death

> *'Under the law almost everything is purified with blood, and without the shedding of blood there is no forgiveness of sins.'*
> Hebrews 9:22

### Blood on his hands

In the Bavarian village of Oberammergau, most of the inhabitants are involved in the performance of the Passion Play, when the story of the last week of Jesus's life is acted out on a huge stage. During the season when the play was performed, a visitor to the village asked whether he could hire a bicycle to get around. He was recommended to try the village carpenter, and visited his workshop. The carpenter found a suitable bicycle, and started to adjust the saddle to the right height. 'Stop,' gasped the horrified visitor, 'you've got blood on your hands! Have you cut yourself?' 'No,' laughed the carpenter. 'That's the blood of Christ! I act the part of one of the soldiers who nail him to the cross at every performance, and it's difficult to wash all the stage blood away when the show's ended!'

### Guilt

Even when you know it's not real, what must it feel like to have the blood of Christ on your hands every day for five months? It's a cliché in thrillers to describe someone who's guilty as having the blood of the victim on their hands. Lady Macbeth's feelings of guilt led her into the delusion that she couldn't wash her hands free from the blood of the murdered king – 'Out, damned spot; out I say', she cried. Pontius Pilate tried to wash the guilt from his hands when he'd condemned Jesus to death. In fact the Bavarian carpenter was far too hearty a man to be disturbed by such morbid thoughts. But then, he's no different from the rest of us. Haven't we all got blood on our hands? For all the times we've connived at wrong and failed to stand up for what's right, for our public sins and our secret sins, we all share in the common guilt of the human race down the ages. And Jesus died for the sins of the world.

## Blood

Some people get a bit queasy when blood's mentioned in the Bible and in our worship. We have to remind ourselves that the word's being used in a metaphorical way. Even so, the imagery of William Cowper's great hymn, 'There is a fountain filled with blood, drawn from Emmanuel's veins', is quite hard to take. Yet the wording's taken directly from the book of Revelation: 'These are they who have come out of the great ordeal; they have washed their robes and made them white in the blood of the Lamb.' So what's the significance of mentioning the blood of Christ so much in our services?

## The blood is the life

Well, anyone can see that a live animal has blood pulsing through its veins, whereas dead meat on the butcher's slab has none. So the Old Testament says that 'the blood is the life'. That's why they were forbidden to eat meat, until the blood had been drained out of it. And when they sacrificed an animal in the Temple, they not only sacrificed something expensive, they were offering a life to God. As the animal's blood poured out over the altar, it symbolized for them the offering of their own lives to God. God doesn't wish sinners to die, so the animal became their representative, showing God how sorry they were for their misdeeds.

## The blood of Christ

When Jesus, then, was crucified, his followers compared his death to those Old Testament sacrifices. The shedding of his blood reminded them of his willing offering of his life to God, to save others. He became our representative. Nothing we have to offer is worthy enough to compensate God for our disobedience; but if we feel penitent, Jesus has promised us that we shall be forgiven. We offer our own life to God in obedience, and Jesus sums up our little sacrifices in his great act of sacrifice, and we're forgiven. Today we seldom handle human blood or even animal blood, so it's an uncomfortable metaphor; but in times past, forgiveness resulting from the death of Christ on the cross was naturally described as 'washed in the blood of the Lamb'.

## Saving blood

Yes, in that sense, we've all got blood on our hands. But it's not blood-guilt, it's the saving blood of forgiveness. Even the crowds who shouted, 'His blood be on us and on our children', were unwittingly claiming the cleansing power of Christ's sacrificial death. May that purifying forgiveness be the experience of each one of us this Holy Week.

### Suggested hymns

*Glory be to Jesus; There is a fountain filled with blood; Were you there when they crucified my Lord?; When I survey the wondrous cross.*

## Maundy Thursday  1 April
## A Sacrament to Meet All Needs

Ex. 12:1–4 [5–10] 11–14 The Passover; Ps. 116:1, 10–17 The cup of salvation; 1 Cor. 11:23–26 The last supper; John 13:1–17, 31b–35 Foot-washing

> 'For I received from the Lord what I also handed on to you, that the Lord Jesus on the night when he was betrayed took a loaf of bread, and when he had given thanks, he broke it and said, "This is my body that is for you. Do this in remembrance of me."' 1 Corinthians 11:23–24

### Dom Gregory Dix

Born in 1901, Dom Gregory Dix was a monk of the Anglican Benedictine Abbey of Nashdom in Buckinghamshire. His great book, *The Shape of the Liturgy*, which took him 15 years to write, influenced the revision of all subsequent versions of the Holy Communion service, Eucharist or Mass. He suggested that the first half of the service should be patterned on synagogue worship, with its readings, songs and prayers. Then the second part should follow the fourfold pattern which, he pointed out, can be seen in the Last Supper, where Jesus

1 took bread and wine
2 gave thanks

3 broke, and
4 gave.

In the final chapter of his book he gives a lyrical description of the central place of Holy Communion in the history of Christian prayer. Jesus broke bread, and gave them wine to drink, and told his disciples, 'Do this in remembrance of me.' Gregory Dix points out the variety of circumstances in which the sacrament has been celebrated, in each of which, in different ways, it exactly meets the needs of the people present. I shall read the passage through slowly; please forgive me if I get a bit emotional, as I find it deeply moving.

### 'Do this in remembrance of me'

'Do this in remembrance of me.' Was ever another command so obeyed? For century after century, spreading slowly to every continent and country and among every race on earth, this action has been done, in every conceivable human circumstance, for every conceivable human need from infancy and before it to extreme old age and after it, from the pinnacles of earthly greatness to the refuge of fugitives in the caves and dens of the earth. Men have found no better thing than this to do for kings at their crowning and for criminals going to the scaffold; for armies in triumph or for a bride and bridegroom in a little country church; for the proclamation of a dogma or for a good crop of wheat; for the wisdom of the Parliament of a mighty nation or for a sick old woman afraid to die; for a schoolboy sitting an examination or for Columbus setting out to discover America; for the famine of whole provinces or for the soul of a dead lover; in thankfulness because my father did not die of pneumonia; for a village headman much tempted to return to fetish because the yams had failed; because the Turk was at the gates of Vienna; for the repentance of Margaret; for the settlement of a strike; for a son for a barren woman; for Captain so-and-so, wounded and prisoner of war; while the lions roared in the nearby amphitheatre; on the beach at Dunkirk; while the hiss of scythes in the thick June grass came faintly through the windows of the church; tremulously, by an old monk on the fiftieth anniversary of his vows; furtively, by an exiled bishop who had hewn timber all day in a prison camp near Murmansk; gorgeously, for the canonisation of Saint Joan of Arc – one could fill many pages with the reasons why men have done this, and not tell a hundredth part of them. And best of all, week by week and month by month, on a hundred thousand successive Sundays, faithfully, unfailingly, across all the parishes of Christendom, the pastors have done this just to *make* the *plebs sancta Dei* – the holy common people of God.

## Meaningful to all

That's the end of the quotation, and there's really nothing left to say. I hope it's given you a new insight into how this service takes on new meanings in different circumstances. And I pray that the sacrament of Holy Communion may meet your needs, this day and every time you join in the celebration, wherever you are and whatever is happening in your life. God bless you.

### Suggested hymns

*An Upper Room did our Lord prepare; Let us break bread together; Lord Jesus Christ, you have come to us; Sing my tongue the glorious body.*

(The quotation from *The Shape of the Liturgy* is reprinted by permission of the Abbot of Elmore Abbey.)

## Good Friday   2 April
## Rigoletto

Isa. 52:13—53:12 The suffering servant; Ps. 22 Why have you forsaken me?; Heb. 10:16–25 *or* Heb. 4:14–16 Jesus the priest; John 18:1—19:42 The blood of the covenant

> *'He was wounded for our transgressions, crushed for our iniquities; upon him was the punishment that made us whole, and by his bruises we are healed.' Isaiah 53:5*

## Rigoletto

Like most operas, Verdi's *Rigoletto* has a very complicated plot. Rigoletto loves his daughter, Gilda, and is horrified to discover that she's been kidnapped and handed over to the Duke. What he doesn't know is that Gilda has already met the Duke and fallen in love with him. Rigoletto offers to pay a hired assassin to kill the Duke, but the assassin spares the Duke, and agrees to murder Rigoletto instead. Gilda overhears this and decides to sacrifice herself to save her father. In the darkness Gilda is stabbed and, while she is dying, placed in a sack which is handed over to Rigoletto as if it contained the Duke's body. He is appalled to find that the Duke's still alive and it's his dying daughter in the sack. They sing a final duet as she dies. The audience is in tears.

## Substitutes

This story's typical of one of the great themes running through tragic literature: that of the person who offers their own life as a substitute for someone else's. Christians see the death of Jesus on the cross as an act of self-sacrifice. We deserve to die because of our sins, but Jesus died in our place. You mustn't push the metaphor too far, because you can't in fact transfer guilt from one person to another. It's better to say that Jesus died as our representative; when we offer to God our tiny acts of self-sacrifice, Jesus takes them up into his great act of obedience and offers them to our Father as if they were part of his own sacrifice.

## Sacrifice

Jesus himself described his life as a sacrifice: 'The Son of Man came not to be served but to serve, and to give his life as a ransom for many.' It's not that God's forgiveness needs to be bought at the cost of a life; it's more a question that the supreme act of self-sacrifice, which Jesus made on the cross, benefits us by changing our whole attitude to life, death, and God. In between the end of the Old Testament and the beginning of the New Testament, some Jews of the family of the Maccabees had died rather than make pagan sacrifices. Their martyrdom was described as a sacrifice: 'through the blood of those devout ones and their death as an atoning sacrifice, divine Providence preserved Israel, that previously had been mistreated.'

## The Suffering Servant

Even before that, however, an anonymous prophet had written about vicarious suffering, suffering on behalf of others, in what are known as the Servant Songs. The book of Isaiah's in at least two parts. The second part, written centuries after the first half, was designed to encourage the Jewish exiles in Babylon who'd lost hope. It promised them that one day soon they'd return from Babylon to Jerusalem. This message was so subversive that the new book was 'tacked on' to the end of the older scroll, to hide it from the Babylonian police. It contains four great poems about the 'servant of the Lord', who's called to be a light to lighten the Gentiles, but at the cost of his own suffering. Some people suggest that the author was describing his own vocation; others think it might be some historical figure like Jeremiah. Commonly, however, readers have seen the suffering servant as an image of the nation of Israel, who suffered during the exile in Babylon, in order to set an example to other nations of their loyalty to God, at whatever cost to themselves.

## Servanthood

Not only the nation of Israel, though, but anyone who's a servant of God may be called to suffer for the sake of others. When Jesus came to earth, he saw himself as fulfilling Second Isaiah's prophecy of the Suffering Servant. His disciples also described his crucifixion in words borrowed from Second Isaiah:

> Behold, my servant . . . is despised and rejected of men; a man of sorrows, and acquainted with grief . . . Surely he hath borne our griefs, and carried our sorrows . . . he was wounded for our transgressions, he was bruised for our iniquities: the chastisement of our peace was upon him; and with his stripes we are healed. . . . the LORD hath laid on him the iniquity of us all . . . when thou shalt make his soul an offering for sin, he shall . . . be satisfied . . .

Who was the Song of the Suffering Servant describing? Israel? Jesus? Rigoletto's daughter? Or you and me? Or all of the above? Think about it, this Good Friday.

## Suggested hymns

*Hallelujah, my Father; In the cross of Christ I glory; Meekness and majesty; Thank you, Jesus, for loving me.*

## Easter Vigil  3–4 April
### Why Seek the Living among the Dead?
*(A minimum of three Old Testament readings should be chosen. The reading from Ex. 14 should always be used.)*
Gen. 1:1—2:4a Creation, Ps. 136:1–9, 23–26; Gen. 7:1–5, 11–18; 8:6–18; 9:8–13 Noah, Ps. 46 Our refuge and strength; Gen. 22:1–18 Sacrifice of Isaac, Ps. 16 The path of life; Ex. 14:10–31; 15:20–21 The Exodus, *Canticle*: Ex. 15:1b–13, 17–18 The song of Moses; Isa. 55:1–11 Come to the waters, *Canticle*: Isa. 12:2–6 Great in your midst; Bar. 3:9–15, 32—4:4 God gives the light of Wisdom, *or* Prov. 8:1–8, 19–21; 9:4b–6 Wisdom, Ps. 19 The heavens declare God's glory; Ezek. 36:24–28 I will sprinkle clean water on you, Ps. 42 and 43 Faith and hope; Ezek. 37:1–14 The valley of dry bones, Ps. 143 A prayer for deliverance; Zeph. 3:14–20 I will bring you home, Ps. 98 Salvation and justice; Rom. 6:3–11 Baptism, death and resurrection, Ps. 114 The Exodus; Luke 24:1–12: The empty tomb

> *'The women were terrified and bowed their faces to the ground, but the men said to them, "Why do you look for the living among the dead? He is not here, but has risen."' Luke 24:5*

## Were you there?

If you've been at any of the Holy Week services, you probably feel as though you've been through a mangle. The services make you want to cry 'Yes', when you hear the hymn, 'Were you there when they crucified my Lord?' Even if you couldn't get to church, but have been reading your Bible, or watching any of those depictions on stage or television, still, by using your imagination, you felt you'd actually been present through all those terrible events. Now, as we come to Easter, try to picture that you're actually present at the empty tomb. *Were you there when he rose up from the tomb?* Yes, yes; I haven't quite got there yet, but I want to be; I want to see the risen Christ clearly in my mind's eye.

## The right place

Well, even if you've only a part-formed wish to meet Jesus, you've come to the right place. Because here, in this church, a bunch of people are on the same quest. Each of us wants to believe that Jesus is risen. Our faith is feeble, and our hope is halting, but our love for him leads to deep longing. Here, among people like us, you're sure to encounter the resurrection. Only to those who believed did Jesus appear. Even a half-formed faith's enough; Jesus wants to reveal himself. Faithless people don't have the right sort of eyesight to see the risen Christ. But here, among the community of faith, comes the amazing realization that Jesus lives in us. That's where you look for him and find him, in the hearts of your fellow Christians.

## Among the dead?

The angels asked the women at the tomb, 'Why do you look for the living among the dead? He is not here, but has risen.' Yet we persist in looking for Jesus in the wrong place. We look for him in libraries, or laboratories, or among unbelievers, and of course, we don't find Jesus there. Books and scientific experiments are very good things, but they're dead things. Reason points to the probability of the resurrection, but to be sure it's true you have to meet him for yourself. Science reveals the vigorous life surging through creation; but it tells you nothing about the source of that life. Doubters argue and debate, but they never have an encounter with the living Christ, because he can only reveal himself to those who believe. There's no point in seeking the living among the dead. But by coming to church today, you've come to the right place, because here Jesus is alive in the community gathered to worship him.

## The living proof

Many sages and prophets claimed to tell us about life after death. Many people claimed to be the new Messiah, bringing in the kingdom of God; but when they died their frightened followers vanished. The fact that the Church of Christ continues to meet and worship him, in spite of persecution, is the proof of the resurrection, because Jesus, alone of all these religious leaders, lives on after his death in the hearts of those who pray to him. Jesus said, 'Seek, and you will find.' The risen Christ's all around us, we just don't look in the right places. Why do you seek the living among the dead?

## Worship and prayer

Don't expect a flash of light. Just worship Jesus along with other Christians, and talk to him in prayer as though he was alive, and it'll dawn on you that Jesus isn't dead, but alive and well in the hearts of his people.

### Suggested hymns

*Jesus Christ is risen today; Light's glittering morn bedecks the sky; Thine be the glory; We have a gospel to proclaim.*

## Easter Day   4 April
*Principal Service*   **New Life**
Acts 10:34–43 Peter and other witnesses to the resurrection; or Isa. 65:17–25 New heavens and a new earth; Ps. 118:1–2, 14–24 I shall not die but live; 1 Cor. 15:19–26 The last enemy destroyed is death, or Acts 10:34–43 Peter and other witnesses to the resurrection; John 20:1–18 Magdalene at the tomb, or Luke 24:1–12 The women see Jesus

*'I shall not die, but live!' Psalm 118:17*

## Easter eggs

Look at this Easter egg! I'll divide it later between the children who have been best behaved during this service, a little bit for each of you. Now, I want to ask you a peculiar question: is this egg alive or dead? Easy one, that. It's made from cocoa beans, ground down and cooked up in the chocolate factory. The beans were once alive, but the chocolate egg's definitely dead. It certainly won't jump up and start running around the table. Now look at these eggs bought from the local shop. They look dead too, don't they? But if you visit a chicken farm, where they breed new generations of poultry, the mother hen will be allowed to sit on some of the new-laid eggs to keep them warm. Although those eggs *look* dead, after a week or two you'll hear a quiet sound, chip, chip, chip. Then suddenly the shell will break, and out will pop – a baby chick! New life, out of something which seemed to be dead.

## New life

Easter's always in springtime, when there's new life all around us. The leafless trees which looked dead all winter begin to burst into bud. The dead-seeming bulbs you planted in the ground last autumn burst into new life with yellow daffodils. The fields are full of baby lambs, bouncing with fresh vitality. Some children won a pair of rabbits in a raffle, and decided one of them was going to have some babies, so they put her in a comfortable hutch with lots of room and warm straw, and banished the other to a bare box. One morning in springtime, they found that the rabbit in the bare box had given birth to a large litter of baby rabbits! The children realized they'd got the parent rabbits the wrong way round! So flowers, lambs and bunnies are all signs of fresh life in springtime. Like the Easter egg – the Easter bunny, the lambs and flowers are used as symbols for new life at Easter.

## Jesus

Easter's the time when we think about what happened to Jesus. Jesus died, and his friends were very sad. They knew he was dead, and they thought that was the end. In those days they used to bury dead bodies in a cave. They put the body of Jesus in a cave near to Jerusalem, and rolled a huge stone across the entrance to stop anybody getting in. Picture the scene: a dead body, hidden in a cave in the lifeless rock; and the stone blocking the doorway emphasizes the deadness of everything. That was on a Friday; on the Sunday, some women came very early in the morning to finish the care that was given to a body when it was buried. They found that somebody'd already rolled the stone away before they got there. One of the women, called Mary Magdalene, stayed behind at the tomb because she was crying. She saw a man standing there and slowly realized it was Jesus. Jesus, who had been dead, was now alive again! The cave, which had been a place of death, was now filled with new life. New life at Easter. That's why the Easter egg reminds us of Jesus; out of something that seemed to be dead has come new life.

## Us

The story doesn't stop there. The new life grows and grows. Jesus promised to give new life to everybody who believes in him. That means you and me, and everybody here today. Because we love Jesus, and know that Jesus loves us, our dull old boring life becomes full of joy and happiness. Our selfish way of treating other people becomes filled with the new life and love of Jesus, and we love other people like he loves us. This bubbling new life never stops. Even when we die, Jesus has promised, we shall still be filled with new life, and live with him for ever in heaven. Out of our death comes new life. And it's all because Jesus defeated death and came alive again at Easter. The egg, which seemed dead, was filled with new life when the chick came out. So it's a reminder that we too can pass through death into new life. Happy Easter!

### All-age worship

*Tell the story of the chick coming out of the egg, and Jesus coming out of the tomb, using movable cardboard cut-out figures.*

### Suggested hymns

*Come, ye faithful, raise the strain; Good Joseph had a garden; I will sing, I will sing a song unto the Lord; Now the green blade riseth.*

## Easter Day
*Second Service*   **The Leap of Faith**
Morning Ps. 114 The Exodus, 117 Praise the Lord; Evening Ps. 105 The Exodus, *or* 66:1–11 God holds our souls in life; Isa. 43:1–21 You are my witnesses; 1 Cor. 15:1–11 Witnesses of the resurrection, *or* John 20:19–23 Sunday evening appearance

> *'[Jesus] said to Thomas, "Put your finger here and see my hands. Reach out your hand and put it in my side. Do not doubt but believe."' John 20:27*

### The leap of faith

A photographer was trying to understand what faith means. He'd taken the cable car to the top of one of the mountains in the Bavarian Alps, and there he was trying to get a good photograph of the paragliders, those brave people who soar like a bird into space, supported by nothing except a narrow parachute. But the weather seemed to be turning nasty: a big black cloud hung over the end of the valley. The photographer was wondering whether it was safe to jump in these conditions, when one of the sportsmen, in a yellow jumpsuit with a bright yellow parachute, took his run across the ridge of the mountain and launched himself into space. At that moment the sun came out, and a beautiful rainbow stretched from mountain to mountain in front of the black cloud. The camera clicked, and the photographer had captured the image of a lifetime: the paraglider trusting his fragile 'chute to support him as he leapt into the rainbow. It was the perfect illustration of what we call 'the leap of faith'.

### Relationships

There has to be a leap of faith in any relationship. When a couple fall in love, they discover a lot of facts about each other. She's beautiful (in his eyes); he has a great sense of humour; she's affectionate; he's headstrong; she hates cooking; he can boil an egg in an emergency; and so on. None of these facts is enough to make a person fall in love, still less are they sufficient reason for getting married. Before taking that decisive step, you decide at some level deeper than reason that you trust the other, and would like to spend the rest of your life together. You can't prove that the one you love is trustworthy, and will go on being so in the years to come. You have to step out in faith, and gamble your whole future on your belief that everything's going to work out. It's not blind faith – you have reasons to make you believe that you're probably right. But those who cling to their doubts and refuse to make the leap of faith never make deep relationships with anybody.

## Thomas

Poor doubting Thomas was one of those. He *nearly* believed in Jesus, but couldn't quite bring himself to trust the reports that Jesus was now alive again. Part of his brain told him that resurrection was impossible; yet, another part whispered that he'd already seen Jesus do many things which up until then he'd thought were impossible. Wasn't it probable that a person like Jesus would surprise them again? Yes, probable, thought Thomas, but not certain. He wanted visible proof. Then he put his doubts on hold for a while, went to the upper room with the others, the place where Thomas had last seen Jesus, and there was Jesus. Jesus, who was alive again and inviting him to touch the wounds. Thomas had no need to; instead, he made the leap of faith, and claimed Jesus as 'my Lord and my God'. He didn't wait for absolute proof; he trusted the Saviour.

## Us

It's the same for you and me. We study the evidence and decide it's probable that Jesus is alive – probable, but not certain. At some point, we have to let go of the old certainties, and make the leap of faith. Faith isn't unreasonable; it doesn't fly in the teeth of the evidence. Faith looks at the probabilities, and decides that the moment's come to put your life on the line and simply rely on Jesus. He told us that there's life after death, and that he was going to prepare a place for us. Now we have to take him at his word and trust him. Like the paraglider who trusts his life to that thin strip of material, we have to leap into the rainbow and trust Jesus to hold us up from now to eternity. Being a Christian's taking a risk, the risk that we could be mistaken – that's what faith means. But when you've taken that leap, and found that Jesus does uphold you, you know that the gamble was worth it. Then you trust the rest of your life to Jesus, and spend the remainder of your days finding out what Jesus wants you to do, and doing it. Happy Easter!

*Alleluia, alleluia, alleluia! O sons and daughters; Jesus stand among us in thy risen power; That Eastertide with joy was bright (Part 3 of Light's glittering morn); The day of resurrection.*

## Second Sunday of Easter   11 April
### Principal Service   Secularism

Ex. 14:10–31; 15:20–21 The Exodus (*if used, the reading from Acts must be used as the second reading*), *or* Acts 5:27–32 Peter and other witnesses to the resurrection; Ps. 118:14–29 I shall not die but live, *or* Ps. 150 Praise in heaven; Rev. 1:4–8 The firstborn from the dead; John 20:19–31 Thomas' doubt and faith

> 'Jesus said to [Thomas], "Have you believed because you have seen me? Blessed are those who have not seen and yet have come to believe."' John 20:29

### Well done!

Well done! Yes, you. Jesus is talking about you, and he says, 'Congratulations'. I'm pleased with you. If he'd been Australian, he'd have said, 'Good on yer, mate!' What he actually said was, 'Blessed are those who have not seen and yet have come to believe.' That's you, isn't it? You haven't seen Jesus with your own eyes. But you believe in Jesus, even if your faith's a bit half-hearted sometimes. He doesn't seem like the sort of person who'd lie when he told the disciples that he'd rise again, to give eternal life to all who believe in him. So you and I, we want to believe, and we try to pray. And sometimes we get the feeling there's someone there listening to us and loving us. So we're the people Jesus was talking about who 'have not seen, and yet have come to believe'. It's not easy, and believing's a bit of a struggle sometimes, but when we manage to believe, Jesus says, 'Well done!'

### A believing society

We're not alone, by any means. When they hold a public opinion poll in the UK, time and again the result shows that around 70 per cent believe in God; other countries come up with similar results. Some of us have odd ideas about what God's like, but the majority would call themselves Christians. They've not seen Jesus alive, but in some way they believe in him. Well done, says Jesus. We're a believing society, on the whole. And that needs to be taken into account when we plan our life together. Christianity's a tolerant religion. There should be respect for Christianity, the majority religion, and for other religions too. There should also be respect for atheists, but they mustn't be allowed to call the tune. Religious schools, religious charities, and places of worship, should be acknowledged by the state for the good work they do among the underprivileged, and neither the legal system nor taxation arrangements should discriminate against religious people. The moral standards of religious people shouldn't be undermined by legislation, and care for the family and the needy should be at the heart of the social framework of a believing nation.

## Secularism

Religious people don't demand special privilege. Respect, yes, but it would be dangerous to construct a theocracy, where religious leaders impose their standards on others. Turkey under Ataturk, and India at Independence, realized that once sectarian violence starts, everybody suffers. So they declared themselves secular societies, so that no religion should claim predominance over any other. But secular societies aren't opposed to religion, nor are they irreligious.

## Leading article

Some of the attacks on religion recently have come from people who call themselves secularists – mostly evolutionary biologists – who blame religion for all the evils in the world. But, as a leading newspaper recently pointed out, by the rules of Darwinism, religion is shown to have survival value, because religious societies thrive, whereas the experiment of non-religious communism has collapsed in chaos, or, in China, is being quietly abandoned. By the logic of natural selection, then, religion is shown to confer benefits which other societies lack; religion, in fact, is in our genes.

## Easter faith

So we should proclaim our Easter faith boldly, sharing it lovingly with those who find faith difficult. We haven't seen Jesus ourselves, but we believe he sacrificed his life for us on the cross, was dead and buried, but somehow came to life again. We believe he hears our prayers, and gives us the strength to face life's challenges and overcome them. We believe he loves us, and wants us to love him, and to love our neighbours for his sake. We believe he wants that love to continue into eternity, so that we may live for ever with him in heaven. To anyone who comes to believe that, Jesus says, 'You've won the jackpot, for you've gained for yourself a place in heaven. Well done!'

### All-age worship

*Draw Thomas kneeling to call Jesus, 'My Lord and my God!' Write underneath, 'I believe Jesus is alive'.*

### Suggested hymns

*Good Christians all, rejoice and sing; Jesus stand among us in thy risen power; This is the day; This joyful Eastertide.*

## Second Sunday of Easter
*Second Service*   **Odessa**
Ps. 16 The path of life; Isa. 52:13—53:12 *or* 53:1–6, 9–12 The Suffering Servant; Luke 24:13–35 The road to Emmaus

> *'They told what had happened on the road, and how [Jesus] had been made known to them in the breaking of the bread.' Luke 24:35*

### Odessa

A story's told about Odessa, in the south of Russia on the Black Sea coast. Nowadays it's a popular holiday resort. It's always been a strongly Christian town. At Easter the people would greet each other with the traditional words from the Russian Orthodox Liturgy, 'Alleluia, Christ is risen', to which the response is 'He is risen indeed. Alleluia!' When the Communist Party came to power in

1918, they found there was strong resistance in Odessa to their atheistic creed. So they arrested the Russian Orthodox priest of the town. The communists thought that if they could get the priest to proclaim that communism's true and Christianity's false, they could win the people that way. They tortured the priest until he was ready to say anything they asked, and then sent him out to the town square, not realizing that it was Easter Day. The moment the priest saw his former flock standing around him he gasped out, 'Alleluia! Christ is risen', and the people shouted with one voice, 'He is risen indeed. Alleluia!' Then the communists realized they'd never make many converts in that town.

## Shared faith

The Odessa Christians knew that shared faith in the resurrection of Jesus unites a community, and strengthens them to resist attacks. The two disciples who met the risen Christ on the road to Emmaus knew the importance of shared faith. They rushed back to Jerusalem to share their experience with the others. 'Then they told what had happened on the road,' writes St Luke, 'and how he had been made known to them in the breaking of the bread.' It's often when we meet together round the Lord's table, to break bread in Holy Communion, that we realize most strongly that Jesus is alive, because he's alive in this church community, in the mesh of human relationships that join us to each other in love.

## Shared communion

There's a prayer in a very old Christian document called the *Didache*, which refers to this. It's a book which may have been written in the first century after Christ, but never made it into the New Testament. The prayer is for use the night before we receive Holy Communion, and it asks of Jesus:

As this broken bread was once seed scattered on the hills,
and has now been brought together in one loaf,
so may your church be gathered from the ends of the earth
into your Kingdom.
Come with the dawning of the day,
and make yourself known to us in the breaking of the bread.

By using that phrase, the first Christians obviously saw the meal in the home at Emmaus as a foretaste of the Holy Communion. The evidence for the resurrection isn't something we look for on our own; it's a corporate experience which we find when we gather together for fellowship and worship.

## Emotion

John Wesley wrote that when he was converted, his heart was 'strangely warmed'. The disciples at Emmaus asked each other, 'Weren't our hearts burning within us?' They had obviously been in the grip of powerful emotion. We're sometimes suspicious of strong feelings, and it's true that people in the grip of emotion, who don't place their feelings under the control of their reason, can do themselves a lot of harm. But then cold logic never gets us going, until we're moved by our emotions. Reason and feelings should be harnessed together. Sometimes we've a very strong sense that Jesus is alive, and listening to our prayers. Maybe it's Jesus who causes these feelings. It's certainly an emotional experience to realize that you're loved.

## Preparing for communion

So you should prepare yourself mentally and spiritually before you come to Holy Communion. You should tell yourself the night before, 'Tomorrow I'm going to meet Jesus.' Remind yourself when you reach the church: 'I'm going to meet Jesus.' Then, with awe, as you go forward to receive the sacrament, say to yourself, 'Jesus loves me, and he's promised to meet me when I eat the bread and drink the wine.' Jesus is alive, so tell him when you return to your seat how happy you are that he's met you. But then look around. Jesus isn't just recognized in the bread *you* have received. He's in everybody else, because they too have received the sanctified bread. The risen Christ is known when we break bread together. When you say to each other, like the people of Odessa, 'Alleluia. Christ is risen', and 'He is risen indeed, Alleluia', remember that the proof of his resurrection lies in our fellowship together.

### Suggested hymns

*Abide with me, fast falls the eventide; Be known to us in breaking bread; I come with joy, a child of God; Light of the minds that know him.*

# Third Sunday of Easter   18 April

*Principal Service*   **153 Fish**

Zeph. 3:14–20 The Lord is in your midst (*if used, the reading from Acts must be used as the second reading*), or Acts 9:1–6 [7–20] Paul's conversion; Ps. 30 God brought me up from death; Rev. 5:11–14 Worshipping the Lamb; John 21:1–19 The lakeshore

> *'Simon Peter went aboard and hauled the net ashore, full of large fish, a hundred and fifty-three of them; and though there were so many, the net was not torn.' John 21:11*

## 153 fish

One hundred and fifty-three fish! That's a very large number. And a very precise number. The fact that the number of fish that the disciples caught when they went fishing on Lake Galilee, after Christ had risen, is recorded so exactly, tells us a number of important things.

## Eyewitness

Only a fisherman would have taken the trouble to count the catch. For other people, fishing is a charming sight and a mine for metaphors. For fishermen it's a business. Anyone else would have exclaimed, 'Goodness, what a lot of fish!' A fisherman would sit down at once and count them. They must be counted before they can be divided up between the crew of the boat; they must be counted before they can be sold. So this story at the very end of the Gospels isn't a legend or a myth. It's an eyewitness account, told by people who knew what they were talking about.

## The generosity of Christ

That's where Jesus meets us, in situations where we already think we know it all, but then he shows us something unexpected. The water's shallow near the shore of Lake Galilee. The fishermen were carrying on their trade at night-time, with lighted flares to attract the fish; but with all their expertise they'd caught nothing. In the grey light of dawn, a man standing on the shore could avoid the reflection of the light and the sky which the men in the boat would see. So Jesus told the professional fishermen how to fish, which must have been humiliating for them. 'Cast the net on the right.' Grudgingly they obeyed him, and they caught 153 fish. The generosity of Jesus in helping them to catch so many reminds us how God often surprises us with the showers of blessing he pours upon us.

## He really is alive

We're dealing here not with a myth. We're dealing with a down-to-earth God who tells people how to do their job better; provides overflowing resources of food, enough for everyone; and cooks breakfast. That's what the eyewitnesses reported – not a vision or a hallucination, but a person whom they'd recognized and shared a meal with. The careful counting of the fish reassures us that Jesus is really alive.

## The number of the nations

St Jerome lived for many years in a cave in Bethlehem, to get to know the way the people in the Holy Land think, so that he could translate the Bible accurately into Latin. Speaking to the Galilean fishermen, he made a surprising discovery. They boasted that there were many types of fish in their lake – 153 different species. St John's Gospel was reporting real events, but it's very quick to recognize their symbolic meaning. Jesus, who told his followers to fish for people, had helped them to catch one of each kind. Nobody knew then how many tribes of people there were on the earth, but maybe this memorable number was to reassure us that there's room in Christ's Church for people from every race and language.

## The net's not broken

St John's Gospel then tells us that in spite of the large catch, 'the net was not broken'. A striking experience for a fisherman; for many people believe that the Gospel was written by John son of Zebedee, who was one of those in the boat. But a striking simile for the Church of God; it's not destroyed by receiving new converts from all over the world, and its unity is precious. It's good that people from each ethnic grouping should set up their own congregations, worshipping God in the language they use to tell their family that they love them. Yet no congregation can do its own thing and ignore the rest. And with more and more people speaking English these days, we must make sure that the English-speaking congregations have a welcome for everybody. Don't be afraid because other people have other ways of doing things and expressing things; the Church is built to cope with that. But we must be careful to preserve the unity of God's family; even when people from 153 different races worship together, the net of the Church will not be broken.

### All-age worship

*Write on little paper fish the names of as many nations and languages as you can think of. Make a cardboard model of a fishing boat with a net big enough to pull them all in.*

### Suggested hymns

*Come, living Lord, when least expected; God is working his purpose out; Hark, my soul, it is the Lord; Jesus calls us: o'er the tumult.*

## Third Sunday of Easter
### Second Service   I Nearly Died
Ps. 86 You have delivered me from death; Isa. 38:9–20 The living thank you; John 11:[17–26] 27–44 The raising of Lazarus

'The living, the living, they thank you, as I do this day.' Isaiah 38:19

### I nearly died

Robert Benchley was an American humorist. Probably his most famous saying was, 'Opera is where a guy gets stabbed in the back, and instead of dying, he sings.' He also spoke about the difficulty of earning one's living by making people laugh – he said, 'In Milwaukee last month a man died laughing over one of his own jokes. That's what makes it so tough for us outsiders. We have to fight home competition.' It's become a catchphrase, hasn't it? People say, 'I laughed so much, I nearly died.' But the words can also be said quite seriously: 'I nearly died.' How many of you here could say that about some moment in your life? As in, 'I was so ill, that if it hadn't been for the skill of the doctors I would have died.' Or,

'I slipped on the mountain, and if somebody hadn't grabbed me, I might have died.' Or, 'I stepped in front of the lorry, and if the driver hadn't braked quickly, I should certainly have died.' Or in a dozen situations, some of which you may not have been aware of at the time, when, if it hadn't been for a lucky chance, you wouldn't be here now. Except that, if you believe in God, there's no such thing as coincidence. The Psalmist wrote:

> I will thank you, O Lord my God, with all my heart,
> and glorify your name for evermore;
> For great is your steadfast love towards me;
> for you have delivered my soul from the depths of the grave.

Do you remember to thank your God for all the many times when, but for his timely intervention, you would almost certainly have died?

## Isaiah

The prophet Isaiah is very emphatic that every one of us ought to thank God regularly for the quite undeserved privilege of life:

> Surely it was for my own benefit that I suffered bitterly;
> but you have held back my life from the pit of destruction,
> for you have hidden all my sins behind your back . . .
> The living, the living, they thank you,
> as I do this day . . .
> The LORD will save me,
> and we will sing to stringed instruments all the days of our lives,
> in the house of the LORD.

## New life

We should also thank God for the gift of new life. When we know that Jesus is our friend and that he loves us, our life's filled with fresh joy and purpose; we feel as if for the first time we've really come alive. 'This is really living,' we say. Charles Darwin suggested that only those variations in a species which make it more likely to win in the struggles of life will enable it to survive – 'the survival of the fittest'. Biologists argue these days as to whether human nature is more likely to survive if we're completely selfish, or whether there is in fact survival value in caring for others. Christians have never been optimistic about human nature, left to our own devices. But when we know that we're loved, we're motivated to love others – and Christians know that we're loved by God. The resurrection of Jesus proves to us how much Jesus loves the human race; through him we receive what he called 'life in all its fullness'. For this, too, we should thank God.

## Eternal life

Then there's life after death to thank God for too. What Jesus called 'eternal life'. The raising of Lazarus was a sort of acted parable, to show us that each of us will be raised to a better life after we die. The raising of Jesus is the proof for us that we, too, shall live with God for ever in heaven. Surely this certainty is a cause for great rejoicing and thanksgiving. Not only at Easter, but whenever we remember the Easter message of eternal life for all, we should sing 'Alleluia'.

## Thank God

There are so many things we should thank God for. For the many times, remembered or almost forgotten, when we might have died. For the abundant life that he gives us in this world, and the promise of eternal life in heaven. Let's never forget to be grateful, not just for an hour on Sunday. Whenever we have a moment's leisure to reflect on our life, we should offer up a mental 'Alleluia!' 'The living, the living, they thank you, as I do this day.'

## *Suggested hymns*

*Alleluia, alleluia, give thanks to the risen Lord; Alleluia, alleluia, hearts to heaven and voices raise; Come, let us with our Lord arise; Now is eternal life.*

# Fourth Sunday of Easter   25 April

(St Mark the Evangelist)

*Principal Service*   One, Holy, Catholic, Apostolic

Gen. 7:1–5, 11–18; 8:6–18; 9:8–13 Noah's flood (*if used, the reading from Acts must be used as the second reading*), *or* Acts 9:36–43 Peter raises Tabitha; Ps. 23 The Lord is my shepherd; Rev. 7:9–17 The Lamb their shepherd; John 10:22–30 My sheep hear my voice

*'The Father and I are one.' John 10:30*

## One

Jesus said that when a couple wed, they become 'one flesh'. That doesn't mean Siamese twins. They still have their separate personalities, and can make their own decisions. But because they're in love, share a house together and have shared dreams for the future, their friends treat them as an item. They're two people, but in another way they're a unit. So what did Jesus mean when he said, 'The Father and I are one'? Perhaps he meant that, like a married couple, they shared a unity of love and purpose. Jesus also said: 'Holy Father, protect them . . . that you have given me, so that they may be one, as we are one.' Jesus asks that his followers may be united in the same way as Jesus is united with his Father. Not giving up their distinct personalities, but one in love and purpose. So the leaders who summarized the Christian faith in the Nicene Creed described the followers of Jesus as 'one, holy, catholic and apostolic Church'. We're not asked to give up our individual personalities, but we *are* called to be at least as united as Jesus was with his Father – and as united as a husband and wife are when they're one in love and purpose. Of course, the Christian Church isn't like that – yet. But at least we're reminded, every time we say the Creed, how Jesus prayed that we should be one. We're working on it, in each congregation, in each denomination, and between denominations, trying to bring about the unity for which Christ prayed.

## Holy

Those four words, 'one, holy, catholic and apostolic', are called the Marks, or Notes, of the Church. Nearly all of them are mentioned in today's readings. After Peter had raised dead Tabitha to life, the Acts of the Apostles says that 'calling the saints and widows, he showed her to be alive'. The congregation in Joppa are called 'the saints'; yet I'm sure they were the same as any other congregation; and that the church members, just like you and me, were sometimes good, and sometimes not, but struggled with God's help to be better. The word 'saints' means holy, but that doesn't mean they were Holy Joes, either. It's best defined as meaning 'different'. Christians are called to be different from the people around; giving their whole lives to serving God and their neighbours; aiming at higher standards than the run of people are satisfied with. Just as oneness is a unity of love and purpose, holiness is a different standard of love and purpose. The Church isn't very holy yet; but a loving, laughing holiness is what we're aiming at.

## Catholic

Just after Peter raised Tabitha to life, in next week's reading from Acts we read how he welcomed Cornelius, the Roman army officer, into the Church. It caused a row, because then, as now, many people didn't want to mix with other races, and thought their church should be restricted to 'people like us'. Peter showed that the Church is meant to welcome the whole human race. Now, the word 'whole' gives rise to other words which sound a bit like it: 'HOL-istic medicine'; a 'HOL-ogram' on your credit card, the 'HOL-ocaust', meaning a whole-burnt-sacrifice. Another word derived from 'whole' is when we talk about the 'cath-WHOLE-ic Church'. It means the *whole* Church, with a welcome for the *whole* human race. Unfortunately, one section of the whole Church has appropriated this word to apply to their part only, so that when we mention 'the catholic Church' in the Creed, some people think we're talking about the Roman Catholic Church. But the phrase was written before the Church was divided, and it applies to the whole, worldwide Church, which welcomes everybody.

## Apostolic

I've left hardly any time to mention the fourth mark of the Church: 'apostolic'. It means, 'sent out by God to be a missionary'. St Peter the apostle was sent to many places to spread the good news of God's love, and the church today is called to do the same. So the Church isn't yet one, holy, catholic or apostolic. But every time we say the Creed, we're reminded that, with Christ's help, those are the targets we should be aiming for.

### All-age worship

*Search for images of Christ the King. Some show him holding an orb or globe, representing the whole earth. Copy one, and write underneath, 'Jesus wants us to be one, holy, catholic and apostolic Church'.*

### Suggested hymns

*Come, risen Lord, and deign to be our guest; Firmly I believe and truly; O thou who at thy Eucharist didst pray; The Church of God a kingdom is.*

## St Mark the Evangelist
### Staying-power

Prov. 15:28–33 Good news, *or* Acts 15:35–41 Paul rejects Mark; Ps. 119:9–16 How can young people keep their way pure?; Eph. 4:7–16 The gift of an evangelist; Mark 13:5–13 Staying-power

*'The one who endures to the end will be saved.' Mark 13:13*

### Stickability

You know those advertisements for batteries, which show one toy rabbit keeping on going after all the others have run out of power? Well, Christians are meant to be like that. According to St Mark's Gospel, Jesus said, 'The one who endures to the end will be saved.' We must keep on going after the others give up. What we need is staying-power; or to use a modern word, 'stickability'. Staying-power in saying our prayers; staying-power in going to church week by week; staying-power in serving our neighbours, even those who don't seem particularly grateful. Not every Christian has these powers of endurance; but those who have are the salt of the earth, and pillars of the Church: God depends on people like that to build his kingdom on earth.

## St Mark

It's ironic, then, that this passage is set to be read on St Mark's Day, the 25th of April, because at first, poor young Mark was distinctly lacking in stickability. He went on a preaching tour with St Paul and his Uncle Barnabas, when Paul showed signs of departing from the planned itinerary, and going up-country to preach to non-Jews. Then Mark did a runner. 'John [Mark], however, left them and returned to Jerusalem.' He gave up too easily. But later, when he realized what he'd done, he was truly sorry, and eventually he and Paul were reconciled. Paul, near the end of his life, wrote to Timothy, 'Get Mark and bring him with you, for he is useful in my ministry.' Perseverance, even if it comes rather late in the day, is an essential qualification for being useful.

## The first Gospel

One way in which Mark made himself useful was by writing the first Gospel. When I say the first, I don't mean that it comes first in the New Testament, because it doesn't. But it was the first one to be written. Nobody'd ever thought of doing such a thing before. The good news of God's love was spread by word of mouth alone, for many years. People gossiped to their neighbours and friends about Jesus, and what he's done for us. Travelling missionaries walked from town to town telling people about the Saviour of the world. Why had nobody thought of writing it down, until Mark had his brainwave? Of course, it took time to gather the information. Writing the first manuscript was a slow and laborious business, and every copy had to be written out by hand. Jewish boys learn to read Hebrew in the synagogues, but in the rest of the Roman Empire, reading and writing were skills that few people possessed. So a book was always going to need word-of-mouth to supplement what it said with eyewitness evidence. But, as you know, the word 'Gospel' means 'good news', and Mark starts his book by writing, 'The beginning of the good news of Jesus Christ, the Son of God.' Others followed his example and wrote longer accounts. But without Mark's staying-power in seeing through his idea until it was finished, you and I might never have heard of Jesus.

## Alexandria

So much is history. The next step in Mark's story can't be proved, but there's a very strong tradition that after Peter and Paul had been martyred, young Mark – though he must have been over forty by now – travelled across the Mediterranean from Rome to Egypt, and became the leader of the church in the great port city of Alexandria. It was the port from which all of Rome's corn supply, grown in the Nile delta, was exported to feed the Empire. It had the world's greatest library, and a group of Jewish scholars were commissioned to translate the Old Testament into Greek there. Paul's colleague Apollos came from Alexandria; he was 'well versed in the [Old Testament] Scriptures', but didn't know much about Jesus, so the Alexandrians needed Mark to teach them. The Coptic, or Egyptian, church today counts Mark as one of its founders.

## Venice

He may have been martyred in Alexandria during the persecution under the Emperor Trajan, but his bones weren't left in peace for very long. In 829 they were dug up and shipped to Venice, where they were buried in the original church of San Marco, in St Mark's Square. His symbol of a lion, one of the four beasts which represent the four Evangelists, became the logo of Venice. We can all learn from his example, because he may have been a bit of a mouse to begin with, but he learnt staying-power, and became a powerful lion at the end.

### *Suggested hymns*

*Awake, my soul, and with the sun; Father, hear the prayer we offer; Lord, thy word abideth; The saint who first found grace to pen.*

# Fifth Sunday of Easter   2 May
## *Principal Service*   Love and Acceptance
Bar. 3:9–15, 32—4:4 Wisdom, *or* Gen. 22:1–18 Abraham willing to sacrifice Isaac *(if used, the reading from Acts must be used as the second reading)*; *or* Acts 11:1–18 Baptism of the Gentiles; Ps. 148 Nature praising God; Rev. 21:1–6 Death will be no more; John 13:31–35 The commandment to love

134

*'[Jesus said,] "I give you a new commandment, that you love one another. Just as I have loved you, you also should love one another. By this everyone will know that you are my disciples, if you have love for one another."' John 13:34–35*

## Cambodia

*INTRO* *then*

In a recent novel, *The King's Last Song* by Geoff Ryman, the author points to the parallel between the Cambodians of today and the people who lived there when Angkor Wat was built. Today, the Cambodian people include former members of the Khmer Rouge, and also those who fought against them. In your own village or your workplace, you may have to live side by side with those who killed your own parents. You also have to live with the knowledge that you yourself may have done equally terrible things. In the twelfth century, the King of Cambodia spread the gentle religion of Buddhism; but he came to power by means of bloody battles, and kept power by having several of his sons killed. A surviving son hates his father, and treats him abominably. But eventually he realizes that seeking revenge achieves nothing; we have to respect people as they are, and, even harder, we have to accept ourselves. The novel ends with the realization that we must learn love, and the words, 'Love, which is acceptance'.

## Jesus

Jesus, too, taught us about the need for love. 'I give you a new commandment,' he said, 'that you love one another, just as I have loved you.' Don't you think that 'acceptance' defines accurately what Jesus meant by love? Notice that Jesus tells us to love others 'as I have loved you'. Jesus explained that he doesn't only love perfect people – if he did, he wouldn't find many people to love! He's described in the Gospels as 'the friend of sinners'. He enjoyed going to parties with people whom others rejected, as being beyond the pale. He accepted them with all their faults. Then, when they repented, he forgave them everything. After that, he set them on the road towards improvement; but he didn't wait until they were good before he loved them; he took them as he found them, and loved them just as they were.

## Jesus loves you

That's a great comfort to us, because it means that this is the way Jesus loves me and you. Very few of us haven't done something in the past, either malicious or just plain thoughtless, which hurt somebody else. We may hide it from other people, because we think they wouldn't love us if they knew. We may hide it from ourselves, because feeling guilty makes us uncomfortable. We don't mention what we've done when we pray to God, because we imagine he'd find us quite unacceptable if he knew. But that's not what Jesus said. He spoke repeatedly about God's forgiveness, to show us that God accepts us as we are, loves us, and helps us to change. And that's how the Son of God loves us; with 'love, which is acceptance'. Isn't that good news? He doesn't condemn us, or punish us; instead, he takes us as he finds us, and helps us to change.

## Love as you are loved

If that's how we're loved, then that's how we're to love other people: accepting them with all their faults, and loving them un-conditionally, as Jesus has loved us. It's no use waiting until people deserve our love, for they never will, any more than we could ever be worthy of the love which Jesus pours upon us. It's no use trying to punish them, or seek revenge for the harm people have done us; Jesus told us to forgive others as we ourselves have been forgiven by God: fully and unconditionally. That's the only condition for being a Christian: we must want to love and forgive others as Jesus loves and forgives us; though we've a long way to go before we reach his level of love. 'By this everyone will know that you are my disciples,' said Jesus, 'if you have love for one another.'

## Loving yourself

But you must learn to accept yourself. It's not easy, living with the knowledge that you're a sinner. But 'all have sinned, and fallen short of God's glory'. So there's the comfort: you're no worse than anybody else. We're all forgiven sinners; and we're all loved by God. If God can accept us, we can accept each other. For 'Love is acceptance.'

## All-age worship

*Find out about Cambodia. Is it possible for people to accept those who have been their enemies?*

## Suggested hymns

*A new commandment; Come down, O Love divine; Jesus, take me as I am; Love divine, all loves excelling.*

# Fifth Sunday of Easter
## Second Service   Who Moved the Stone?
Ps. 98 God has done marvellous things; Dan. 6:[1–5] 6–23 The lions' den; Mark 15:46—16:8 The resurrection

> *'[The women] had been saying to one another, "Who will roll away the stone for us from the entrance to the tomb?" When they looked up, they saw that the stone, which was very large, had already been rolled back.' Mark 16:3–4*

## Frank Morrison

Frank Morrison was a young English journalist who set out to disprove the resurrection of Jesus. He started from the position taken by many scientists, that miracles simply cannot happen, and therefore any account of a miracle must be a lie. After pondering for some years about what he saw to be the lies contained in the four Gospels, Morrison decided to write a book. He wanted to focus on the last seven days of the life of Jesus, because they seemed to be the least miraculous part of the Gospels; the four Gospels were in fairly close agreement as to what happened; and the amount of contemporary documentary evidence supported the hypothesis that the crucifixion of Jesus, at least, was historical fact. Added to this was the fact that a group of followers emerged after his death who were all convinced that Jesus had been crucified, and none of their enemies denied it.

## Why?

So Frank Morrison examined the accounts of what Jesus said and did in those seven days from the eve of Palm Sunday up to Good

Friday. He soon realized that apparent discrepancies could easily be reconciled without impugning the reliability of the witnesses. What puzzled him, however, were the motives of the participants. Why did Judas betray his Master? Why were the Pharisees so opposed to him? Why did the High Priests take so much trouble to arrest Jesus secretly? Why did they hold an illegal, secret trial by night, and then hand Jesus over to Pontius Pilate? Why did Pilate decide to crucify him? Above all, why did Jesus go submissively to his death, without defending himself by words or actions? Frank Morrison saw that a lot more needed to be explained than he'd realized.

## Hindsight

The people who wrote the Gospels hadn't understood what was happening at the time, either. It was only in retrospect that the meaning became clear to them. So Morrison decided that the seven days couldn't be taken in isolation. He had to consider also what happened in the next 36 hours after the crucifixion. Then, perhaps, with hindsight he'd be able to understand. Many people, who can only dimly discern the pattern of events as they are occurring, have twenty-twenty vision when they look back with hindsight. So why, asked the journalist, did the disciples all share the delusion that Jesus, who had died, was now alive again?

## Evidence

Then he decided to examine the evidence that was presented in favour of this miracle. The reports of the eyewitnesses, Mary Magdalene and the other women, Peter, John, James. Even, some years later, Paul of Tarsus. Could all these people have been lying? Even if they were all deluded, which seems unlikely, why didn't they own up and retract their testimony when they were threatened with ridicule and martyrdom? Could they have invented the story? Why didn't the priests present them with the dead body of Jesus, then, to prove them wrong? Did the disciples come secretly by night to steal the corpse and hide it somewhere? But there was a guard of Roman soldiers placed there with the deliberate intention of foiling any such plot. Added to which, a stone weighing several tons had been placed across the entrance to the tomb, which would have taken a gang of strong men to move it – scarcely the sort of thing a scattered group of disheartened fishermen could achieve without making a noise and waking the neighbourhood. So Frank Morrison came to the crunch question, which gave him the title for his book: if Jesus hadn't been raised to life again, *Who Moved the Stone?*

## A change of heart

The young journalist discovered that he had no answer to this question. He'd set out to disprove the miracles, and had convinced himself that the resurrection of Jesus, the biggest miracle of them all, must indeed have happened exactly as it was described in the Gospels. Morrison had had a change of heart. He'd come out with exactly the opposite conclusion to the one he'd intended. His book, *Who Moved the Stone?*, became a classic defence of the Christian belief in the resurrection. If only more doubters would look honestly at the evidence as he did, they'd find their doubts evaporating like the morning dew. If only we Christians would look clearly at the foundation documents of our faith, we'd be more convinced of the love of God in Jesus, and the truth of his promise of eternal life.

### Suggested hymns

*At the lamb's high feast we sing; Jesus lives! Thy terrors now; Love's redeeming work is done; The strife is o'er.*

## Sixth Sunday of Easter (Rogation Sunday)    9 May
*Principal Service*   **Do You Want to Change?**
Ezek. 37:1–14 The valley of dry bones (*if used, the reading from Acts must be used as the second reading*), *or* Acts 16:9–15 The baptism of Lydia; Ps. 67 Let the peoples praise you; Rev. 21:10, 22—22:5 The heavenly Jerusalem; John 14:23–29 Going to the Father; *or* John 5:1–9 The paralysed man at the pool

> '*When Jesus saw [the paralysed man] lying there and knew that he had been there a long time, he said to him, "Do you want to be made well?"' John 5:6*

### Light bulbs

As you probably know, there are dozens of light-bulb jokes. The original was probably this one: how many idiots does it take to change a light bulb? Answer: 100; one to hold the bulb and 99 to

turn the ceiling! My favourite, however, is: how many psychotherapists does it take to change a light bulb? Answer: only one, but the
light bulb must really want to change.

## Change in ourselves

Many people go to healers and helpers, asking them to change
the circumstances in which they have to live. The wise healer
will gradually bring them to understand that the problem's in the
patient. Things will only get better for them if they're willing to
make changes in themselves. Alcoholics Anonymous include this
as one of their 12 steps to healing. The same goes for other addic-
tions, to smoking, drugs, gambling or shopping: you *can* break the
habit, but only if you really want to change. If simply changing the
surroundings solved problems, Adam would have stopped sinning
once he left paradise.

## The paralysed man

Jesus visited the Pool of Bethesda (or Bethzatha) and found a paralysed man lying at the water's edge, who didn't want to change.
The remains of that pool can still be seen today in Jerusalem,
though it's several meters below street level. It had five porticos;
one on each edge of the rectangular pool and one on the causeway
across the middle. Due to the complicated water-supply system,
sometimes water would gush out of an underground pipe and stir
up the pool – it's called the siphon effect. Superstitious people
thought this was done by an angel or a spirit, and that then the
water would heal the first person to climb in. But the paralysed
man couldn't be healed, because he couldn't get into the water
quick enough. Jesus asked him a very surprising question: 'Do
you want to be made well?' Of course he did, that's why he was
lying there. Many paralysed people would dearly like to be healed,
and can't be, because their illness is due to an irreversible physical
change. But this man was different; Jesus saw into his heart, and
realized that he'd got used to being paralysed, and enjoyed having other people making a fuss of him. Being healed would mean
taking responsibility for his own life, and he was scared of that.
The original cause of the paralysis may have been in his mind; or
it may have been something physical which cleared up years ago
– anyway, Jesus recognized that the man could move now, if he
wanted to. So Jesus said to him: 'Stand up and walk.' The man

faced the challenge, changed his attitude, and with a bit of help from Jesus he stood up and walked away.

## Facing change

Most of us are sick, in mind, or body, or just sick of the circumstances we live in. Jesus asks us, 'Do you want to be healed? If so, are you prepared to face the required changes?' Nobody likes change. I don't like change. The older we get, the less we want to change our ingrained habits. But if you're thinking that you can't teach an old dog new tricks, remember that Abraham was over seventy when God told him to leave his home, go to a new country and found a new nation. Refusal to change results in slow death – if you won't change, you're dead already. If you plough the same furrow year after year, the furrow becomes a rut and you're stuck in it.

## Change in the Church

The Church in this country's sick, fewer people go to church. Eventually it'll die, unless we attract new members. To do that, we must share with them the gospel that God loves them, and let them experience God's love in our fellowship. The gospel's unchanging; but the world's changing all the time, and we have to find new ways of sharing God's love with the people of today. Jesus asked the paralysed man, 'Do you really want to be healed?' He asks the same question of the Church today, and of me and of you. If the answer's yes, we have to accept the necessity of change, and then stand up and walk.

## *All-age worship*

*Make a jointed paper cut-out of the paralysed man lying on his mat, then standing up, rolling up the mat, and carrying it on his shoulder.*

## *Suggested hymns*

*I danced in the morning; Have faith in God, my heart; Make way, make way; O for a thousand tongues to sing.*

# Sixth Sunday of Easter

## Second Service    God is in Your Midst

Ps. 126 The Lord has done great things for us, 127 Unless the Lord builds the house; Zeph. 3:14–20 God is in your midst; Matt. 28:1–10, 16–20 The ascension command

> 'The LORD has taken away the judgements against you, he has turned away your enemies. The king of Israel, the LORD, is in your midst; you shall fear disaster no more.' Zephaniah 3:15

### Loss

The hardest part of bereavement is learning to accept your loss. You keep expecting the one who died to come round the corner and say it never really happened. You can't get used to not having them visibly there beside you. Christians have an answer to that, which I'll come to in a minute. But Jesus's disciples had got used to having him with them as they walked the dusty roads of Galilee. Jesus, their Master, told them about God his Father, and it almost felt as though the Lord God was there in their midst – and then Jesus died. Their sense of loss was unbearably greater than that of other bereaved people, because Jesus had been so close to them, and his friendship was more precious than any other. But on the third day he was alive again, part of their fellowship, their family group around the table. They knew that, as the prophet Zephaniah had said, the Lord was in their midst. They had forty days of euphoria. Then, on Ascension Day, which we celebrate next Thursday, Jesus left them again, to be with his Father in heaven. Or that's what they thought, for they couldn't see him any more. The symptoms of loss began all over again.

### Pentecost

Still, thank God, they went on meeting together, probably in the same upper room where Jesus had celebrated the Last Supper. There, ten days later, on the Feast of Pentecost, they received the gift of the Holy Spirit. God the Holy Spirit was now within them, dwelling in their hearts. It was fairly dramatic the first time they realized this, but the first excitement seems to have settled down eventually. It was replaced by the steady joy of knowing that God was still in their midst every time they met together to pray, and in their hearts when they needed his power. The Holy Spirit is the power of God working in people's hearts, giving them a strength they wouldn't have on their own. Power to resist temptation; power to pray and to heal; power to speak about God to other people; and power to cope with disaster and loss. The Holy Spirit's the Spirit of Jesus; when we let the Holy Spirit use us as God's messengers to bring God's love and peace to others, then the Lord Jesus is truly in our midst.

## The last enemy

When we let Jesus into our hearts, then he takes away the 'guilty' verdict which God had awarded to us as sinners, and turns away the temptations to sin which are the enemies we fight. St Paul said that the last enemy is death, and it's true, because the presence of death tempts us to give up hope, and fall into the sin of despair. But Paul goes on to say that by his death, Jesus submitted to the worst that death could do to him, and by his resurrection he defeated death: death is swallowed up in victory. Death is the worst disaster that can happen to us; and because of Jesus's resurrection we need fear disaster no more. The Holy Spirit in our hearts gives us courage in the face of death, for Christians know that death will take us to be with Jesus and his Father in heaven.

## Bereavement

So what can Christians say to bereaved people in their feelings of loss? Well, we must be very sympathetic and understanding, and not push the conversation any further than they want us to. Often the best thing is simply to sit with them in silence. But if they ask us, this is what we have to say. Jesus promised that when people die, they go to be with him in heaven. Not just good people; he welcomes all forgiven sinners, like me and you. And where's Jesus? Right here, in our midst. So in a real sense, the dead never leave us; they're right here in our midst. Whenever we speak to Jesus, we can feel them here with us. I don't mean just an airy-fairy thing, 'the memory lingers on' and all that. The resurrection of Jesus and the gift of his Holy Spirit to us proves that God's in our midst; so all those who are with God in heaven are close to us every time we pray.

'The LORD has taken away the judgements against you, he has turned away your enemies. The king of Israel, the LORD, is in your midst; you shall fear disaster no more.'

### Suggested hymns

*Do not be afraid; Glorious things of thee are spoken; Lord, it belongs not to my care; Ye choirs of new Jerusalem.*

## Ascension Day  13 May
### The Unseen Presence

Acts 1:1–11 The Ascension (*must be used as either the first or second reading*), or Dan. 7:9–14 The Son of Man; Ps. 47 God has gone up, or Ps. 93 The Lord is king; Eph. 1:15–23 Christ is seated beside God; Luke 24:44–53 The ascension

> *'[Jesus said at the ascension] "Remember, I am with you always, to the end of the age."' Matthew 28:20*

### Shackleton

Sir Ernest Henry Shackleton was a famous Antarctic explorer at the beginning of the twentieth century. He was born in County Kildare, in Ireland, and was a junior officer in Sir Robert Scott's National Antarctic expedition from 1901 to 1903, which explored the Ross Sea area, and discovered King Edward the Seventh Land. In 1909 Shackleton led his own Antarctic expedition, climbing Mount Erebus, reaching the south magnetic pole for the first time, and only stopping a hundred yards from the South Pole itself. In 1915 he sailed south again in a ship called *The Endurance*. His ship was crushed in the ice, and he trekked across the snow with two others for a day and a half to fetch relief for his starving crew. He was knighted in 1909, and died at South Georgia during a fourth expedition in 1922.

### The Presence

Shackleton wrote several books. One of them he called *The Presence*, describing that long walk through the snow to fetch help in 1915. In it he wrote:

> When I look back upon those days, with all their anxiety and peril, I cannot doubt that our party was divinely guided both over the snowfields and across the storm-swept sea.
> I know that during that long and racking march of thirty-six

hours over the unnamed mountains and glaciers of South Georgia, it seemed to me often that we were not three, but four. I said nothing to my companions on the point, but afterwards Worsley said to me: 'Boss, I had a curious feeling on the march that there was another Person with us.'

## We are not alone

We are not alone. This sort of experience is not uncommon. Many people, when they're most alone, become clearly aware of the presence of God with them. They don't see anybody, but they're vividly conscious that Someone's there, keeping an eye on them. The unseen God may not remove the dangers, but he makes it possible to face them bravely. Those in peril often feel a strength coming into them from without, a strength without which they couldn't have surmounted their challenges. What's more, while they do their best for themselves, they no longer worry whether they're to die or to live. Because God is with them, they no longer fear death, for death would merely be drawing back the veil, and making the unseen presence visible at last. Very often people who have this experience tell nobody about it, for fear of being thought 'peculiar'. But they'd strongly deny that it was only a hallucination. Rather, it seems as though for the first time they've come face to face with the truth that God's always with us. We're never alone when God's our friend.

## The ascension

When Jesus died and rose again, for forty days he appeared visibly to his friends, and taught them about the mammoth task he was setting them, of converting the whole world to Christ. Then he withdrew his visible presence from them. They described it as his ascension into heaven, but they knew as well as we do that heaven isn't a place 'up there'. It's a higher level of existence, life lived in full fellowship with our heavenly Father. The point was to make the disciples realize that they were no longer going to be able to see Jesus on earth. But that didn't mean Jesus would no longer be with them; they'd have to learn to believe in his invisible presence. The account of the ascension varies subtly in the Gospels of Matthew and Luke and the Acts of the Apostles, because when you've had a spiritual experience you don't remember the details. The underlying meaning's clear in all of them, however: the followers of Jesus wouldn't be able to see him again. But they'd know that he's here, because they'd receive the power of the Holy Spirit, giving them strength to overcome their challenges, and courage when things go badly. The message is the same for you and me today: we're never alone. We may have a vivid sense, as Shackleton did, of the unseen presence, or we may be deadened and feel nothing. But the simple fact is there, whether we realize it or not: we're never alone. Jesus says to me and to you, 'Remember, I am with you always, to the end of the age.'

### Suggested hymns

*Be still, for the presence/Spirit of the Lord; Immortal, invisible, God only wise; Hail the day that sees him rise; See the conqueror mounts in triumph.*

## Seventh Sunday of Easter
(Sunday after Ascension Day)    **16 May**
*Principal Service*    **That the World May Believe**
Ezek. 36:24–28 I will put my Spirit in you (*if used, the reading from Acts must be used as the second reading*); or Acts 16:16–34 Baptism of a jailer; Ps. 97 The Lord is king; Rev. 22:12–14, 16–17, 20–21 Come!; John 17:20–26 Church unity and love

> '*[Jesus prayed, saying,] "I ask not only on behalf of these, but also on behalf of those who will believe in me through their word, that they may all be one. As you, Father, are in me and I am in you, may they also be in us, so that the world may believe that you have sent me."' John 17:20–21*

### Overseas travel

More and more people these days can afford an overseas holiday. Some people bring back with them nothing more than a suntan, which fades, and a few souvenirs. They never sample the local food, and they make no attempt to learn even a few words of the local language. But for others, travel broadens the mind. How amazing, they say, to find that there are people who look different from us, wear different clothes and speak a language that's unfamiliar to us, yet underneath, they're people just like us! With the same feelings, the same needs and desires, and the same dreams of happiness!

## Jesus and the world

Jesus never travelled further than a few miles outside Judaea, to visit the other side of Lake Galilee, and the regions around Tyre and Sidon. Yet he had a vision of the whole world, and God's plan for everybody in it. 'I am the light of *the world*,' he said, so 'you are the light of the world.' 'For God so loved *the world* that he gave his only Son, so that everyone who believes in him may not perish but may have eternal life.' 'Father, I desire that *those also* . . . may be with me where I am, to see my glory.' Jesus prayed that far-off nations, in ages yet to come, might be welcomed into God's glory. But the kingdom of heaven begins here and now, when we share a common table with people who are different from us.

## Table fellowship

Many varied people sat at table with Jesus. He went to dinner at the home of a Pharisee – and the Pharisees were upright, law-abiding people. Then the Pharisee found he was expected to welcome to his meal table 'a woman in the city, who was a sinner'. Among his disciples was Simon the Zealot, and those were extreme nationalist freedom-fighters. Yet he also included among the Twelve, Matthew the tax-collector, a traitor to his nation who collected taxes to pay the hated Roman army of occupation. Jesus smiled around the table to see Pharisees and prostitutes, terrorists and quislings sharing a meal together, and said, 'The kingdom of God is among you.' The Romans and Jews hated each other, and yet, when a Roman centurion expressed his faith in Jesus, Jesus said, 'I tell you, many will come from east and west and will eat with Abraham and Isaac and Jacob in the kingdom of heaven.' When some Greek foreigners came looking for Jesus, he said, 'Now is the Son of man glorified.' The vision of Jesus was of nothing less than the whole human race living together as one family.

## Church unity

What an impossible dream! How on earth did Jesus expect to bring it about? Jesus foresaw a world united in love, brought into being by a Church united in love. So he prayed for his disciples, that they might be one; and for you and me, 'I ask . . . on behalf of those who will believe in me through their word, that they may all be one. As you, Father, are in me and I am in you, may they also be in us, so that the world may believe that you have sent me.' The Christian Church becomes one as we learn to love those who are different from us. 'By this everyone will know that you are my disciples,' said Jesus, 'if you have love for one another.' Christians from different cultural backgrounds will never organize their churches in the same way, worship God in the same way, nor agree on every detail of the faith. But we can learn – despite our differing traditions – to accept, welcome and love Christians who are radically different from us, as sisters and brothers in Christ. Then the vision of Jesus, of a world united in love, will come a little nearer, and the whole human race will have an opportunity to enter into God's glory.

## *All-age worship*

*Collect pictures and recordings of Christian worship by people of a different culture from our own.*

## *Suggested hymns*

*All hail the power of Jesus' name; Crown him with many crowns; Let us break bread together, we are one; The head that once was crowned with thorns.*

# Seventh Sunday of Easter
## *Second Service*   **Maturity**
Ps. 68 Let God arise; Isa. 44:1–8 I will pour my Spirit; Eph. 4:7–16 Gifts of the ascended Christ; *Gospel at Holy Communion*: Luke 24:44–53 I am sending upon you

> *'Building up the body of Christ, until all of us come to the unity of the faith . . . to maturity, to the measure of the full stature of Christ.' Ephesians 4:12–13*

## Maturity

When you were a kid, did you long to be grown-up? Sometimes you dream of the day when you stop making childish mistakes; when you've enough confidence to mix with grown-ups, and to speak in public. Childlike trust's a virtue in adults; but childishness is only appropriate in children. Grown-ups need to behave with maturity.

One dictionary defines maturity as 'having the mental, emotional and social development appropriate to an adult'. The Letter to the Ephesians describes the work of ministers in the church as 'Building up the body of Christ, until all of us come to the unity of the faith and of the knowledge of the Son of God, to *maturity*, to the measure of the full stature of Christ.' In other words, every member of this congregation should be aiming for an *adult* mental, emotional and social development in our life as Christian disciples, and in our fellowship together. Whenever a Christian speaks or behaves in a petty, intolerant or judgemental way towards others; when we're quick to take offence and go off in a huff; when we're proud, and cling to some object or position in the church as though it was ours by divine right; when we're lazy and don't want to pull our weight – then we're being childish and immature. St Paul defines Christian maturity as reaching 'the measure of the full stature of Christ'. Imagine Jesus standing by the wall with a book on his head and someone marking with a pencil on the wall his height. Then imagine yourself taking his place, so as to see how you compare. Then suppose it's not physical height which is being measured, but spiritual maturity. We all love God and our neighbours a little bit. But if that love were compared to the love of Jesus, it would be seen as lamentably inadequate. Never mind, Jesus still loves us; but Christlike maturity is what we should be aiming at.

## Doctrine

One sign of immaturity which St Paul warns us against is fickleness in doctrine. 'We must no longer be children,' he writes, 'tossed to and fro and blown about by every wind of doctrine, by people's trickery, by their craftiness in deceitful scheming.' It's so tempting to go wandering off after the latest theory or fad which you've read in a book somewhere, and make this the most important thing in your belief system, and the acid test to judge whether somebody else is 'a *real* Christian'. To leave your home church and join another which is more to your liking. To set up your own church, where membership is restricted to true believers, 'people like us'. Someone who feels overlooked in the church they attend can become a VIP when they leave and join a smaller one. But it's immature behaviour; instead, you should stay and love the people in your church until you mature together like a vintage wine, 'building up the body of Christ, until all of us come to the unity of the faith and of the knowledge of the Son of God'.

## Speaking the truth in love

It's not congenial companions that we're looking for, but the truth. St Paul says we should speak the truth in love. We should be open and honest; but we should also be tactful. There are those who say, 'I'm a plain-spoken, blunt person', and hurt others deeply by not considering what effect their words will have on somebody else's feelings. If you're blunt back to them, they don't like it at all. No, truthfulness must always be coupled with discretion.

## Growth of the body

For our only object is to create a fellowship united by love. As St Paul puts it, 'We must grow up in every way into him who is the head, into Christ, from whom the whole body, joined and knit together by every ligament with which it is equipped, as each part is working properly, promotes the body's growth in building itself up in love.' Have you thought of your love as an essential ligament to bind other Christians firmly together in the body of Christ?

## Waiting for the Spirit

This Sunday comes between Ascension Day and Pentecost. Jesus ascended into heaven, and poured down the gift of the Holy Spirit on us, his followers. The Holy Spirit gives us power to love, builds us up towards maturity, true doctrine and unity in our fellowship together. Pray for the Spirit to lead you to a fully developed love, comparable to that of Jesus.

## *Suggested hymns*

*All praise to our redeeming Lord; Christ triumphant, ever reigning; Hands that have been handling; Jesus is Lord! Creation's voice proclaims it.*

## Day of Pentecost (Whit Sunday)   23 May
*Principal Service*   **First-fruits of God's Harvest**
*(The reading from Acts must be used as either the first or second reading.)* Acts 2:1–21 The day of Pentecost, *or* Gen. 11:1–9 The tower of Babylon; Ps. 104:26–36, 37b The Spirit in creation; Rom. 8:14–17 Adoption; John 14:8–17 [25–27] The Spirit of truth

> *'When the day of Pentecost had come . . . all of them were filled with the Holy Spirit.' Acts 2:1–4*

### Pentecost

The word 'Pentecost' means 'fiftieth'; it's the name given in the Jewish calendar to the fiftieth day after Passover. The feast's better known to Jews as the Feast of Weeks, because it was seven weeks and a day after Passover. It was the Jewish Harvest Festival – the book of Leviticus describes how the first grain reaped from the fields, the first newborn lambs and calves, and the first of the new vintage of wine, were brought to the Temple, to be offered to the Lord. It was also called the Day of the First-fruits, using 'fruit' in the widest sense for all the produce of field and flock. In gratitude for the new harvest, the first items to be gathered in were dedicated to God.

### The Church's birthday

Pentecost, for Christians, is remembered as the day when the Holy Spirit came upon the disciples. In the power of the Holy Spirit, tongue-tied Simon Peter preached his best sermon yet, and about three thousand new converts joined the Church. Pentecost is there-fore often called the Church's birthday: this is the day when the body of believers first came together, which we now call the Christian Church. So, Happy Birthday, all of you. I mean you as a congregation, as a fellowship of followers of Jesus. This congregation's spiritually descended in a direct line from those three thousand men, women and children who began the movement in about AD 30, one thousand nine hundred and eighty years ago today.

## First-fruits

It's very appropriate that the birthday of the Church should fall on the Day of the First-fruits. Those first three thousand converts were the beginning of God's harvest, the harvest of souls. God's a farmer, and the world's his farm. In this soil he's growing people who'll one day inhabit the kingdom of heaven. God rejoices when even one sinner joins his kingdom. He rejoiced on the day when you first decided that you wanted to be a Christian, because that's what he made you for. He designed you as someone who'd one day live with God for ever in heaven. When you joined the Christian Church, God gathered you in, as part of his harvest.

## Farm-workers

Actually, God doesn't do the harvesting all on his own. He employs farm-workers to bring in the harvest of souls on his behalf. That includes preachers and writers, and all who proclaim to others that God loves them, drawing them into the great fellowship of those who know they're loved. To speak and write effectively, they need God's help and inspiration, in the form of the Holy Spirit. It's very humbling for a preacher to realize that listeners are moved by sermons, not because of the power of the preacher's oratory, but by God secretly working in their hearts. But you, too, are a farm-worker in God's harvest. Many people don't listen to sermons, and seldom read a Christian book. So it's up to you to tell them about your experience of God's love, and show it to them by the way you love them for God's sake. Don't blench at this challenge, and make the excuse that you can't do anything like that. Of course you can't, God knows that. But he doesn't leave you to do it on your own. God comes into your heart, and God's Holy Spirit helps you to grow, changes your character, makes you more loving, and puts words into your mouth of which you never thought you were capable.

## Thanksgiving

So on the Day of Pentecost, you should thank God

- for the great harvest of souls he's reaping all over the world;
- for the first-fruits, those first three thousand who founded the movement we know as the Christian Church;

- for the Church as you've experienced it here;
- for pouring down his Holy Spirit on the Church;
- for the first-fruits of your own harvesting, those children and adults who've learnt of God's love by seeing it reflected in your life.
- Above all, thank God that you've received the Spirit of God, inspiring you and empowering you, bringing you and those you influence into God's heavenly barns for the last great harvest.

Perhaps we should end by singing 'Happy Birthday' to the Church throughout the world.

### All-age worship

*Draw or model Peter preaching to the crowd at Pentecost. Label it 'God begins his harvest'.*

### Suggested hymns

*Come Holy Ghost, our souls inspire; Spirit of God, unseen as the wind; Spirit of holiness, wisdom and faithfulness; Spirit of the living God, fall afresh on me.*

## Day of Pentecost (Whit Sunday)
### Second Service   God Speaks Face to Face
Morning Ps. 36:5–10 In your light we see light, 150 Everything that breathes; Evening Ps. 33:1–12 The breath of his mouth; Ex. 33:7–20 My presence will go with you; 2 Cor. 3:4–18 Letter and Spirit; *Gospel at Holy Communion*: John 16:4b–15 The Spirit of truth

> *'Thus the LORD used to speak to Moses face to face, as one speaks to a friend.' Exodus 33:11*

### Celebrities

Is there a celebrity whom you secretly admire from afar? Perhaps you wish you had a chance of meeting him or her, and telling them what you feel. But most of us, given an opportunity like that, would simply blow it. Meeting somebody really, really famous, we'd probably be struck dumb with awe, or stammer and be tongue-tied, mouth trivialities, or be terribly stiff and formal. There'd be no meeting of minds, for sure.

## Meeting God

If, on the other hand, you're utterly self-confident, and certain you could carry off an interview like that calmly and with panache, congratulations. How then would you feel about meeting God? Now that really would be awesome! What sort of a conversation do you think you'd be able to have in those circumstances? Yet the Bible says that 'The LORD used to speak to Moses face to face, as one speaks to a friend.' How did Moses achieve such intimacy with the Creator of the universe?

## The presence of God

The answer surely lies in the fact that Moses knew that God was always with him. In whatever land he pitched the Tent of Meeting, God would come to him and talk to him. Moses made God promise this, when he said:

> 'If your presence will not go, do not carry us up from here. For how shall it be known that I have found favour in your sight, I and your people, unless you go with us? . . .' The LORD said to Moses, 'I will do the very thing that you have asked; for you have found favour in my sight, and I know you by name.' He said, 'My presence will go with you, and I will give you rest.'

## Pentecost

The same promise that God made to Moses, of his perpetual presence, God made to the Christian Church on the day of Pentecost. For the Holy Spirit's the Spirit of God, and wherever the Spirit dwells, there God is. We believe in the real presence of Jesus in the sacrament of Holy Communion, and when you receive the bread and wine, God's within you. In this place we're inspired by the love of God, and the Holy Spirit dwells within us. This building's our Tent of Meeting with God. But you don't have to be in a church; once we leave here, God's promised that his presence will go with us, and every time we pray, we know that through the Holy Spirit, God's 'closer to us than breathing, nearer than hands or feet'.

## The human face of God

Then why aren't we shrivelled up by the sheer majesty of God whenever we pray? Ah, that's because Jesus came to show us the human face of God. As the disciples discovered, Jesus is the easiest person to talk to in all the world, because he's so loving, and understands us completely. Anybody can chat with Jesus – you can, I can, any time, any place. We can talk to Jesus as a friend; we don't need to dissemble with Jesus. But, 'God was in Christ, reconciling the world to himself.' So when we talk to Jesus, we're talking to God. We can present our true face to God, with no need to be ashamed, for God's already forgiven and forgotten all the things we repent of. Through the work of the Holy Spirit in our hearts, the Lord can speak to us 'face to face, as one speaks to a friend'.

## Your prayer life

Think what a difference this will make to your prayer life! Prayer will be no longer a duty to be grudgingly performed; it'll be a pleasure to be anticipated, as you chat with God your friend. There'll be no need to speak in perfectly grammatical sentences; you can use colloquialisms, just as you do in conversation with your friends. No longer will you worry whether it's appropriate to pray for something you want; you'll just speak your mind, and trust God to decide whether to answer yes or no. You won't wait for the right time or hunt for the right place to pray; you can pray as you're walking along or while you're doing your work. And never will you struggle to achieve a certain standard in your prayers. No, the Holy Spirit will be praying through you 'with yearnings too deep for words'. Through the Spirit's work, you'll speak with God 'face to face, as one speaks to a friend'.

## *Suggested hymns*

*Breathe on me, breath of God; Come down, O Love divine; God is love, and where true love is; Gracious Spirit, Holy Ghost.*

## Trinity Sunday   30 May
*Principal Service*   **Faith Transcends Knowledge**
Prov. 8:1–4, 22–31 Wisdom in creation; Ps. 8 Stewardship of
nature; Rom. 5:1–5 God's love and Spirit; John 16:12–15 Spirit,
Father and Jesus

> *'[Jesus said,] "When the Spirit of truth comes, he will guide you
> into all the truth . . . because he will take what is mine and declare
> it to you. All that the Father has is mine."' John 16:13–15*

### St Augustine

St Augustine was puzzling over how he could understand the doctrine of the Trinity. Walking along the seashore, he came across a
child, scooping up the seawater in a seashell, and pouring it into
a hole which he'd dug in the sand. The saint asked him what he
was doing. 'I'm going to take all the water out of the sea,' the child
replied, 'and pour it into this hole.' The saint smiled at the child's
folly in thinking he could get the whole ocean into such a small hole.
Then he realized that he himself was being no wiser, in imagining
that he could get the whole nature of God into his own little mind.

### Faith and reason

Yet if we're to pray to God, and know his love, we must at least
believe that God exists. An atheist wrote in a newspaper recently
that belief in God is utterly unreasonable, so a Christian wrote a
letter to the editor, outlining a number of observations which are
much easier to explain if there is a God than if there isn't. A friend
remonstrated with him, asking what he was doing, applying reason
to questions about God, when the Church teaches that all you need
is faith. 'Ah, but,' replied the Christian, 'faith is not unreasonable. The Christian faith doesn't fly in the faith of reason. Nobody
can prove that God exists, and nobody can prove that there's no
God. But each of these observations – the beauty, complexity and
efficiency of the world in which we live; the number of intelligent
people who believe in God; the words of Jesus claiming that God is
revealing himself through him, and so on – each is hard to explain
if there's no Supreme Being. Arguing from any one of these observations, you can show that it's more probable that God exists. It
would be unscientific to take the less likely explanation, that these

156

things happened by chance; it would be sheer folly to prefer the more improbable explanation in every case.' Bishop Hugh Montefiore published a book with the title, *The Probability of God*, in which he examined each of these arguments in detail, showing that it's more reasonable to believe in God, than not.

## Faith

So where does faith come in? Faith isn't believing in unreasonable things because the Church tells you, like the Queen boasting to Alice that she could believe as many as six impossible things before breakfast. Faith follows a logical line of reasoning as far as it'll go, and then goes further because we trust what God has said about himself. We're using the word faith with two meanings here. You can talk about the Christian faith which is summarized in the Creeds; we believe *that* these things are true, because God's revealed them to us. But we have faith *in* God because we've found God to be trustworthy.

## Trusting what we cannot prove

In daily life, we believe in many things which are not contrary to reason, but go beyond it. We believe things we can't prove, which we can't understand, or which we've no personal experience of, because we trust the person who told us. We believe the bus is going to the place named on the destination board; but the only way to prove it is to get on the bus in faith. An elderly scientist took a young colleague fishing with him, who asked the older man, 'How do you explain the constant flow of this river, the same in dry and wet weather?' 'I don't,' replied the scientist. 'I just fish in it.' One of the early Kings of Siam was told by a Dutch traveller that in some seasons, the water in his country becomes so hard that an elephant could walk on it. The King was at first doubtful, because he'd never seen ice; but he realized at length that the traveller was trustworthy.

## The Trinity

So on Trinity Sunday, we're reminded of the teaching of the Church, based on the words of Jesus, that the Father is divine, Jesus is divine, and the Holy Spirit is divine, and yet there's only one God. We can't understand this, because God's greater than the human mind. But like the scientist who didn't need to understand the river in order to fish in it, it's not unreasonable to worship the Almighty God through faith, though he surpasses our reasoning.

### All-age worship

*List things you trust to be true, though you can't prove them.*

### Suggested hymns

*Holy, holy, holy, Lord God almighty; I the Lord of sea and sky; Thank you, O my Father; There is a Redeemer.*

## Trinity Sunday

(*For Corpus Christ, the Thursday after Trinity Sunday, see page 322.*)

### Second Service   Give Unto the Lord

Morning Ps. 29 The Lord enthroned; Evening Ps. 73:1–3, 16–28 Hard to understand; Ex. 3:1–15 I AM; John 3:1–17 God so loved

> 'Ascribe to the Lord, you powers of heaven,
> ascribe to the Lord glory and strength.'
> Psalm 29:1 (Common Worship)

### Choral rehearsal

A well-known choral society was rehearsing for a concert of music by Sir Edward Elgar. They were preparing a piece in which the composer sets to stirring music the words of Psalm 29:

> Give unto the Lord, O ye mighty,
> give unto the Lord glory and strength.
> Give unto the Lord the glory due unto his name:
> worship the Lord in the beauty of holiness.

As they sang the words 'the voice of the Lord is upon the waters', there began the heaviest rainfall any of them could ever remember. The rain hammered on the roof of the rehearsal room as they sang 'the God of glory thundereth'. It almost seemed as though the building would be washed away, while they sang 'It is the Lord that ruleth the sea'. The humour of the situation was not lost on them as they sang 'The voice of the Lord is mighty in operation; the voice of the Lord is full of majesty . . . The Lord sitteth above the water flood: and the Lord remaineth a King for ever.' Scarcely able to contain their mirth, the singers continued with Elgar's music, as the rainstorm gradually subsided, till, when they were singing 'the Lord shall give his people the blessing of peace', it stopped completely and there was complete calm! The conductor laughed, asking, 'Do you think the Lord was listening to what we were singing?' One of the chorus replied, 'How can anyone deny that God has a sense of humour?' They then abandoned the rehearsal, as everyone was laughing too much to be able to sing.

## Psalm 29

It was a coincidence that the choral society should be singing those words during a rainstorm, because Psalm 29, like several others, is indeed a song about God ruling over the storm. The Psalmists had lived through violent thunderstorms themselves, often under the flimsiest of shelters, a truly frightening experience. Some of them might have been caught in a terrifying storm at sea. Then they cried to the Lord in their distress, and God caused the storm to cease. Which increased their awe in the presence of the Almighty. They were amazed, saying, 'What sort of god is this, that even the winds and the sea obey him?' Exactly what the disciples asked when Jesus stilled the storm on the lake: 'What sort of man is this, that even the winds and the sea obey him?' It began to dawn on them that Jesus wasn't just a man, at all; in some way he was one with the God of the Psalmist, who ruled over the storms at sea or on land.

## The holy Trinity

We mustn't forget, also, that at the beginning of Genesis, the Bible describes the Spirit of God brooding over the face of the deep. So God the Father, Jesus the Son of God, and the Holy Spirit are all described as ruling over the storm. I'm not suggesting that this 'proves' the doctrine of the holy Trinity; that would be too trite. But it does suggest that, in struggling to find words to describe the indescribable God, we can hardly avoid using language like 'three Persons in one God'.

## Wartime

Elgar wrote his setting of this psalm in 1913, when the great powers were engaged in an arms race, and the secure Edwardian world which he'd known was slowly breaking apart. As he composed his music on the very brink of the Great War, it's all the more remarkable that he was able to describe the Lord God as mightier than any other power, who's able to bring out of the chaos the blessing of peace.

## Awe

But the use of this psalm on Trinity Sunday also teaches us something very profound. Jesus is our friend, come to put a human face on God. He described God as our loving heavenly Father. The Holy Spirit is described in one of our hymns as 'that gentle voice we hear, soft as the breath of even'. Yet, together with these intimate portraits of the Trinity, we must remember that God is awesome in his power. All the power in the universe comes from him – that's what 'almighty' means. Thank God, he uses that power benevolently as far as he can. Yet God isn't to be trifled with. You don't take lightly the power behind the Big Bang which created the universe. All we can do is fall down in reverence before him, singing, 'Ascribe to the Lord, you powers of heaven, ascribe to the Lord glory and strength.'

## Suggested hymns

*Bright the vision that delighted; Father of heaven, whose love profound; Immortal, invisible, God only wise; Our blest Redeemer, ere he breathed.*

## First Sunday after Trinity (Proper 5)   6 June
### *Principal Service*   Jesus and Elijah

(*Continuous*): 1 Kings 17:8–16 [17–24] The widow's jar; Ps. 146 God upholds the widows; *or* (*Related*): 1 Kings 17:17–24 Elijah heals the widow's child; Ps. 30 Resurrection from death; Gal. 1:11–24 Paul's conversion and authority; Luke 7:11–17 The resurrection of a child at Nain

> *'The dead man sat up and began to speak, and Jesus gave him to his mother. Fear seized all of them; and they glorified God, saying, "A great prophet has risen among us!"' Luke 7:15–16*

### *The Once and Future King*

*The Once and Future King* is a novel by T. H. White. It's not the only book to be based on the old legend that King Arthur will one day return from the dead to fight for his country. In a similar way, Jewish people expect Elijah to return some day. Elijah never in fact died: at the end of his life on earth he was taken up to heaven in a chariot of fire. In the Old Testament book of Malachi, God says, 'Lo, I will send you the prophet Elijah before the great and terrible day of the LORD comes.' The people of Jesus's day, therefore, firmly expected Elijah to reappear on earth to prepare for the coming of the Messiah. When Jesus raised the widow's son at Nain, the people exclaimed, 'A great prophet has risen among us.' Was Jesus then a reincarnation of Elijah, the once and future prophet?

## The rich woman's son

Now, Elijah had once done something very similar to what Jesus did on that day. There was a rich woman in the village of Shunem, whose only son died, and she sent for Elijah. The prophet gave God a telling-off for causing evil; then breathed into the child; the child came to life again; and Elijah gave him back to his mother. The amazing thing is that Nain's only a couple of miles from Shunem. No wonder the people wondered whether Jesus was Elijah, come back to life to repeat the miracles Elijah did centuries earlier.

## The widow's son

Jesus arrived at Nain in Galilee, just as the funeral was taking place. Funerals are not uncommon; we all have to die sometime; death's the price we pay for the privilege of life. But what made it doubly tragic for the young man's mother was that she was a widow. Now that her husband and her only son were both dead, she had nobody to support her. A woman couldn't survive on her own in those days; she could either become a prostitute, or she'd die of starvation. When Jesus saw her, he realized what an awful situation she was in, and St Luke tells us 'he had compassion for her'. Jesus wasn't some lofty, detached superhuman figure; he was human, one of us, and he knew how unbearably sad life can be for some people. So he felt for the woman; and shared her feeling of grief. And because the character of Jesus reflects that of God our heavenly Father, we know that God isn't remote and uncaring, either. When humans go through the depths of sadness and the agony of grief, it helps to remember that heaven's weeping with us.

## Resurrection

Then, like Elijah before him, Jesus raised the dead son to life, and gave him back to his mother. It was a miracle, which showed the bystanders that Jesus was at least as great as Elijah. People in those days expected prophets to perform miracles; today some people would suspect that the son in each case was only in a trance; but the important thing is that they returned to life. This prefigured the resurrection of Jesus, the king who rules over life and death. The sons whom Jesus and Elijah raised weren't like Jesus; they were resuscitated or revived to earthly life, and later they'd really die. Jesus died, but was raised to a new sort of life; breathed new life into his apostles; and then ascended into heaven like Elijah, where he lives and reigns for ever. Everybody dies sometime: first our parents, then our partner, then ourselves and lastly our children. We hope and pray it may be in the right order. God doesn't cause evil, but sometimes it seems even God can't prevent it. But God has compassion on us, strengthens us, breathes new life into us. So we're never alone; Jesus is always with us. When we're bereaved, our dead are with Jesus – and so they're close to us every time we pray. Jesus is the once and future king: he conquered death once and for all two thousand years ago; he reigns over our lives now, and he'll see us safely through the gateway into eternity when our turn comes to die. Eventually we shall be all one happy family reunited in heaven.

### All-age worship

*Make a sympathy card for someone who has been bereaved.*

### Suggested hymns

*O for a thousand tongues to sing; Restore, O Lord, the honour of your name; Sometimes a light surprises; Thine arm, O Lord, in days of old.*

## First Sunday after Trinity
### Second Service   Ecology
Ps. 44 Come to our help; Gen. 8:15—9:17 God's covenant with Noah; Mark 4:1–20 Parable of the Sower

> *'God blessed Noah and his sons, and said to them, "Be fruitful and multiply, and fill the earth."' Genesis 9:1*

## Turkana pastoralists

Since 1999, there's been virtually no rainfall in north-west Kenya. The Turkana people who lived there survived as nomads, herding their cattle from place to place, wherever there was grass. When there was rain, they and their cattle could build up their strength until the next drought. But since climates around the world started to change, the drought in the Turkana region has been continuous. There was fighting over the few remaining water holes; some families moved away; others were too attached to their nomadic life to change, and their situation is dire. Aid workers have realized, as never before, how interdependent are the worlds of plants, animals and human beings.

## Noah

Something of this is reflected in the story of Noah and his sons after the flood: God commanded them to multiply and fill the earth, and gave them the animals and plants for food. Sure, it may only be a legend. But these primitive stories often tell profound truths which are valid for every period. So let's take the opportunity once again to have a look at our relationship with our environment – at how we handle the problems of ecology.

## Inter-racial

The first thing to note is that the sons of Noah – Shem, Ham and Japheth – are described in the story as the ancestors of all the nations of the earth. Roughly, Shem represents the Semitic people, the Hamites are in Africa and the descendants of Japheth are in Europe. Of course, modern genetics have taught us a lot more about how the different races in the world are related to each other. But even in the Bible it was recognized that we're all descended from common ancestors. So the races are dependent on each other. You can't say that drought's a problem for the Africans, and nothing to do with us. The Africans and the Europeans are cousins; we should think of each other as brothers and sisters. Most people today accept that drought in Africa's caused by global warming, which is the result of carbon emissions in the industrialized nations.

## Biodiversity

Secondly, we learn from the story of Noah that human beings depend on the well-being of the plants and animals for their food supply. Whether or not you're a vegetarian, you have to recognize that the healthiness or otherwise of the world of nature affects our own survival. So the demands of biodiversity and the protection of endangered species are not just the concern of a few cranks; they all affect the food chain somewhere, and the extinction of species may rob us of so far undiscovered medicines. Genetic engineering may be good if it increases food supplies to poor nations, but if poor people can't afford to grow the new strains, then once again the rich will become richer at the expense of the poor. The developed nations produce something like twice as much food as we can eat, but instead of sharing the rest with the poor, we throw it away and further pollute the environment with landfill sites.

## The Bible and ecology

So the Bible teaches that ecology's the concern of us all. Our little gestures like switching to low-energy light bulbs and inflating our car tyres may not make much difference, but at least they show that we're concerned, and the experts can help us put it all into perspective and face up to the major challenges. Most people in Bangladesh farm land which is only inches above sea level, and in the monsoon season it's covered by floods. They're being taught to grow crops on floating rafts of water-hyacinth, but if global warming causes sea levels to rise only a fraction of an inch, they'll starve and Bangladesh will be uninhabitable. If the industrialized nations make life impossible in the poorer countries, they'll have no moral grounds for resisting the demands of poorer people to emigrate to countries where they can make a living.

## What God expects

So God expects you and me to be concerned about these problems, and to do something about them. Whether or not the story of Noah's flood's historical, it conveys a stark message to us:

- sinful behaviour creates ecological disaster;
- the races are dependent on each other;
- the poor suffer from the profligacy of the rich;

- and when God told our ancestors to multiply and cultivate the earth, that included a responsibility to care for and protect all species as well as our own.

May God give us the grace to see our perilous situation, in time to leave an inhabitable world for our grandchildren. May he give us the strength and wisdom to do something about it before it's too late.

### Suggested hymns

*God of mercy, God of grace; God, whose farm is all creation; Great is thy faithfulness, O God my Father; You shall go out with joy.*

## Second Sunday after Trinity (Proper 6)    13 June
*Principal Service*    **Galatians**
(*Continuous*): 1 Kings 21:1–10 [11–14] 15–21a Naboth's vineyard; Ps. 5:1–8 God's justice; *or* (*Related*): 2 Sam. 11:26—12:10, 13–15 David's repentance; Ps. 32 Forgiveness; Gal. 2:15–21 Law, faith and grace; Luke 7:36—8:3 A woman's repentance

> *'We have come to believe in Christ Jesus, so that we might be justified by faith in Christ, and not by doing the works of the law, because no one will be justified by the works of the law.'*
> *Galatians 2:16*

### St Paul

Saul of Tarsus was a Jew and a Pharisee, and tried very hard to be good. To please God, he believed, you have to obey all the commandments found in the Hebrew Scriptures. Yet over and again he failed to measure up to his own ideals. So he was very angry with himself; and he took out his rage on the Christians, a new Jewish sect, who seemed to say that obeying the law was less important than faith in Jesus. 'That's all wrong,' thought Saul, until on the road to Damascus he saw the light. After that, he changed his name to Paul, and tried to persuade his fellow Jews to believe in Jesus, like he did. Of course it's still important to be good, he said, but Jesus taught a more relaxed sort of goodness, based on love rather than rules and regulations.

166

## Galatia

Paul was sent on a preaching tour, with Barnabas, around the Jewish synagogues in Cyprus. Unexpectedly, the Governor of Cyprus, a Roman diplomat, became a believer in Jesus. Paul wondered whether perhaps he shouldn't restrict his preaching to Jews; maybe he should try to interest the non-Jews in Jesus too. He sailed from Cyprus to the mainland, in what we now call Turkey, and climbed up onto the high Anatolian plain, which was then called Galatia. Galatia got its name because it was settled by large numbers of Gallic people – Gauls from France – who fought bravely against the Romans before they were conquered and became part of the Empire.

## Synagogues

Paul preached about Jesus in the synagogues of Galatia, but the Jews there refused to listen to him. In despair he 'turned to the Gentiles', as he put it – non-Jews, who knew nothing about the Jewish law, but were attracted by the idea of modelling their lives on the love of Jesus. After St Paul left, some Jewish Christians turned on the new Galatian converts. 'Paul misled you,' they told them. 'God's judging you, like in a law court, and he's found you guilty. The only way to get a not-guilty verdict from God is to obey every letter of the Jewish law. In other words, you've got to become Jews.'

## A furious letter

St Paul heard about this and was incandescent with rage. He fired off a furious letter – 'You stupid Galatians,' he wrote, 'why did you let them cast an evil spell on you?' It's in our New Testament; we call it 'The Letter (or Epistle) to the Galatians'. Paul took up his enemies' image of the law court. The word he uses for a good, upright person's translated into English as 'righteous'. The Jews, even those who became Christians, thought the only way you could become righteous was by avoiding all the things forbidden by the Old Testament. But Paul had tried that, and failed. He wanted his readers to see that there's no point in making Gentiles become Jews, because even Jews don't deserve a not-guilty verdict. God judges everybody, Jews and Gentiles alike, as guilty, unless they trust Jesus to get the verdict reversed. God will treat us as righteous, if we have faith in the death of Jesus on the cross as a sacrifice for our sins.

## Justification

Unfortunately we've got no English word for declaring somebody not-guilty, so we have to make do with the cumbersome term 'justification'. When we deserve a guilty verdict, but God in his kindness and mercy declares us not-guilty, we say we're justified by the grace of God. So a simple and beautiful idea gets lost in translation, and comes out as the cumbersome phrase: 'We have come to believe in Christ Jesus, so that we might be justified by faith in Christ, and not by doing the works of the law.' Think of the argument going on between the Jewish Christians and the non-Jewish Galatians, and you'll see why this phrase is the crux of Paul's teaching, and so important to you and me. If Paul hadn't insisted on this, we'd have to become Jews and keep the whole Jewish law before becoming Christians. But if Paul's right, God treats us as not-guilty, and takes us to live with him for ever in heaven, simply because we trust in Jesus. It's just a pity there's no simple way to explain that in English.

### All-age worship

*Cut cards into the shape of a cross. On one side write 'Jesus I'm sorry', and on the other 'My child, I forgive you'.*

### Suggested hymns

*And can it be?; Great is thy faithfulness; Hail, thou once-despised Jesus; To God be the glory.*

## Second Sunday after Trinity
### Second Service    Stories

Ps. 52 A tree in God's house [53 Fools say]; Gen. 13 Abram and Lot; Mark 4:21–41 Parables and a storm

> 'With many such parables [Jesus] spoke the word to them, as they were able to hear it; he did not speak to them except in parables, but he explained everything in private to his disciples.'
> Mark 4:33–34

## Stories

Don't you just love a good story? It's been the same since we were kids, begging to be told a story at bedtime, demanding to be read to, until we were able to read for ourselves and open the world of stories. Maybe you like to curl up with a good book nowadays; or you're a film buff, eager to see the latest action hero; or a telly addict, desperate never to miss an episode of your favourite soap opera. Any story must have a beginning, a middle and an end, with a plot that develops and keeps you wanting to learn more, believable characters and an interesting setting. Stories play an important part in our learning about life.

## The purpose of parables

Jesus told many stories. We usually call them 'parables', and they've been described as 'earthly stories with heavenly meanings'. We all know the parables of the prodigal son and the good Samaritan, but altogether there are over eighty parables in the Gospels, and probably Jesus told other stories which never made it to the written page. Undoubtedly he composed attention-grabbing fiction, but all that comes down to us is a brief summary in a single sentence; perhaps this was the punchline at the end of a long tale. Jesus himself explained the purpose of the parables: he preferred to teach by telling a memorable story, because most people can accept new ideas through imaginative and challenging fiction, more readily than by exhortation or reproof. Very often Jesus's first hearers must have thought his stories were hilariously funny, and then have suddenly stopped laughing, when they realized their own behaviour was just as ridiculous as that being satirized in the parable. Sometimes the stories begin or end with a question: 'What do you think?' In this way they force us to make up our own minds about the characters, and thereby to judge our own actions. Many of the parables are about the kingdom of God, which doesn't mean a place on earth, or even where we go when we die. The parables of the kingdom describe what earth would be like if we all obeyed God as our king. They also describe the growth of the Christian community who are already trying to do this.

## Lamp under a bushel

Even in today's short reading from St Mark's Gospel there are five parables. The first is the saying about hiding a light under a bushel. A faithful elderly Christian was astonished to discover she'd been misunderstanding it for years because she thought a bushel was a small bush! Actually it's a measure for grain, probably a basket. You don't light a lamp in order to hide it under a basket, but to spread its light throughout the house. Neither does God reveal his love in Jesus for it to be kept as private information for the in-crowd, but for them to spread it far and wide for everyone to hear.

## Hidden to be revealed

Nobody hides anything away for ever, says Jesus; we hide things so that we can bring them out later. Similarly, God doesn't deliberately keep things secret from us, though he may wait to reveal them until we're able to understand.

## The measure you give

The third parable in this passage is hidden away in a short saying about the measure you give and the measure you receive. If a cheating corn merchant uses small measuring baskets to sell his grain, he'll be cheated by those who sell to him. So we can't expect God to be generous and forgiving when he judges us, if we're mean-minded and prejudiced in the way we judge other people.

## The sleeping farmer

The story of the farmer whose crop goes on growing while he's asleep, reminds us that we have to work hard at serving God, and leave the results to him.

## The mustard seed

The parable of the mustard seed which grows into a big plant warns us not to be depressed when Christians seem to be a small minority; so long as our faith is growing, we can achieve what God wants us to.

## Remembered truths

We all love a good story. It's been said that the legacy of Greek civilization lies in the Greek myths, because Greek stories survived, when Greek science had been forgotten. The teaching of Jesus will last through his parables, provided that whenever we hear one, we ask ourselves, 'What does that say about me?'

## Suggested hymns

*A man there lived by Galilee; Break thou the bread of life; For the fruits of his creation; Tell me the stories of Jesus.*

## Third Sunday after Trinity (Proper 7)   20 June
*Principal Service*   **Facing our Inner Demons**
(*Continuous*): 1 Kings 19:1–4 [5–7] 8–15a The still small voice; Ps. 42 & 43 Faith and hope; *or* (*Related*): Isa. 65:1–9 God's judgement; Ps. 22:19–28 Salvation; Gal. 3:23–29 The Law our tutor till faith comes; Luke 8:26–39 Demons sent into pigs

> '*Jesus . . . commanded the unclean spirit to come out of the man . . . for many times it had seized him.*' *Luke 8:29*

### Losing control

We're all afraid of losing control. A control freak's someone who's obsessively reluctant to share power or responsibility with others. This egocentric behaviour's a form of pride. But there's a darker and deeper fear which haunts almost everyone. There are, within each one of us, desires and psychological forces which we're afraid might take us over. For some people it's the demon drink: 'After a couple of glasses I'm not responsible for my behaviour.' For others there are different desires, lurking in the background to take over if you give them half a chance. It may be an uncontrollable desire to overeat. Maybe you see a handsome man or a beautiful woman, and it's almost impossible to keep your hands off them. Then there are those who go berserk if anyone prevents them having their own way. Those with a filthy temper, who are absolute demons when they're angry. All these temptations can eventually be resisted, but it's a struggle. We all have this deep fear, which we may even be afraid to admit to ourselves, that one day the fatal flaw within us may become irresistible – and then we're lost.

## Possession

To be manipulated by your own dark psychological forces is worse, much worse, than being enslaved by somebody else. But there's a solution. Like the alcoholic, each of us has to admit first that we have a problem, and then face up to it. A newspaper article wrote about people's fear of the devil – historically regarded as a superhuman being with horns and hooves, but even today in the widespread fascination with horror films, the belief that there may be some creatures so evil that they desire to possess us, body and soul. The writer concluded that 'In the end it seems the Devil might not be a devil at all, but something worse – a symbol for every human being's fear of possession; of the deep black stain inside their heart spreading outwards and claiming them.'

## Demon possession

Which brings me to the man described in today's Gospel. He was quite convinced he was possessed – controlled by a whole regiment of demons, so that he said, 'My name's Legion.' He may have been right, or he may have been deluded, but Jesus didn't stop to question his self-diagnosis, he just healed him. Nearby was a herd of pigs, grazing near the cliff-edge, and pigs are regarded by Jewish people as 'unclean'. Jesus either sent the demons into the pigs, or caused the sick man to imagine that he had. The pigs panicked, and tumbled over the cliff. The man felt that he was no longer possessed, and his behaviour became rational. There's no need to decide whether these were 'real' demons, or a figment of his imagination; who could ever answer such a question? What matters is that Jesus took charge; and the power of Jesus is greater than any other power.

## Facing our inner demons

So this isn't just a story of a mentally disturbed man in ancient times: it's a symbol of what besets every one of us. First we need to face up to the dark side of our own personality: for me to acknowledge that I'm often tempted, and some of these temptations are extremely powerful. Admit it: I'm afraid that one day I might not be able to resist any longer, and then I'd lose control. I'd be possessed by a force that's stronger than I am. But there's a solution. The power of Jesus is greater than any other power. Once you've faced up to your own, personal, inner demons, and cried out to Jesus for help, you've beaten them. They're totally powerless. There's no longer any need to be afraid that one day you'll lose control; keep close to Jesus, and he'll deal with that. Pray regularly, and Jesus will give you the will-power to say no to temptation. Say, in the words of the hymn by Isaac Williams,

And if I tempted am to sin,
and outward things are strong,
do thou, O Lord, keep watch within,
and save my soul from wrong.

If you allow yourself to be possessed by Jesus, there's no need to fear that you could be possessed by any lesser power.

### All-age worship

*Practise arm-wrestling to find who is stronger. If an adult helps you, you are stronger than anyone. Write on a poster, 'Jesus is stronger than anything'.*

### Suggested hymns

*Be thou my guardian and my guide; Lord Jesus, think on me; Praise to the Holiest in the height; To God be the glory.*

## Third Sunday after Trinity
### *Second Service*   **Rebecca**
[Ps. 50 A sacrifice of thanksgiving] 57 In the shadow of your wings; Gen. 24:1–27 Isaac and Rebekah; Mark 5:21–43 Jairus' daughter

*'Before [Abraham's servant] had finished [praying], there was Rebekah . . . coming out with her water jar on her shoulder.' Genesis 24:15*

(NB The Old Testament spelling is 'Rebekah'; today most people spell it 'Rebecca'.)

## Great women of the Bible

The Bible tells the story of some famous men. But although it was written by men in a very patriarchal society, it also pays a good deal of attention to a number of women, who are highly praised. Yes, they play an apparently subservient role as home-makers, which wouldn't satisfy a modern feminist. But in many respects the Jewish mother's always dominated her family, and still does. So instead of arguing about which form of society is best, let's have a look at the character of one of the great women of the Old Testament. The list includes Sarah, the wife of Abraham; Leah and Rachel the wives of Jacob; Ruth the wife of Boaz; and Abigail and Michal the wives of King David. Today's reading focuses on Rebecca, the wife of Isaac.

## Choosing a daughter-in-law

The story comes from a nomadic desert tribe beginning to settle into land-ownership, a very different society from ours. The way Rebecca was chosen seems very strange to us. Abraham had been called by God to leave his ancestral homelands in Mesopotamia and settle in the Promised Land. God had a purpose for Abraham and his descendants, which would change the way people think about God for ever. So Abraham thought it was essential that his family should remain distinct from the Canaanite people among whom they lived. For any expatriate or immigrant community, there's a tension between the older generation who want to preserve their cultural distinctiveness, and the younger folk who want to adopt the customs, and marry the children, of the people round them. The fact that the Jewish people have resisted the temptations to assimilation for so many centuries may be a good thing or a bad thing. But if they hadn't done so – to begin with, at least – God's plan to bless the world through them could never have been realized. So Abraham chose that his son Isaac should marry one of their own. As it happened, Rebecca was the granddaughter of Abraham's brother Nahor, making her Isaac's first cousin once removed.

## The girl at the well

Abraham's servant, having returned to the home country, prayed for the right girl, and before he'd finished praying, Rebecca appeared at the well with a water jar on her shoulder. We learn that she was good-looking; of marriageable age but not yet married; and above all kind. Before attending to her own needs, she offered to draw water for the stranger and his camels, and then invited him to her home. The duty of hospitality's emphasized in desert communities, but Rebecca went above and beyond the call of duty. The fact that she showed such an open kindness convinced the servant that she was the right girl to marry Isaac. The negotiations were all carried on by the older generation, as was usual in those days, but when Isaac and Rebecca eventually met, and were married, they fell in love. It often happens that way round in arranged marriages, though we in the West value our right to choose our own partners too much ever to go back to that system.

## A mother in Israel

Rebecca, the wife of Isaac, became the mother of twin boys, Jacob and Esau. Jacob cheated Esau out of his birthright, the share of property belonging to the first-born. Then Rebecca, showing disgraceful favouritism, helped Jacob to cheat Esau out of their blind father's blessing by disguising himself. Rebecca insisted that her son Isaac should find a wife from the old country, where she herself had come from. All we know after that is that when Isaac was about to die, he asked to be buried in the cave of Machpelah at Mamre, because 'There Abraham and his wife Sarah were buried; there Isaac and his wife Rebecca were buried; and there I buried Leah.' They were obviously a close-knit family, despite the rivalry between Rebecca's two sons. The burial place is now called the Ibrahimi Mosque in Hebron, because Abraham's also regarded as their ancestor by Arab Muslims. To be near the tomb, a group of Jewish settlers moved into the Arab town, and it has been the scene of bloody battles between Israelis and Palestinians. Rebecca was chosen because of her kindness to strangers. How sad that these two groups, both claiming descent from Abraham, are riven by fratricidal strife. Mind you, Christians, who claim to be the spiritual descendants of Abraham and the other patriarchs and matriarchs of the Bible, daren't criticize Jews and Arabs until different groups of brother and sister Christians can learn to get along.

## *Suggested hymns*

*Christ is the King! O friends rejoice; Let there be love shared among us; Make me a channel of your peace; The God of Abraham praise.*

## Fourth Sunday after Trinity (Proper 8)  27 June
*Principal Service*  **Fruit of the Spirit**

(*Continuous*): 2 Kings 2:1–2, 6–14 Elijah's spirit given to Elisha;
Ps. 77:1–2, 11–20 Remembering God's saving acts; *or* (*Related*):
1 Kings 19:15–16, 19–21 Elijah calls Elisha; Ps. 16 The path
of life; Gal. 5:1, 13–25 The fruit of the Spirit; Luke 9:51–62
Endurance in following Christ

> *'The fruit of the Spirit is love, joy, peace, patience, kindness,
> generosity, faithfulness, gentleness, and self-control.'* Galatians
> 5:22–23

### Fruit tree and Christmas tree

What's the difference between a Christmas tree and a fruit tree?
Well, a Christmas tree has gifts tied onto it, specifically chosen to
meet the needs of a particular individual at a particular moment.
A fruit tree bears fruit continuously, year after year, because of the
life flowing from its roots through its trunk and branches. Gifts and
fruit. St Paul writes about the gifts of the Spirit and the fruit of the
Spirit, and the words are very well chosen.

### Gifts

The gifts of the Spirit are talents needed by a particular individual
at a particular moment. The church in Corinth had many gifted
people among its members. They had gifts of wisdom, knowledge,
faith, healing, miracles, prophecy, discernment of spirits, speaking
in tongues, the interpretation of tongues, and love. The trouble was
that each claimed that his or her gift was more important than anybody else's. Some even said, if you haven't got my gift, you aren't
a real Christian. This dispute was tearing the church apart. So the
Apostle insisted that our gifts are nothing to boast about: they're
all given to us by the Holy Spirit, whenever we need them to do a
particular job for the Lord. For instance, most Christians have no
need at all for the ability to heal others, most of the time. Thank
God the Holy Spirit bestows on some people that gift. But those
who have different gifts are in no way inferior to those who can
heal. Love is the greatest gift, and we must use it to preserve the
unity of the Church at all costs. Like the gifts on the Christmas tree,
spiritual gifts are there for a purpose, and when that need's been
met, the gifts may no longer be required.

## Galatia

The situation in the church in Galatia was quite different. This was a newly founded community of inexperienced Christians. Most of them were non-Jews, and they'd been delighted when St Paul told them that God loves them. God wants you to live with him for ever in heaven, Paul told them, and all the sins you've committed will be graciously and immediately forgiven, as soon as you repent. Then you can begin your spiritual growth, gradually becoming more loving as the Holy Spirit builds your character. But some Jewish Christians had been teaching the very opposite of what St Paul taught. God will only listen, they said, to people who obey every one of the commandments in the Old Testament. You can only earn God's forgiveness if you obey every detail of the law of Moses. This, too, was splitting the church in Galatia.

## Fruit

So a better picture than the Christmas tree, in this situation, was the apple tree. Fruit grows on it because the sap brings nourishment up from the roots. St Paul writes about the fruit of the Spirit which grows slowly but naturally on the branches. The Holy Spirit's like the sap in the tree, causing the fruit to grow. The fruit are the characteristics which grow in the soul of every Christian who prays: love, joy, peace, patience, kindness, goodness, faithfulness, gentleness and self-control. 'For such there is no law,' adds St Paul – qualities like that can't be created by battering people with commandments. The law tells you what you mustn't do, but it doesn't make you any more loving.

## 'Inna my heart'

'I want to be a Christian inna my heart', sings the old spiritual. Are the fruits of the Spirit growing inna *your* heart? Are you becoming more loving, more joyful, more at peace in your heart as time passes? I'm sure you'd humbly admit that you're nothing like as loving as you should be. But if you pray regularly, these qualities should be growing in you slowly – oh so painfully slowly – as the years go by. Ask yourself whether your heart's a spiritual growth area, a living fruit tree, as I read again the list of the fruits of the Spirit. If they're showing a slow but steady increase, thank God. If not, pray eagerly to become a growing fruit tree, bearing a bumper crop of love, joy, peace, patience, kindness, goodness, faithfulness, gentleness and self-control.

### All-age worship

*Make a cardboard cut-out Christmas tree and a fruit tree. Hang on the Christmas tree parcels labelled with the gifts in 1 Corinthians 12—14. Draw on the fruit tree fruits labelled from Galatians 5:22–23.*

### Suggested hymns

*For the fruits of his creation; Gracious Spirit, Holy Ghost; Lord, dismiss us with thy blessing; Spirit of holiness, wisdom and faithfulness.*

## Fourth Sunday after Trinity
### Second Service    Vulnerability
Ps. [59:1–5, 18–20 You are my fortress] 60 Human help is worthless; Gen. 27:1–40 Jacob cheats Esau; Mark 6:1–6 Jesus rejected at Nazareth

> *'[Jesus] came to his hometown . . . and many . . . said . . . "Is not this the carpenter, the son of Mary and brother of James and Joses and Judas and Simon, and are not his sisters here with us?" And they took offence at him . . . And he could do no deed of power there.' Mark 6:1–5*

### Homecoming

Jesus returned on a visit to Nazareth, the town where he'd been brought up as a kid. You'd have expected a joyful homecoming, a celebration of the local boy who'd made good. But their horizons were too limited. All they saw was the village carpenter, who thought Nazareth wasn't good enough for him, and had deserted them to do something different. They were tripped up by their own narrow prejudices. Worse, they were totally materialistic in their assessment of the world around them. Somebody who made money was important, but a travelling preacher had no value, because the things he was talking about – love and faith – didn't appear on their balance sheets. So the homecoming was a failure, and Jesus couldn't heal any of the sick people there; he'd always said, 'Your faith has made you well', and they had no faith.

## Vulnerability

Yet, in a sense, Jesus had asked for it. They'd have respected the Son of God if he'd appeared among them in his heavenly glory. Instead, he decided to come down to earth and live among them as an ordinary human being. He deliberately made himself indistinguishable from his neighbours, because that was the only way to win their love. But it made him vulnerable, and by becoming human he ran the risk that he'd be ignored. If he'd claimed the privileges of his heavenly birth, he wouldn't have been crucified. Seeking to gain the understanding of human beings by becoming just like us, Jesus took a gamble – and apparently he lost, in Nazareth and in Jerusalem.

## Defeat is victory

Yet paradoxically, by his willingness to be defeated, Jesus won his greatest victory. By refusing to accept the material standards of the world, he overcame them, showing that there are many things in life more important than money. By submitting to death rather than betraying his friends, he drew the sting of death, transforming it into the gateway to life. By insisting that God is our loving heavenly Father, he demonstrated that materialists, who restrict their interest to things which can be measured and weighed, miss out on everything that makes life worthwhile. It was Jesus's very vulnerability which was his triumph.

## Failure is success

That means that for us, too, the moments of our apparent failure may turn out to be our greatest successes. Like Jesus, we may find we get nowhere with our family and neighbours. They hear us talking about our experience of God's love, and they dismiss us as silly old fools. 'There's no point in reasoning with him (or her),' they say. 'He won't listen to reason, and he's so-o-o last-century. Everyone with any sense is an atheist these days.' Like Jesus in Nazareth, we're rejected by those closest to us. Of course, some of their criticism of us may be justified; after all, they know us well. But like the people of Jesus's hometown, they won't lift their eyes above the merely material. They talk about love, truth and beauty, yet by their rejection of the Christian faith, they imply that none of these supernatural things exist. By our insistence on prayer and worship, we bear witness to the supreme importance and eternal significance of the supernatural; and in that our broadness of vision triumphs over our narrow-minded neighbours.

## Influence

The influence of Jesus has spread around the world, and down the ages, because of his willingness to accept failure. We too, when we try to make the world a better place, and our best efforts seem to come to nothing, feel that we've failed. But nobody knows how much influence you've had on the hearts of people whose names you may not even know, by your persistence in the service of others. By your insistence on the importance of love and honesty, truthfulness and faith, you may have won a victory over those who are simply interested in making their pile.

## Paradox

So from the failure of Jesus in Nazareth, we learn a very paradoxical message, which applies to our own lives too. What appears to be failure is very often really success; what appears to be defeat is often really victory. By our willingness to accept our own vulnerability, and to gamble with the possibility of disappointment, we've won a victory over the sceptics, which may last long after we have passed on to our final reward in heaven.

### Suggested hymns

*Lord of all hopefulness; O Jesus, I have promised; The Son of God his glory hides; There in God's garden stands the tree of wisdom.*

## Fifth Sunday after Trinity (Proper 9)   4 July
*Principal Service*   **Boasting**

(*Continuous*): 2 Kings 5:1–14 Naaman healed from leprosy; Ps. 30 Healing; *or* (*Related*): Isa. 66:10–14 The motherhood of God; Ps. 66:1–8 God's grace; Gal. 6:[1–6] 7–16 Righteousness; Luke 10:1–11, 16–20 Sending out the seventy disciples

> *'May I never boast of anything except the cross of our Lord Jesus Christ, by which the world has been crucified to me, and I to the world.' Galatians 6:14*

### Proud of his humility

An old monk lay dying, and his brothers gathered round his death-bed, praising his intelligence, his singing and his devotion. When they'd all gone, he turned to the nurse and said, 'You see that? Typical. None of them praised the characteristic of which I'm most proud.' 'What's that?' asked the astonished nurse. The monk replied, 'Why, my humility, of course!' It's a silly story, because if he'd been really humble he couldn't have been proud at the same time. But the story points up how foolishly proud we are about unimportant things.

### St Paul

Many of the Pharisees were proud of their righteousness. By this they meant how successful they were at keeping the laws in the Old Testament. In his younger days, Saul of Tarsus was a Pharisee. But he set himself such impossibly high standards to aim for that he realized he could never be truly righteous by obeying the law. When he became St Paul the Christian, he realized that the only righteousness that pleases God is the spirit of gentleness, working for the good of all, and a willingness to bear one another's burdens. That requires genuine humility, so nobody could possibly boast about it. Moreover, Paul writes to the Galatians that loving care for our neighbours can't be achieved by our own efforts, but it's the gift of the Holy Spirit of God. So we can't take any credit for it ourselves, or boast about it.

## Boasting

Paul calls boasting a temptation. Especially when we're tempted to compare other people's behaviour unfavourably with our own. If good behaviour's the gift of the Holy Spirit, it's nothing to boast about. Everybody's tempted to do wrong. If some people are more successful in resisting temptation than others, the credit should go to God. Anyone who boasts obviously hasn't resisted the temptation to the sin of pride. If we boast of our race, or our parents, or our nationality, we only make fools of ourselves, because the accident of our birth is not an achievement which we deserve any praise for. Jewish Christians in Galatia were boasting about belonging to God's Chosen People, the only people who tried to obey the laws of God; but the Gentiles despised the Jews, whom they considered vastly inferior to themselves. So St Paul writes to the Galatians: 'May I never boast of anything except the cross of our Lord Jesus Christ, by which the world has been crucified to me, and I to the world.'

## Boasting about the cross

The cross seems a strange thing to boast about. But when you think about it, it's amazing that Jesus should think of sacrificing his life for other people. Paul regarded the death of Jesus as a sacrifice, and his experience, which could be echoed by millions of other Christians, is that when we realize how much Jesus loves us, we feel our burden of guilt lifted, and a wonderful sense of freedom and forgiveness. Sinful human beings don't deserve this; logically, God would do well to write us off as a bad lot and destroy us. So the fact that, sinful as I am, God loves me, is surely a true cause for boasting, and one which we share with anyone who has faith in Jesus.

## Crucified to the world

Once we realize this, all the other things we used to boast about pale into insignificance. If God loves us and accepts us just as we are, it no longer matters whether we're rich or poor, famous or unnoticed, come from a famous family or completely humble origins. St Paul expresses this by saying that by 'the cross of our Lord Jesus Christ . . . the world has been crucified to me, and I to the world'. The world of the rich and famous could be dead as far as I'm concerned, and I'm dead to all of that. All that matters is that

God loves me, Jesus died for me, my past is forgotten, and God and I are friends for evermore. Most people boast about what *they've* done – Christians boast about what God has done for us. To boast about anything else is to be puffed up with vanity and pride.

## All-age worship

*Make a cross from card wrapped in silver foil, and write on it with a felt-tip pen, 'Jesus loves me'. Hang it proudly from a string round your neck.*

## Suggested hymns

*Beneath the cross of Jesus; For the healing of the nations; In the cross of Christ I glory; When I survey the wondrous cross.*

# Fifth Sunday after Trinity
## Second Service   The Herod Mob
Ps. 65 God in nature [70 Don't delay]; Gen. 29:1–20 Jacob loved Rachel; Mark 6:7–29 The death of John the Baptist

> 'Herod himself had sent men who arrested John, bound him, and put him in prison on account of Herodias, his brother Philip's wife, because Herod had married her.' Mark 6:17

## The Herod family

The story of the Herod family is nastier than anything dreamt up in a crime novel. If you submitted the plot to an editor, it'd be turned down as unrealistic. No real family of thugs and gangsters, they'd say, could possibly behave as badly as that. But the Herod family were appalling – I prefer to call them the Herod Mob. Many of them appear in the New Testament, and their relationships to each other are distinctly complicated.

## Herod the Great

Today's reading from St Mark's Gospel tells the story of a girl who danced in front of one of the Herods, and demanded as her reward the head of John the Baptist. Most manuscripts name her

## Outline family tree of all the Herods mentioned in the New Testament

(There were many more wives and offspring than there is space for here.)

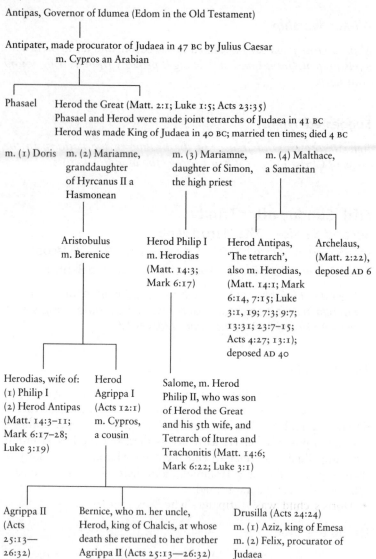

Antipas, Governor of Idumea (Edom in the Old Testament)

Antipater, made procurator of Judaea in 47 BC by Julius Caesar
m. Cypros an Arabian

Phasael

Herod the Great (Matt. 2:1; Luke 1:5; Acts 23:35)
Phasael and Herod were made joint tetrarchs of Judaea in 41 BC
Herod was made King of Judaea in 40 BC; married ten times; died 4 BC

m. (1) Doris

m. (2) Mariamne, granddaughter of Hyrcanus II a Hasmonean

m. (3) Mariamne, daughter of Simon, the high priest

m. (4) Malthace, a Samaritan

Aristobulus
m. Berenice

Herod Philip I
m. Herodias
(Matt. 14:3;
Mark 6:17)

Herod Antipas, 'The tetrarch', also m. Herodias, (Matt. 14:1; Mark 6:14, 7:15; Luke 3:1, 19; 7:3; 9:7; 13:31; 23:7–15; Acts 4:27; 13:1); deposed AD 40

Archelaus, (Matt. 2:22), deposed AD 6

Herodias, wife of:
(1) Philip I
(2) Herod Antipas
(Matt. 14:3–11;
Mark 6:17–28;
Luke 3:19)

Herod Agrippa I
(Acts 12:1)
m. Cypros, a cousin

Salome, m. Herod Philip II, who was son of Herod the Great and his 5th wife, and Tetrarch of Iturea and Trachonitis (Matt. 14:6; Mark 6:22; Luke 3:1)

Agrippa II
(Acts
25:13—
26:32)

Bernice, who m. her uncle, Herod, king of Chalcis, at whose death she returned to her brother Agrippa II (Acts 25:13—26:32)

Drusilla (Acts 24:24)
m. (1) Aziz, king of Emesa
m. (2) Felix, procurator of Judaea

(From Michael Counsell, *Every Pilgrim's Guide to the Journeys of the Apostles*, Canterbury Press, 2002)

Herodias, but they're wrong; later manuscripts corrected it to read 'Herodias's daughter', whose name was Salome. But the history of family wickedness stretches back to her grandfather, King Herod the Great. This was the Herod whom the wise men visited while looking for baby Jesus, the newborn King of the Jews. Herod the Great thought *he* was the king of the Jews, so he responded with the Massacre of the Innocents – all the baby boys in Bethlehem were slaughtered to get rid of the rival claimant to his throne. This was completely in character: Herod the Great had many of his own family assassinated, including his young wife Mariamne, whom he loved but suspected of adultery, and three of his sons. This led to the Emperor Augustus's witticism that he'd rather be Herod's pig than Herod's son. Herod the Great wasn't Jewish, but came from Edom; it was the Romans who made him king of the Jews.

## Wives

The appalling Herod the Great married at least ten times. Only five of the wives of Herod the Great need concern us here. Their names were:

1 Cleopatra of Jerusalem
2 Doris
3 Mariamne, who was descended from the Hasmonean royal family
4 another Mariamne, daughter of Simon the High Priest, and
5 Malthake, a Samaritan.

## Children

By each of these wives, Herod the Great had one or more children:

- Philip the Tetrarch was the son of Cleopatra, and ruled over areas to the East of the River Jordan. He it was who married Salome.
- Doris's child was Antipater, who was murdered by his father Herod the Great.
- The first Mariamne had two sons, Alexander and Aristobulus, both of whom were murdered by their father, though before that happened, Aristobulus had become the father of Herodias and of Herod Agrippa the First.
- The other Mariamne was the mother of Herod Philip, who

185

married Herodias his niece; they were the parents of Salome.

- Malthake had two sons, Herod Antipas and Archelaus. Herod Antipas was the ruler of Galilee – he was the Herod who heard the case against Jesus before his crucifixion. He had seduced and married Herodias, the wife of his half-brother Herod Philip, and it was for marrying his brother's wife, which was against the Jewish law, that John the Baptist rebuked Antipas. Finally, Archelaus ruled Judaea after the death of his father Herod the Great, and Joseph and Mary were so scared of what he might do to their son Jesus that instead of returning to Bethlehem they moved to Nazareth in Galilee. He was such a bad king that the Romans were obliged to depose him.

## Grandchildren

Finally, a word about the grandchildren in this ghastly clan. Salome, the girl who danced for her stepfather, eventually married her uncle, Herod Philip the Second. Herod Agrippa had two daughters, Bernice and Drusilla. Bernice married her uncle, Herod, King of Chalcis. After he died she moved in with her brother, Agrippa the Second; the two of them sat in judgement on the apostle Paul, and Agrippa said sarcastically that Paul had almost persuaded him to become a Christian. Drusilla married, as her second husband, the Roman Procurator Felix, and they, too, sat in judgement on St Paul. I warned you it was complicated.

## Punishment

Sometimes Christians imagine that everybody's basically nice, like us. The reality is that there are many thoroughly evil people in this world. The Herod Mob were punished when their kingdoms were taken from them by the Romans. What happened to them in the afterlife we don't know; if they repented of their wickedness, God could have forgiven them, but there's no sign they ever did. They're a warning to us of the sort of people Christians may find themselves up against, and of the insidious grip which evil can get on anyone who's not prepared to stand up against it.

## *Suggested hymns*

*Christian, dost thou see them?; In vain the cruel Herod's fear; O Lord, the clouds are gathering; Unto us a boy is born.*

## Sixth Sunday after Trinity (Proper 10)    11 July
*Principal Service*   **Every-Member Ministry**
(*Continuous*): Amos 7:7–17 The plumb line: judgement on the city; Ps. 82 Justice; *or* (*Related*): Deut. 30:9–14 The word is near you; Ps. 25:1–10 Truth and guidance; Col. 1:1–14 Prayer, faith and works; Luke 10:25–37 The good Samaritan

> *'This you learned from Epaphras, our beloved fellow servant. He is a faithful minister of Christ on your behalf.' Colossians 1:7*

### Epaphras

St Paul founded churches in the provincial capitals of the Roman Empire, then trained the converts he made there. When they were strong enough in their faith, they travelled out from the capital cities, to found new churches in the smaller towns around. This strategy made sense, for Paul would never have had time to visit the little towns himself. But handing over the work to new converts was a stroke of genius – nothing establishes new Christians in their faith so much as giving them some responsibility. Epaphras was one of these. Paul spent three years in Ephesus, the capital of the Province of Asia. The River Meander reaches the sea near Ephesus. One of its tributaries is the River Lycus. In the Lycus valley were three towns: Hierapolis, Laodicea and Colossae. Colossae was the home town of Epaphras. He travelled to Ephesus, and met Paul there; soon he was ready to go back home and establish a church in Colossae. He was thoroughly successful – because Paul had trained him well. Paul never visited Colossae, but he wrote a letter to the Colossians, saying how pleased he was with what Epaphras had done. The Christian hope of heaven, he wrote, 'you learned from Epaphras, our beloved fellow servant. He is a faithful minister of Christ on your behalf.' Later he writes:

> Epaphras, who is one of you, a servant of Christ Jesus, greets you. He is always wrestling in his prayers on your behalf, so that you may stand mature and fully assured in everything that God wills. For I testify for him that he has worked hard for you and for those in Laodicea and in Hierapolis.

Here was a Christian who put the parable of the good Samaritan into practice, by loving his neighbours in the Lycus Valley churches.

## Ministry

What St Paul and Epaphras had in common was a burning desire to serve God by serving their neighbours, telling them of God's love for them. 'Ministry' simply means service, and that's something any Christian can do, not only those we call ministers. The love of God's best understood by people who've experienced a loving Christian community. Every member of the local church has a part to play in making that loving community a reality. Yes, some people are good at public speaking, and some have natural gifts of leadership. But every member of the church can do something to make it run smoothly, if they'll only think what it is. Unfortunately, some people get stuck in positions in the church which they hold down for years, because nobody else will volunteer. Nobody should feel obliged to do the same thing, even flower-arranging, for more than, say, six years unless they want to, before somebody else offers to take over and free that person to do something else. Every congregation needs to draw in new members, to replace those who fall ill or move away, and hopefully to grow larger year by year. The ordained ministers can't do that on their own – every member of the church must invite their friends and neighbours to come to church with them if it's to be a vibrant and living fellowship. Today people talk about 'every-member ministry', recognizing that the ordained ministers simply haven't time to minister to every single person in their congregation and the area around. Their task's to train others to do it, like St Paul did with Epaphras. Ministry, serving others, is something every member of the church can and must do. They must all be prepared to accept some training, and then take responsibility. If you always leave everything for somebody else to do, nothing ever gets done at all. Do you know the popular saying about teamwork?

There are four people named Everybody, Somebody, Anybody and Nobody. There was an important job to be done and Everybody was asked to do it. Anybody could have done it, but Nobody did. Somebody got angry about that, because it was Everybody's job. Everybody thought that Anybody could do it, but Nobody realized that Everybody wouldn't do it. It ended up that Everybody blamed Somebody when Nobody did what Anybody could have done.

That's what happens in a church which hasn't thought about every-member ministry!

## All-age worship

*Have older children guide the hands of younger ones as they write out the words 'Jesus Loves You'. Then have the younger ones deliver this message to members of the congregation.*

## Suggested hymns

*I the Lord of sea and sky; Lord, pour thy Spirit from on high; Make me a channel of your peace; O thou who camest from above.*

# Sixth Sunday after Trinity
## *Second Service*  **Memory**
Ps. 77 Remembering the past; Gen. 32:9–30 Wrestling Jacob; Mark 7:1–23 Tradition

*'I will remember the works of the Lord; and call to mind your wonders of old time.' Psalm 77:11 (Common Worship)*

## Loss of memory

A guide was showing some visitors round Bateman's, the house where Rudyard Kipling lived, and suddenly went silent because, to his chagrin, he'd forgotten the name of the other house where the novelist had lived previously. Later one of the guests saw the name under a picture of the house concerned, and tactfully drew the guide's attention to it. 'Ah well, you know what they say,' sighed the guide. '"There's only two disadvantages to growing old: one's loss of memory – and I can't remember what the other one is!"'

## Value of memory

There's another saying: 'You never miss the water till the well runs dry.' And most people don't realize what a useful thing memory is until it begins to fail them. There are short-term memories and long-term memories. The former concern what you've just done, like where you put your reading glasses, and this is the first to fail in old age. Long-term memories, like things you did when you were young, often become more vivid as you grow older, and elderly people get a lot of pleasure by sharing their memories of days gone by.

## Types of memory

Most memories are described in words, and some experience of memorizing poems, or acting on a stage, improves your ability to memorize the things that have been said to you. Other memories consist of a mental image of something you've seen, and fortunate are those who have a photographic memory. Dancers learn movement memory, and can repeat complicated sequences of steps almost without thinking, which makes people wonder whether some memories are stored not in the brain cells, but in the nerves and muscles themselves. Memory can also be stored in books, paintings or music, or digitally on a computer, which is simply a machine for sorting memories.

## Personality

René Descartes said, 'I think, therefore I am.' Thinking mostly consists of rearranging your memories and making links between them. Who I am, my personality, consists of what memories I have stored in my brain, and how I arrange them and link them. Someone suffering from total amnesia ceases to be a person at all. A community's often bound together by their shared memories. Anthropologists who study remote tribes say you can't be accepted as a member of the tribe until you've 'learnt their songs' – meaning the account of the events which formed them into a community. In Psalm 77, the author sings, 'I will remember the works of the Lord; and call to mind your wonders of old time.' The people of God are formed by shared memories of what God's done for us; we come together in worship to recite those memories, so establishing our membership in the community. The Israelites remembered the crossing of the Red Sea every year at Passover, and Christians remember the death and resurrection of Jesus when they eat bread and drink wine 'in remembrance of' him.

## Living on

After we die, we hope that we shall live on in the memories of those who've known us. Often we feel as though those in authority have forgotten all about us. Archbishop Rowan Williams once described the Church as 'the forgotten people whom God remembers'. Everything we do is stored in the memory of God – except for the sins which we confessed and which he has promised to forget. So perhaps we could be described as living on in the memory of God.

## God as a computer

If it's not too irreverent, we could compare God to a super-computer. Really big computers are capable of multi-tasking – they can do more than one thing at a time. So God can give his whole attention to every person who prays to him, even if they all speak at once. God's a massive memory, into which, if we believe in God, we can download all our memories. As a computer saves information into its memory, so God saves us when he remembers us, and we live in him for ever because God's memory's timeless and eternal. What we're doing now – worship – is important. In worship we remember what God's done for us, and tell him our thoughts and memories. Our personality's the sum of our memories, so the whole of me and the whole of you can be stored in the mind of God, after our bodies are finished with. Our soul lives on in the mind of God, and we can recognize each other, and continue to talk to each other, and continue to love, after we've died. It's only a metaphor, but perhaps this can give twenty-first-century people a way of thinking about eternity.

### Suggested hymns

*Come, O thou traveller unknown; Lord Jesus, think on me; To God be the glory; We have a gospel to proclaim.*

# Seventh Sunday after Trinity (Proper 11)   18 July
*Principal Service*   **Human Biodiversity**
(*Continuous*): Amos 8:1–12 Justice for the needy; Ps. 52 Justice for the needy; *or* (*Related*): Gen. 18:1–10a Abraham welcomes three guests; Ps. 15 Justice; Col. 1:15–28 Christ the head of the Church; Luke 10:38–42 Martha and Mary, works and prayer

> *'As they went on their way, he entered a certain village, where a woman named Martha welcomed him into her home. She had a sister named Mary, who sat at the Lord's feet and listened to what he was saying.' Luke 10:38–39*

### Mary and Martha

Jesus was walking up from Galilee to Jerusalem, and was exhausted by the journey. There was bound to be trouble when he arrived in

Jerusalem, and he needed peace and quiet to think about how he'd handle it. So he turned off the road to a small village called Bethany. He'd good friends there – Lazarus and his two sisters Mary and Martha. Surely they'd give him a place of stillness to recover his strength, and sort out his ideas. But as soon as he arrived, Martha started fussing over him. She did it with the best intentions, but it was the last thing he needed at that particular moment. She wanted to be kind to Jesus, and her way of being kind was to lay on a big meal. Her dinners were famous in Bethany. Any other time, and Jesus might have been honoured and delighted to accept her warm hospitality. But not right now! The two sisters, Mary and Martha, were as different as chalk from cheese. Mary was the quiet one; while Martha bustled and complained, Mary sat in silence near Jesus and listened to what he had to say. Jesus praised her for doing the only thing that was necessary – necessary for her, so that she could come close to God, and necessary for him, to give him time for reflection.

## Personality types

Psychologists tell us there are many varieties of human personality. Martha would have found it difficult to adopt Mary's stillness, and it would have been hard for Mary to be busy like Martha. It was simply a clash of temperaments; neither was right and neither was wrong. Martha would have echoed the words of the poem called 'The Divine Office of the Kitchen', variously ascribed to Fay Inch-fawn or Cecily Hallack, which begins:

> Lord of the pots and pipkins, since I have no time to be
> A saint by doing lovely things and vigilling with Thee,
> By watching in the twilit dawn and storming Heaven's gates,
> Make me a saint by getting meals and washing up the plates.

Her sister Mary, on the other hand, was a contemplative. It's an effort for the extrovert to be sensitive to the introvert, and it's hard for introverts to turn themselves into extroverts. Extroverts are party animals; introverts regard gatherings of more than about five people as a painful form of purgatory. Sometimes you have to force yourself to behave out of character, if God calls you to do something which doesn't come naturally. But you must always try to understand those who are different from you.

## Tolerance

When Jesus came to call, Martha should have been sensitive to his needs. She wanted to help him, but in her way, not his; she should have learnt to understand that other people may think, and feel, quite differently from us, and waited for the right moment to be busy. This was quite definitely not it. So we must discover how to tolerate people with whom we may have little in common. More than that, we should learn to enjoy the many varying types of people that God's put on this earth. Perhaps God made us so different from each other because he appreciates what makes each one of us unique. Maybe we should learn to do the same.

## Human biodiversity

So I'll end with a little bit of doggerel which a retired clergyman called Michael Counsell wrote recently. Just as the ecologists try to preserve biodiversity in animals and plants, he called this 'Human Biodiversity':

> Since Jesus likes the likes of you
> and likes the likes of me,
> though you and I, to tell it true,
> are unlike as could be,
>
> then why should I not like you too,
> and learn to share our dreams,
> that we may love alike, we two,
> unlikely though it seems?
>
> And if you think that you could see –
> since God loves everyone –
> your way to like me, we'd agree
> to do as God has done.
>
> So let's be kind to humankind,
> and undervalue none,
> enjoying difference, and find
> God's likeness in each one.

## All-age worship

*Make up a questionnaire to discover who prefers being in a crowd or being on their own, outdoor sports or reading a book, and so on. Talk about loving people who are different.*

## Suggested hymns

*In Christ there is no east or west; O love divine, how sweet thou art; Seek ye first the kingdom of God; When we walk with the Lord.*

## Seventh Sunday after Trinity
### Second Service   Any Dream Will Do

Ps. 81 I rescued you; Gen. 41:1–16, 25–37 Interpreting dreams; 1 Cor. 4:8–13 Fools for Christ; *Gospel at Holy Communion*: John 4:31–35 Ripe for harvesting

> *'Pharaoh said to Joseph, "I have had a dream, and there is no one who can interpret it. I have heard it said of you that when you hear a dream you can interpret it." Joseph answered Pharaoh, "It is not I; God will give Pharaoh a favourable answer."'* Genesis 41:15–16

## Musical

*Joseph and his Amazing Technicolor™ Dreamcoat* is an amazingly successful musical by Tim Rice and Andrew Lloyd-Webber. As you probably know, it's based on the story of Joseph from the Bible, but it's not at all solemn. It was written as a cantata for a school in London in 1968, and originally only lasted 20 minutes. For the third performance at St Paul's Cathedral later in the same year, it was expanded. *Joseph* was finally professionally produced in 1972. It's been performed by over twenty thousand amateur groups, in schools and churches all across the world.

## The plot

At the opening of the show, the narrator, encouraging children to dream, tells the story of Joseph the dreamer in 'Any Dream Will Do'. Jacob has 12 sons, but the brothers are jealous because their father's given Joseph, his favourite, a coat of many colours. Joseph has dreams implying that he's going to rule over them. The brothers sell him to some Ishmaelites, who sell him on in Egypt as a slave to Potiphar – but Potiphar's wife attempts to seduce him. Potiphar throws Joseph into jail, where he interprets dreams for his fellow prisoners. Pharaoh, the king, a parody of Elvis Presley, is having dreams that no one can interpret, until Joseph predicts the seven years of famine. He's then promoted to become the second most powerful man in Egypt. Back home, Joseph's brothers decide to go to Egypt, and – not realizing that he's their own brother – they beg Joseph for food. He tricks them to test their sincerity, and each of them offers his own life as a prisoner if Joseph will set Benjamin free. Joseph sees their change of heart and their growing awareness of family loyalty, and reveals himself. The whole family's reunited for a happy ending.

## Pastiche

The music contains parodies of many styles of singing which were popular at the time it was written, including French ballads in 'Those Canaan Days', Elvis-type rock and roll in 'Song of the King', western in 'One More Angel In Heaven', 1920s ragtime in 'Potiphar', and disco in 'Go, Go, Go Joseph'.

## Tribes

The story of Joseph and his seven brothers goes 'way, way back, many centuries ago'. How much of it's historical we can't tell, yet it was obviously popular because it's a rattling good yarn. But another purpose was served by repeating the story. Each of the brothers is said to be the ancestor of one of the 12 tribes of Israel. In the course of the story they learn the importance of family solidarity; so the tale was told to encourage the tribes to co-operate and be loyal to each other. It also teaches that betrayal is serious, but it can be forgiven, if there's genuine repentance and a desire for reconciliation.

## Lessons for today

These lessons are still important in the changed society of today. Even young members of amateur groups performing the musical can recognize this, and learn in a very acceptable and deep way the importance of loyalty to their friends and family. Jealousy's a fatal flaw in the life of any family or society, whether it's jealousy of brothers, people at work, or the rich and famous. Betrayal's a sin, and even if we're undiscovered, we shall suffer pangs of conscience for the rest of our lives over the harm we do to other people – people who should have been able to trust us. Yet even the worst sins can be forgiven. If we apologize to those we've harmed, and try to make up to them the damage we've caused, then maybe our friends will forgive us, though we don't deserve it. Or maybe they won't, but God certainly will. We can also all learn the importance of dreaming big, planning an ambitious future for ourselves, and following that dream with determination and perseverance. Yes, it's true, any dream will do. But if it's a dream of attempting great things for God, and using the power he gives us in serving others, then God's promised to love us, forgive us and strengthen us. Then we can work together, loyal to each other and faithful to God, in his service. He'll clothe us in the dream-coat of his Holy Spirit, not to create jealousy and rivalry, but to show that his fatherly love is equally available to all his children.

## Suggested hymns

*Blest be the tie that binds; Brother, sister, let me serve you; In heavenly love abiding; Jesus, stand among us.*


# Eighth Sunday after Trinity (Proper 12)
# (St James the Apostle)   25 July
*Principal Service*   **How to Pray**
(*Continuous*): Hos. 1:2–10 Hosea's family; Ps. 85 Forgiveness; *or* (*Related*): Gen. 18:20–32 Abraham's prayer for Sodom; Ps. 138 Prayer for grace; Col. 2:6–15 [16–19] Resurrection with Christ; Luke 11:1–13 Ask, seek, knock

> '*Ask, and it will be given you; search, and you will find; knock, and the door will be opened for you.*' Luke 11:9–10

## How to hug

A shy young man saw a volume in the window of a bookshop, and on the spine were the words 'HOW TO HUG'. He thought this was just what he needed to achieve success with the girl he admired, and rushed in to buy it. But when he got home he found it was volume

18 of an encyclopaedia, covering the entries from Howler Monkeys to Huguenots – HOW to HUG! The disciples asked Jesus 'how to pray'. Jesus's answer was much more helpful to them, and to us, than the encyclopaedia was to the bashful lover.

## How to pray

First Jesus taught them how to say the 'Our Father', which we call the Lord's Prayer. The novice, beginning the journey of prayer, can resolve never to go to bed without having said the Lord's Prayer by heart; but then you can begin to elaborate the prayer in your own words, using each phrase as a 'headline' for the things you want to ask. Jesus followed this with the parable of 'the friend at midnight', where even the man who's already gone to bed answers his friend's request for help. This is an ironic rebuke to those who are tempted to give up on prayer because God never seems to answer – keep going, says Jesus, and the answer will come in God's good time. So he follows this with a little piece of poetry:

Ask and you'll receive;
Search, and you'll find,
Knock, and the door will be opened;
For everyone who asks receives;
Everyone who searches finds;
And the door is opened to everyone who knocks.

It's a perfect poem; no, I know it doesn't rhyme, but rhyme wasn't invented until several hundred years later. But Jesus the poet produced a perfect six-line verse, where the last three reflect the first three.

## Why pray?

So why do we pray? Even in countries where church attendance is in decline, surveys find that 70 per cent of the people believe in God and 80 per cent pray. For many, personal difficulty's often what moves us to pray: no one's an atheist when their car's hurtling at 60 miles an hour towards a lamp-post. Others want to thank God for the good things he's given us. Every one has their own way of praying; there's no wrong way to pray – whichever way's helpful to you is pleasing to God. Jesus taught that prayer should be as natural as a child chatting with their parent. Even though we can't hear God speaking, we know what he's saying to us. For the Bible tells us that God is love: he expects those who love him to treat others with the same love and consideration as he shows us, and his nature is to forgive. To pray to a God like that's a lifelong delight. Yet just as a child needs time to learn how to talk, so the art of prayer's something which takes years of practice before you're good at it. You're never too old to learn more.

## Chatting and learning

Only after you've mastered the habit of praying in a structured way can you move on to a more informal approach to prayer. This begins with thoughtful reading of the Bible. Then you meditate on what you've read, using your imagination to put yourself into the middle of the scene described. We can easily imagine the sights, sounds, smells, tastes and feelings that we'd have if we were there. Then you can ask yourself what this Bible passage teaches you to pray about.

## ACTS

Try thinking of the word Acts, ACTS; the letters stand for Adoration, telling God how much you love him; Confession, telling him you're sorry; Thanksgiving for the good things that have happened to you; and Supplication, asking God for the supplies you need, of physical necessities and spiritual grace, to cope with the day to come. What do the verses you've just read tell you to praise God for? To say sorry for? To thank God for? And to ask of him? Then make a list of other people to pray for, asking God to supply their needs too. Growing in prayer is a great adventure, which doesn't finish till we meet God face to face in heaven. Ask, and you *will* receive.

### All-age worship

*Learn by heart, 'Ask and you'll receive' (above).*

### Suggested hymns

*Come, my soul, thy suit prepare; Jesus, where'er thy people meet; Prayer is the soul's sincere desire; What a friend we have in Jesus.*

## St James the Apostle   25 July
### Compostella

Jer. 45:1–5 Seeking greatness; Ps. 126 Sow in tears, harvest in joy; Acts 11:27—12:2 Herod kills James (*if the Acts reading is used instead of the Old Testament reading, the New Testament reading is* 2 Cor. 4:7–15 Treasure in clay pots); Matt. 20:20–28 Seeking greatness

> *'About that time King Herod laid violent hands upon some who belonged to the church. He had James, the brother of John, killed with the sword.' Acts 12:1–2*

### Legend

According to the Gospels, the apostles were commissioned by Christ to take the good news into all the world. Undoubtedly some of them did travel outside Palestine, but where each one went to is dependent entirely on unreliable legends. In later centuries, different countries would promote the story that the church in their nation had been founded by one of the 12 apostles, so that they might hold their heads up proudly as being of equal importance with other nations which also claimed apostolic foundation. Spain claims St James the Great, whose day it is today. The legend there is that, soon after the crucifixion of Christ, St James came to bring the message of Jesus's death and resurrection to the Celts of the Iberian peninsula. He then returned to Jerusalem, where he was killed by King Herod Agrippa in AD 44. The Acts of the Apostles reads: 'About that time King Herod laid violent hands upon some who belonged to the church. He had James, the brother of John, killed with the sword.'

### Relics

Yet the Spanish legend doesn't end there. They claim that his remains were brought back to Spain and buried in Galicia, the north-west corner of the country. But the Roman emperors persecuted the Spanish Christians, and the tomb of St James was abandoned in the third century, and they even forgot where he was buried. In AD 814, a hermit called Pelayo saw a star hanging above a particular field, which he called the Field of the Star – in Latin, *campus stella*. He reported that this was where St James's body had been buried, and when digging began, what was claimed to be the tomb of the apostle was found, and a chapel was erected over it. Now the original Hebrew word for James was Jacob; it was translated into Greek as *iakobos*. Somehow the English language distorted this into James; the Spanish are nearer the mark when they call him 'Iago'. So in Spanish, the Field of the Star where St James's tomb was found becomes *Santiago de Compostela*. King Alfonso II of Asturias became the first pilgrim to the site, and built a church. As the number of pilgrims increased, larger churches were built, until the present building was begun in 1170. It's in granite, in the Romanesque style, known in England as Norman architecture, with round arches. The Cathedral of Santiago de Compostela is the largest Romanesque building in Spain, and one of the largest in Europe.

## Pilgrims

Pilgrimages were made in the Middle Ages, either to visit a place where prayers were answered, or as an act of penance showing true penitence for your sins. Well-marked pilgrim routes from all over Europe led to Santiago, and still thousands of pilgrims every year walk the Road to Compostela. One of the highlights of a visit to the cathedral is if you can see the huge incense burner, the Botafumeiro, weighing 80 kilogrammes, which on special occasions is swung by a special pulley mechanism from the roof of the nave, almost reaching the roof of the two transepts on either side, pouring out clouds of incense.

## The Moors

At one time there were many Moors in Spain, Muslims from North Africa. Once, Muslims, Jews and Christians lived together in peace and mutual respect, discussing science, religion and tolerance. Tragically, under King Philip II in the sixteenth century, the Spanish Inquisition killed or expelled the majority of the Muslims, together with the Jews and Protestants, making St James their patron and alleging that his spirit had returned to earth to fight and kill on their behalf.

## Praise and blame

St James the Apostle can't be blamed for this misuse of his name. But the medieval devotion to St James showed that prayers are answered, God can heal, and the effort of journeying to a place of historic holiness can produce lives of great sanctity. This is a jubilee year at Compostela, when St James's day falls on a Sunday. Maybe as we praise St James today, some of that medieval sanctity will rub off onto us, until we see all life as a pilgrimage, a journey along a road leading to our final destination in heaven with all the saints.

### Suggested hymns

*For all thy saints, O Lord; He who would valiant be/Who would true valour see; O for a closer walk with God; Who are these, like stars appearing?*

# Ninth Sunday after Trinity (Proper 13)   1 August
## *Principal Service*   **Generosity**
(*Continuous*): Hos. 11:1–11 Fatherhood of God; Ps. 107:1–9, 43 Guidance; *or* (*Related*): Eccles. 1:2, 12–14; 2:18–23 Vanity and wisdom; Ps. 49:1–12 Wisdom and death; Col. 3:1–11 Selfishness or unity; Luke 12:13–21 The rich fool

> *'God said to him, "You fool! This very night your life is being demanded of you. And the things you have prepared, whose will they be?"' Luke 12:20*

### A selfish man

A Latin proverb says that money's like sea water – the more you drink the thirstier you become! Jesus described a man like that. He'd already stored up more than enough to live on for the rest of his life, but he wasn't satisfied. His granary was full to bursting, so he knocked it down, intending to build bigger and better barns. But that night he had a dream: God said to him, 'You fool! This very night your life is being demanded of you. And the things you have prepared, whose will they be?' The rich fool lived within the tiny world of his own comfort and desires. He never saw the people outside, each with their own needs and wishes. All he could talk about was I, me, my and mine. He'd more wealth than he needed, yet he knew nothing of the richness of relationships, nor the pleasure of giving anything away to those who need it.

## Afterlife

The rich fool's horizons were also limited to the present time. What would happen when he died? His sons would inherit the heaps of grain, which had stood out in the weather while he built bigger barns. Yet all they'd wanted from him was a little affection, which he'd never given them. What, then, would he say when he met his Maker? He'd never been generous towards God; maybe he thought that nobody can prove that God exists. But if an atheist dies and finds there is a God after all, he'll be in for a nasty shock.

## Stewardship

Jesus told this story when asked to arbitrate in a dispute over a will. It gave him a chance to outline the Christian attitude to money. Money's for giving away, he said. When John Wesley was at Oxford he had an income of £30 a year; he lived on £28 and gave £2 away. When his income rose to £120, he still lived on £28 a year and gave the rest away. Jesus didn't demand such heroic self-denial as that, but he does expect us to be generous. In his day everyone was expected to give a tenth of their income to the Temple. Today every local church needs a lot of money to maintain the buildings, and pay and house the minister and other workers. Without generous giving by their members, many churches will have to close. Most churches only suggest giving a twentieth, or 5 per cent of your after-tax income to the church. You may not manage that at first, but it's a target to work towards, and it'll still leave you with some to give to other charities. Most churches find that those on low incomes are proportionately more generous than those who are rich.

## Time and talents

But Christian teaching about stewardship isn't only about money. We're also asked to think about time and talents. God's given us 16 waking hours a day, 365 days a year, all through our life. How much of that do we give back to God, to show our gratitude? An hour a week? That sounds rather mean. Of course, we all live busy lives, nobody ever has enough time. But churches and charities survive only because of the time gladly given by their members to keep the show on the road. Then, God's given each of us various skills; we're far too modest in assessing our own talents. God's given us those abilities so that we can enjoy them; but also to make ourselves useful to others. Have you done an audit of your own talents and how you use them? Could you manage a target of giving 5 per cent of your leisure time and talents to the church, the same as you're aiming towards with your money?

## Life audit

Nobody's giving you orders about how much you should give; that's between you and God. But when you look back over your life and assess what you've achieved, your generosity's what counts. God won't ask how much you own; if that's your yardstick of success, you're no better than the rich fool. But if you've given generously of your time, talents and money to the church and to people worse off than yourself, you need have no fears when you stand before your God.

### All-age worship

*Find out what each person is clever at. Could they give a short demonstration, to bring pleasure to others?*

### Suggested hymns

*Glorious things of thee are spoken; O Lord of heaven and earth and sea; O worship the Lord in the beauty of holiness; Take my life, and let it be.*

## Ninth Sunday after Trinity
### *Second Service*   A Splendid Funeral
Ps. 107:1–32 Thanksgiving for deliverance; Gen. 50:4–26 Deaths of Jacob and Joseph; 1 Cor. 14:1–19 Tongues and prophecy; *Gospel at Holy Communion*: Mark 6:45–52 Walking on water

> *'Both chariots and charioteers went up with him. It was a very great company . . . When the Canaanite inhabitants of the land saw the mourning . . . they said, "This is a grievous mourning."'* Genesis 50:9–11

203

## A splendid funeral

So Jacob died, having asked his children to bury him next to Abraham and Sarah in Canaan. His body was embalmed, and his children wept for him for 70 days. Then his 12 children, their entire households, together with many of the Egyptian leaders and of Pharaoh's servants, took his body to Hebron, accompanied by chariots and charioteers. There they buried Jacob, and you can imagine them congratulating each other. In modern slang, they'd have said something like, 'What a splendid funeral! We gave the old boy a good send-off, didn't we?'

## Modern funerals

Those phrases ring a bell, because we've heard them said after funerals today. Sometimes a great deal of the deceased's estate is spent on the funeral. Now, it's good to tell the world how much you love somebody. Yet the departed either knows nothing about it, or else is too preoccupied with the joys of the afterlife to care very much. Maybe there's an element of guilt, because the mourners never told the deceased they loved them while they were alive.

## After the funeral

Sometimes the family have been scattered, and haven't met for a while until after the funeral, when long-buried tensions may rise to the surface. In the case of Jacob's sons, they took care to deal with this. Joseph's 11 brothers apologized to him for the harm they'd done him when they sold him into slavery in Egypt. Joseph wept, and the brothers wept on his shoulders. Then Joseph forgave them and promised to look after them and their children. That's a much better way to cope with a difficult time than by squabbling over the will.

## Oral tradition

The story of Jacob's splendid funeral must have been passed on by word of mouth for several centuries; very few things like that were committed to writing in those days. We need to remember, too, that the 12 sons of Jacob were considered to be the ancestors of the 12 tribes of Israel. Just as tensions and misunderstandings can arise in a family, so there were divisions from time to time between the tribes. For a long time the Joseph tribes were a separate kingdom from those descended from the other brothers. So this story must have been passed on to teach the importance of honouring their common ancestry. It also emphasizes the importance of defusing tensions as soon as they arise, without being ashamed to apologize and forgive.

## Today

So this ancient story has an important message for us today. In great nations and in humble families, disagreements can fester if they aren't dealt with promptly. It's good to have splendid national occasions, and happy family festivities too. But what matters much more than how much money you spend, is how much effort is put into harmonizing any misunderstandings that may exist. It's much better to bring them out into the open; then probably both sides in the argument ought to apologize, if only for not understanding how much hurt they were causing by whatever caused the squabble in the first place. Then both sides will need to unconditionally forgive. This applies at family funerals and other times as well. It applies even more to the life of the nation. Tensions arise between political parties, classes and ethnic groups. It's a fallacy to suggest that anyone can apologize for what their ancestors did, but we can, and should, say sorry for the way we've allowed the resulting inequalities to persist. We have to be prepared to apologize publicly for our own prejudices, our words and actions, then forgive, and let bygones be bygones. Only so can brothers and sisters, and generations and nations, live together in harmony. Then, if everybody's willing to bury the past, there's every justification for holding a splendid funeral, to say goodbye to the departed, with love; and also to bury our misunderstandings – and good riddance to those.

## Suggested hymns

*Be still, my soul; Brother, sister, let me serve you; 'Forgive our sins as we forgive'; O God of earth and altar.*

## Tenth Sunday after Trinity (Proper 14)  8 August
*Principal Service*  **Faith is the Compass**

(*Continuous*): Isa. 1:1, 10–20 Justice is better than sacrifice; Ps. 50:1–8, 23–24 Covenant; *or* (*Related*): Gen. 15:1–6 Promise to Abram and his faith; Ps. 33:12–22 Faith; Heb. 11:1–3, 8–16 Abraham's faith; Luke 12:32–40 Treasure in heaven

> '*By faith Abraham obeyed when he was called to set out for a place that he was to receive as an inheritance; and he set out, not knowing where he was going.*' Hebrews 11:8

### Abraham's journey

If I was told to travel over a thousand miles across semi-desert countryside to a place I had never seen before, the first thing I would do would be to go out and buy a compass. But Abraham was 75 years old, and had never left home before, when he was told to travel, on foot though with a few donkeys, taking his family and dependants and their herds with him, from Ur on the Persian Gulf to find the Promised Land. This was about 1900 BC, and compasses weren't invented until AD 1117 in China! Until then, travellers had to rely on rough observations of the sun and the stars, and seldom travelled out of sight of human habitation.

### Faith is the compass

So what had Abraham got, to take the place of a compass in guiding him along his pilgrimage? The Letter to the Hebrews tells us it was his faith: 'By faith Abraham obeyed when he was called to set out for a place that he was to receive as an inheritance; and he set out, not knowing where he was going.' He trusted that God would show him the way to go, and each day, before he set out, instead of consulting a compass he consulted God. Sometimes God spoke to Abraham, which probably means in a vision or a dream. But the Bible nowhere says this happened every day. Mostly he had to rely on those little coincidences, and the inner conviction in his heart based on what God had said in the past, which is God's normal way of guiding us through life. If Abraham hadn't had faith for his compass, he'd probably have gone round in circles.

## What is faith?

The Letter to the Hebrews tells us that faith is the assurance that God will give us the things we hope for, and the certainty that the things we can't yet see really do exist. Sometimes faith means believing that certain forms of words are true. More often, faith means believing in a person – believing that God's trustworthy. There's nothing illogical or unreasonable in that. People sometimes attack religion as though it demands belief in things which are clean contrary to reason. But God is a logical God, and if logic tells us that something's untrue, then God doesn't expect us to believe it. There are limits to reason, however, and many things that you cannot prove to be true, and neither can you prove them to be untrue. So you have to trust God to tell you all you need to know. Faith goes beyond reason, but it doesn't contradict reason.

## A moral compass

Just like Abraham, we all need faith as a compass to guide us through life. Everybody has faith in something, even an atheist. Everyone consults something before they plan their day, or when they have a difficult decision to make. They may call it their conscience, or their sense of right and wrong, or the greatest good of the greatest number. The trouble with those compasses is that they're all internal. If you've no external authority to guide you, you can twist your conscience any way you choose. But if you have faith in a Supreme Being, you can trust him to reveal his guidance to those who believe in him down the centuries. God's guidance gives us a moral compass, which never changes.

## Morality

Yet, when we talk about morality, we never make ourselves popular. It's true that Christians have sometimes used what the Bible says about God's will as a means of condemning other people and giving themselves a pat on the back. But Jesus told us not to judge. The purpose of moral teaching is to guide us on how to treat other people lovingly. If that means being unselfish, we may fight against God's guidance because we don't like it. But we know deep down that following God's advice is the right way to live, because God's trustworthy. It would be as foolish to begin each day on life's pilgrimage without faith in God, as it would be to set off into the desert without a compass.

## All-age worship

*Practise map-reading your way around the building with the help of a compass.*

## Suggested hymns

*Lead us, heavenly Father, lead us; My soul, there is a country; One more step along the road I go; When we walk with the Lord.*

# Tenth Sunday after Trinity
## *Second Service*   An Ensign for the Nations

Ps. 108 Love as high as heaven [116 The cup of salvation]; Isa. 11:10—12:6 Return from exile; 2 Cor. 1:1–22 God's 'Yes'; *Gospel at Holy Communion*: Mark 7:24–30 The foreign mother

> 'On that day the root of Jesse shall stand as a signal to the peoples; the nations shall inquire of him, and his dwelling shall be glorious.' Isaiah 11:10

## Rally round the flag

An American patriotic song begins:

Oh, we'll rally round the flag, boys,
We'll rally once again,
Shouting the Battle Cry of Freedom.

In every nation, in the days before trench warfare and tanks, the national flag, or sometimes the regimental standard, was carried into battle at the centre of the troops. From the place where their banner was, they launched their attacks, and to it they withdrew. Brave men would give their lives to prevent their flag being captured. Sometimes the flag was called an ensign, because it was a sign or signal marking the focus of their loyalty; today we talk about the ensign as the national flag on a ship. The sight of their national ensign would give them fresh courage, such is the power of symbolism.

## Isaiah

The book of Isaiah refers to the Messiah as an ensign for the nations. Isaiah was a prophet in Judah in the eighth century BC. He rebuked God's Chosen People for their lack of loyalty to the Lord, yet promised them that God would forgive them if they repented. Though the kings descended from King David had been a grievous disappointment, Isaiah promised that one day there would be a better king, who would lead his people to victory. This king would be known as 'the Anointed One' – in Hebrew 'the Messiah', in Greek 'the Christ'. King David's father was called Jesse, so the royal family were the tree of Jesse. But the kings had been such a failure that all that was left of the tree was more like a tree stump. Don't despair, said Isaiah: like a fresh shoot growing out of an apparently dead tree stump, the Messiah will be a branch from the root of Jesse. Then comes that strange phrase, which in the King James or Authorized Version reads: 'And in that day there shall be a root of Jesse, which shall stand for an ensign of the people.' The NRSV translation calls the Messiah 'a signal to the nations'; the Good News Bible calls him 'a symbol to the nations'. However you translate it, the picture is of a flag round which people rally.

## Editing

As the centuries passed by, the book of Isaiah was reverently edited and expanded, to show that his message of justice and forgiveness still applied to later ages. Based on the suggestions of a Jewish scholar called Ibn Ezra, it's been widely recognized in Europe since the eighteenth century that chapters 40 onwards were added at the time when the Jews were exiles in Babylon, two hundred years after Isaiah died. The anonymous editor wanted to give the Jewish exiles fresh hope that God still had a purpose for his Chosen People: 'Comfort, comfort my people, says your God.' Not only this, but suitable changes were also made in the first 39 chapters: in chapter 11, the Lord promises to bring back the Jewish exiles from Mesopotamia and all the other places they had been taken to. The Messiah is to be the ensign or flag round which the returning exiles will rally.

## All nations

Another subtle change was also coming over Hebrew thinking at this time too. In Babylon they had come into contact with a culture older than their own, and learnt that God's power isn't restricted to the Holy Land; God's interested in the rest of the world too. Among those who edited the book of Isaiah were some who wondered whether, perhaps, the Chosen People had not been chosen just for their own sake. Maybe God had chosen them as a tool for bringing the Jewish knowledge of the just and forgiving God to the whole world. The Messiah is to be the rallying flag for *all nations*. That means the non-Jews, the Gentiles; their former enemies; you and me. The Jewish people, and their Messiah, were to be a 'Light to lighten the Gentiles'. Not all of the Jewish people accepted that this was their destiny; but the followers of Jesus saw that this was why the Christ had come. Jesus has chosen you and me too, not for privilege, but for service; to care for others, and share with each of them the message of a God who demands justice, but is willing to forgive.

### Suggested hymns

*Crown him with many crowns; Faithful vigil ended; God is working his purpose out; Lord, enthroned in heavenly splendour.*

## Eleventh Sunday after Trinity (Proper 15)
## (The Blessed Virgin Mary)   15 August
*Principal Service*   **Dividing Families**
(*Continuous*): Isa. 5:1–7 The song of the vineyard; Ps. 80:1–2, 9–20 The vine; or (*Related*): Jer. 23:23–29 The word of God; Ps. 82 Justice; Heb. 11:29—12:2 Faith and perseverance; Luke 12:49–56 Interpreting the time

> '[Jesus asked his disciples,] "Do you think that I have come to bring peace to the earth? No, I tell you, but rather division!"' Luke 12:51

### Mei and Lee

Mei was a young Chinese girl, who came to a priest in Singapore. She said, 'I want to marry a Christian boy called Lee. I'm a Buddhist, so I'd like you to baptize me.' 'I can't do that,' answered the priest, 'unless your parents give permission. Christians are commanded to honour their parents.' 'My parents will never give permission,' answered Mei. 'But all Buddhism can offer me is an endless cycle of reincarnation. I want to get off that wheel, and Lee tells me that Christians receive eternal life in heaven. What can I do?' All the priest could tell her was to wait till she was 21, then she'd no longer have to obey her parents in everything. Tragically, a few months later, Mei and Lee were in a car crash, and both were thrown out of the car. When Lee regained consciousness, he realized that Mei was dying, so he scooped up some water in his hand from the monsoon ditch where they lay, and poured it on her forehead, saying, 'Mei, I baptize you in the name of the Father, and the Son, and the Holy Spirit.' He knew that in an emergency, lay people are also allowed to baptize. Mei's parents accepted what had happened, and she was given Christian burial.

## Family unity

It's a true story, though the names have been changed. Christians accept the Bible's teaching about family unity, and that children should obey their parents, at least until they're of age to decide for themselves. United families give children support and nurture, with guidance and example on behaviour. Adults find in their family a secure emotional base from which to venture into a hostile world. But Jesus taught us that there are no hard-and-fast rules, except for the law of love, which overrides all other commandments. In some circumstances, every law needs to be broken, even the commandment to honour your parents. Jesus asked his disciples:

> Do you think that I have come to bring peace to the earth? No, I tell you, but rather division! From now on five in one household will be divided, three against two and two against three; they will be divided: father against son and son against father, mother against daughter and daughter against mother, mother-in-law against her daughter-in-law and daughter-in-law against mother-in-law.

It's a hard saying, and difficult to understand. But sometimes the family becomes a tyranny. Fathers dictate to their sons which jobs they shall do; mothers tell their daughters whom to marry; and daughters-in-law are told exactly how they're supposed to look after their mother-in-law's darling boy. So, while Christianity upholds the unity of the family, in some circumstances loyalty to God's more important.

## Bunyan and Lovelace

John Bunyan wrote *Pilgrim's Progress* when he was in prison, for refusing to obey what he considered an unjust law. But it was agony to him not to be able to care for his family – 'like tearing the flesh from my bones,' he wrote. '*And especially my poor blind child . . .* O the thought of the hardship . . . my blind one might go under, would break up my heart to pieces.' Yet he knew that God expects us to stand by our principles, whatever it costs. Richard Lovelace was a Cavalier soldier, who wrote to his beloved Lucasta, when he was ordered to go to war:

> I could not love thee (Dear) so much,
> loved I not honour more.

## Context

Jesus understood the pain he'd give to some, by bringing division into families. His own mother, whom he loved, tried to stop him going up to Jerusalem to die, and he had to be quite firm with her. Remember that on this day, when we honour the Virgin Mary. Circumstances change from day to day, and today's obedience may need to be put on hold tomorrow, if God requires it. Then understanding and tolerance must eventually bring about reconciliation. So it's impossible to say that Jesus was pro-family or anti-family. It all depends on the circumstances. What we need most is to support each other whenever a difficult decision has to be made, and try to understand the dilemmas which those we love may sometimes find themselves torn by. Then promise to go on loving them, whether we agree with their decisions or not.

### All-age worship

*Make a collage of pictures of families cut from a magazine. Older children can divide them into 'Happy Families' and 'Unhappy Families'.*

## Suggested hymns

*For the beauty of the earth; Forgive our sins as we forgive; Help us to help each other; O thou who camest from above.*


# The Blessed Virgin Mary   15 August
## Honouring Mothers

Isa. 61:10–11 As a bride; *or* Rev. 11:19—12:6, 10 A woman in heaven; Ps. 45:10–17 You shall have sons; Gal. 4:4–7 Born of a woman; Luke 1:46–55 Magnificat

> *'When the fullness of time had come, God sent his Son, born of a woman, born under the law, in order to redeem those who were under the law, so that we might receive adoption as children.'*
> *Galatians 4:4–5*


## Short story

In a short story by William Trevor, called *Death in Jerusalem*, a Roman Catholic priest takes his brother on a pilgrimage to the Holy Land. The brother, Francis, is middle aged but still tied to his mother's apron strings. A telegram arrives for the priest, to tell him their mother has died. Unwisely, he decides not to tell his brother until later, so as not to spoil his pilgrimage. When eventually he finds out, Francis is shattered. He feels as though his brother, a priest, by taking their mother's death so casually, represents a church which scorns his mother – although the same church honours so steadfastly the mother of its founder.


## Festivals of the Virgin

Francis is right in that, though he's wrong in almost everything else. The whole of Christianity, Protestant as well as Catholic, honours the Blessed Virgin Mary. Today's her festival. The Byzantine Church had a number of festivals dedicated to the memory of the Mother of God, of which today was one. In the Roman Church they were universally observed from about the eighth century, and today was kept as the Feast of the Assumption of the Virgin Mary into heaven, a doctrine which first appeared in the fourth century, but was not defined by the popes until 1950. Members of Protestant Churches are left to decide for themselves whether to accept this tradition, but in the Church of England, in 2000, today was chosen as the principal day for commemorating the Virgin Mary.

## Honouring mothers

So, as the man in the story said, a church which honours the Mother of our Lord ought equally to honour all mothers. A baby depends almost entirely on its mother to nurture it and care for it during its infancy; children who lose their mothers urgently need to find a substitute. From our mothers we learn how to feed ourselves and care for ourselves; they teach us to live in a way that won't offend our neighbours, and how to get on with our relations. It's from our mothers that we discover what love is, and we learn to love others in the same way as we have been loved. No matter how much we pick up later from our fathers, our schools and our friends, our basic training in living comes from our mothers. That's why Mother's Day or Mothering Sunday has become so popular around the world, as a day for saying thank you to our mothers for all they've done for us.

## Honouring Mary

Christians, above all, should honour motherhood because Jesus honoured his mother Mary. We read in the Bible that he was obedient to her throughout his childhood; and as he hung dying on the cross, he commended her to the care of his beloved disciple, saying, 'Son, behold your mother.' The Church has taken that as a command to all of us to honour Mary as though she were our own mother – which, because Jesus calls us brothers and sisters, in a sense she is. St Paul, wanting to emphasize that Jesus was fully human, like the rest of us, wrote that 'When the fullness of time had come, God sent his Son, born of a woman . . . so that we might receive adoption as children.' In other words, our status as children of God depends on the fact that Jesus was the child of Mary. It's sometimes pointed out that by choosing the words 'born of a woman', Paul implies that he knows that Jesus, being divine, had no earthly father, though he nowhere else refers to the Virgin Birth. But being human, and having put aside his divine omniscience, Jesus had to learn from Mary how to obey and how to love. Which emphasizes once again how much we owe to Mary, and how much we owe to our own mothers. Henry Baker wrote in 1868:

Shall we not love thee, Mother dear,
whom Jesus loves so well?
And to his glory year by year
thy joy and honour tell? . . .

Thy Babe he lay upon thy breast,
to thee he cried for food;
thy gentle nursing soothed to rest
the incarnate Son of God . . .

And as he loves thee, Mother dear,
we too will love thee well;
and to his glory year by year
thy joy and honour tell.

Amen to that, say I!


### Suggested hymns

*Her Virgin eyes saw God incarnate born; Lord of the home, your only Son; The angel Gabriel from heaven came; The God whom earth and sea and sky.*

For the full words of the hymn quoted, go to http://www.oremus.org/hymnal/s/s101.html


## Twelfth Sunday after Trinity (Proper 16)
### 22 August
*Principal Service* **The Mediator**
(*Continuous*): Jer. 1:4–10 Jeremiah's call; Ps. 71:1–6 Providence; *or* (*Related*): Isa. 58:9b–14 The needy; Ps. 103:1–8 Forgiveness and healing; Heb. 12:18–29 The mediator of a new covenant; Luke 13:10–17 Healing on the Sabbath

> *'You have come . . . to Jesus, the mediator of a new covenant, and to the sprinkled blood that speaks a better word than the blood of Abel.' Hebrews 12:22, 24*


### Matchmaker

An English bachelor working in the Far East employed a Chinese cook, an 'amah'. He had a six-month leave back home, and she asked him, 'You come back with wife, no?' 'No,' he replied; 'six months isn't long enough to find the right girl and persuade her to marry me.' 'Your Mummy arrange one for you,' laughed the amah. When he reached England his mother introduced him to some of the nice girls in the neighbourhood. Returning to the East, the newly married Englishman was teased by his amah, who was convinced she'd been right all along. Perhaps she was. Unlike other countries, Britain has no formal system of arranged marriages, but friends and relations still find ways to ensure that suitable couples meet. From Jane Austen's *Emma* onwards, many people have appointed themselves unofficial matchmakers to bring others together.

## The Mediator

The concept of the matchmaker, or go-between, shows us the meaning of the word 'mediator'. In the New Testament Letter to the Hebrews, Mount Sinai's contrasted with Mount Zion. Sinai represents our fear of God as a harsh judge, who'll destroy us if we break his commandments. Zion symbolizes the gospel promise of heaven, where we shall be forgiven, and washed clean by the sacrificial blood of Jesus, the Mediator bringing us and God together in love.

## Displeased

God's instructed us to love one another, and of course he's displeased when we break this commandment. Sin's what prevents harmony and love between human beings, and between us and God. Harmony and love are what God made us for, so anything that gets in the way has to be dealt with. But punishing us only drives us into a state of terror and resentment. God prefers us to understand the harm our sin's done, to others and to ourselves, and to repent. Then God can forgive us, as he wishes to. But many people are too frightened of God to come anywhere near him. So a mediator's needed to bring us together.

## Covenants

In the world of business, too, two powerful industrialists or corporations are sometimes both looking for a merger. But neither's willing to make the first move. Some consultant's called on to negotiate between them, and draw up a draft contract. If they agree, it's often the mediator who's to thank. The word the Bible uses for a contract is 'covenant'. Covenants were often drawn up in the ancient world between neighbouring nations, agreeing to co-operate for their mutual benefit. The Israelite rabble, who squabbled their way across the wilderness, were brought together by a covenant; but what was completely new about the covenant at Mount Sinai was that one of the signatories to the contract was the Lord God. The idea of an agreement binding human beings and the Almighty together in a commitment of mutual loyalty was breathtaking in its daring novelty, but that's what the Ten Commandments were. By the sacrificial blood poured over the altar and sprinkled on the Israelites, they signed up to a contract that they'd be his people and obey his commands, and he'd be their God and protect them on their journey.

## The new covenant

The next daring move was when Jesus at the Last Supper, some-where on Mount Zion, poured out the wine saying, 'This is my blood of the new covenant.' When you drink the wine at the Holy Communion, you're signing up to a contract with God. You prom-ise to obey God's command to love God and love your neighbour, and God promises to give you the grace making that possible. It's a bit like a marriage contract, with mutually binding commitments on both sides. Maybe you thought you could never be as close to the Creator as husband and wife. But with Jesus as the matchmaker and go-between, it can be brought about, though only at the cost of his own blood. He's the bridge between us and God. A bridge needs firm foundations on both sides of the chasm; so Jesus was com-pletely human and completely divine. Being human, he understands the temptations we live under. Being divine, he can hold our hands and introduce us to his Father. That sort of intimate relationship of mutual love with the Creator of the universe is only possible through Jesus, the mediator of the new covenant. When you receive the bread and wine, thank God for the heavenly matchmaker.

## *All-age worship*

*Write out ten commandments for parents, and ten commandments for children.*

**Suggested hymns**

*Bind us together, Lord; Glory be to Jesus; Peace, perfect peace, in this dark world of sin?; Rejoice! The Lord is King.*

# Twelfth Sunday after Trinity
## Second Service    The Sat-Nav

Ps. 119:49–72 I was humbled that I might learn; Isa. 30:8–21 This is the way; 2 Cor. 9 A collection; *Gospel at Holy Communion*: Matt. 21:28–32 The two sons

> *'When you turn to the right or when you turn to the left, your ears shall hear a word behind you, saying, "This is the way; walk in it."' Isaiah 30:21*

## The sat-nav

To people who are used to them, the satellite navigation system which you carry in your car and which tells you which road to follow is a most useful piece of technology. To those who are unfamiliar with them, they're absolutely terrifying. A passenger in a taxi late one night had his mouth open to tell the driver the way to his home, when this computerized female voice suddenly interrupted him, to advise the driver to follow a completely different route. 'Can I argue with her?' he asked the taxi-driver. 'No,' answered the driver, 'but at least she doesn't call me a bloomin' idiot if I disobey her instructions!'

## A tutor in hope

The Chief Rabbi, Sir Jonathan Sacks, in a newspaper article, described the sat-nav as a tutor in hope. He imagines a driver protesting that he knows more than the machine does. He's been driving for 20 years, and knows the area like he knows his own mother. Anyone knows that you turn left here. The computer's response if you disobey its instructions, wrote the Rabbi, is an education in politeness. It goes quiet for a moment, perhaps reflecting on the greatness of human foolishness, and then says 'Recalculating the route'. In a few seconds, it gives you a new route, based on how to get to where you wanted from where you are now, ignoring the fact that you got there by disregarding the wisdom it first gave you. This is one of life's great lessons, concludes Rabbi Sacks. If you know where you want to be, then no matter how many wrong turnings you've taken, there's always a route from here to there. This should always be a source of hope to us, no matter how lost we feel!

## Ants

The Chief Rabbi, in his newspaper column, contrasted this with the behaviour of certain species of army ants. They're genetically programmed, if a group of them gets separated from their colony, to follow the ant in front of them. But if that ant's lost too, the group sometimes forms a circle and they follow each other round and round for a couple of days until most of them are dead. Human beings also follow the crowd, through reluctance to think for themselves. We need dissenting voices to speak out against the received wisdom, and warn us that the majority isn't always right. Religious people are the prophets who dare to speak out and warn the crowd that they're going round in circles. Like the sat-nav, which bounces a signal off something outside the earth and listens carefully to how it returns, religious people bounce a prayer off God, asking how their situation now appears from his point of view. Rabbi Sacks points out that human societies have a poor record with regard to 'protecting the environment, preserving species, conserving resources, promoting justice, respecting strangers and pursuing peace'. Yet most of them were convinced at the time that what they were doing was right. That's why we need the satellite navigation system's message of hope: no matter how many wrong turns the human race has taken, 'if we know where we want to be, there *is* a route from here to there'.

## Isaiah

A newspaper's no place to quote verses from Scripture to support your thesis, as most of the readers will remain unconvinced by that sort of argument. But I'm sure that at the back of the Rabbi's mind was the verse from Isaiah we heard read in the Old Testament reading in this service: 'When you turn to the right or when you turn to the left, your ears shall hear a word behind you, saying, "This is the way; walk in it."' God, standing outside the muddled affairs of earth, does have a view on where we are at present, and how to get to our desired destination. If we'll only ask him, his answers come to us through Bible reading, an inner conviction of God's loving nature and his purposes for us, the advice of our friends and discussions with our family. If we listen carefully, we shall hear his voice within us, telling us which way to turn. We can ignore the advice of the satellite navigation system if we choose to, but we disregard the advice that God gives us at our peril.

## Suggested hymns

*Amazing grace; God moves in a mysterious way; O Jesus, I have promised; There's a quiet understanding.*

# Thirteenth Sunday after Trinity (Proper 17)
## 29 August
### Principal Service   Humble Goodness
(*Continuous*): Jer. 2:4–13 Living water; Ps. 81:1, 10–16 God's justice; *or* (*Related*): Ecclus. 10:12–18 Pride and judgement; *or* Prov. 25:6–7 Pride and humility; Ps. 112 Righteousness; Heb. 13:1–8, 15–16 Righteousness; Luke 14:1, 7–14 Pride and humility

> '[Jesus said,] "All who exalt themselves will be humbled, and those who humble themselves will be exalted."' Luke 14:11

## How to be humble

That verse was printed in a service sheet, but due to a printing error it appeared as: 'Whoever exalts himself shall be humbled, and whoever humbles himself shall be *exhausted*'! It's true, exhaustion follows any attempt to behave and speak in a humble way, if it doesn't arise naturally from an inner attitude. There's a much less exhausting way of becoming humble. It has three phases:

1 Face the facts.
2 Compare yourself with those who are better than you.
3 Compare yourself with Jesus.

First, look at yourself realistically. However much you know, it's tiny compared with what you still have to learn. However much you've achieved, it'll soon be forgotten. However important we consider ourselves, others will carry on with our work, and maybe do it better, when we retire or die.

Second, compare yourself with those who do the things you pride yourself in, but do it better. A schoolboy saw his teacher, who played the French horn, coming out of a concert given by the great Dennis Brain. 'Didn't he make it sound effortless?' exclaimed the boy. 'How did that make you feel?' 'I felt like throwing my horn on the ground, and trampling on it,' exclaimed the amateur horn-player. Fortunately, when he calmed down, he kept his horn and practised all the harder, now that he had the humility to compare himself with an expert.

Third, compare yourself with Jesus. He had all the virtues, yet he lived humbly among the poor. He never thrust himself forward, but let people draw their own conclusions about him, based on the evidence. Whenever you feel like boasting about your good deeds, remember that you're nothing like as loving as Jesus.

## Be good

When you've acquired humility, that'll motivate you to serve other people. A worshipper said to a preacher after the service, 'Thank you so much for giving us a teaching sermon. They're so much more effective than a "Be good" sermon!' Goodness which is an attempt to show off is false. But when you humbly consider yourself no greater than those around you, and serve them because you understand that they have the same needs as you, then you may earn genuine respect for your humility.

## Hebrews

It may seem surprising, therefore, that our reading today from the Epistle to the Hebrews looks at first sight like a 'Be good' sermon. We're exhorted to show hospitality; care for those in prison; avoid sexual sins and love of money; respect our leaders; be regular in worship; be good, give sacrificially, and share what we have. All good advice, but what chance is there that people will go away and put it into practice, just because they've heard it read from the Bible and preached from the pulpit? Not much, in many cases. But put it in context, as the conclusion of a long description of how humble Jesus was, and how much he sacrificed to show you how much he loves you – even sacrificing his own life for you – then temptation appears in a different light. We're all naturally greedy, but when we remember how generous Jesus has been to us, how could we refuse to give generously to others? How could we fail to go to church regularly, for the joy of thanking him? It's easy to love law-breakers, when we remember that, compared with the perfect love of Jesus, we're all of us sinners. When we see positions of authority as opportunities of service, we shan't be envious, but respect the sacrifices our leaders make in caring for those under them. There's nothing unusual in feelings of sexual desire. Sex as an expression of long-term commitment to mutual love is one of God's most beautiful gifts. But used casually for self-gratification, while riding rough-shod over the feelings of others, it shows an appalling lack of humility. Jesus had the same temptations as we have, but he overcame them, and Jesus 'is the same yesterday and today and for ever'. So if your goodness springs naturally out of your humility, and your humility comes from comparing yourself to Jesus, then being good will be the most delightful thing in the world, and not at all exhausting.

### All-age worship

*Learn the nursery rhyme about Jack Horner. Was he really a good boy?*

### Suggested hymns

*Jesus, humble was your birth; Meekness and majesty; My God, and is thy table spread?; Tell out, my soul, the greatness of the Lord.*

## Thirteenth Sunday after Trinity
*Second Service*   **The Best Man**
Ps. 119:81–96 Like a wineskin in the smoke; Isa. 33:13–22 To see the king in his beauty; John 3:22–36 I must decrease

'He who has the bride is the bridegroom.' John 3:29

### The best man

At Jewish weddings in the old time, I discover, the best man had a very important part to play. He was known as the friend of the Bridegroom. Once the betrothal was agreed by the two families, the best man acted as the liaison between the bride and the bridegroom. The best man arranged the wedding ceremony. He sent out the invitations; he presided at the wedding feast. When the ceremony was over, the best man had one last task: to guard the bridal chamber, the room where the bride awaited her new husband. In the darkness, the best man could only recognize that the man at the door was the correct bridegroom, and not some cheeky impostor, by the sound of his voice. When he heard the bridegroom's voice, he let him in, and went away happy – his job was completed, and the lovers were together. He didn't begrudge the bridegroom his wedding night. His only job had been to bring the two of them together, and now he was content to fade into the background.

## John the Baptist

Now that I've learnt all that, suddenly the words of John the Baptist come vividly alive:

> [His disciples] came to John and said to him, 'Rabbi, the one who was with you across the Jordan, to whom you testified, here he is baptizing, and all are going to him.' John answered, '. . . I am not the Messiah, but I have been sent ahead of him. He who has the bride is the bridegroom. The friend of the bridegroom, who stands and hears him, rejoices greatly at the bridegroom's voice. For this reason my joy has been fulfilled. He must increase, but I must decrease.'

So that's what he meant! John's taking the best man's role. The crowds who'd flocked to John, when he started baptizing, were now deserting him and going over to Jesus. But that's what was meant to happen. Jesus was cast as the bridegroom, and the people were the bride. John had introduced them to each other; Jesus loved the people and the crowds loved him. Now John's job was done, and he was content to leave centre-stage to Jesus. It's an astonishing display of humility, and an example to all of us when we long to be noticed. Our job's to introduce people to Jesus, and then give them time to get to know each other.

## Idolatry is adultery

That's not all we can learn from this metaphor, however. Several prophets describe Israel as the bride of God, and God as Israel's bridegroom. The relationship between God and his Chosen People was so close, it could only be described as a marriage. It was astonishing, in an age when most people were terrified of the gods, to talk of the God of Israel being in love with his people. Like the best of husbands, God wanted to make his people happy, and ensure they lacked nothing. What a contrast with the idols, who needed to be propitiated lest they destroy you! Such was God's love, however, that he wanted his beloved all for himself. If they started worshipping other gods as well, that was as shattering to their relationship with the one true God as if they'd committed adultery with someone who was not their husband.

## The Bride of Christ

John the Baptist took this picture over, and described the growing band of disciples as the Bride of Christ, the ones he loved, and the ones he had come to win. Only, the description of Israel as the Chosen People had been a bit nationalistic and exclusive. The difference now was that other races started to become disciples, slowly at first, and then in a great wave, until the Gentile Christians began to outnumber the original Jewish disciples. St Paul's ministry was trying to teach these two groups to live together as one Church, and he spoke more than once of the Church as the Bride of Christ. There's no way of putting that picture that's non-gender-specific, so I'm afraid the men here will have to think of themselves as brides for this purpose. But cheer up, it's the whole Christian community which is described in this way. The husbandly love of Jesus is for us all when we come together as his disciples, but also for each individual Christian. Every Christian must love Jesus as deeply as any love-sick bride adores her handsome husband. Like any metaphor, the image is not to be taken literally, but to set us thinking. John the Baptist's imagery about the best man, the Bride and the Bridegroom gives us plenty to think about on the subject of God, love, humility and faithfulness.

### Suggested hymns

*Deck thyself, my soul, with gladness; Now from the heavens descending; O Love divine, how sweet thou art; The Church's one foundation.*

# Fourteenth Sunday after Trinity (Proper 18)

## 5 September

*Principal Service*   **Slavery Today**

(*Continuous*): Jer. 18:1–11 The potter; Ps. 139:1–5, 12–18
God knows us; *or* (*Related*): Deut. 30:15–20 Choose life; Ps.
1 Righteousness; Philemon 1–21 The runaway slave; Luke
14:25–33 The call to take up the cross

> *'Perhaps this is the reason [your slave] was separated from you for
> a while, so that you might have him back forever, no longer as a
> slave but more than a slave, a beloved brother.'* Philemon 15–16

## Slavery

The Roman Empire was based on slavery. Like most ancient civilizations, from China to Egypt to South America, the prosperity of Rome depended on a regular supply of free labour, so prisoners of war were taken into slavery. Paupers were sold as slaves; so were penniless widows and divorcees. The children of slaves became slaves in their turn. Unless a generous slave-owner was willing to set you free, the only way out was to save up a great sum of money from your tips – slaves earned no wages – give it to a temple, and have the god buy you from your master and set you free. This was called redemption; Christians use this word to describe how our God redeems us from slavery to sin and death.

## The runaway slave

Once, a slave called 'Useful' escaped from his owner, somewhere near Ephesus, and ran all the way to Rome. There he met St Paul, who was in prison. 'Useful' heard about Jesus our Redeemer, was converted, and became a Christian. Then Paul wrote a letter to the slave-owner, called Philemon; Paul's Letter to Philemon is the shortest book in our New Testament. In his letter, Paul asks him to welcome back the runaway slave, yet not as a piece of property, but as a Christian brother. This was revolution! If people started treating their slaves as equals, that was the end of slavery. The mind-bending idea originated with St Paul; it took nineteen hundred years to take effect.

## From Paul to Wilberforce

For slavery continued in the Middle East and Africa, and even parts of Europe: St Patrick was an English boy captured and taken as a slave to Ireland. Serfs in feudal society had little more freedom than slaves had had. Few people questioned, when the European nations opened the labour-intensive sugar plantations of America and the Caribbean, that they'd need slaves to work them. They bought them from the Arabs, who bought them from slave-owning African chiefs and marched them to the slave ships. It was readers of St Paul's Letter to Philemon who first opposed slavery: American Quakers, English Evangelicals and a few freed slaves. William Wilberforce was a member of the 'Clapham Sect', a small Evangelical group who reacted against eighteenth-century immorality, and urged that Christian moral standards must be applied in every department of life, including social morality.

## Guilt and blame

So if citizens of any nation today want to be proud of the good things their ancestors did, we must also be ashamed of the harm they caused. British people can be proud of the legacy of the aboli-tionists, but ashamed of the deeds of the slave-traders. Every other nation and racial group has some things to boast of, and others to hang their heads over. But we mustn't condemn anybody for what their ancestors did – guilt and blame aren't inherited. We *can* be blamed, however, if we go on benefiting from what our ancestors did, without trying to help the descendants of those they harmed.

## Slavery today

For situations which are almost as bad as slavery continue today. Even where it's officially illegal, hidden slavery remains widespread. Most prostitutes are slaves. Many wealthy people around the world employ domestic servants for despicable wages with little chance of escaping, and so do some hotels. Many of the clothes we wear are made in sweatshops which pay pennies for hours of toil. The trag-edy of the cockle-pickers of Morecambe Bay uncovered an industry in immigrants, whose passports are taken away until they've paid the cost of their passage; much of the cheap fruit and vegetables we buy are gathered by immigrants under the same yoke. Anybody who buys cheap Third-World goods profits indirectly from modern slavery – the only way to avoid it is to buy fair-trade products whenever we can.

## Equality

For as St Paul recognized, when the Son of God came to live as an ordinary poor working man, he showed that all are equal in the eyes of God, rich and poor, captives and free. What that meant then, and means today, is that we must treat all the oppressed as our brothers and sisters. We can't call ourselves followers of the Suffering Servant, unless we do all in our power to set free the modern slaves whose hard work provides our prosperity.

### *All-age worship*

*Arrange a stall to sell fair-trade goods after the service, and find out about the people who produce them.*

### *Suggested hymns*

*Brother, sister, let me serve you; From heaven you came; God's Spirit is in my heart; When Israel lived in Egypt's land.*

## Fourteenth Sunday after Trinity
### *Second Service*   Search the Scriptures

Ps. [120 Deliver me] 121 I lift my eyes; Isa. 43:14—44:5 A new thing; John 5:30–47 Search the Scriptures

> *'You search the scriptures because you think that in them you have eternal life; and it is they that testify on my behalf. Yet you refuse to come to me to have life.' John 5:39–40*

### Sticking in a pin

A Christian promised to do exactly what the Bible told him. He opened the Scriptures at random, and stuck in a pin – the verse he found said, 'Judas went out and hanged himself.' Puzzled about how to apply this, he opened the Bible again and stuck his pin in at the good Samaritan, where he read, 'Go and do thou likewise'! He realized that a literal reading of the Bible's instructions isn't the best way to interpret it. From the earliest days, Christians saw that any verse in the Bible can be understood in four ways:

- You can look at the literal meaning of the words, to see what happened.
- You can look to see what the verse tells you to believe.
- You can learn from the words about how to behave.
- And you can ask what it tells you about our hopes for eternity.

If the literal sense of the words is illogical or offensive, God's telling you to look for a deeper level of meaning.

## Critics

Jesus respected the Hebrew Scriptures; but he always went deeper than the surface meaning of the words. He believed the law was given by God to show us how we should live. But the Ten Commandments aren't like the law of the state, which define what's legal and lay down punishments for what's not. No, they outline areas in which moral choices have to be made. Sometimes different laws point in different directions: if your parents are starving, one commandment says you mustn't steal; another tells you to keep them alive at all costs. Jesus taught that the law of love overrides all other laws. But he had his critics. He met a paralysed man on the Sabbath day, and healed him there and then. Those who took a literal interpretation of the Jewish law said he was working on the Sabbath. Jesus replied that healing a sick man is one way of showing God's universal love, which is far more important than observing the Sabbath.

## Search the Scriptures

So Jesus sent them back to the source of all guidance, the Holy Bible; but he warned them to be careful how they interpreted it. 'You search the scriptures', he said, 'because you think that in them you have eternal life; and it is they that testify on my behalf. Yet you refuse to come to me to have life.' Jesus was trying to drum into his critics that God gave us the Bible to teach us that he loves us, and to love him in return. Then God would be able to give us eternal life. That's what God made us for, so that we can live with him in mutual love in eternity. Petty rules and regulations about how we keep the Sabbath mustn't get in the way of that. This shocked his fellow Jews to the core: to them, preserving the traditional inter-pretation of the Scriptures was the heart of religion. They thought Jesus was destroying their faith, so they set out to destroy Jesus.

## Bible knowledge

The statement, 'You search the Scriptures', could equally as well be translated as a command: 'Search the Scriptures – go on, do it.' It's a command to you and to me too. We don't understand the Bible, because we don't spend enough time reading it. No Christian should let a day pass without reading at least a couple of verses from the Bible. That can be when you wake up, or before you go to sleep, or when you're among your books. You can follow a reading scheme, so that over time you've read the whole Bible; or you can follow a simple set of Bible reading notes, or a commentary on the text, to make sure you understand what you've read. After a year or more of regular Bible reading, you'll understand a lot about how to interpret what you read.

## Knowing Jesus

But knowing about the Bible is only a means to an end; what matters is to know Jesus. If we come to him, we can have eternal life. The Scriptures are a springboard to prayer. Allow the words of God on the page to lead you to know Jesus, the Word of God, who became like us so that we might become like him. Becoming familiar with the Bible is to know Jesus; to talk to Jesus is to talk to God. Read the Bible regularly, then pray for the right way to understand it, so that it may lead you to eternal life.

## *Suggested hymns*

*Break thou the bread of life; God has spoken to his people, alleluia; Lord, thy word abideth; Tell me the old, old story.*

# Fifteenth Sunday after Trinity (Proper 19)

## 12 September

*Principal Service*    **God the Storyteller**

(*Continuous*): Jer. 4:11–12, 22–28 Judgement; Ps. 14 The fool
has said; *or* (*Related*): Ex. 32:7–14 The golden calf and a prayer
for forgiveness; Ps. 51:1–11 Prayer for forgiveness; 1 Tim.
1:12–17 Christ brings salvation; Luke 15:1–10 A lost sheep, a
woman's lost coin

> *'[Jesus] told them this parable: "Which one of you, having a
> hundred sheep and losing one of them, does not leave the ninety-
> nine in the wilderness and go after the one that is lost until he
> finds it?"' Luke 15:3–4*

## Storytellers

Children love storytellers. They'll gather round the infant-school
teacher gladly when she begins to tell them a story. Preachers are
listened to when they tell a story, more willingly than when they
spout theology. Some television programmes deal in ideas, but most
people prefer to watch a good drama. It was the same with Jesus:
he told his disciples many things about God, but what they remembered best were the parables. Stories of sowers and shepherds; of
fig trees and fishing; of wine and of wedding feasts; and 'the people
heard him gladly'.

## God the storyteller

The Bible's full of stories. Sometimes in the Old Testament it's not
easy to tell where the history ends and the fiction begins. And really
it doesn't matter. Deciding whether or not Jonah was swallowed
by a fish doesn't make a great deal of difference to how we live our
lives today. But the *message* of the book of Jonah does. Jonah was
told to proclaim God's love even for the sinners of Nineveh, but he
didn't want to, so he ran away. But God put an end to that when
Jonah was swallowed by a fish, and was then spewed out on the
shore he'd just left. So the message for us is that you can't refuse
when God calls you to do something, and nobody's beyond the
pale to the God of love. Exactly the same message as the parable of
the lost sheep. The heavenly Father's like Jesus. So perhaps God's
a storyteller too.

## Romantic fiction

If so, God told some rattling good yarns. Perhaps we should regard the whole Bible as a tremendous work of romantic fiction. That's not to denigrate the Bible; it's a comfort to know that many parts of it are historically very accurate. But recounting history's not the point of the Bible. The Bible's there to tell us that God loves us – all of us, even the most disreputable. Worrying about historical accuracy's just a distraction which stops us looking at the real message.

## Lovers

When two people are in love, they tell each other stories. Not lies, but stories about what happened to them in their childhood, what made them the people they are today, and what their hopes and dreams are for the future. If you want someone to fall in love with you on a date, don't go to a philosophy lecture; go instead to a slushy romantic movie, cry together over the misfortunes, and kiss each other when the happy ending comes! When you want to tell someone you love them, don't talk about your pulse rate and adrenalin flow: facts like that impress nobody. No, use poetic language about mountains you'd climb and rivers you'd swim to prove your love. It doesn't much matter whether it's true or not; it's a way of using fiction to say 'I love you'.

## A love-letter

So if you regard the whole Bible as a love-letter from God, that changes the way you read it. The parables of Jesus are fiction; perhaps fiction's the only way God's got to persuade us how much he loves us. If God wanted to tell us he made the world just so he could have people in it to woo, and who'd respond by loving God in return, how would he set about it? Would he describe the Big Bang with which the universe began? I very much doubt it. For a start, that wouldn't mean anything to people who lived before the twentieth century. The Big Bang theory's probably true, though future generations may regard it as hopelessly naive and simplistic. But it doesn't tell you *why* it happened, or where all that colossal outburst of energy came from. So the alternative story, which starts 'In the beginning God created . . .', is a better way of persuading you and me that God loves us. Worrying about the details is irrelevant

231

– what matters is that we should hear the call of God the master storyteller, who loves us however rotten we are, and respond by loving God and all the varied people that God loves. The message of the lost sheep goes all through the Bible from beginning to end.

### All-age worship

*Make a card for everyone in church, reading, 'Memo: God loves you.' Give it to each of them after the service.*

### Suggested hymns

*Amazing grace; Faithful Shepherd, feed me; O the deep, deep love of Jesus; The king of love my shepherd is.*

## Fifteenth Sunday after Trinity
*Second Service*   **You Can't Reason with Them**
Ps. 124 If the Lord were not on our side, 125 Those who trust in the Lord; Isa. 60 Arise, shine; John 6:51–69 I am the living bread

> *'[Jesus said,] "It is the spirit that gives life; the flesh is useless. The words that I have spoken to you are spirit and life."' John 6:63*

### Robbers and teenagers

If a robber demands your money, it's wiser just to hand over the money; you can't reason with robbers. Many parents of teenage youngsters feel the same about their offspring: you can't reason with them, much better to set them as good an example as you can of how a good and loving person should live, assure them of your love whatever they do, then just let them get on with their lives and learn by their mistakes. You can't argue addicts out of their addiction, or selfish people out of their selfishness. It's a fact of life: if someone's decided on a course of bad behaviour, rational argument's quite ineffective to divert them from their chosen path. If, on the other hand, someone really wants to be good, then a discussion about what constitutes good behaviour can help them to decide which actions are best. But when you've decided how you want to behave, it's not always easy to put your resolutions into practice. Most people would say with St Paul, 'I do not do what I want, but I do the very thing I hate.' So if reason doesn't change people, what's the answer? Is it religion?

## NewScientist

A few years ago the *NewScientist* magazine had an article headlined: 'If Morality is Hard-Wired in the Brain, What's the Point of Religion?' Evolutionists say that, in the genetic information passed from generation to generation, physical characteristics which enable humans to survive better, and have children of their own, always predominate. Does this apply to our behaviour also? Identical twins, even if brought up separately, show many similarities in the way they behave. So some aspects of our behaviour must be inherited from our parents, and their parents before them, but surely not all? Even animals *learn* behaviour by watching others; some even learn by trial and error. Each of us feels as though, when we have to make a decision, we're free to choose for ourselves which path to follow. Some, but not all, scientists believe that's a delusion – they think our behaviour's predetermined by our genes. But that's not how it feels. The Jewish humorist Isaac Bashevis Singer wittily observed, 'We *must* believe in free will. We have no choice!' Another thinker challenged the behaviourists by pointing out that if all our thinking's predetermined by our genes, and your genes make you an atheist and make me a Christian, we have no way of telling which is true. The scientific way of studying behaviour's to write a questionnaire and get thousands of people to answer it; but the answer you get depends very much on how you word the questions, and different sociologists come up with opposite answers. The article reported some who think that we're born with an innate sense of right and wrong. Then why do we so seldom follow it? One survey reported in *NewScientist* showed a difference between

- people who saw belief in God and attendance at church as an end in itself, whose religion made them more tolerant and compassionate;
- people who go to church for the social benefits it brings, whose religion makes them behave worse; and
- questioning people who search out a faith for themselves, who have high standards of personal behaviour, but are more tolerant of others than anybody.

## The Spirit

So some of what the atheists say about religion is true: it can be very dangerous if it's merely external, and doesn't result in a change of behaviour for the better. Jesus was saying the same, when he told those who criticized him, 'It is the spirit that gives life; the flesh is useless. The words that I have spoken to you are spirit and life.' The externals of religion do us no good; it's the Holy Spirit within that changes lives. Putting it another way, reasoning with someone who behaves badly won't change them – only love will do that. Jesus told us that God loves us, however much we reject him; Jesus died for saying that, and went on loving us as he hung on the cross. When you realize that's how much God loves you, your gratitude's a strong enough motive to change the way you live. God knew all along that you can't reason with a sinner; love's the only thing that'll change us.

### Suggested hymns

*I am the bread of life; Lord, I have made thy word my choice; Let me have my way among you; There's a quiet understanding.*

## Sixteenth Sunday after Trinity (Proper 20)
### 19 September
*Principal Service*   **Politics and Prayer**
(*Continuous*): Jer. 8:18—9:1 Balm in Gilead, healing the nation; Ps. 79:1–9 Suffering, prayer for forgiveness; *or* (*Related*): Amos 8:4–7 The needy; Ps. 113 The needy; 1 Tim. 2:1–7 Those in authority; Luke 16:1–13 The shrewd manager

> *'First of all, then, I urge that supplications, prayers, intercessions, and thanksgivings be made for everyone, for kings and all who are in high positions.'* 1 Timothy 2:1–2

### Politicians

Winston Churchill was asked what are the qualities needed to become a politician. He replied, 'It is the ability to foretell what is going to happen tomorrow, next week, next month, and next year. And to have the ability afterwards to explain why it *didn't* happen.'

We're very critical of our politicians. It's healthy that their policies, and the way they carry them out, should be under constant public scrutiny. Whether their private lives need to be commented on in the media is another matter altogether. In fact politicians are the object of such a constant barrage of criticism that it's a wonder why anyone should want the job in the first place. Perhaps they dream that it'll give them power. One well-known MP complained that, whereas when he was a local councillor he could point to this hospital or that school and say 'I got that built', now he was in Parliament there was nothing he could do except vote for his party. Even party politics has become a slanging match. Party leaders ask people to vote for them because they've rubbished their opponents; and many voters cast their ballot for the politician whose face looks best on television, ignoring the question of which party's policies will be best for the country – and the world – in the long run. Stanley Baldwin, who became Prime Minister in 1923, felt so criticized that he said, 'There are three classes which need sanctuary more than others – birds, wild flowers and Prime Ministers.'

## St Paul

So let's criticize policies, but not personalities. St Paul, writing to his friend Timothy, recommended a quite different way of treating people in positions of authority. 'First of all, then,' he wrote, 'I urge that supplications, prayers, intercessions, and thanksgivings be made for everyone, for kings and all who are in high positions.' Don't treat your politicians as punchbags, then, but as people to pray for. Pray that they may have wisdom to see which policies will be best for everyone. Then ask God to give them the courage to put these policies forward, and the skill to persuade the electorate that they're to their advantage. Ask God to make our politicians tolerant, so that they'll not bully their colleagues. Pray that they may not succumb to the temptations of wealth, or destroy their bodies by an unhealthy lifestyle. 'Power tends to corrupt', we know, so pray for strength for our leaders to resist opportunities for corruption.

## Tyrants

When St Paul wrote asking his friend to pray for 'kings and all who are in high positions', remember that the Roman emperor at the time was the notorious Emperor Nero, the one who 'fiddled while Rome burned', conveniently clearing a space where he wanted to build himself a new palace, and then transferred the blame onto the Christian minority, crucifying hundreds of them beside the highways, and setting fire to them to hasten their death. It was under Nero, in fact, that St Peter was later crucified, and St Paul, who couldn't be crucified because he was a Roman citizen, was beheaded with a sword. And yet it was for this monster that the apostle told his friend to pray. Nero must have already shown signs of incipient madness; and Paul had already experienced life under the Emperor Caligula, so he knew that Roman emperors weren't all nice people. But he told us to pray for them. There are still tyrants around the world today, and while we hate what they do, we shouldn't hate the perpetrators, but pray for them. Hitler, Stalin, Pol Pot, Idi Amin and others, have done terrible things. Yet, while we may pray earnestly for them to be removed from power, Jesus told us to love our enemies, so we should also pray for them personally. Pray that the tyrant may see the harm he's causing to others, repent and seek God's forgiveness.

## Thick skins

After that, it'll seem quite easy to pray for the ordinary people who represent us on the local council, in Parliament, and internationally. God, give them wisdom to discern your will and follow it, and a thick skin to withstand all the criticism which is piled on them. Amen.

### All-age worship

*Cut out of the newspaper pictures of the government ministers, and your local parliamentary and council representatives. Make a collage, and write on it, 'God bless our leaders'.*

### Suggested hymns

*For the healing of the nations; Judge eternal, throned in splendour; Mine eyes have seen the glory; O God of earth and altar.*

# Sixteenth Sunday after Trinity
*Second Service*  **Ezra**

Ps. [128 Domestic Bliss] 129 Cursing the persecutors; Ezra 1
Permission to rebuild; John 7:14–36 The one who sent me

> *'Thus says King Cyrus of Persia: The L*ORD*, the God of heaven, has given me all the kingdoms of the earth, and he has charged me to build him a house at Jerusalem in Judah.'* Ezra 1:2

## Two Testaments

While rehearsing a choral work with words from the New Testament, a Jewish singer turned to her Christian neighbour saying, 'This sounds more Jewish than Christian to me.' Obviously she had always been told that the two religions were in stark opposition. The Christian tried to explain that everything in Christianity has its roots in Judaism. 'Imagine a Bible laid on a table face downwards,' he said. 'The New Testament's resting on the Hebrew Scriptures. We Christians owe everything to you Jews.' The Jewish woman was astonished at this unexpected affirmation of the importance of Judaism.

## Jewishness

But Jewishness itself evolved slowly. Abraham and the other patriarchs learnt loyalty to one God; Moses taught of a God who saves his people, and makes a covenant with them. King David and King Solomon united the worship of the twelve tribes at the Temple in Jerusalem, and the prophets protested against those who compromised with foreign religions, or who oppressed the poor. Then most of the Jews were exiled to Babylon, so they assumed their God had forgotten about them. The book of Isaiah contains comforting words, promising them a return to Jerusalem. This happened, beginning around 538 BC, thanks to a change in the politics of the super-powers of the day. The Persians, under King Cyrus, took control of Assyria and its capital city of Babylon. Cyrus allowed the exiled Jews to return home. The Jews said that Cyrus had been anointed by their God to do this for him.

## Ezra-Nehemiah

The story of the return from exile is told in the two books called Ezra and Nehemiah in our Bible, though in the Hebrew Bible they're only one book. The chapters may have got out of order, so it's not easy to sort out the exact sequence of events, but Nehemiah was the Governor, who organized the rebuilding of Jerusalem and its walls, and Ezra was the priest. The rebuilding of the Temple took place in two phases, and when it was completed, Ezra organized the worship in the Temple, and the laws. In this way, he defined for all time what it means to be Jewish, and so he was also an important influence, both positive and negative, on the development of Christianity.

## Worship

The first thing that Ezra emphasized was that the life of God's people must be focused on worship. Although the Second Temple, as the Jews called it, was destroyed by the Romans, elements of its ritual survive in the description of heavenly worship in the book of the Revelation, in the synagogue services, and in the Christian liturgy. Ezra and his colleagues taught that the people of God were not to be seen as different tribes, each with its own place of worship; there was to be only one sanctuary in Jerusalem, with local synagogues. Our life depends on regular worship in our local church. Yet however varied and indigenous our local churches may be, the Christian Church is one family under one Lord.

## Law

Ezra's other contribution was to develop Jewish observance of the law, the sacred Torah. Standing on a platform – the King James Version calls it a pulpit – he read the law of Moses to the whole people; they confessed their sins, and entered into a covenant to keep it strictly. This was essential so that the Jews should survive as a distinct people through periods of persecution – the law's been called the hard shell of the nut, to protect the living kernel of faith in God. But Jesus opposed the legalism of the Pharisees, which had become a substitute for love. Worse still, Ezra tried to preserve the racial purity of his nation by compelling men who'd married foreign wives to divorce them. The book of Ruth is thought to have been written in protest against this kind of racism, for she was a foreign wife who became the great-grandmother of King David. The book of Jonah, too, denounced nationalistic Jews who rejected God's call to share their knowledge of God with other nations.

## Legacy

The Christian faith draws nourishment from its Jewish roots. The legacy of Ezra the priest, then, still teaches the importance of devout worship and total obedience. His narrow rigidity, however, warns us not to let the outward show of religion become a substitute for loving service to God and our neighbours.

### Suggested hymns

*Angel voices ever singing; Christ is made the sure foundation; They shall come from the east; We love the place, O God.*

# Seventeenth Sunday after Trinity (Proper 21)
## 26 September
*Principal Service* **Afterlife**

(*Continuous*): Jer. 32:1–3a, 6–15 Buying a field; Ps. 91:1–6, 14–16 Providence; *or* (*Related*): Amos 6:1a, 4–7 Possessions; Ps. 146 The needy; 1 Tim. 6:6–19 Possessions; Luke 16:19–31 A rich man and Lazarus

> 'If they do not listen to Moses and the prophets, neither will they be convinced even if someone rises from the dead.' Luke 16:31

## Not just now

A bride had just put on her wedding dress, and was ready to leave her father's house for the church. Her father, who was 'giving her away', had just struggled into his smartest clothes, when the door-bell rang. Outside the door they found an evangelist from one of the sects, who asked, 'Would you like me to save you from the fires of hell?' 'Well, that's very kind,' stammered the bride's father, 'but could you please save us some other time? It's not very convenient just now.' They had just got rid of the evangelist, when the doorbell rang again. The furious father flung open the door, to be met by a salesman, who asked, 'Can I sell you a fire extinguisher?' 'Not just now,' snapped the father. 'But a fire extinguisher might be just what that man ringing the doorbell of the house across the road needs!'

## Hellfire

Some Christians talk a lot about hellfire – indeed in the Middle Ages most Christians thought that the description of hell that Jesus gave, in the parable of the rich man and Lazarus, was literally true. Did Jesus expect us to make a literal interpretation? After all, it was a parable, and parables are stories. All the others are clearly fiction; there's nothing to suggest that this one alone was a literal description of the afterlife. In fact it may have been an old folk tale, which Jesus adapted to give a single clear message: you can't evade your responsibility of compassion towards the needy by claiming that tomorrow we die, and that's final. Abraham in the story predicted that people won't be convinced even if someone rises from the dead. When Jesus himself returned from the dead, many people still refused to believe in life after death.

## Hades

In the parable, the rich man, Lazarus and Abraham are all in a place called Hades, though on either side of a deep chasm. Hades is a Greek word for where people go when they die; neither Greeks not Jews regarded it as a place of punishment. There's another word, *Gehenna*, which was the name of the municipal rubbish incinerator just outside Jerusalem. Prophets would tell their hearers that they were a load of rubbish, fit only to be thrown onto the rubbish tip. Both these words are sometimes translated as hell, but it's misleading. When Jesus showed himself alive after his resurrection, it wasn't 'life as we know it'; he could pass through closed doors, and appear or disappear at will. It was better than earthly life, and Jesus said that at the resurrection we're not worried about material things like marrying and giving brides away in marriage, but 'like the angels in heaven'. It's beginning to sound as though Jesus didn't mean us to take any of this literally, neither the flames nor Abraham's bosom. Probably he used picture language and stories to attract the attention of the doubters, because it was the best way of describing the indescribable.

## Charitable interpretation

From the earliest times, Christian writers insisted that texts from the Scriptures must always be interpreted in the most charitable way possible. Bible verses aren't meant to be sticks to hit other people over the head with – as Jesus said, the whole Bible can be summed up in the commands to love God and love our neighbours. So would a loving God condemn some of his children to being burnt alive for ever? Some Christians say yes, because it's there in the Bible. But others reject any literal description of eternal life, which is in another dimension altogether. The Bible tells us that God made us so that we could live with him in another life, outside space and time. Jesus said we judge ourselves, if we refuse to accept God's love. Some believe that in that case, those who reject God are snuffed out like a candle when they die. Others say God's love is irresistible, and he'll find a way to make everyone love him in the long run. I don't think the parables help us to decide which view's nearest to the truth; I don't think they're meant to. Literal interpretation just distracts us from the real point of the story, which is that God's made us to enjoy a non-material, non-temporal life with him after we die; but that's no excuse for ignoring the needy.

### All-age worship

*Draw Lazarus outside the rich man's gate. Find out what happens to homeless people near you. Could you do anything to help?*

### Suggested hymns

*All my hope on God is founded; Blest are the pure in heart; God is our strength and refuge; When I needed a neighbour.*

## Seventeenth Sunday after Trinity
### *Second Service*   The Truth Will Make You Free
Ps. 134 Night-time in the Temple, 135 The acts of God; Neh. 2 Surveying the walls; John 8:31–38, 48–59 Jesus and Abraham

> '[Jesus said,] "You will know the truth, and the truth will make you free."' John 8:32

## Freedom

In recent years many groups have fought for and gained their freedom: black people, women, the subjects of dictators and tyrants, and many other oppressed people. If they weren't able to fight for themselves, others have fought for them. The results have been mixed, to say the least. The violence has sometimes been terrible, and some people found themselves worse off with their freedom than they were before. During the French Revolution, the battle cry was 'Liberty, Fraternity and Equality'; and Lamartine commented, 'O Liberty! What crimes are committed in your name!' The end doesn't justify the means, and though the struggle for liberty may turn violent, the violence must be proportionate. When you demand liberty, you should always ask first, 'Liberty *from* what? And liberty *for* what?'

## The truth will make you free

Jesus said to some Jews who believed in him, but weren't fully committed, 'You will know the truth, and the truth will set you free.' He was offering them liberty, but it wasn't necessarily the type of liberty they were looking for. Jesus offers to all of us who trust him freedom from fear, freedom from self, freedom from other people, and freedom from sin. We're often slaves to these things, without realizing it. Let's look at these offers one at a time:

- Jesus offers us freedom from *fear*. We live in fear of failure, of suffering, of death and of the unknown. It's true that any of these things could happen to us at any time, but terror freezes us so that we're unable to cope with them when they strike. If we believe in Jesus, however, we're never alone. He'll hold our hands, and share our burdens with us. With a friend like that, fear's something we can survive.
- Jesus offers us freedom from *self*. We look for a solution to our problems, when often we're ourselves part of the problem. We become trapped within our own image of ourselves. 'Oh, I'm not the sort of person who could deal with a situation like that,' we whine. 'I can't change. I've tried to be strong, but coming from my background, it's impossible.' But Jesus can change us, if we let him; he can re-create us, so that we discover inner strength that we never knew was there.
- Jesus offers us freedom from *other people*. Some people's lives are dominated by the fear of what other people will say or think

242

about them. So they do nothing, from fear of being misunderstood. If we know that God approves of us, it doesn't matter a jot what other people think.

- Jesus offers us freedom from *sin*. Sin's not a popular word these days. The siren voices tell us we're free to do what we like, without anyone else telling us we mustn't. And yet we know full well that many of the ways in which we misuse our freedom do great harm to ourselves and to other people. Often, we become slaves to our bad habits, crippled by guilt, and our attempts to free ourselves from them only dig us deeper into the hole we've made. Yet one word of forgiveness from Jesus can set us free. God still loves you, whatever you do, and he'll give you the strength to resist sin, if you ask him.

## Truth

So Jesus says that the truth will set you free. If you know the truth about the things you're afraid of, you'll fear them no longer. If you know the truth about yourself, and your worth in the eyes of God, you'll gain a new confidence. If you know the truth about the world around you, you won't care what other people think of you. If you face up to the truth that you're a sinner, you'll be ready to accept God's forgiveness. Freedom is God's gift to those who believe in the truth. That doesn't mean ticking a series of statements and saying, 'I agree that these are true.' People can be trapped in a straitjacket of rigid doctrines and dogmas, forgetting that truth is a person, not a theory. 'I am the way, the truth and the life', said Jesus. The way to freedom lies in immersing ourselves in the words of Jesus by reading them daily, until we realize that Jesus is Love incarnate, and nothing else matters. 'Jesus said to the Jews who had believed in him, "If you continue in my word, you are truly my disciples; and you will know the truth, and the truth will make you free."'

### Suggested hymns

*God forgave my sin in Jesus' name; I will sing, I will sing; Rise and hear, the Lord is speaking; Thou art the way.*

## Eighteenth Sunday after Trinity (Proper 22)
## 3 October
(Alternatively the Dedication Festival)

*Principal Service*   **Believe and You'll Achieve**

(*Continuous*): Lam. 1:1–6 The nation, suffering; *Canticle*: Lam. 3:19–26 New every morning; *or* Ps. 137 Suffering in Babylon; *or* (*Related*): Hab. 1:1–4; 2:1–4 A watchman; Ps. 37:1–9 Faith and justice; 2 Tim. 1:1–14 Faith and justice; Luke 17:5–10 Faith and obedience

> *'[Jesus said,] "If you had faith the size of a mustard seed, you could say to this mulberry tree, 'Be uprooted and planted in the sea' and it would obey you."' Luke 17:6*

### Space

After the Second World War, the Russians determined that they would put a man into space. It seemed impossible, they had little money or advanced technology at their disposal, but using the simplest materials, they launched Yuri Gagarin into earth-orbit in April 1961. A month and a half later, President Kennedy announced that the USA would send a man to the moon and also bring him back. The debate still rages over whether the space programme was an appalling waste of resources, or the boldest adventure in history and the key to the future of the human race. But the fact remains that the scientists of NASA believed they could achieve the seemingly impossible. A mere nine years after President Kennedy's speech, Neil Armstrong was walking on the surface of the moon.

### Believe and you'll achieve

In many other fields, human beings have achieved what previous generations would have dismissed as impossible, because they believed it could be done. Believe and you'll achieve. It's a recipe for success in every human endeavour. Undreamt of scientific discoveries have been made, incredible surgical procedures have been developed, long-standing records have been broken, and complex techniques have been mastered, just because some people believed that they could do it, and set out to prove they were right. Faith is the key to progress; without belief, nobody can succeed. At first sight, it doesn't appear to matter what you believe in, whether it's self-confidence, or trust in your colleagues, belief in a blind fate or faith in a loving God.

## Trust in God

But when you look deeper, it does matter. Self-confidence makes you insufferably proud, and can easily lead to self-delusion. Belief in other people's always liable to be let down. If you trust the fortune-tellers, you lay yourself open to abuse by the unscrupulous. But trust in a heavenly Father opens you up to all the resources of his power. God sometimes works unexpected miracles; much more often, though, his way of intervening in history is by using somebody who believes in him.

## A grain of mustard seed

According to St Luke, Jesus said, 'If you had faith the size of a mustard seed, you could say to this mulberry tree, "Be uprooted and planted in the sea" and it would obey you.' St Matthew has a similar saying: 'If you have faith and do not doubt . . . even if you say to this mountain, "Be lifted up and thrown into the sea," it will be done.' There's an echo of this in St Paul's First Letter to the Corinthians, where he talks about having 'all faith, so as to remove mountains'. The Bible teaches that to those who have faith, nothing's impossible. That's an extravagant promise, and undoubtedly it's spoken in exaggerated language to make an impression. Jesus told us that whatever we ask for in his name, he'll give it to us. Now it's perfectly obvious that if you asked him for something which would do you harm, or which you could use to harm others, the answer would be no. Similarly faith isn't a blind assumption that we can achieve anything we've set our heart on. We have to ask first whether it's something that God would approve of. If you think he would, and you're willing to work at it in God's way, then through your faith he'll give you the strength to achieve your heart's desire. But without your faith in God, there's precious little that he can do to help you.

## Moving mountains

A village in Korea was surrounded by productive fields. But a steep mountain stood between the village and the markets where they could sell their crops. At harvest time, they were exhausted by carrying the produce on their shoulders up one side of the mountain and down the other, and it was as much as they could do to get all the perishables to market before they were spoilt. The villagers explained their predicament to an American army chaplain whose unit was stationed nearby. Then the chaplain persuaded the engineers to use their bulldozers to drive a road, wide enough to take a heavy truck, right across the mountain. In that instance, faith moving mountains was more than just a metaphor. Believe and you'll achieve.

### All-age worship

*Find a toy bulldozer and make a model of the Korean village.*

### Suggested hymns

*Father, hear the prayer we offer; Give us the wings of faith to rise; Have faith in God, my heart; Strengthen for service, Lord, the hands.*

## Eighteenth Sunday after Trinity
*Second Service*   **The pool which means 'Sent'**
Ps. 142 My portion in the land of the living; Neh. 5:1–13 Social Justice; John 9 Spiritual blindness

> *'[Jesus said,] "Go, wash in the pool of Siloam" (which means Sent).' John 9:7*

### Waterworks

King David besieged the Jebusite city of Jerusalem, and captured it by sending his men 'up the water-shaft'. This was a way for the people inside the city to lower buckets into the only water supply, the Spring of Gihon, which was outside the walls. The spring was covered over during a siege and hidden from the attackers, but when David found it, his troops could enter the city. Three hundred years later, King Hezekiah decided to solve this weakness in the city's defences, and built a tunnel. Today you can walk by torchlight along Hezekiah's Tunnel, in the dry season, when the water comes up to about waist level. Hezekiah's builders started digging from both ends, and left an inscription at the point where the two groups met up in the middle. Hezekiah's Tunnel sent the water from the Gihon Spring, which was then permanently covered over, to a pool just inside the walls on the south of the city. Because the water's sent there through the tunnel, this pool was called by the Hebrew word for 'sent', which is Siloam.

## Siloam

The pool of Siloam's been a landmark from Hezekiah's day until now. Isaiah mentions the waters of Shiloah, which 'flow gently'; in other places in the Old Testament it's called the Lower Pool, the Upper Pool, the King's Pool and the Pool of Shelah; in Arab times it was called Birket Silwan. Jesus mentioned the 18 men 'who were killed when the tower of Siloam fell on them' – probably casualties of an accident during repair works to the pool. And in the ninth chapter of St John, Jesus healed a man who was born blind, saying to him, '"Go, wash in the pool of Siloam" (which means Sent).' Now St John could have been adding a curious topographical detail by naming the pool; but the fact that he translates the Hebrew name suggests that he saw something symbolic in it.

## Jesus is sent

A few verses previously, Jesus had replied to those who blindly attacked his teaching, 'We must work the works of him who sent me while it is day; night is coming when no one can work. As long as I am in the world, I am the light of the world.' Jesus was contrasting the man who was physically blind, but had spiritual insight, with the Pharisees, who had 20/20 physical vision, but were totally blind to what God was doing through Jesus. Jesus said he was doing the works of 'him who *sent* me'. Jesus had been *sent* on a mission into the world, just as the waters were *sent* down the tunnel into the pool of Siloam. And the one who *sent* him to heal the world's blindness was God his heavenly Father.

## We are sent

So the man who was born blind symbolized all the disciples, and you and me. We were blind to the light of God's love. But Jesus came and shone the light of his love on us; we 'saw the light', and discovered that God loves us. And then Jesus sends us to wash, to be baptized, in the pool whose name means 'Sent'. Jesus said, 'As the Father has sent me, so I send you.' Jesus was sent on a mission into the world, and as soon as Christians have been healed of their spiritual blindness, we too are sent on a mission to bring sight to the blind.

## Missionaries

Siloam, as I said, comes from the Hebrew word meaning 'sent'. The Greek word for somebody who's sent is 'apostle'; the Latin word's 'missionary'. Missionaries aren't only people who go to work overseas; every Christian's a missionary, because Jesus sends us to bring the light of God's love to other people. You don't have to go to a foreign land to be a missionary; your own household may well contain people who are blind to the fact that God loves them. You're sent by Jesus to enlighten your friends and family; you don't need clever words to do it; all you need to do is speak out of your own experience: 'One thing I do know, that though I was blind, now I see.' Your commissioning as a Christian missionary was when you were baptized – when Jesus said to you, '"Go, wash in the pool of Siloam" (which means Sent).' You were given the wisdom and the tact to choose the right words to say to each individual, when you were confirmed, when the Church's representative laid hands on your head, saying 'Receive the Holy Spirit.' Because we've seen the light of God's love, we *must* share it with others.

### Suggested hymns

*Amazing grace; God's Spirit is in my heart; Lord, the light of your love is shining; Thou whose almighty word.*

## Nineteenth Sunday after Trinity (Proper 23)
### 10 October
*Principal Service*   **Lepers**
(*Continuous*): Jer. 29:1, 4–7 Support the city; Ps. 66:1–12 What God has done; *or* (*Related*): 2 Kings 5:1–3, 7–15c Naaman healed from leprosy; Ps. 111 The works of the Lord; 2 Tim. 2:8–15 Suffering and perseverance; Luke 17:11–19 The healing of a leper and his thanks

*'[Jesus said to the lepers], "Go and show yourselves to the priests."*
*And as they went, they were made clean.' Luke 17:14*

## Leprosy today

Leprosy is a medical condition, known as Hansen's disease, which still affects millions of people. It's caused by a bacillus, spread by airborne droplet infection. The first sign that someone has leprosy is when an area of skin loses the sense of touch and feeling. If diagnosed early, it's completely curable with what's called 'Multidrug therapy'. If it's left untreated, Hansen's disease attacks the nerves under the skin. Then if the patient injures themselves, they may not feel it. This leads to infections, swellings and loss of circulation; then eventually deformity and paralysis. Leprosy, which used to be thought of as terrifyingly contagious, is actually quite difficult to catch. Over 95 per cent of people are naturally immune to it. If you do catch it, after a couple of days of treatment it's no longer infectious. Yet people who have the disease are scared to report it, so it often goes untreated. It principally survives in India, Brazil, Indonesia and Myanmar (Burma) – in these four countries there are over sixteen hundred new cases every day. Those who report for treatment are completely cured, but they still have difficulty in being readmitted to society, because their neighbours suspect they're still contagious. Their situation isn't helped by the Bible's use of the word 'leprosy' to apply to a whole range of quite unconnected conditions.

## Naaman

The story of Naaman the leper is told in the second book of Kings. Elisha told him to go and wash in the River Jordan; yet he was a Syrian, and far too patriotic to use one of these nasty foreign rivers. Then, when he did, and was cured, he decided to worship the God of Israel, who'd cured him – but secretly. So he asked for a sack of earth from Israel to take back with him, to kneel on, because a god could only be worshipped on his own soil!

## Jesus heals lepers

Jesus often healed lepers. Because leprosy was thought to make you ritually 'unclean' and disqualified sufferers from entering the towns, healing them was called 'cleansing'. Jesus cleansed the lepers by laying his hands on them. People thought that for Jesus to touch them and not catch it was a miracle.

## Social leprosy

Once, Jesus healed ten lepers, yet only one returned to say thank you, 'and he was a Samaritan'. Which takes us on to the other aspect of leprosy. 'Jews have no dealing with Samaritans', says St John's Gospel. They treated them as untouchable; as, so to speak, social lepers. For Jesus to make the good Samaritan a hero was a deliberate provocation to Jewish racists. But then Jesus was always dealing with social lepers; Jesus treated them all, quite unexpectedly, as human beings. He dined with 'publicans and sinners', people who worked for the enemy and those who couldn't be bothered to keep the law. So Jesus healed physical leprosy, but he also healed social leprosy. He favoured the outcasts of society, people whom nobody else would speak to. Jesus taught us that it's wrong to exclude people, because those we won't speak to often have a lot to teach us. In many ways the disreputable ones may be better people than us respectable folk – Jesus said they'd march into the kingdom of heaven ahead of us. If you love people and respect them, there's a chance that they may change; slowly at first, perhaps never completely, but nevertheless, the social leper's a person like you and me.

## Outcasts today

Who are the social lepers today? Whom wouldn't you like to be seen mixing with? Is Jesus calling you to do something about healing them? Do we ostracize whole races, like the Jews did the Samaritans? Or religious groups; have we turned Muslims into lepers? What about countries? When their leaders behave badly, is the best response to exclude them from the society of nations, impose sanctions and forbid anyone from having dealings with them? Or could we do as Jesus did with the lepers in his day, take them by the hand and try to help them? Could we treat the social lepers as though they were already cured, in the faith that with God's love and our help, they'll soon be fit again? I only raise the question. It's up to you to work out the answer. And may God have mercy on us all.

## All-age worship

Find out as much as you can about the work of the Leprosy Mission, <www.leprosymission.org.uk>.

## Suggested hymns

A man there lived in a Galilee; From thee all skill and science flow; Fight the good fight; Where cross the crowded ways of life.

# Nineteenth Sunday after Trinity
## Second Service    Aelred
Ps. 144 Prayer for peace; Neh. 6:1–16 Rebuilding the Temple; John 15:12–27 Friends of Jesus

> '[Jesus said to his disciples,] "You are my friends if you do what I command you."' John 15:14

## Rievaulx Abbey

Rievaulx is one of the beautiful ruined Cistercian abbeys for which Yorkshire's famous. The ruins are picturesquely set in a romantic wooded valley. It was founded by the Cistercian monks in the twelfth century. The Cistercian order was founded by St Bernard in Clairvaux, in France. When they first came to England, Rievaulx was one of the first monasteries they built, starting in about 1132. They chose a remote setting to help them to meditate. The land was fertile, and they introduced new agricultural methods, so that they soon became very wealthy. Thus they could afford to erect large buildings. The nave, from about 1135–40, still stands to a good height, and is of an austere, simple design. The presbytery, still standing three storeys high, is by contrast of an ornate Early English design. Enough survives of the domestic buildings, with kitchens, infirmary and warming-house, to give a good idea of how the monks lived their life. The first abbot was called William, and the remains of his shrine, which was visited by many pilgrims, is in the west wall of the chapter house. Later the tomb of one of Williams's successors, Abbot Aelred, was also honoured.

## Aelred of Rievaulx

Aelred was the son of a priest of Hexham – celibacy wasn't yet compulsory for secular priests – and educated at Durham. He was a high official at the court of King David of Scotland, and in 1134 he became a monk of the new abbey at Rievaulx. He was trusted as a delegate to Rome to settle the dispute over the election of the Archbishop of York, and in 1147 he was appointed Abbot of Rievaulx. Under his guidance it grew to 150 monks and 500 lay brothers, and five other Cistercian houses were founded in England and Scotland. He was an advisor to kings, but also a friend to the other monks in his community. His writings were always sensitive and charitable, softening the harshness of Cistercian discipline.

## Friendship with Jesus

Based on the Roman orator Cicero's book *On friendship*, Aelred wrote a book called *On Spiritual Friendship*, which is regarded as his greatest work. Jesus said to his disciples, 'I have called you friends', and friendship with Jesus was at the heart of Aelred's spiritual life. No friendship can ever be taken for granted; friendship needs working at. So it is with the friendship with Jesus. Aelred wrote:

> Dear Jesus, there are times when I wander away from you. I don't deliberately turn away from you. But my mind is so fickle. I really want to offer you my whole life, but then my determination to serve you goes all weak. I begin to think all over again that I'm in control of my own life. But whenever I wander away from you, life becomes burdensome. Inside me, it's all darkness and despair, fear and worry. So I'm coming back to you. I admit that I've sinned against you. But I'm sure that you'll forgive me.

## Friendship with others

Aelred's friendship with Jesus was the source of his friendships with other people. He believed that human friendships are one of the most precious gifts that God can give us – a cause of endless joy. It's friendship which makes us human. Yet friends can fall out with each other, and as the leader of a community, who spent many hours of each day in each other's company, he was constantly having to mediate in petty squabbles. Ruling over the community was often a pain and a worry to him, and he prayed:

O God, you know what a fool I am. I can't hide my stupidity from you. And so, dear Lord, I'm not asking you for gold, silver, or jewels – only, please give me wisdom, to make me a good leader for your people.

## Passionate friendships

A deep and abiding friendship is a wonderful thing. But the monks of Rievaulx were all men who had vowed to live a life of celibacy, so they could not form deep friendships with women, and sometimes their friendships with other men became passionate. Even when such love is given no sexual expression, it can become very disruptive in a close-knit community. Aelred handled the issue of deep friendship between people of the same sex within a celibate community with great sensitivity. Quite remarkable for the Middle Ages was his encouragement of the monks to find in their deepest friendships an impetus to deeper friendship with Jesus Christ.

### Suggested hymns

*He wants/lacks not friends that hath thy love; Jesu, lover of my soul; Jesu, the very thought of thee; O Jesus, I have promised.*

# Twentieth Sunday after Trinity (Proper 24)
## 17 October
(Eve of St Luke the Evangelist, see page 347.)
### Principal Service   The Word of God
(*Continuous*): Jer. 31:27–34 The new covenant; Ps. 119:97–104 Love for God's law; *or* (*Related*): Gen. 32:22–31 Wrestling Jacob; Ps. 121 Providence; 2 Tim. 3:14—4:5 The word of God; Luke 18:1–8 Perseverance in prayer

> 'From childhood you have known the sacred writings that are able to instruct you for salvation through faith in Christ Jesus. All scripture is inspired by God and is useful for teaching, for reproof, for correction, and for training in righteousness.' 2 Timothy 3:15–16

## Inspiration

St Paul writes to Timothy about the Scriptures, by which of course he means the Old Testament, as the New Testament wasn't written yet. Paul says they're 'inspired by God'. But what does 'inspired' mean? Does it mean, as some people believe, that God spoke from heaven and dictated the Hebrew words that he wanted his people to write down? Alternatively, does it mean what a poet or composer means when they say they were inspired as they wrote: that the words were their own, but the ideas came from somewhere beyond? Does it mean God caused certain events to happen to a group of tribes in the Middle East, and inspired them to understand what that revealed about God's character? St Paul doesn't say that the Old Testament's an infallible textbook of history or science, but that 'the sacred writings . . . are able to instruct you for salvation through faith in Christ Jesus.'

## What did happen?

So what did happen four thousand years ago? Frankly, I don't know; but by studying the words of the Bible alongside the archaeology and the writings of neighbouring nations, we can get a pretty good idea. It goes something like this.

Around 2000 BC some of the tribes in the area cultivated the fields, some were sheep-farming nomads. Most worshipped local gods whom they called the Elohim, the plural of El, their word for God. They each collected the history of their tribe as poetry and song. Two tribes, probably no more, became slaves in Egypt and were led out by a man called Moses. What was remarkable was the interpretation of these events. God inspired them to see that he could act anywhere, not only on his own turf; he didn't stop his followers being stupid, and getting into a fine mess as a result; but God saved them out of it. But in return, he expected them to obey him and treat each other kindly. So, out of these experiences, they got the idea that there's one God, who can save us, but expects us to treat each other lovingly. We call this 'ethical monotheism', and it's the main contribution of the Old Testament to world philosophy.

## Twelve tribes

These two tribes, under David, attacked and conquered Jerusalem, and they called their God 'Yah', or something like that. They gathered ten other tribes and made a covenant, with each other and with Yah. They promised to obey Yah, and he promised to protect them. But the twelve tribes were only briefly united: after the death of Solomon they split, ten tribes in the north and two in the south. Those in the north worshipped Elohim in temples at Samaria, Dan and Shiloh; they collected and edited the old songs of their ancestors. But they only lasted a couple of hundred years before the Assyrians destroyed them; we sometimes call them the Lost Tribes. The two in the south worshipped Yah in Jerusalem. They collected the same songs, which is why we often get two versions of the same story in the Old Testament; and both kingdoms had some remarkable poets and prophets. The southern tribes were exiled for some fifty years in Babylon. During that time, and just before and after, they edited the two collections into one library of holy writings. These tended to elaborate the law, claiming that it all went back to Moses; and to recount visions in which God still gives his judgement on how we treat each other, such as the book of Daniel.

## Jesus the Jew

Into this culture, Jesus was born. Without it, nobody would have understood what he meant, when Jesus talked about one God, who cares how we treat each other (ethical monotheism) and who intervenes in history (if only we'll recognize it), saving us out of the messes we get ourselves into. That's what Jesus was doing in his teaching, death and resurrection: saving us from the results of our sin and selfishness, and showing that God cares how we treat other people. The New Testament grows out of the Old, and both of them are inspired poetry. 'The sacred writings . . . are able to instruct you for salvation through faith in Christ Jesus.'

### All-age worship

*Make two imitation books. Write on one 'Story of the Jews, word of God'; on the other 'Story of Jesus, Word of God'. Show how the second book rests on the first.*

### Suggested hymns

*Lord, for the years; Lord, thy word abideth; Thou whose almighty Word; Thy hand, O God, has guided.*

# Twentieth Sunday after Trinity

*Second Service*　**Rejoicing in the Law**

Ps. [146 Freedom] 149 Justice; Neh. 8:9–18 Rejoice in the law;
John 16:1–11 The Spirit of truth

> *'Day by day, from the first day to the last day, he read from the book of the law of God . . . And there was very great rejoicing.'*
> *Nehemiah 8:18, 17*

## Growing up

When children are small, you give them warnings, for their own benefit, to save them from hurting themselves: 'Don't play with fire'; 'Don't cross the road without looking'; 'Wash your hands before you eat'. Later on, the reasons behind these warnings may be more subtle: 'Don't annoy your sister.' 'Why not?' protests the child. You really haven't got time to explain that life's much more fun when the siblings aren't squabbling with each other, so you make the lame response, 'Because I say so.' You know as you say the words that they're not actually an adequate reason, and you have a guilty feeling that you're really thinking of your own comfort. But children need boundaries. In the early years, you may reinforce the warnings by threatening to withdraw privileges: 'If you don't do your homework, I won't cook you your favourite meal.' When they're teenagers, you start on the battleground of 'Don't stay out late'; 'Don't have too much to drink'; 'Do you have to wear those appalling clothes?' And so on. Because bringing up children's like subduing wild tribesmen: you hope to instil some standards of civilized behaviour before they're beyond your influence. Growing up, on the other hand, is a process of becoming a new person, with your own standards and principles, and you discover those by rebelling against everything your parents have ever told you, and testing the boundaries. But if there are no boundaries to rebel against, youngsters won't know where to stop. Wise parents will warn them that the rules are for their own benefit, but that they'll still be loved, even if they transgress them. It's too late now to hold out any threats of punishment. With luck and patience, the parents may be surprised, when all the tussles are over, to discover what nice people their children have grown into.

an exaggeration of the trials of parenthood, in some
ent punishment only turns naughty children into vio-
en people become parents, they begin to understand
to call God 'Our Father'. Each one of us has tested
at some point in our lives. We've certainly deserved
ent, and the amazing thing is that he never does pun-
he often can't save us from the results of our folly
le's wickedness). So God treats the human race like
by setting firm boundaries in the early days, though
love us even when we transgress. The Jews discov-
of civilized behaviour, and rejoiced. Nehemiah and
rst reading, read God's law to the people, and then
dapted a festival to celebrate it. 'Day by day . . . he
book of the law of God . . . And there was very great
y should they rejoice? Children don't say 'thank you'
them what they mustn't do. But children have never
seen the results of lawlessness; the Jews had. When everyone does
'what is right in their own eyes', nobody's safe from the spiralling
revenge attacks of their neighbours. When rulers punish arbitrarily,
nobody knows where they stand. But where there's a developing
legal code, even if it's not perfect yet, they enjoy the benefits of clear
boundaries.

## Law or love

Yet the human race, too, has to grow up. St Paul described the law
as a schoolmaster, keeping an eye on us until we're ready to make
our own decisions. Jesus said that he'd fulfilled the law and the
prophets, not by obeying them slavishly, but by bringing them to
their logical conclusion in the law of love: 'Love God and love your
neighbour . . . there is no other commandment greater than these.'
In other words, the law of love overrides all the rules of the Old
Testament; you should always behave lovingly, even if it appears
to contradict one of the old regulations. Now we're adults, under
grace, not under law. We still need the laws to give us early warning when we're going off the road. But we're not slaves to the law;
we rejoice in the law as one of God's merciful gifts, useful when
we haven't the maturity or the time to work out the best way to
behave. We don't fear God's punishment, though we shall be wary
of displeasing him. We rejoice in the gift of the Holy Spirit, which
has replaced the law as our guide on how to be loving.

## Suggested hymns

*A new commandment I give unto you; God moves in a mysterious way; Gracious Spirit, Holy Ghost; When God of old came down from heaven.*


## Last Sunday after Trinity (Proper 25)   24 October
(Alternatively Bible Sunday or the Dedication Festival)
### Principal Service   I Finished the Race
(*Continuous*): Joel 2:23–32 Harvest; Ps. 65 Harvest; *or* (*Related*): Ecclus. 35:12–17 Justice for the needy *or* Jer. 14:7–10, 19–22 Repentance; Ps. 84:1–7 The Temple; 2 Tim. 4:6–8, 16–18 Fight the good fight; Luke 18:9–14 Pharisee's pride, taxman's humility

> *'I have fought the good fight, I have finished the race, I have kept the faith. From now on there is reserved for me the crown of righteousness, which the Lord, the righteous judge, will give me on that day, and not only to me but also to all who have longed for his appearing.' 2 Timothy 4:7–8*


### Imagine an athlete

Imagine you're an athlete at the end of an event. There'll be great weariness, even exhaustion. Yet there'll also be quite justified pride in your achievement, and the feeling that all those months of training and self-denial have been worth it. Now you can look forward to going up on the platform to receive the gold medal, cup or shield – the moment you've been working for.


### Ephesus

This is the image conjured up in the New Testament reading from the Second Letter to Timothy. Timothy's told to remain in Ephesus, which was a great city on the coast of what we now know as Turkey. You can visit the extensive and impressive remains there today. There's a fine theatre, where the people rioted against St Paul – the story's told in the Acts of the Apostles. The great Temple of Artemis was larger than St Paul's Cathedral in London – now only one pillar remains. And, like every ancient city, Ephesus had a stadium, built by the Emperor Nero between AD 54 and 68. The *stade* was a Greek measure of length, 202 yards or 184 metres, and a stadium gets its name because it was an arena holding a running track one *stade* long. So this letter was written to people who'd seen many athletic events in the stadium, and had cheered on the runners they supported.

## I finished

St Paul compares his life to that of sportswomen or sportsmen who sacrifice everything to concentrate on their training. Hours a day are spent practising; they eat and drink wisely, and there's little time for socializing if they want to win. Paul's life had been a long-distance race, with many obstacles in the way, and he had to make sacrifices. He'd undertaken long journeys so that he could preach the gospel in new places. He'd survived shipwrecks and riots, and opposition from fellow Jews and even fellow Christians. He could have had a comfortable life as the father of a family and a respected scholar and rabbi. Instead he sacrificed his comfort, his time, energy and money, and the respect of his contemporaries, all for the sake of the gospel. We too may have to make sacrifices. Yet, as we approach the end of our lives, most Christians feel the sacrifice was worth it. There are many joys in being a Christian, chiefly the pleasure of being able to help other people and influence them for good. It's said that being a Christian's a job where the pay's lousy, the hours are long, but the retirement benefits are 'out of this world'! So Paul compares the joys of heaven with the crown of laurel leaves which was placed round the brow of the successful athlete in the ancient games.

## Must we win?

Keen athletes focus on winning. But when it's all over, the real satisfaction comes from knowing you've done your best. The results may not be as good as you'd hoped, but to have got as far as you did was an achievement to be proud of. Some schools have races where points or prizes are given to encourage those who can never hope to come in first. The judges are just beginning to pack up after the cross-country run, or the two-mile walk, or the half-mile swim, when into sight comes some faithful plodder who decided to finish the course no matter how long it takes, and the spectators reward them with a cheer for their grit and determination. Perseverance in the Christian life is rewarded – perseverance in loving other people, saying your prayers, going to church and sharing the good news of God's love – though it may never bring you fame and fortune. An American sports writer, Grantland Rice, wrote a poem in 1941 using a metaphor from football. It's fashionable in some quarters to sneer at these lines. But there's truth in the poetry nonetheless. He wrote:

> For when the One Great Scorer comes to mark against your name,
> He writes not that you won or lost but how you played the Game.

### All-age worship

*Make a prize for perseverance and give one to each of the congregation.*

### Suggested hymns

*Be still my soul; Fight the good fight; Guide me, O thou great Redeemer; Who would true valour see.*

## Last Sunday after Trinity
### Second Service    David's Son

Ps. 119:1–16 How can young people be pure?; Eccles. 11, 12 Remember your Creator in your youth; 2 Tim. 2:1–7 Crowning an athlete; *Gospel at Holy Communion*: Matt. 22:34–46 Love God and love your neighbour

> 'Jesus asked [the Pharisees], "What do you think of the Messiah? Whose son is he?" They said to him, "The son of David."' Matthew 22:42

### King David

King David was remembered as the anointed king who united the country and drove out their enemies; the ideal king, and the founder of the royal dynasty. But his successors were a great disappointment. Eventually the Jews were defeated and exiled to Babylon. No descendant of King David sat on the throne in Jerusalem. But the dream lived on, that one day a descendant of King David would seize power and drive out their enemies. Jesus was just one of many descendants of the royal family living in Judaea; which would it be? They called the one they hoped for 'the anointed one', the Messiah, or 'the Son of David'. Some people called Jesus by that name, but he'd no wish to become a military leader and battle against the Romans. So the Pharisees rejected him. He might or might not be descended from the royal family, but as far as they were concerned he wasn't *the* Son of David.

## Dialogue

So the dialogue between Jesus and the Pharisees went something like this. Jesus asked, 'Whose son will the Messiah be?' The Pharisees answered, 'He'll be the Son of David.' 'Is a son greater or lesser than his father?' 'Nobody could be a greater general than King David.' 'So why did King David call the Messiah his lord? That implies that the Messiah's greater than David.' 'What? Impossible! When did David ever call the Messiah his lord?' 'In the book of Psalms,' replied Jesus; 'when he wrote, "The Lord God said to my lord, Sit at my right, in the place of honour".' 'Oh yes,' admitted the Pharisees, crestfallen; 'we'd forgotten that.' 'So if the Messiah's King David's Lord,' continued Jesus, 'he must be greater than David; not a greater general, but greater in some other way. Whom did David call 'Lord', and accept as his superior?' Eventually the Pharisees admitted, 'The Lord God was the only one whom King David called Lord.' 'So King David must have been talking about the Messiah,' said Jesus, 'who's vastly greater than King David. So I ask you again, whose son is the Messiah?' Deathly silence. The only possible answer to Jesus's question was, 'The Lord Messiah's the Son of the Lord God.' The Pharisees didn't want to admit that; they changed the subject and slunk away.

## God's Son

Game, set and match to Jesus! But he wasn't interested in winning obscure arguments. He wants us to change our idea of what 'Messiah' means. The Messiah's a king, as David was, and everyone must obey the Christ as their all-powerful king. He's going to defeat our enemies, and bring in a kingdom, as David did. But he's not going to war with the Romans, or any other human enemies. He's going to defeat our spiritual enemies of sin, hatred, jealousy and despair, and bring us to his eternal kingdom of heaven.

## Manipulating the Messiah

We all try it on, don't we, like the Pharisees did? I mean, trying to manipulate the Messiah for our own purposes. But our king isn't our slave, to do what we tell him to. They wanted him to drive out the Romans; we want him to solve all our personal, national and international problems. 'I can't accept that Jesus was the Son of God,' we say, 'because look at the world today. How could a loving God allow war, and terrorism, and hunger? Why would he allow the people I love to suffer and to die?' That's what all of us feel on our bad-hair days, but won't admit to. But who's boss, you or Jesus? You can't tell him how you'd like him to run the universe. He never promised you a rose garden; indeed he warned you you'd have to suffer as he did, when he called you to take up your cross and follow him. But he also told us where the way of the cross leads us to, and when we get to heaven, all the pain and grief will be forgotten.

## Thank God

So thank God Jesus is the Messiah, on his terms and not on ours. He's the Son of our Father God, and loves us as our Father does. So he serves us, comforts us and fills us with hope for eternity. He's our Saviour and our Friend. Isn't that the sort of Messiah you'd follow, rather than any miserable old general? Thank God for Jesus, as he really was, not in the mould that I or anyone else would have liked to manipulate him into.

## Suggested hymns

*Lord Jesus Christ; Make me a channel of your peace; O Jesus, I have promised; Take my life, and let it be.*

# All Saints' Sunday   31 October
## Whatever Next?

*(These readings are used on the Sunday, or if this is not kept as All Saints' Sunday, on 1 November itself; see page 352.)* Dan. 7:1–3, 15–18 The people of God will receive power; Ps. 149 The victory of God's people; Eph. 1:11–23 Christ rules with the saints; Luke 6:20–31 The sermon on the plain

> *'I pray that the God of our Lord Jesus Christ, the Father of glory, may give you a spirit of wisdom and revelation as you come to know him, so that, with the eyes of your heart enlightened, you may know what is the hope to which he has called you, what are the riches of his glorious inheritance among the saints.' Ephesians 1:17–18*

## Whatever next?

When something unexpected happens to someone, they often exclaim, 'Would you believe it? Whatever next?' Surprising things happen to us all the time, some bad, some good. Life's always unpredictable, and often quite different from what we'd expected. So if life's like that, what happens when it comes to an end? When we die, what happens next? You'd think we'd have learnt by now that whatever happens next is always quite outside our experience of life so far.

## A month about death

November seems to be a month for thinking about the afterlife. November 1st is All Saints' Day, though this is preceded by Halloween. The next day we have All Souls' Day. Some churches celebrate the saints of our own nation on November 8th, and then on the Sunday nearest November 11th comes Remembrance Sunday. Halloween means the evening before All Hallows, all holy ones or All Saints, but it's derived from a pre-Christian winter festival of the dead. Our ancestors feared that those who died might return to threaten us as ghosts, so witches were paid to appease the spirits. Irish immigrants took to America the 'trick or treat' custom, the trick often being a violent attack on those unwilling to pay. Fortunately, the festival was commercialized, making money out of people's love of dressing up. Most children love pretending to be scared, and handled carefully Halloween doesn't seem to harm them despite its pagan origins. All Saints and the other Christian festivals proclaim that some people, at least, go to a better world after death – that whatever is next is better than what's gone before.

## Afterlife

Where does this belief in a benign afterlife come from? Greeks, Romans and Jews believed that our souls sleep after death. Then Jewish prophets predicted the kingdom of God – at first they hoped for a period of earthly history when everyone would behave justly and obey God as their king. This was followed by a belief in resurrection, when those who'd died unjustly would return to earth to enjoy their deferred reward. The resurrection of Jesus convinced his followers that the kingdom of God is here and now, but when his long-awaited return to earth didn't happen, they turned their expectation to an afterlife in heaven.

## Eternity

'Everlasting life' sounds boring, but 'eternal life' reminds us of those timeless moments on earth when we're really enjoying ourselves, and time seems to stand still. Maybe it's only with Einstein's teaching about multiple dimensions that we've begun to conceive what a life unlimited by the constraints of space or time could be like. But of course we can't describe it; it'll surprise us so that we exclaim, 'Whatever next?'

## Justice

One of the attractive things about believing in an afterlife is that it means that injustices will be corrected. Life's full of undeserved suffering; it could hardly be otherwise when God's given us free will to disobey him. But that's bearable if we believe that in the hereafter all wrongs will be righted, and faithfulness rewarded. That doesn't mean we can evade our responsibility to treat others fairly in this life by escaping into a dream of 'pie in the sky when we die'. The thought that we shall have to answer to our Maker as to how we've used or abused his creation, and that we shall meet face to face with those whom we've harmed in this life, makes us more anxious to behave well here on earth.

## Relationships

Yet the only way to paint the indescribable bliss of heaven is in terms of relationships. The loves we've known here on earth continue when one of us dies, and come into full flower when we meet again in the world of eternal love. And since God can't have made us for any other reason than that he wants us to know his love and to love him in return, he's not going to allow the death of the body to interrupt our glorious relationship with him. Well, would you believe it? Whatever next?

### *All-age worship*

*Photocopy pictures of people you love and dress them up as saints or angels.*

### *Suggested hymns*

*Blest be the tie that binds; Give us the wings of faith to rise; Let saints on earth in concert sing; There's a quiet understanding.*

## Fourth Sunday before Advent   31 October

(*For use if the Feast of All Saints is celebrated on 1 November, see page 263.*)

### Sins as Scarlet

Isa. 1:10–18 Forgiveness; Ps. 32:1–8 Forgiveness; 2 Thess. 1:1–12 Justice; Luke 19:1–10 Salvation for Zacchaeus

> 'Come now, let us argue it out, says the Lord: though your sins are like scarlet, they shall be like snow; though they are red like crimson, they shall become like wool.' Isaiah 1:18

### Sins like scarlet

Red's the colour of sin, for red's the colour of blood. 'Caught Red Handed!' scream the newspaper headlines in condemnation. Lady Macbeth longs for a way of wiping the blood from her guilty hands. If there's political strife, we warn that there'll be 'blood on the carpet'. So God reasons with his people: our sins are like scarlet; they're red like crimson. We're all guilty as sin. We're as bad as the people of Sodom and Gomorrah, who'd committed every imaginable sin, and some that we'd rather not imagine. Our hands are dripping with blood. The actual sins Isaiah condemns are sins of omission – social sins and political iniquity. We haven't learnt to do good; to seek justice, rescue the oppressed, defend the orphan, or plead for the widow. It's our failure to care for the hungry in the developing nations, and the underprivileged in our own society, which God is laying to our charge. We can only hang down our heads and plead that the whole of our society is guilty; we haven't lived up to the example of care and compassion for others set us by Jesus. 'All have sinned and come short of the glory of God.'

## True remorse

Not that God wants us to flagellate ourselves with remorse. We can't be held guilty for the sins of our ancestors, or for oppression that we may benefit from without our knowing anything about it. All that can be said is that we ought to have found out sooner, and we ought to have done something about it. There's no such thing as corporate guilt. But there *is* corporate responsibility to put wrongs right when it lies within our power. In a democracy, that may consist simply of giving our vote to those who promise to help the needy, even though it may be to our personal disadvantage. Sin's not breaking the rules, but lack of love. Jesus told us to love one another as he loves us. By that standard all of us have failed; our love is faint and feeble compared with his. To love as Jesus loves is our target, and we've all missed.

## White as snow?

If only we could start all over again, and begin with a clean sheet! Many an Evangelical sermon has been preached on the text, 'though your sins are like scarlet, they shall be like snow; though they are red like crimson, they shall become like wool'. Indeed, this is the single greatest promise of the gospel: that total forgiveness by God is a real possibility for everyone. God's willing to forgive and forget. But there are two big 'IFs'.

## The big 'if'

Our scarlet sins, our blood-stained hands, can become like snow, *if* . . . If what? God says, '*If* you are willing and obedient, you shall eat the good of the land.' We must accept responsibility for our actions, and intend to do better in the future. In one way God's forgiveness is unconditional, because we don't have to earn it. But it does depend on our repentance. God can't forgive those who are always saying, 'It wasn't my fault.' Such people are unwilling to accept forgiveness when it's offered, because they don't know they need it.

## Washed in the blood of the Lamb

The other condition is that Jesus had to die on the cross before we could be forgiven. It's not until we see what human sin did to Jesus that we realize the awfulness of our own sin, as we crucify him again daily by our carelessness. When he offers his perfect life as a sacrifice to the Father, we can unite our feeble love and repentance with his, and he'll offer us to God. Red's the colour of sin, for red's the colour of blood. But red blood was what Jesus shed on the cross, and blood's become a shorthand symbol for his love, so that metaphorically, we are washed clean in the blood of the Lamb. Then our sins which were as scarlet can become white as snow.

### All-age worship

*Use an artist's brush and red wine to write the word 'Naughty' on a white cloth. Pour white wine on it. Wash it in cold water, until it is white again. Discuss.*

### Suggested hymns

*'Forgive our sins as we forgive'; Glory be to Jesus; Guide me, O thou great Redeemer; How shall I sing that majesty.*

## Third Sunday before Advent    7 November
*Principal Service*   **Contemporary Language**
Job 19:23–27a My redeemer lives; Ps. 17:1–9 Prayer for salvation; 2 Thess. 2:1–5, 13–17 Perseverance; Luke 20:27–38 The wife of seven brothers

> *'[Jesus said,] "Now he is God not of the dead, but of the living; for to him all of them are alive."' Luke 20:38*

## Sadducees

Jesus was in the middle of an argument. He often argued with the Pharisees; today it was the Sadducees' turn. The Pharisees were a religious movement, intent on imposing their interpretation of the Old Testament laws on everybody else. The Sadducees were more like a political party. The priests and the wealthy aristocrats were all Sadducees – they made sure to keep on good terms with the ruling Roman authorities, so they opposed revolutionary ideas which might offend them. They accepted the laws of Moses, but rejected the teachings of the prophets, who proclaimed that when the Messiah came, the dead would rise from their graves and return to earth in the kingdom of God. The Pharisees believed in resurrection; the Sadducees rejected it, because it's nowhere mentioned by Moses, and would upset the status quo. Pharisees and Sadducees were often at each other's throats; the only thing that united them was their shared hatred of Jesus. So some Sadducees invented a preposterous story about seven brothers, who all, one after the other, married the same woman. 'What would happen if they all returned to earth?' they asked with a sarcastic sneer, 'Which would be her husband? All seven?' One bride for seven brothers? It's too ridiculous to imagine, they thought. So there's no resurrection: the Pharisees and Jesus are wrong.

## God of the living

Jesus answered this absurd argument courteously. He didn't question their assumptions, though he easily could have done. Instead, Jesus started from the books which they believed in. In the story of the burning bush, the Lord's described as 'the God of Abraham, the God of Isaac, and the God of Jacob'. 'Now,' Jesus continued, 'he's God, not of the dead, but of the living.' Putting that into today's language, God's not interested in presiding over a kingdom of corpses. He wants living people to love, who'll love him in return. So there must be life after death, because that's what God made us for.

### Ad hominem

It's a complex answer to a dry and twisted question. But Jesus took them on in their own terms. He fought the battle on their ground, and spoke their language. The words that Jesus spoke wouldn't convince many people today; you'd have to update it into contemporary language. But Jesus was concerned about the people in front of him, and left the updating to us. He was using what's known to philosophers as an *ad hominem* argument – Latin for one addressed 'to the man'. The dictionary defines it as one 'directed to the feelings or prejudices of the hearer'. That was what Jesus was doing all the time: talking to real people and using the words most likely to persuade them. He couldn't speak twenty-first-century English words, nor could he use the way of thinking that we use.

## Contemporary language

So it's up to us to translate the words of Jesus into today's English, if we want anyone to listen to us. There's great beauty in the language of the Authorized Version and the Book of Common Prayer, and when we're offering the best of everything to God in our worship, that includes the best possible language. But if there's even one person present who doesn't understand it, we owe it to them to let them speak to Jesus in their own words, and we owe it to Jesus to let him speak to that person in terms that they'll understand. That doesn't mean we abandon the lovely old words altogether; but we *must* explain them in contemporary language, for God's sake.

## By all means win some

St Paul said, 'When I'm among Jews I behave like a Jew, and when I'm speaking to Greeks, I speak like a Greek. I have become all things to all people, that I may by all means win some.' Jesus wants us to persuade everyone that he loves them, and we must stop at nothing to do so. We must put ourselves in the shoes of those who listen to us, so that we can choose words which will appeal to them. God loves us as real people, with all our quirks and oddities; so we should be free to love God without trying to be somebody different. God put us here to learn love, so that we should go on giving and receiving his love after we die. So there must be life after death, as Jesus proved to the Sadducees, whichever words you choose to explain it.

## *All-age worship*

*Make a collage of pictures of people who have died. Write underneath, 'Jesus is God of the living.'*

*Forth in the peace of Christ we go; Jesus, stand among us; Now is eternal life; Thine be the glory.*


# Third Sunday before Advent
## *Second Service*   The Love of God in Christ

Ps. 40 I waited for the Lord; 1 Kings 3:1–15 Solomon's prayer for wisdom; Rom. 8:31–39 The love of God in Christ; *Gospel at Holy Communion*: Matt. 22:15–22 The tribute money

> '[Nothing] will be able to separate us from the love of God in Christ Jesus our Lord.' *Romans 8:39*


## The Gospel according to Paul

The eighth chapter of Paul's Letter to the Romans is one of the finest in the New Testament – some call it 'The Gospel according to Paul'. Paul had travelled around half the Roman Empire, founding new churches, but he'd never been to the capital city yet. He was hoping to go to Rome, and wrote a letter preparing them for his arrival. In the melting-pot which was Rome, there were many Jewish Christians, and many Christians from other nations also; they were suspicious of each other, and suspicious of St Paul. Had he, a Jew, lowered the standards of the Chosen People, by admitting non-Jews to the Church without making them obey the complete Jewish law? Paul points out, in his defence, that the Holy Spirit unites us with Jesus – all of us, of whatever race – and that gives us new life. The law of Moses tells us how to live in the flesh; life in the Spirit is about our relationship with God, who has adopted us as his sons and daughters. The whole created world is groaning under the effects of sin; but the fact that we've received the fruit of the Spirit proves that eventually we shall live with God in glory. That makes our sufferings bearable, because of our hope of heaven. St Paul's message applies to us all, and reaches its climax at the end of this chapter; let's look at each verse in turn:

*Verse 31: What then are we to say about these things? If God is for us, who is against us?*
Does God judge us guilty because we haven't kept every detail of the law? Is suffering his punishment? No, God's on our side.

*He who did not withhold his own Son, but gave him up for all of us, will he not, with him, also give us everything else?*
God gave us his Son Jesus, to die on the cross for our sake, and bring us new life – he's not going to take that away by denying us life in heaven. If there's a court case when we die, and we're put on trial for our sins, who'll be the prosecuting counsel?

*Who will bring any charge against God's elect? It is God who justifies. Who is to condemn?*
God's already declared us 'not guilty'; nobody's going to argue against that. Particularly when Jesus is speaking for the defence:

*It is Christ Jesus, who died, yes, who was raised, who is at the right hand of God, who indeed intercedes for us.*
Roman law was famous, and the law-court metaphors are piling up. Jesus, as St John also said, is our Advocate. But now Paul turns from law to personal feelings, and writes about the love of God in Christ:

*Who will separate us from the love of Christ?*
St Paul knows, from what others told him, and from his own experience, that Jesus loves us. Love's the most powerful force in the universe, and nothing can get in its way:

*Will hardship, or distress, or persecution, or famine, or nakedness, or peril, or sword?*
St Paul had suffered greatly as a travelling missionary, but it only made him feel closer to Jesus; he quotes Psalm 44:

*As it is written, 'For your sake we are being killed all day long; we are accounted as sheep to be slaughtered.' No, in all these things we are more than conquerors through him who loved us.*
His experience of suffering had only shown Paul how much he was loved, and nothing in life or death can come between the Christian and our heavenly Father. People in those days believed that the earth was suspended between the underworld of hell and the heavenly spheres, where the stars were thought to influence our lives. Yet even these powerful spirits, says Paul, are powerless, to-day or tomorrow, against the love of God, who is drawing us to himself:

*For I am convinced that neither death, nor life, nor angels, nor rulers, nor things present, nor things to come, nor powers, nor height, nor depth, nor anything else in all creation, will be able to separate us from the love of God in Christ Jesus our Lord.*

So that's the gospel, the good news that Paul had been trying to spread. It applies to Jew and Gentile, to you and to me. There's nothing to be afraid of; God loves us, and even though we're sinners, God will make it possible for us to live with him in eternity.

## Suggested hymns

*O Lord my God, when I in awesome wonder; Oft in danger, oft in woe; Soldiers of Christ, arise; There is a green hill far away.*

# Second Sunday before Advent    14 November
## The Power of Music

(*For a service which is not a Service of Remembrance.*)
Mal. 4:1–2a Judgement; Ps. 98 A new song; 2 Thess. 3:6–13 Perseverance in good works; Luke 21:5–19 Perseverance

'Sing to the Lord a new song.' Psalm 98:1 (Common Worship)

## The power of music

'Music expresses that which cannot be said, and on which it is impossible to be silent,' wrote Victor Hugo. William Congreve wrote that 'Music has charms to soothe the savage breast.' The amazing power of music over human behaviour depends on its appeal to our deepest emotions. When music's linked to fine words in song, then it appeals to the mind as well as the heart. Yet the brain alone can't control how somebody behaves. Music's needed – or in the totally unmusical, some other form of beauty – to arouse the emotions which can change a person's actions. No matter how often you tell somebody how they should behave, nothing alters, until some strong motivating force overcomes our selfishness.

## Music in the Bible

That's why music's mentioned so often in the Bible. The book of Psalms was the hymn book of the Jerusalem Temple. It calls on us to 'Sing to the Lord a new song', and to play musical instruments too: 'Make music to the Lord with the lyre . . . with trumpets and the sound of the horn, sound praise before the Lord, the King.' The Virgin Mary sang the Magnificat, and at the end of the Last Supper, Jesus didn't leave the Upper Room until 'after they had sung a hymn'. St Paul quotes poetry, apparently from early Christian hymns; he sang hymns when he was in prison in Philippi, and he exhorted his friends to 'Let the word of Christ dwell in you richly . . . and with gratitude in your hearts sing psalms, hymns, and spiritual songs to God.'

## National ballads

Andrew Fletcher, a Scottish politician of the seventeenth century, wrote, 'I knew a very wise man . . . [who] believed, if a man were permitted to make all the ballads, he need not care who should make the laws of a nation.' This is sometimes quoted more concisely as, 'Let me but make the songs of a nation, and I care not who makes its laws.' This encapsulates the difference between the Old Testament religion of law and the New Testament gospel of grace. Laws can tell us what we ought not to do, but they can't give us the strength to do what we ought. The Holy Spirit acts like music on our emotions, moving us and empowering us to behave lovingly.

## Limits of reason

Emotion's needed because reason alone can't stir us to loving behaviour. God's given us the power of reason, so that we can think out the best way to behave. There's no excuse for behaving unreasonably, just because some inner hunch or prejudice tells us to. But when you've worked out what to do, you need the grace of the Holy Spirit to empower you. Otherwise, as St Paul said, 'The good that I would, I do not; and the evil that I would not, that I do.'

## Music in church

That's surely why we use so much music in church. An army sings marching songs as it goes to war, to encourage each other and strengthen their resolve. Christians are engaged in a battle against evil in the world and temptation in their own hearts, and we need all the motivation we can get. Some people find they're attracted to churchgoing because of the beautiful music, and the chance to have a good sing. They may not think deeply about the doctrines which are taught, but the spirited singing moves them to behave in a more Christian way when they go home.

## Music in heaven

So the Bible describes heaven in terms of music – saints and angels praising God in endless song:

> Then I looked, and there was the Lamb, standing on Mount Zion! And with him were one hundred and forty-four thousand who had his name and his Father's name written on their foreheads. And I heard a voice from heaven like the sound of many waters and like the sound of loud thunder; the voice I heard was like the sound of harpists playing on their harps, and they sing a new song before the throne and before the four living creatures and before the elders.

This isn't to be taken literally, or those with no voice would feel left out! But it's a sign that we should all be prepared to use our emotions in the praise of almighty God, so that God can use us to love and serve our neighbours. 'For such there is no law.' 'Let me but make the songs of a nation, and I care not who makes its laws.'

### All-age worship

*Learn to sing a favourite hymn or chorus by heart.*

### Suggested hymns

*How shall I sing that majesty?; I will sing, I will sing, a song unto the Lord; Joy to the world, the Lord is come; Sing to God new songs of worship.*

## Remembrance Sunday   14 November
## Does Religion Cause Wars?

*(The readings of the day, or those 'In Time of Trouble' can be used. These readings are for 'The Peace of the World'.)*
Micah 4:1–5 Swords into ploughshares; Ps. 85:8–13 God
will speak peace; James 3:13–18 The harvest of peace; John
15:9–17 No greater love

> *'They shall beat their swords into ploughshares, and their spears into pruning hooks; nation shall not lift up sword against nation, neither shall they learn war any more.' Micah 4:3*

### Richard Dawkins

A campaign against religion has been waged over recent years by Richard Dawkins, a professor of genetics. On closer examination it turns out to be a criticism of fundamentalism in all religions, and he's reluctant to enter into dialogue with thinking mainstream Christians. He rejects the excellent reasons for believing that God probably exists, but which he dismisses as 'the God delusion'. His main reason for attacking religion, however, is that he says that religion causes war.

### Atheist wars

The obvious answer to this accusation is to point out that atheists, too, cause wars. In the twentieth century, Joseph Stalin, Adolf Hitler, Mao Tse Tung and Pol Pot between them caused the deaths of many millions; a total death toll far exceeding the number killed in all the so-called 'religious wars'. To sustain Professor Dawkins' criticism, you'd have to redefine religion so as to include communism and fascism: something like 'a belief system that controls the whole of one's life'. But then, on that definition, atheism would count as a religion too!

### Is he right?

This doesn't close the argument, however. There's enough truth in Professor Dawkins' denunciation for us to take it extremely seriously. Why is it that so many Christians down the centuries claimed that they went to war in God's name, because God wanted them to? Does God really want us to kill those who disagree with us? Today we remember those who've died as a result of wars, and we celebrate the courage of those who fought to defend our lives and our liberties. Most people would say that to fight for your country in a defensive battle is an honourable thing to do. When war is declared on another nation which hasn't first attacked us, however, many people would have doubts, not about the bravery of the combatants, but about the morality of those who sent them into battle. When we think of the many civilians who've died as a result of war, we can only wring our hands at the folly of it all.

## History

How did we get into this mess? To answer this, we have to look, not just at history, but at how we view the people of the past. They were all human beings like us, with a mixture of good and bad in each of us. But, to do them justice, we must realize that on many matters they had very different opinions from ours. In the religious wars of the Reformation era, for instance, almost everybody believed that the kindest thing you could do for those of a different denomination was to torture them until they recanted of their heresy, and make them suffer by burning them at the stake, to lessen their sufferings hereafter in hell. We believe our ancestors were wrong in this, but we can't entirely blame them, because everybody was doing it, and nobody questioned its rightness. It makes you wonder how many of the things we take for granted in our own day will appal subsequent generations.

## Progressive revelation

Our primitive ancestors regarded it as natural to fight over fertile land, which they needed if they were to stay alive. Through much of the Old Testament, it was believed that God approved of such behaviour, and only a few prophets cried for swords to be beaten into ploughshares. Jesus said, 'Blessed are the peacemakers', and told us to love our enemies, but many Christians ignored this aspect of his teaching. It seems that fighting's inborn in human nature, and people use religion as a peg to hang their weapons on. But you can't blame religion for that; if anything, God's used religion to show people the folly of their ways. Human beings are so stubborn, God can't reveal the whole of his will to them all at once. He has to hand it down bit by bit, in a process we call 'progressive revelation'. God promises that his Holy Spirit will lead us into all truth, but it's a slow process, and we haven't learnt the half of it yet. Maybe those who've died in battle have died in a good cause, as part of the process by which God teaches us that there's a better way of resolving our disputes than by fighting over them.

## All-age worship

*Stick red paper onto a plain background to form the petals of a poppy.*

## Suggested hymns

*Almighty Father, who for us thy Son didst give; Christ is the world's true light; For the healing of the nations; Peace is flowing like a river.*

## Christ the King   21 November
*Principal Service*   **When You are King**
Jer. 23:1–6 Bad and good shepherds; Ps. 46 God is our refuge and strength; Col. 1:11–20 Forgiveness in the Son through the cross; Luke 23:33–43 The thief on the cross

> *'Jesus, remember me when you come into your kingdom.' Luke 23:42*

## We kings

In 1896, Prempeh, King of the Ashanti tribe in Ghana, was exiled by the British to the Seychelles Islands in the Indian Ocean. He stayed there until 1924, heard the message of the gospel, and decided to be baptized. Asked whether he wanted to be a member of the Roman Catholic Church or the Church of England, he asked which King Edward was. Told that King Edward was definitely Church of England, King Prempeh replied, 'We kings must stick together.' He was baptized in the Anglican church; the column in the baptism register for his occupation reads 'Ex-king'!

## Types of king

There have been many different types of king. Prempeh was an enlightened educator, but many kings have been notoriously blood-thirsty. There are romantic kings in popular legend, and kings in disguise. We even have the childish vision in the rhyme, 'When you are King, dilly, dilly, I shall be Queen.' Today we celebrate the feast of Christ the King. What sort of a king was Jesus? Pilate asked him, 'Are you a king, then?' and Jesus replied, 'You say that I am a king. For this I was born, and for this I came into the world, to testify to the truth.' So he was not a king in the sense that Pilate meant it. He had previously said, 'My kingdom is not from this world. If my kingdom were from this world, my followers would be fighting to keep me from being handed over to the Jews. But as it is, my kingdom is not from here.'

## A king who brings the truth

Jesus wasn't a violent king, but one who brought the truth. Even the thief crucified next to Jesus recognized something regal in his manner. 'Jesus,' he called out, 'remember me when you come into your kingdom.' What faith! Nobody else thought that the prophet from Nazareth, dying there in agony, could ever become a king. But the thief cried out, 'When you are King . . .' as though he really believed it would happen one day. This wasn't a childish fantasy, 'When you are king, dilly, dilly'. This was the beginning of faith. The thief saw beyond his own inevitable death, and the death of the man on the next cross, who'd so recently befriended him, to a kingdom not of this world. Jesus brought the truth that there is a paradise waiting for all those who have faith in him. Even thieves and murderers, for he said, 'Truly I tell you, today you will be with me in Paradise.'

## Winning subjects

Jesus wasn't competing with Pilate for a kingdom based on force; violence wasn't his way. And that's what makes him a greater king than all the others, for violence never wins the loyalty of its victims, whereas truth lives for ever. So Christ is the king of every nation, over despots and democracies alike. Jesus is the ruler of the whole earth, but he doesn't force or frighten his subjects into submission. Instead he loves them, until they love him in return. He doesn't only love good people; he loves robbers and bandits. For love is the only thing that can make us change our ways. Once we realize that we're loved, even though we don't deserve it, we fall in love with Jesus. Then nothing's too great or difficult for us to do, to show how much we love our Saviour. That's the sort of obedience that Christ our King wants of us: not forced, not the fruit of fear, but the willing offering of love.

## Faith

The day when Jesus rules over all other authorities on earth sometimes seems as far off and impossible as it must have seemed to the dying thief. Like him, we must have faith. 'When you are king', we must say – 'when', not 'if'. Gradually Christ is extending his rule over all the godless authorities of this world. One by one, those who don't believe in him realize that Jesus loves them. Eventually they respond to his love by their obedience. The final culmination of his kingdom may not come in this life, however, but in the better world that he told us about, the world beyond the grave. Even when we've died, Jesus will remember us; so we can say with the dying thief, 'Jesus, remember me, when you are king.' For when you are king, dilly, dilly, we shall be reigning with you . . . 'in paradise'. We kings, and queens, must stick together!

### All-age worship

*Make paper crowns for everyone who wants to be in Paradise with Jesus when they die.*

### Suggested hymns

*According to thy gracious word; Meekness and majesty; 'The kingdom is upon you'; Thy kingdom come, O God.*

# Christic the King

## Christ the King

*Second Service*   **Charles, King and Martyr**

Morning Ps. 29 Enthroned, 110 The king at your right hand;
Evening Ps. 72 An ideal king; 1 Sam. 8:4–20 The demand for a
king; John 18:33–37 My kingdom is not of this world

*'In that day you will cry out because of your king, whom you have
chosen for yourselves; but the LORD will not answer you in that
day.' 1 Samuel 8:18*

### A saintly man but not a wise king

On the Feast of Christ the King, I want you to think about King
Charles the First of England. He was a saintly man but not a wise
king. He never bothered to explain to Parliament why his disastrous war against Spain was costing the country so much, and tried
to impose an illegal loan to pay for it, as well as the unpopular 'ship
money' tax to pay for the navy. Then, through mismanagement by
his adviser Buckingham, he was drawn into a war against France as
well. When Parliament condemned his arbitrary conduct, he ruled
without calling a parliament for eleven years. He tried and failed
to impose the Book of Common Prayer on the Scottish Presbyteri-
ans, and consequently became involved in a war against the Scots
'Covenanters'. He opposed the Puritan majority in the House of
Commons, defending the ritual and ceremonial of the Church of
England against those who wished to abolish all traces of 'popery'.
When Civil War broke out between the Parliamentarian and Royal-
ist armies, he showed himself a brave man but no general.

### Trial and execution

His dignity at the time of his trial and execution entitle him, however, to be numbered among the noble army of martyrs. He was
tried before Parliament, although he denied that they had any right
to judge him, protesting that he stood for 'the liberty of the people
of England'. On the night before he was executed, after spending
two hours in prayer, he remarked to Sir Thomas Herbert: 'Herbert,
this is my second marriage day; I would be as trim today as may
be; for before night I hope to be spoused to my blessed Jesus . . .
I fear not death! Death is not terrible to me. I bless my God I am
prepared.'

## Speech from the scaffold

King Charles was executed on January 30th 1649, on a scaffold outside the Banqueting House in Whitehall. In his speech from the scaffold he said:

> In troth, sirs, my conscience in religion, I think, is very well known to the world, and therefore I declare before you all, that I die a Christian according to the profession of the Church of England as I found it left me by my father . . . I have a good cause, and I have a gracious God. I will say no more . . . I shall say but very short prayers, and then thrust out my hands.

## Burial

After he'd been beheaded, his head was carried in procession around London. In the Deanery at Windsor, not open to visitors, is the table on which his body was laid out in the meanwhile. Charles Dickens wrote about a character who was obsessed with locating King Charles's head. Don't worry, both head and body are buried together! If you go into St George's Chapel in Windsor Castle on January 30th, you may find a small delegation from the Royal Stuart Society laying a wreath on his grave. Until the nineteenth century there was a service for that day in the Book of Common Prayer, which clergy were enjoined by law to use.

## Leadership

We can learn, from King Charles the First, lessons that apply not only to kings, but to anyone in a position of authority, from parents to popes. First, he always acted on principle, whatever it cost him. He would never do anything that he conscientiously believed to be contrary to the will of God. But he failed to educate his conscience, so that he was often mistaken in what he took to be God's will. All leadership, like politics, is the art of the possible. It's no use having wonderful ideals if you can't put them into practice. The main reason for failure is when those who seek to influence events fail to carry others with them. You must patiently persuade those whose co-operation you need, until they come round to your point of view. Finally, King Charles rightly recognized that our Lord Jesus Christ is the 'King of kings and Lord of lords'; but he thought that gave him the 'Divine right of kings' to be an autocratic and absolute monarch. Christ the King, however, came not to abolish the law but to fulfil it. That means that nobody, however great their power, is above the law. Too many people in positions of authority have come a cropper through failing to realize that.

## Suggested hymns

*How beauteous are their feet; How bright these glorious spirits shine; I vow to thee, my country, all earthly things above; Palms of glory, raiment bright.*

# Sermons for Saints' Days and Special Occasions

**SAINTS' DAYS**

*When his friends describe the martyrdom of St Polycarp in about AD 156, they declare their intention of 'celebrating the birthday of his martyrdom' every year in the future. When churches could be built to enshrine the bodies or relics of the martyrs, they were often dedicated on the anniversary of their death, and an annual dedication festival was held on that date. Other churches dedicated to the name of a saint soon celebrated the saint's day as their 'patronal festival'. The Bible describes the heroes of the Old Testament as a 'cloud of witnesses' around us, and all believers as being united in the body of Christ, as 'fellow citizens of the saints, and of the household of God'. Since the time of the Maccabees it had been held that those who had died heroically are praying for those who are alive, the Church Triumphant interceding for the Church Militant. It seemed natural to ask the departed for their prayers, and to talk to our dead friends just as we did when they were alive. But superstition grew up around devotion to the saints in the Middle Ages, and it was rejected by most Protestants. Yet many congregations wished to continue honouring the saints, especially on their own patronal festival. When the Book of Common Prayer was printed in two colours, the more important saints' days were listed in the Calendar as 'Red Letter Days'. This book provides sermons for all the 'Festivals' in the modern calendars, including the patron saints of England, Scotland, Wales and Ireland, and Corpus Christi; as well the 'Principal Feasts' commemorating the Epiphany, the Annunciation and All Saints' Day; Harvest Festival, and sermons for baptisms, weddings and funerals.* The Christian Year: Calendar, Lectionary and Collects *(with later amendments),*

## St Stephen, Deacon, First Martyr

26 December 2009

**Reality**  2 Chron. 24:20–22 The stoning of Zechariah; or Acts 7:51–60 The death of Stephen; Ps. 119:161–168 Persecuted without a cause (*if the Acts reading is used instead of the Old Testament reading, the New Testament reading is* Gal. 2:16b–20 Crucified with Christ); Matt. 10:17–22 Persecution

> *'"Look," [Stephen] said, "I see the heavens opened and the Son of Man standing at the right hand of God!"' Acts 7:56*

### Reality

Suppose a young man's suggesting a plan of action which his friends think is hopelessly idealistic. They'll tease him, saying something like 'Get real, man! Things just don't happen like that in the real world.' This suggests that there's a world of the imagination, a world of dreams and ideals, and over against that there's the world we live in, which is quite different. But that begs the question, which one of them is the real world? 'Reality television' is very popular these days. In some programmes the cameras are trained on people placed in a challenging situation for which they've had no preparation or previous experience. The suggestion here is that other television programmes, where actors perform according to a script, are somehow less real than the unscripted ones. I'm not sure that's so. It seems to me that when people know there's a camera watching them, they behave in a most unnatural manner. Once again, which is real and which is false?

## Stephen

The day after Christmas we commemorate St Stephen, the first martyr. The real world in which he lived was bitterly opposed to Stephen, because he didn't conform to their established norms. His accusers said that he was set on destroying the Temple and the law of Moses. More likely he was preaching that moral codes and priestly systems don't bring us any closer to God; it's only faith in Jesus, who offered God's unqualified love to sinners and foreigners alike. Stephen's long speech of defence trawls through the Jewish Scriptures to show that Moses had promised another prophet, by whom, Stephen implied, he meant Jesus; but the Jewish leaders had always rejected the prophets whom God had sent them. So the members of the Jewish council stoned Stephen to death as a blasphemer, the same crime they'd accused Jesus of before they sent him to Pilate to be crucified.

## The heavens opened

But before he died, Stephen had a vision. 'Look,' Stephen said, 'I see the heavens opened and the Son of Man standing at the right hand of God!' The question was, which was real? The world that had condemned Stephen and Jesus to death, or the world which Stephen saw in his vision? He was quoting from the book of Daniel, as they well knew:

> As I watched in the night visions, I saw one like a human being [literally, one like a Son of Man] coming with the clouds of heaven. And he came to the Ancient One and was presented before him. To him was given dominion and glory and kingship, that all peoples, nations, and languages should serve him. His dominion is an everlasting dominion that shall not pass away, and his kingship is one that shall never be destroyed.

Jesus, whom they'd crucified, said Stephen, was really the Son of Man who would welcome all races into his kingdom.

## The open heavens

But even more significantly, Stephen said he had seen the heavens opened. Heaven, he believed, was reality; the 'real world', so-called, was only a delusion. Here he was following the line taken by Isaiah, who called on God to 'tear open the heavens and come down'; Ezekiel, who proclaimed, 'the heavens were opened, and I saw visions of God'; and Jesus at his baptism, when 'Suddenly the heavens were opened to him and he saw the Spirit of God descending like a dove.' The phrase 'the open heavens' always introduces in the Bible, and in many other Jewish books from the same period, a vision of reality. Here Stephen, who spoke Greek, must also have been thinking of the philosopher Plato. Plato described the world of ideals, contrasted with the objects in the physical world, which are merely imperfect copies of the heavenly prototypes.

## The reality of Jesus

The reality of Jesus, Stephen proclaimed, was that the man who was born in Bethlehem, and brought up in Nazareth, was really the longed-for Messiah. He is really enthroned next to God the Father, as ruler and judge of the whole earth. And Jesus wants to welcome each one of us out of this world of shadows into the bright light of the real world of heaven. If you still think that the only world which really exists is the material world, all we can say to you is, 'Get real. The only real world is the world where Jesus is, in heaven. Get a life. Move into the real world.'

### Suggested hymns

*Immortal, invisible, God only wise; O worship the King; Son of God, eternal Saviour; The great God of heaven is come down to earth.*

## St John, Apostle and Evangelist   27 December
(*See page 34.*)

## Holy Innocents   28 December
## When Children Die   Jer. 31:15–17 Rachel weeping for her children; Ps. 124 When our enemies attacked us; 1 Cor. 1:26–29 God chose what is weak; Matt. 2:13–18 The massacre

*'Rachel is weeping for her children . . . because they are no more.'*
*Jeremiah 31:15*

## The Brothers Karamazov

John Hick, in his book *Evil and the God of Love*, quotes from the Russian author Fyodor Dostoyevsky. In his novel, *The Brothers Karamazov*, Dostoyevsky describes two brothers arguing about God. The atheist brother Ivan challenges Alyosha, who's a priest, asking how he can possibly believe in God when there's so much evil in the world. The usual answer is that we can't reach heaven without knowing the reality of good and evil. We must experience suffering at the hands of evil people, so that we can understand the greatness of love, and freely choose between them. Alyosha could have pointed to people whose characters were refined by the patient way they've responded to a long life of suffering. But Ivan says, 'I'm not talking about the sufferings of grown-up people.' What about the suffering of children, he asks. Is it necessary that children should scream with pain, so that other people should learn to choose between good and evil? Is the result worth the price that has to be paid? And would you be willing, he challenges his saintly brother, to be God, the architect of an unjust universe like that? Softly, Alyosha says, 'No, I wouldn't consent.'

## Children in pain

Ask that same question of any parent. Ask it of a parent who's lost a child. If you were God, would you create a world in which children have to suffer so that other people can learn a lesson? No, of course not. Parents will do anything to protect their children, and if a child dies, the first question they ask is, what sort of God would allow a thing like that? So, from Rachel weeping for her children, because they are no more, to the mothers of Bethlehem, grief-stricken by King Herod's murder of their innocent children, and on again to the present day, the cry rises up, what sort of God would create a world in which children have to suffer? And to that, religious people have no answer.

## What is death?

Or so it seems. But then, answers may not be what grieving parents want. It's no help to reason with somebody in the pit of despair, or to argue with someone in the depths of grief. All we can do is put an arm round them, and let our tears fall with theirs. As Jesus said, 'weep with those who weep'. What someone who's been bereaved needs is not answers but love. Of course they'll never forget their little ones, but as time goes by they may understand that life has to go on – there may be other children to care for. The agony of grief may subside into dull numbness, and then into resigned acceptance. And then they may begin to ask the question, 'What is death?' Over the course of time, they turn back to the teaching of Jesus, with its message that death is a bridge into a better, happier life. Then they may gradually change their attitude. What if our little ones are in fact happy now, and with Jesus? Of course we miss them, and maybe they miss us, but in that timeless world it won't be very long before we're together again. Children are very quick to forget pain. If they go on to a better life when they die, the pain they endured may be forgotten as quickly as all the other yesterdays.

## A God who suffers

You find that hard to believe? So do I. But what you and I need, the same as the bereaved parents, is not explanations but love. Jesus didn't say, 'I have explained the world', but 'I have overcome the world'. Jesus does that by putting his arm around us and weeping with us. That's why he died on the cross. Jesus was revealing a God who can't prevent evil people from hurting and killing others, even from hurting and killing children. But we have a God who comes right in and suffers with us, and grieves with us, and dies with us. And in that way he takes us all to rejoin those for whom we grieve, to live with him in joy for ever, in a world where there is no more pain or death.

## John Hick

John Hick ends the book I mentioned at the beginning by posing the ultimate question:

> Can there be a future good so great as to render acceptable, in retrospect, the whole human experience, with all its wickedness and suffering as well as all its sanctity and happiness? I think that perhaps there can, and indeed perhaps there is.

### Suggested hymns

*Lully, lulla, thou little tiny child; Morning glory, starlit sky; Once in Royal David's city; Unto us a boy is born.*

# Naming and Circumcision of Jesus   1 January 2010
## Hallowed Be Thy Name   Num. 6:22–27 Aaron's blessing;
Ps. 8 From the mouths of babes; Gal. 4:4–7 Born under the law;
Luke 2:15–21 Naming and circumcision

> *'After eight days had passed, it was time to circumcise the child;
> and he was called Jesus, the name given by the angel before he
> was conceived in the womb.' Luke 2:21*

### The Chinese evangelist

Almost a century ago, there was a Chinese man, living in China,
who had become a Christian. He tried to tell the people in the town
where he lived about the Jesus he loved. On one occasion, they
laughed at him, used foul language about the Jesus-god he worshipped, tied his hands together behind him and strung him up on a
high pole. When he was eventually taken down, his bishop came to
see him and found him crying. 'The pain must have been terrible,'
murmured the bishop sympathetically. 'I'm not crying because of
the pain,' answered the Chinese evangelist. 'It's because the name
of Jesus was taken in vain and dishonoured.'

### What is your name?

A person's name's something unique to him or her. It's what shows
that they are different from anyone else. It indicates that they've
a character which they've built up over the years, which is unlike
anybody else's. With a few exceptions, when somebody's given
their name, it's chosen because nobody else in their neighbourhood
has exactly the same first name, surname and middle names, or if
so they're given nicknames to distinguish them. There's nobody else
in the whole world who has the same moniker as you. So when we
honour somebody's name, we're celebrating their uniqueness and
distinction. 'What is your name?' means 'What makes you different
from anybody else?' God values us as individuals, so it's good to
celebrate our difference.

### Jesus

A week after the baby was born in Bethlehem, he was circumcised
and given the name of Jesus. It was actually quite a common name,
a later form of the word Joshua, which means 'God saves'. Jesus

was given that name to show he is the Saviour, the one who will save us from our sins. Usually in those days people with the same first name were distinguished by being described as 'son of . . .' and then the name of their father. There were probably many 'Jesus son of Joseph's in Bethlehem. Those who knew that Mary wasn't married will have described him as 'Jesus son of Mary', and there can't have been many of those. But those who knew the secret of his birth could call him, 'Jesus Son of God', and nobody else shares that name.

## Dishonouring the name

The third commandment tells us not to dishonour the name of the Lord our God. Imagine what you'd feel if another person took the name of someone you love and used it as a swear word. Then you'll understand why the Chinese evangelist wept at the dishonouring of the name of Jesus. Of course most people who say 'O Christ' when they're cross don't realize what they're doing. A vicar was helping a plumber to do some work in the church when the plumber did just that, and then said, 'I suppose I shouldn't say that word in here.' 'It's quite all right,' said the vicar, 'neither of us will notice.' 'What do you mean, neither of us?' asked the plumber. 'Well, I've been in the army,' answered the vicar, 'and God will think you're praying!'

## Hallowed be thy name

The opposite to dishonouring the name of God, of course, is when we say in the Lord's Prayer, 'hallowed be thy name'. May God's name be regarded as holy. A building which is regarded as holy is a building which is separate from all other buildings, and protected from profane and sinful use. So when we pray that God's name may be hallowed, that means that we should regard him, his unique character and essence, as separate from, and higher than, any other being.

## Reverence

The first thing we ask for in the Lord's Prayer is reverence. This is to believe that God exists, that he is love, that he is everywhere present, and that we must obey and worship him. Jesus was given a special name, to show that he's unique, and we must reverence him for it. Every human being has a unique name, to show that God loves them for their unique character, making them distinct from anybody else. So if we reverence Jesus, the Son of God, we should also reverence every child of God, and celebrate their difference, their unique qualities. Happy New Year, everybody!

## Suggested hymns

*God is working his purpose out; How sweet the name of Jesus sounds; Lord, for the years; To the name of our salvation.*


# Epiphany   6 January
*(or may be transferred to Sunday 3 January)*
**Kings Bow Down**   Isa. 60:1–6 Bringing gold and incense; Ps. 72:[1–9] 10–15 Kings will bow before him; Eph. 3:1–12 Preaching to Gentiles; Matt. 2:1–12 Visit of the Magi

*'All kings shall fall down before him, all nations shall do him service.' Psalm 72:11 (Common Worship)*

## Charles II

A certain Revd Dr South was preaching to a congregation which included King Charles the Second. He interrupted his sermon, asking someone to wake up Lord Lauderdale, who had fallen asleep. When the noble Lord had been woken up, Dr South rebuked him, saying, 'My Lord, you snore so loud you will wake the King!' Evidently his sermon must have been unusually soporific, but his respect for the monarch was so great that he wouldn't presume to rouse the royal head from its slumbers.

## Monarchy

Up until fairly recently, whatever the personal failings of the king at the time, everybody respected the institution of monarchy. Anthony Trollope wrote that if a people wished to be held high in the respect of other nations, then it must hold its monarch high. The king or queen, or someone with an equivalent title, was regarded as the head of state in all nations except briefly during the Greek experiment with democracy, and the short-lived Roman republic.

Any nation that conquered another would expect the king of the client state, even if he remained in office, to come to the court to do homage. Psalm 71 sings about the King of Israel, 'All kings shall fall down before him, all nations shall do him service.'

## Messiah

The psalms were composed for singing in the Temple in Jerusalem, the royal chapel of the successors of King David. Royal psalms, like this one, praised the king who was on the throne at the time. None of the kings deserved it, because none of them was perfect, but people dreamt that one day they'd have an ideal king. He'd be the Messiah, the Anointed One, the descendant of King David, who'd raise the small and often-defeated nation of Judah to a position of international greatness. Even rich nations, the countries with gold mines, would become dependencies:

> The kings of Tarshish and of the isles shall pay tribute;
> the kings of Sheba and Seba shall bring gifts.

## Three kings

Christians see this as a prediction of the visit of the three kings to Bethlehem, which we celebrate at Epiphany time, with their gifts of gold, frankincense and myrrh. The snag with this, however, is that the New Testament nowhere calls them kings, nor does it say there were three of them. St Matthew wrote:

> Wise men from the East came to Jerusalem, asking, 'Where is the child who has been born king of the Jews? For we observed his star at its rising, and have come to pay him homage' . . . On entering the house, they saw the child with Mary his mother; and they knelt down and paid him homage. Then, opening their treasure chests, they offered him gifts of gold, frankincense, and myrrh.

So an unknown number of wise men, or magi, who were Persian astrologers, paid homage to baby Jesus, and offered him three gifts. In Christian legend they've become three kings, and we've even given them names: Caspar, Melchior and Balthasar. How nice! It makes a good story, whether it's accurate or not. And it brings out the point of what Matthew was saying.

## Gentiles

For the magi, coming from Persia, were Gentiles, non-Jews. It's quite striking that Matthew, the most Jewish of the four Gospels, is the only one to report that non-Jews were among the first to worship Jesus. That's because Matthew was fascinated by the fulfilment of prophecy, and never loses a chance to draw our attention to it. And although in the history of the Jews, the Gentiles were often their enemies, the Old Testament again and again holds out a vision of reconciliation. God's servant's to be a 'Light to lighten the Gentiles'. No longer will foreign kings lord it over God's people, they'll bring gifts to the Messiah. That's perfectly symbolized by transforming the Gentile magi into kings, and three of them because there are three gifts.

## Gifts

So this story confirms for us that Jesus really was the Messiah; and that he is the Saviour of the world. Not just for his fellow Jews, but for us Gentiles also. He is above all earthly powers, and stands in judgement on the leaders of the nations. But he also welcomes the gifts that every nation brings to him, the national characteristics of which each of us is so proud. He welcomes the national traditions of every country, with their gifts of language, literature, music, art and science, and their unique achievements in every sphere. So we should offer our own nation to Jesus, and rejoice when other cultures, too, are brought into the service of Jesus, the King of all the earth.

## *Suggested hymns*

*As with gladness men of old; Earth has many a noble city; From the eastern mountains; We three kings of orient are.*

# Week of Prayer for Christian Unity   18–25 January

## That They May Be One   Zeph. 3:16–20 Bring you home; 1 John 4:9–15 We ought to love one another; Ps. 133 Brothers at unity; John 17:11b–23 That they may be one

> *'[Jesus prayed,] "I ask not only on behalf of these, but also on behalf of those who will believe in me through their word, that they may all be one."' John 17:20*

## A mother's pain

Picture a mother with a very large family. She loves them all, and every night she prays for each of them by name, lifting them up in her mind before God and asking him to give each one what they most need. But suppose it's a quarrelsome family, and each one comes to her daily asking, 'Why can't I have what *I* want? Why should my brothers and sisters always have it their way?' In the case of such a family, surely the mother would pray for one thing, and one thing only. She would ask God that her family might learn to love each other and be united. That would be far more important to the mother than that any of them should get what they'd asked for. Their quarrelling would wound the mother's loving heart; she'd feel as though she was being torn apart.

## The family of Christ

I've told that story about a mother, to make you think of it in human terms. Now I want you to apply it to Jesus, and his family the Christian Church. At the Last Supper Jesus prayed for his disciples, and then went on to pray for 'those who will believe in me through their word'. That's you and me. The Christian Church today is made up of Christians who believe in Jesus because of what the first disciples preached and wrote. That means that Jesus, like the loving mother in the story, prays every day to his Father for each one of us by name.

## A quarrelsome family

But wait! The Christian Church is a quarrelsome family. We argue about many things, some of them very important, some of them rather trivial. Sometimes we argue gently and politely, and sometimes with vindictive hatred in our hearts. There's a story about a priest, a minister and a rabbi having a discussion, and God asked each of them what he'd ask for if he had only one request. The priest immediately asked that every Protestant in his town might be destroyed, and the minister asked that there should be no more Catholics there. God turned to the rabbi and asked what he wanted. 'Nothing for myself,' answered the rabbi humbly, 'if you would just kindly deal with these two gentlemen's requests!'

## Denominations

Christians argued in the past over issues which seemed to them so important that they justified splitting the Church into different denominations. Some of those issues appear to us today to be theological matters of principle; with others, we find it hard to understand what the fuss was all about. But we're stuck with the aftermath, in that we're members of different denominations, and nobody seems to regard it as very urgent to overcome the divisions.

## The prayer of Jesus

Yet Jesus is praying for us. And what do you think he is asking the Father for? Is Jesus asking that Catholics, or Anglicans, or Methodists, or Evangelicals might have everything their own way? Is Jesus praying that any one of us should be proved to be entirely right, and all the others completely wrong? Is Jesus asking that we should all muddle along in our own part of his vineyard, and meet up once a year to say how nice it would be if we could co-operate on a few matters? If you think that's what Jesus is praying about, then you haven't understood the pain of the mother in the story I began with. No, Jesus told the disciples at the Last Supper what he'd be requesting for you and for me, when he prays for us. He said:

> I ask not only on behalf of these, but also on behalf of those who will believe in me through their word, that they may all be one. As you, Father, are in me and I am in you, may they also be in us, so that the world may believe that you have sent me.

Our quarrelling, rivalry and disunity all hurt the loving heart of Jesus more than anything else; he feels as though he's being torn apart – crucified afresh – by our failure to agree.

## Urgency

This means that the search for Christian unity is urgent – not because it would make life simpler for us, make us more efficient, and save money and time – no, because we're tearing Jesus apart every day by the lackadaisical way we approach the whole issue. For Christ's sake, let's get a sense of urgency!

### Suggested hymns

*A new commandment I give unto you; Bind us together, Lord; Jesus, stand among us; O thou, who at thy Eucharist didst pray.*

## Conversion of St Paul   25 January

**Paul's Priorities**   Jer. 1:4–10 The call of a prophet; Ps. 67 Let all the peoples praise you; Acts 9:1–22 Saul's conversion (*if the Acts reading is used instead of the Old Testament reading, the New Testament reading is* Gal. 1:11–16a Called me though his grace); Matt. 19:27–30 The reward of eternal life

> *'Immediately something like scales fell from [Saul's] eyes, and his sight was restored. Then he got up and was baptized.' Acts 9:18*

### Principles

A cynic said that when someone claims that they did what they did, not because of the money involved, but as a matter of principle, you can be sure it was the money that decided it! A Victorian humorist defined politics as a strife of interests masquerading as a contest of principles, and as 'the conduct of public affairs for private advantage'. That's because money occupies the prime place in most people's priorities. Money and admiration. It's unusual to find somebody for whom that's not so, even though we cover it up with fine words. But St Paul was one of those rare characters whose priorities were the exact opposite to those of most other people. Paul gloried in what he'd given up, rejoiced in what he'd relinquished, boasted of the blows he'd borne, was proudest of his pain, delighted in what he'd denied himself, and celebrated his sufferings. Each day he faced eagerly the dangers that confronted him, writing to his friends, 'I forget what's behind me and press on towards what lies ahead.' St Paul showed us what human beings can be, and should be if we really mean what we say.

## Scales fell from his eyes

It was, he said, as though his eyes had been covered in fish scales, and suddenly the scales fell from his eyes and he could see clearly. Not only was his physical blindness cured, but he could see what was important in life, and what's trivial. He radically reversed his basic principles of living, and saw for the first time that loving God and loving his neighbour for Christ's sake are far more important than obeying a set of rules and regulations about how you should live.

## A welcome for suffering

Paul regarded his sufferings as blessings, because they would strengthen his character. Whatever traps his enemies set him, he turned them into victories, and thanked God for the opportunity to make sacrifices for Christ's sake. He was glad when people abused him for preaching about love, for it showed that he'd successfully challenged their consciences. He preferred poverty to wealth; hard work to idleness; and contempt to honour. He had no dread of death, for he regarded it as the gateway to eternal life with the Master whom he loved. The one thing he feared was that he might let God down; his primary principle was that he wanted more than anything else to please the Almighty.

## To be loved

What motivated the Apostle, above all, was that he knew that God loved him. To be loved in this way made him, he thought, the happiest man alive, no matter how humble his position. He had no wish to be thought of as the friend of the great and famous; that was no substitute, to St Paul's mind, for the love of his Creator.

## Valuing attacks and death for Christ's sake

In St Paul's opinion, the wealth and renown which most people strive after is worth less than the dust in the streets. Those who thought he'd destroy their reputation for goodness tried to silence him. Rulers who were enraged by their fear that Paul would destabilize the Roman Empire attacked him. He shrugged off these annoyances as though they were unimportant insect bites. The pain and suffering which awaited him, and even his own death, St Paul thought were irrelevant, compared to his hope of sharing eternal life with his Saviour.

## Fight the good fight

We should praise St Paul for his courage, and praise God that he gave, to his servant the apostle, the strength to fight his battle until victory was won. But more important than praising Paul is to imitate him. We should make Paul's principles our own principles. We should be proud to bear suffering as he did, rejoicing that suffering gives us something to offer as a sacrifice to God. Suffering brings with it the same crown of glory that St Paul won for himself at the end of his long and adventurous life. The scales must fall from our own eyes, also, and we must make Paul's priorities our own.

### Suggested hymns

*Fight the good fight; Make way, make way for Christ the King; Onward, Christian soldiers; We sing the glorious conquest.*

# Presentation of Christ in the Temple (Candlemas)

2 February (*or may be observed on Sunday 31 January*)
**Open the Gates**    Mal. 3:1–5 The Lord shall come to his Temple; Ps. 24:[1–6] 7–10 Open the gates for the Lord; Heb. 2:14–18 Jesus became like the descendants of Abraham; Luke 2:22–40 The presentation of Christ in the Temple

> 'Lift up your heads, O gates; be lifted up, you everlasting doors; and the King of glory shall come in.' Psalm 24:7 (Common Worship)

## A procession

Imagine that you're in Jerusalem in the days when it was ruled by the kings of Judah. It's a hot day, and you've just toiled up the mountain road, at the head of a pilgrim procession, up the mountain road to the hilltop city, carrying on your shoulders one of the poles supporting the Ark of the Covenant. This is a wooden box containing two enormous stone tablets in it, the Ten Commandments engraved on them. On top of the box are two carved figures of winged cherubim. These make your load tall and top-heavy, so you're looking forward to putting your burden down at its destination in the Temple. Then you find the gates are shut!

## Annual ritual

Quite likely this procession was repeated every year, and the closing of the temple gates was part of the ritual, so that the Lord God had to ask permission to enter his own Temple. Picture an enormous gateway, shut off by a heavy wooden gate with three parts: one on the left, one on the right and one at the top. Most days only the two lower gates would be opened at dawn; but for the procession with its tall load, the top one would have to be swung open; probably pulled up, by a rope, on the hinges at the top edge. Those who carried the Ark of the Covenant have to give the password, just like any other visitors, to test whether they were friends or foes. So they sing out:

Lift up your heads, O gates;
be lifted up, you everlasting doors;
and the King of glory shall come in.

The priests who are inside then ask the test question:

Who is this King of glory you are talking about?

Those waiting outside make the answer:

The Lord, strong and mighty,
the Lord who is mighty in battle.

But it's the wrong answer, and the gates remain resolutely shut. So they try again:

Lift up your heads, O gates;
be lifted up, you everlasting doors;
and the King of glory shall come in.

The priests inside ask the same question:

Who is this King of glory?

The people in the procession make the correct answer this time:

> The Lord of hosts,
> he is the King of glory.

The top panel of the gate is hauled up, and the procession with the Ark, the symbol of the presence of God, on their shoulders, can pass through at last and take their God into his own house.

## The Presentation

The Ark of the Covenant was only a symbol of God's presence among his people. But Jesus was the Word of God made flesh, and when he was brought to Jerusalem at the tender age of 40 days old, God really was entering his Temple. Yet, just as the Lord of hosts humbly asked permission to be admitted to his own dwelling-place, so the Son of God came to the Temple as a humble and powerless baby. Furthermore, he had to pay for his life. At the Exodus, when Moses led the Israelites out of Egypt, and all the first-born of the Egyptians died, God's people paid for the angel of death to pass over their homes with the sacrifice of the Passover Lamb. For ever after, the oldest male offspring of humans and animals belonged to God; first-born animals were sacrificed, but a human family could buy back their oldest son from God at the cost of a sheep, or in the case of a poor family two pigeons. So God spared the life of his own Son at the cost of two young doves; later the Son would willingly sacrifice his own life to his Father to set you and me free from death.

## Symbolism

So the symbolism of this day shows us the humility of God, who asks permission to enter his own home, and then eventually enters as a newborn baby. Birth and death are linked together in the life-giving sacrifice. Ceremonial, ritual and poetry combine to show us Christ, the Light of the World, who's willing humbly to sacrifice his own life that we may live, and wants to make his home in our hearts. But he won't come in until we give him permission to enter and rule our lives. Have you given Jesus permission yet to enter the temple of your heart and set up his throne there?

## Suggested hymns

*Hail to the Lord who comes; Lift up your heads, you mighty gates; Thou didst leave thy throne and thy kingly crown; Ye who own the faith of Jesus.*

## St David, Bishop of Menevia, Patron of Wales
## c. 601   1 March
**The Celtic Fringe**   Ecclus. 15:1–6 Whoever holds to the law will obtain wisdom; Ps. 16:1–7 I have a goodly heritage; 1 Thess. 2:2–12 Entrusted with the gospel; Matt. 16:24–27 Take up your cross

> *'My share has fallen in a fair land; indeed, I have a goodly heritage.' Psalm 16:5 (Common Worship)*

### Genetic research

According to the latest scientific research, it appears the earliest human beings came from Africa, and developed fair skin in Europe because they no longer needed protecting from the intense African sun. A pale skin was a benefit, because they were able to produce more vitamin D and avoid rickets. During the last Ice Age the Europeans wisely retreated to Spain and the south of France, but some fifteen thousand years ago, before the English Channel was formed, a few hundred hunter-gatherers crossed the land bridge into the peninsula which later became Britain. The earliest fossil skeleton of these people is the so-called 'Red Lady' in a cave in the Gower Peninsula. These Ancient Britons were the earliest inhabitants, and most British people today are descended in part from them. Professor Sir Walter Bodmer, one of the scientists involved in the mapping of the human genome, has done a statistical analysis of the genetic makeup of people from different areas in the British Isles, showing that people from West Wales, Devon and Cornwall, Ireland and Scotland are most likely to have a high proportion of the genes associated with these original 'Ancient Brits'. Much later, only about six thousand years ago, a great cultural change came over these people. No longer hunter-gatherers, they learnt to farm. The new skills swept across Europe from the Middle East, though there was little movement of population or change in genetic makeup. With the spades and ploughs, however, came another vital tool: the development of language necessary when learning to farm in fixed settlements. It was spoken all over Europe, with local differences; because the Romans first came across it in Gaul, they called it the Gallic language. The Welsh language, of course, as spoken by St David, is one of its branches.

## Celtic

You notice that I haven't used the word 'Celtic'. Neither did the Romans: they referred to them by the name of their tribe, or in general as the Britons. Celtic was a Greek word, describing inland tribes who weren't influenced by Greek culture; but there was never a Celtic empire. It's good to use the word Celtic to describe a group of languages and cultural traditions, but there was no 'Celtic people', genetically distinguishable from the rest of the population of Europe.

## Anglo-Saxons

When the Romans withdrew from Britain, in the fifth century AD, the power vacuum was filled with people coming from Germany and Holland, whom we call the Anglo-Saxons. They landed on the East coast of England, whence their language and genetic inheritance gradually spread westwards. There were many local skirmishes, but no great military campaign. The influence of the Anglo-Saxon language hardly reached the remoter parts of these islands, which kept their Celtic culture. Genetically, the people of East Anglia are most likely to have inherited the Anglo-Saxon genes; with Northumbria, Kent and Sussex about 70 per cent more likely to have predominantly Saxon genes; but surprisingly, people from Oxfordshire are about 51 per cent more likely to have the blood of the Ancient Britons running in their veins. So there was no genocide, and no clear boundary, just a gradual spreading of Anglo-Saxon influence.

## Celebrating

It's a strange topic to discuss in a sermon, but I think it's important to clarify just what we're celebrating on St David's Day. *Dewi Sant* was an outstanding orator in the Welsh-Celtic language. He brought much of the ancient British culture into Welsh Christian life, with its sense of oneness with nature and its magnificent artistic gifts. Welsh people share this heritage with the Irish and Scots people, so that we can sing with the Psalmist, 'My share has fallen in a fair land; indeed, I have a goodly heritage.' The fashion arose in the eighteenth century of referring to Wales, Scotland and Ireland as the 'Celtic Fringe'. About 21 per cent of the people of Wales speak Welsh, 41 per cent in Ireland speak Gaelic, but only 2 per cent in Scotland. Celtic art originated in southern Germany in the fifth century BC; the great flowering of Welsh literature dates from the epic poem *Taliesin* in the sixth century AD, and the prose tales of the *Mabinogion* in the twelfth century fused the legends of King Arthur with local stories. Welsh Christianity can be traced back to St David in the sixth century, and so can Welsh enthusiasm in preaching and singing, probably. These are the things we must celebrate and thank God for on St David's day.

### Hymns with Welsh tunes

*Alleluia, sing to Jesus; Guide me, O thou great Redeemer; Jesu, lover of my soul; King of Glory, King of peace.*

# St Patrick, Bishop, Missionary, Patron of Ireland
## c. 460  17 March
**Without Loss of Life**   Deut. 32:1–9 May my teaching drop like the rain; *or* Tob. 13:1b–7 In the land of my exile; Ps. 145:12–13 Make known to all peoples; 2 Cor. 4:1–12 This ministry; Matt. 10:16–23 Warnings for missionaries; *or* John 4:31–38 Ripe for harvest

> *'[Jesus said,] "I am sending you out like sheep into the midst of wolves; so be wise as serpents and innocent as doves."' Matthew 10:16*

### Without loss of life

St Patrick converted the whole of Ireland to Christianity without loss of life. That's remarkable. Christianity's a religion of peace, but when it starts making new converts, the result's very often war and strife. There are all sorts of reasons which account for this. Partly it's due to the controversial nature of the Christian message.

It elevates the underdogs and gives them a position of importance in God's plan of things.

> The vilest offender who truly believes,
> that moment from Jesus a pardon receives.

That's good news for the offenders, but very offensive to the wicked who have to give way to them. So the spread of Christianity's often met with resistance from the rich and powerful, from the wicked who don't like their sinfulness shown up by the virtues of the new converts, and the priests of the old religions who see with dismay their adherents slipping away from them and joining the flock of Christ. Somehow, Patrick managed to calm this opposition from the opponents of Christianity when it arose.

## Colonialism

Sometimes, however, violence and resentment emerge because of those who claim to be Christianity's supporters. Historically, traders have come into a new nation from abroad, hoping simply to buy and sell, making a profit for themselves and a way for local people to earn their living. But they can't trade if the tribes are warring against each other, so they send for troops to defend them, and the soldiers put colonial governors in control. Then, in the new safer environment, the missionaries bring the good news of the Prince of Peace. But even though it means they can live at peace, people won't willingly surrender their freedom by becoming colonial subjects. So the newly colonized people rise in revolt, and the colonists stamp on the uprising. The missionaries are associated in people's minds with the colonists, and they, too, become the objects of popular anger. Thank God there was no colonial power in Ireland at that time to besmirch St Patrick's reputation.

## Culture

A third reason for violence accompanying the Christian message is if there's a conflict of cultures. In some cases missionaries deliberately set aside their home culture, and start learning the way of life and thought of the local people, exploring new ways of expressing the unchanging Christian message in terms of the local culture. In some places, missionaries actually kept alive a local culture which was on the verge of extinction. But some were not so wise, and taught that the way of life in the countries they came from was superior to that of the nation whose guests they were. Such insensitivity naturally arouses resentment. But the converts themselves, seeing that the missionaries' home country was richer than theirs, clamoured to adopt the culture of the foreigners, in the hopes of sharing their prosperity. Then you get a clash of cultures, with people hating the new ways yet strongly tempted to adopt them. Fortunately St Patrick was from the same cultural background as the people to whom he preached, for he came from somewhere on the western coast of Britain. In those days a single culture was shared by all the original inhabitants of Europe, and it was this which Patrick used as a vehicle for spreading the new Christian gospel. He could read and write in Latin, of course, which was not common in Ireland then, but any suggestion that he trained in Gaul and visited Rome comes from a much later tradition. Under his guidance, a distinctively Irish version of Christianity grew up, and Irish monks founded some of the most important monasteries in Europe.

## Peacemaker

Patrick avoided the clashes that come with resentment of social change, of colonialism and of conflicting cultures. But the peaceful spread of the gospel in Ireland came mainly from his own character, 'wise as a serpent, innocent as a dove'. He was a peacemaker and reconciler, and dealt tactfully with new tribes and their chieftains. So Ireland was converted without the loss of a single life. If only we could be as irenic today in the way we proclaim the good news of Jesus, the Prince of Peace. Where Christianity's associated with resentment at loss of power, or at a colonial legacy, or at changing cultures, then you can be sure that the false gospel which is being proclaimed is not the peace-loving gospel which Patrick the peacemaker himself preached.

### Suggested hymns

*Be thou my vision; God is working his purpose out; I bind unto myself this day; To God be the glory.*

# St Joseph of Nazareth   19 March
## Cuckolded?   2 Sam. 7:4–16 Descendants of David; Ps.
89:26–36 David's line; Rom. 4:13–18 Abraham's descendants;
Matt. 1:18–25 Joseph's dream

> *'Joseph, being a righteous man and unwilling to expose [Mary] to
> public disgrace, planned to dismiss her quietly.' Matthew 1:19*

## Betrothal

Joseph of Nazareth was a remarkable man, but he was human.
He was betrothed to his fiancée Mary. Betrothal was a stronger
bond than engagement is today. An engagement can be broken,
and although it's sad when this happens, many people will say it's
for the best: better to find out that you don't get on before you're
married than afterwards. But in the Old Testament betrothal's a
legally binding bond. In the twenty-second chapter of Deuteronomy
it's laid down by law that

> If there is a young woman, a virgin already engaged to be mar-
> ried, and a man meets her . . . and lies with her, you shall bring
> both of them to the gate of that town and stone them to death,
> the young woman because she did not cry for help . . . and the
> man because he violated his neighbour's wife.

It's a good thing we don't have to apply the laws of the Old Testament literally today, or there'd be frequent public stonings. So if
Mary was betrothed to Joseph, and he wasn't the father of the baby
she was expecting, then he was not only permitted but expected to
accuse her publicly and take the lead in stoning to death both her
and the man she'd been unfaithful to him with. Until the angel came
to him, Joseph assumed that some other man was the begetter of
Mary's unborn child. The dilemma he was in wasn't an easy one to
solve, for he didn't know who'd cheated him.

## Cuckolded?

In medieval Europe there was a great deal of ribald humour at the
expense of husbands who had kept so loose a watch on their wives,
or their betrothed, that some other man had stolen a march on
them. They were called 'cuckolds', a word you seldom hear these
days. It comes from the bird called the cuckoo, which as you know

lays its egg in another bird's nest, so that the unsuspecting host can feed and rear its chick for it. The situation's not the same, but a man was described as cuckolded if he was not the father of the child of the wife he was married to. If that sounds complicated, it's because I'm trying not to make any comparisons with contemporary marriage; but I think you know what I mean. So in the medieval mystery plays, when Bible stories were acted in church or on carts around the town, there was usually a comic scene in which Joseph is certain he's been cuckolded. Shakespeare also makes bawdy jokes about men wearing horns, which was the symbolic description of a cuckold.

## Quiet divorce

There was one way open to Joseph. Jewish men could divorce their wives, though a wife couldn't divorce her husband. If Joseph divorced Mary quietly, people might forget that she was an adulteress, he thought, and that might be the best for both of them. St Matthew's Gospel tells us:

> When . . . Mary had been engaged to Joseph, but before they lived together, she was found to be with child . . . Her husband Joseph, being a righteous man and unwilling to expose her to public disgrace, planned to dismiss her quietly. But just when he had resolved to do this, an angel of the Lord appeared to him in a dream and said, 'Joseph, son of David, do not be afraid to take Mary as your wife, for the child conceived in her is from the Holy Spirit . . .' When Joseph awoke from sleep, he did as the angel of the Lord commanded him; he took her as his wife, but had no marital relations with her until she had borne a son.

## A good man

What a good man he was! He didn't know for sure, but he suspected that Mary would be disgraced when people found out what she'd done. So he contemplated a quiet divorce, to spare her that. When he found out what had really happened, he waited till after the baby was born, and then he married her. He had no need to, but if there was to be any shame he wanted to share it with her. Christians disagree as to whether he had what are quaintly called 'marital relations' with her after they were married, but what's beyond all doubt is that he loved her very much, and wanted to do the best thing for her. So although his dilemma was absolutely unique, we can respect him as a loving husband, and try to follow his example of caring tenderly for those who find themselves pilloried by people who ought to know better.

### Suggested hymns

*As Joseph was a-walking; Brother, sister, let me serve you; Joseph dearest, Joseph mine; Lord of the home, your only Son.*


## Annunciation of Our Lord to the Blessed Virgin Mary   25 March
**Nothing's Impossible**   Isa. 7:10–14 The sign of Immanuel; Ps. 40:5–11 I love to do your will; Heb. 10:4–10 I have come to do your will; Luke 1:26–38 The angel's message

*'Nothing will be impossible with God.' Luke 1:37*


### Annunciation

An angel appeared to the Virgin Mary and told her she was going to have a baby. That's impossible, she protested. The angel replied, 'Nothing will be impossible with God.'


### Scientists

Lord Kelvin, when he was president of the Royal Society in 1895, stated that 'Heavier-than-air flying machines are impossible.' Which only goes to show the truth of the remark by Arthur C. Clarke, who wrote, 'When a distinguished but elderly scientist states that something is possible he is almost certainly right. When he states that something is impossible, he is very probably wrong.' The trouble is that science isn't designed to tell us what is and what isn't possible. All science can do is to say, 'We haven't observed such-and-such to happen – yet!'


### Relativity

For instance, when the apple fell on Isaac Newton's head, he suggested as a hypothesis that 'Between any two objects there is an attraction proportional to the product of their masses and inversely proportional to the square of their distance apart.' Such a simple explanation seemed impossible, so Newton did some calculations from which, if it were true, he could predict the distance of the moon from the earth. They didn't work out right, so he put the papers propounding his hypothesis away in a drawer. Years later, more accurate measurements were made, and his suggestion was vindicated – it was universally accepted as the law of gravity. Then Einstein did calculations based on the movements of the planets that couldn't be predicted under Newton's theory. The theory wasn't abandoned, but modified by the law of relativity: you have to take into account the velocity of two objects relative to each other when calculating their mass. Again and again in the history of science, scientists have had to revise their theories in the light of new evidence.

## Nothing's impossible to God

So the most that a scientist could say to the Virgin Mary is, 'Well, my dear, we've never observed a virgin give birth to a baby. But who's to say there may not be new evidence which will make us revise our theories?' The Archangel Gabriel put it more simply, when he said, 'Nothing will be impossible with God.' The laws of science are not regulations forbidding God from doing what he wishes; they're observations of how we have so far observed God to work in carefully controlled laboratory conditions. But God can always surprise us.

## The impossible

There's a slogan in the US Army: 'The difficult we do immediately; the impossible takes a little longer.' By humour, it hopes to challenge the soldiers to imaginative thinking that'll find a way around their problems. We would all do well to cross the word impossible out of our dictionaries. Then we might look again at things which other people tell us are impossible, and have a go at them all the same. There's something of that grit and determination in the Virgin Mary's reply to the angel: 'Here am I, the servant of the Lord; let it be with me according to your word.' In other words, if you say God can do it, I'm willing to do all I can to co-operate. This is the other side of the coin from the rather insipid pictures we usually see of the Blessed Virgin. And it's a lesson to all of us.

309

## Loving your neighbour

For instance, the comedian John Cleese was reported in *The Times* as saying, 'Loving your neighbour as much as yourself is practically . . . impossible . . . You might as well have a commandment that states, "Thou shalt fly".' Quite. The Sermon on the Mount is full of commandments to do impossible things. That's how Jesus works. He tells you that God requires of you impossible standards of love and virtue, which drives you into despair. You know you couldn't do it on your own. Good – at last you've realized your need of God. Even loving your neighbour's possible if you ask God to help you. So that little dialogue which Mary had with the archangel's important to us every day of our lives. God commands you to do the impossible. Don't worry if a scientist tells you it's humanly impossible to achieve such high standards: have a go, like Mary did. 'Dream the impossible dream.' You may never quite reach your target; but you'll arrive a lot closer to it than you would have if you'd never made the attempt. Remember: 'Nothing will be impossible with God.' Nothing's impossible for you, either, if you have the power of God's Holy Spirit in your fuel tank.

### Suggested hymns

*For Mary, Mother of our Lord; Her Virgin eyes saw God incarnate born; Sing we of the blessed Mother; The angel Gabriel from heaven came.*

# St George, Martyr, Patron of England *c.* 304
## 23 April
**Myths and Heroes**    1 Macc. 2:59–64 Be courageous, *or* Rev. 12:7–12 Michael fights the dragon; Ps. 126 Restore our fortunes; 2 Tim. 2:3–13 A soldier of Christ; John 15:18–21 They will persecute you

> *'War broke out in heaven; Michael and his angels fought against the dragon.' Revelation 12:7*

### St George

St George was a Christian who was martyred in the third or fourth century AD, in the town known in the Bible as Lydda, and which has now given its name to Lod airport, the major air terminus in Israel. Nothing else is known about him; as early as the sixth century he was described as a good man 'whose deeds are known only to God'. Yet he was soon widely venerated in that area, and still is today. A few churches in England and Ireland were dedicated to St George well before the Norman Conquest. Not until the late Middle Ages, however, do we find the rest of the well-known story. In the popular book called *The Golden Legend*, George was said to have been a soldier from Cappadocia, in what's now Turkey, who rescued a virgin princess from a dragon at Silene in Libya. Soldiers from England who went to the Middle East to fight in the crusades found that St George was a popular saint, prayed to by Muslims as well as Christians. His emblem of the red cross on the white background was used as an ensign by soldiers as they went into battle, and George, together with another soldier-saint, St Demetrius of Thessalonica, was given the credit for the success of the attack on Antioch. When King Edward III founded the chivalric Order of the Garter with George as its patron saint, meeting in the chapel of St George's, Windsor, the popularity of the saint spread until he supplanted St Alban as England's patron saint. And yet, embarrassingly, nothing is known about him except the place where he was martyred. The story of the dragon's entirely legendary; yet that may be no bad thing.

## Perseus

You see, everybody needs a hero. Not far from Lydda is the port of Joppa, later known as Jaffa, and now a suburb of the metropolis of Tel Aviv–Yafo. There, according to Greek myth, the hero Perseus rescued a maiden called Andromeda from the sea monster known as the Kraken. Andromeda's rock, to which she was tied to await her fate, still stands at the mouth of Yafo harbour. But the power of the Greek myths is still seen in the number of modern books, plays and films which are based on their stories. Everybody likes a good yarn, and especially in the days when few people could read, the legends, often in poetic form, which were recited around the campfire and passed down by word of mouth from generation to generation, filled the place which is now occupied by the soap operas. Because it's from fiction that most people develop their attitude to life, and their view of what's good and what's bad behaviour. The heroes were the role models. No matter that in real life nobody's perfect, human nature needs someone to look up to, and to pattern our own lives on. The stories of the Greek heroes, even when they were based on historical people, provided the people of the Roman Empire with myths and legends which they could inflate into impossible novellas, and use as patterns for daily living. The myth of Perseus, Andromeda and the Kraken taught generations about the importance of men defending their women folk against evil attacks.

## Christianity

Then came Christianity and spoilt it all. The priests told the people that the gods of Olympus didn't exist, and so couldn't be worshipped; and with them the heroes and heroines were proscribed as well. Where were the people to turn to for role models? Why, to the Christian saints, of course. But the yarn of Perseus of Joppa was too good to lose, so he was moved a few miles up the road and became George of Lydda. George certainly existed, but the dragon never did. Yet the same lessons of chivalrous behaviour can be learnt from St George as had been previously learnt from Perseus. Whatever you think of the need for maidenly modesty in the twenty-first century, the need to care bravely for those we love and defend them from all evil is as valid and important today as it ever was. So all honour to St George, about whom we know so little, but who's so important in showing us the virtues of courage and care; and destruction to all the evil dragons of the twenty-first century, no matter what form they take. Everybody needs heroes and heroines, role models and examples of virtue. So, until the day when a better one comes along, the part-fact, part-fiction story of St George is good enough for me.

### Suggested hymns

*And did those feet in ancient time; I vow to thee, my country; O God of earth and altar; When a knight won his spurs.*

## St Mark the Evangelist   25 April
(See Fourth Sunday of Easter, page 132.)

# SS Philip and James, Apostles   1 May

**No Indispensable Man**   Isa. 30:15–21 This is the way; Ps. 119:1–8 The way of the Lord; Eph. 1:3–10 The mystery of forgiveness; John 14:1–14 Show us the Father (I am the way)

*'Philip said to [Jesus], "Lord, show us the Father, and we will be satisfied." Jesus said to him, "Have I been with you all this time, Philip, and you still do not know me? Whoever has seen me has seen the Father. How can you say, 'Show us the Father'?"' John 14:8–9*

## The apostles

The apostles were so full of themselves. Wrangling over who should have the most important seats at the Last Supper, and who'd be Jesus's right-hand-man in the kingdom of God. Philip even challenged Jesus with a question to which he perfectly well knew there was no answer, to show that he was smarter than all of the rest. 'Show us the Father,' he asked, 'then we'll believe you.' The Scriptures told him that nobody can see God and live; he didn't really imagine that Jesus could present him with God on a plate; he just wanted to prove how clever he was. Philip, the great know-it-all. And Little James, or James the Less as he's called to distinguish him from James the brother of John and son of Zebedee. If this James, the son of Alpheus, got his nickname because he was small in stature, perhaps he'd learnt that little people get overlooked unless they speak up for themselves, and had become cocky with it. The apostles all needed taking down a peg.

## Us

But let's not be too hard on them. After all, it's a common human characteristic to have a big opinion of yourself. To some extent it's a good thing; we perform better if we're confident. But taken to extremes, self-confidence becomes egotism, and that's a menace. Yet we all love an ego trip. We just know that we're more intelligent than the others, more skilled at doing useful things, more talented in each of the arts, and it's amazing how other people never recognize our genius. Of course, I'm not referring to you when I say this, but to all the conceited people around you. Perhaps.

## A TV play

A play written for television concerned a retired man, who went back to his workplace a couple of years later to see how they were getting along without him. He'd designed a form, which he was particularly proud of. By showing them how to complete this form regularly, he'd eliminated many of the problems which prevented the organization operating smoothly. 'Are things still going smoothly?' he asked them. 'Oh yes,' they answered. 'So you're regularly filling in form Z47,' he continued. 'Form which?' they asked in astonishment. Not only were they not filling it in; most of them had never even heard of it.

## Leaf by Niggle

J. R. R. Tolkien, the author of *The Lord of the Rings*, wrote a short story about an artist called Niggle. Niggle had painted many huge canvasses, which he was sure would make his memory live for ever. One night he dreamt that all his paintings had been destroyed in a fire, except for one small scrap of canvas. Heartbroken that there was no record of his life's work to ensure his immortality, he visited, in his dream, a great art gallery where a large crowd had gathered excitedly round a small framed painting on the wall. Pushing to the front, he saw that it was the surviving scrap of his life's work, showing only one leaf from a tree. The painting was called *Leaf, by Niggle*. He was remembered, not for his great master-works, but for the care and attention which he'd lavished onto painting this one leaf. It's so easy to be proud of our great schemes. But God cares much more about the little things, our love for our family, our care for some needy but insignificant soul.

## A poem

So I finish with an anonymous poem. It's not great poetry, and it dates from the politically incorrect days when people wrote 'man' when they meant 'person'. But it proclaims a truth which could have been heard to advantage by Philip or James or any of the other apostles. Maybe it'd be good if we also paid it some attention. It goes like this:

Take a bucket and fill it with water,
Put your hands in it up to the wrist;

Pull them out – and the hole that's remaining
Is the measure of how you'll be missed.

You may splash all you please when you enter,
You may stir up the water galore,
But stop; and you'll find in a minute
That it looks just the same as before.

The moral of this is quite simple;
Do just the best that you can,
Be proud of yourself, but remember
There is no Indispensable Man.

### Suggested hymns

*O for a heart to praise my God; Teach me, my God and King; Thou art the Way, by thee alone; To God be the glory.*

## St Matthias the Apostle   14 May

**Suicide**   Isa. 22:15–25 Eliakim replaces Shebna; Ps. 15 Who shall dwell in your house?; Acts 1:15–26 Mathias replaces Judas (*if the Acts reading is used instead of the Old Testament reading, the New Testament reading is* 1 Cor. 4:1–7 Stewards of God's mysteries); John 15:9–17 I have appointed you

> '[St Peter said,] "Friends, the scripture had to be fulfilled, which the Holy Spirit through David foretold concerning Judas, who became a guide for those who arrested Jesus – for he was numbered among us and was allotted his share in this ministry." (Now this man acquired a field with the reward of his wickedness; and falling headlong, he burst open in the middle and all his bowels gushed out.)' Acts 1:16–18

### The sin of Judas

Today we remember St Matthias, who was appointed to bring the number of the apostles up to twelve again, now that Judas was no longer among them. But let's also think about Judas. The sin of Judas was not just that he betrayed Jesus – that could have been forgiven. Jesus would have offered forgiveness even to Judas, if

Judas had come to him. No, the thing that prevented Judas from accepting forgiveness was that he didn't believe he was forgivable. In his despair, he didn't even consider turning to God in penitence. He still hadn't learnt the message which Jesus taught in so many parables, that our heavenly Father's waiting in love to welcome back his prodigal children, no matter what they've done.

## Seeking help

The first thing somebody should do if they're feeling depressed is ask for help. The number of the Samaritans is easy to remember: 0845 7 90 90 90. But before they're ready to do that, people may express their suicidal thoughts and feelings to friends or family. It can be frightening and confusing if somebody close to you shows signs of depression. Here's some advice from mental health professionals.

## Recognizing symptoms

The first thing is to be able to recognize the symptoms of depression. Someone who's feeling suicidal may speak about their feelings of hopelessness. They may stop looking after themselves, stop eating or taking care over their appearance. They may have problems sleeping, and become very withdrawn. They may or may not talk about suicide. The old myth that someone who talks about suicide won't go through with it just isn't true. Take it seriously if you recognize these signs, and be sympathetic without kicking up an unnecessary fuss.

## Encourage them to talk

The first thing to do if you want to help someone is to encourage them to talk. Take what they say seriously, and ask them leading questions about their feelings. If they ask you questions, don't feel you have to answer them; they may not really want advice, and might not take it if it were offered. Reflect the question back at them – 'What do you feel about that?' – and encourage them to find their own answers. Don't dismiss feelings of hopelessness as 'a cry for help'. Some people imagine that just talking about suicide makes it more likely, but the opposite's the case: just listening to somebody patiently and 'being there for them' can help them to feel less scared and isolated.

## Persuade them to seek help

Then persuade them to seek help. Suggest that they contact their GP, or organizations such as the Samaritans, Saneline, Mindinfo-Line, NHS Direct, Cruse for bereaved people, or CALM for men aged 15–35. I've put a list of phone numbers on the noticeboard. Help people liable to depression to make their own list of phone numbers and addresses of people and organizations to call, and keep it by them.

## Address underlying problems

Finally, address the underlying problems. Even when you've got through the crisis, the reason for the suicidal feelings may still be there. So it's important to help the depressed person to seek support and help for these problems, so that they can make some progress at least towards solving them before the suicidal feelings return.

## Look after yourself

But there's one more thing the experts recommend to those who want to help: look after yourself. Helping someone who's depressed may make you feel angry, frustrated, guilty and under enormous pressure. You, the helper, need someone to talk to. Build your own support group, speaking to friends or family, or contact the Carers National Association Help Line. And remember, Jesus has promised that the Holy Spirit will always give you the words to say if you ask him. If only some of the people around Judas had known all this, St Matthias might never have needed to step into his shoes.

### *Suggested hymns*

*All ye who seek for sure relief; Jesu, lover of my soul; Lord Jesus, think on me; O for a closer walk with God.*

☎ **CONFIDENTIAL CONTACT DETAILS FOR THOSE WHO NEED HELP AND THOSE WHO OFFER IT IN THE UK. See <www.helplines.org.uk>.**

**Samaritans** 0845 7 90 90 90. 24 hours, 7 days a week, for anyone in crisis. See *The Phone Book* for the local office.

**Saneline** 0845 767 8000. 12 noon until 2 a.m. daily, for anyone experiencing mental health problems.

**Chinese Wah Sum** Helpline 0845 122 8660.

**NHS Direct** 0845 46 47. 24-hour health helpline – multilingual.

**Cruse National Helpline** 0870 167 1677. For anyone who has been bereaved.

**Child Death Helpline** 0800 282986. For anyone affected by the death of a child.

**CALM** 0800 58 58 58. Daily 5 p.m. to 3 a.m. Confidential helpline for men aged from 15–35.

**MindinfoLine** 0845 766 0163. Monday to Friday 9.15 a.m. to 5.15 p.m. The Mental health charity. Deaf or speech-impaired enquirers can use this number, or with BT Textdirect add the prefix 18001.

**Childline** 0800 1111. Helpline for children and young people to age 18.

**NSPCC Child Protection Helpline** 0808 800 5000. Freetext 18001 0800 056 0566. 24-hour helpline for children and young people or anyone concerned about a child or young person at risk of abuse.

**Carers National Association Help Line** 0808 808 7777. Wednesdays and Thursdays 10–12 a.m., 2–4 p.m. Support for those who care for others.

**Parentline Plus** 0808 800 2222. Support and information for parents and anyone in a parenting role.

318

# Visit of the Blessed Virgin Mary to Elizabeth

31 May

**The Music Makers**   Zeph. 3:14–18 Sing, daughter Zion; Ps. 113 Making her a joyous mother; Rom. 12:9–16 Hospitality; Luke 1:39–49 [50–56] Magnificat

*'Sing aloud, O daughter Zion!' Zephaniah 3:14*


## Magnificat

The Blessed Virgin Mary visited her older cousin Elizabeth when they were both pregnant, and then sang a remarkable song beginning, 'My soul magnifies the Lord', which we call the Magnificat. She must have been a truly unusual woman. Today her song would be banned as dangerously revolutionary, with its talk of throwing down the mighty from their thrones, and replacing them with the humble and meek. But Mary's poem's had more influence on the subsequent history of the world than any other poem in ancient literature. The Magnificat encourages the oppressed to stand up for themselves, and has been the indirect cause of many a tyrant's downfall. But we shouldn't be surprised at the effect Mary's song has had, because art and music can bring about change which political rhetoric totally fails to shift. This is pointed out in a Victorian poem called 'The Music Makers', one line of which everybody knows, about 'movers and shakers'.


## Arthur O'Shaughnessy and Sir Edward Elgar

'The Music Makers' comes from *Music and Moonlight*, a collection of poems by Arthur O'Shaughnessy. He lived from 1844 to 1881, and was employed in the library of the British Museum. In his poem, he argues that it's the artists and musicians who bring about changes in history. Sir Edward Elgar set it to haunting and beautiful music for choir, orchestra and mezzo-soprano soloist in 1912, full of quotations from his own compositions, from *Nimrod* to *The Dream of Gerontius*. Listen to the poem now, and think about the changes which Mary wrought in human thinking with her revolutionary poem.

We are the music-makers,
And we are the dreamers of dreams,

Wandering by lone sea-breakers,
And sitting by desolate streams;
World-losers and world-forsakers,
On whom the pale moon gleams:
Yet we are the movers and shakers
Of the world for ever, it seems.

With wonderful deathless ditties
We build up the world's great cities,
And out of a fabulous story
We fashion an empire's glory:
One man with a dream, at pleasure,
Shall go forth and conquer a crown;
And three with a new song's measure
Can trample a kingdom down.

We, in the ages lying
In the buried past of the earth,
Built Nineveh with our sighing,
And Babel itself in our mirth;
And o'erthrew them with prophesying
To the old of the new world's worth;
For each age is a dream that is dying,
Or one that is coming to birth.

A breath of our inspiration
Is the life of each generation;
A wondrous thing of our dreaming,
Unearthly, impossible seeming . . .
The soldier, the king, and the peasant
Are working together in one,
Till our dream shall become their present,
And their work in the world be done.

They had no vision amazing
Of the goodly house they are raising;
They had no divine foreshowing
Of the land to which they are going:
But on one man's soul it hath broken,
A light that doth not depart;
And his look, or a word he hath spoken,
Wrought flame in another man's heart.

And therefore to-day is thrilling
With a past day's late fulfilling;
And the multitudes are enlisted
In the faith that their fathers resisted,
And, scorning the dream of tomorrow,
Are bringing to pass, as they may,
In the world, for its joy or its sorrow,
The dream that was scorned yesterday.

But we, with our dreaming and singing,
Ceaseless and sorrowless we!
The glory about us clinging
Of the glorious futures we see,
Our souls with high music ringing;
O men! It must ever be
That we dwell in our dreaming and singing,
A little apart from ye.

For we are afar with the dawning
And the suns that are not yet high,
And out of the infinite morning
Intrepid you hear us cry . . .
How, spite of your human scorning,
Once more God's future draws nigh,
And already goes forth the warning
That ye of the past must die.

Great hail! we cry to the comers
From the dazzling unknown shore;
Bring us hither your sun and your summers;
And renew our world as of yore;
You shall teach us your song's new numbers,
And things that we dreamed not before:
Yea, in spite of a dreamer who slumbers,
And a singer who sings no more.

## Conclusion

Well, the Blessed Virgin Mary sings no more on earth, though
I've no doubt she's singing in heaven. But I thought you'd like me
to read that poem in full for her, to remind us what an influence
she has had down the ages with just one revolutionary poem, the
Magnificat.

**Suggested hymns**

*Eternal Ruler of the ceaseless round; How shall I sing that majesty?; Tell out, my soul; The spacious firmament on high.*

# Day of Thanksgiving for the Institution of Holy Communion (Corpus Christi)   3 June

**The Banknote**   Gen. 14:18–20 Melchizedek brought bread and wine; Ps. 116:10–17 The cup of salvation; 1 Cor. 11:23–26 The Last Supper; John 6:51–58 Living bread

> *'[Jesus said,] "Those who eat my flesh and drink my blood have eternal life, and I will raise them up on the last day."' John 6:54*

## The Banknote

In a secure printing works, some words and printing are being applied to a piece of paper. It's only paper with printing on it; but in fact it's a banknote. The materials from which it's made are probably worth a few pence at the most. But the writing says that it's a 20-pound note. Its cost hasn't altered, but now it has a value far beyond the cost of materials and labour. That's because our representatives in Parliament, and through them, you and I, have agreed that this paper shall be equivalent in value to 20 pound coins. It is our words which have given the paper its value. The material hasn't changed, but the worth of it has, through our words.

## The Blessed Sacrament

In this way, the banknote's like the bread and wine in Holy Communion. Without going into a complicated discussion about what Jesus actually meant, there's no disputing that his words gave to ordinary bread and wine a worth far exceeding their material value. It's the value that counts: the meaning that Jesus put upon the bread and wine, and that we put on it when we receive it into our mouths. The bread and wine have no value without the words of Jesus; the words of Jesus have no value until we recognize what they mean.

## Humanity

Most people would agree that the words of Jesus were symbolic. He talks about eating his flesh; the literal meaning would be appalling, so this must be a symbol of something. In his letters, St John insists that Jesus has come 'in the flesh': 'By this you know the Spirit of God: every spirit that confesses that Jesus Christ has come in the flesh is from God.' Here, 'flesh' is obviously symbolic language for the humanity of Jesus. Jesus was not just a god dressed up as a human being; he actually became completely human. This means that he faced our human problems, struggled against human temptations, and worked out human relationships, just like you and me. What we need to do is to take that into ourselves, internalize this knowledge. Jesus understands us, even when we're at our lowest, because he's been there himself.

## Life

The Jews said that blood represents life: when blood is flowing through an animal, that animal's alive; when the blood's drained out of it, it's dead. So Jesus, telling us to drink his blood, doesn't mean it literally; he means we take his life into ourselves. Imagine a book on the shelf; until you read it, it remains external to you. But once you've read it through, it becomes a part of you. The life of the author enters into your life. So Jesus calls us to make his life part of our life. Stop thinking of Jesus as just a character in a book. Make him a part of you, his presence always with you, your life caught up into his sacrificial life of service to others. When we speak the words over the bread and wine in the Sacrament, we give them added value; they become the means by which we can take the humanity and the life of Jesus into ourselves.

## Spirit

Jesus said that mere flesh would do us no good; even his own flesh is useless to us until we add the value which comes from the meaning of his words. So this Sacrament deserves our deepest reverence, because it's the means by which we take the humanity and the life of Jesus into ourselves. In this way it's like the banknote, which is still paper with printing on it, but its value comes from the meaning we put upon the words.

## Eating and drinking together

So when we come to eat bread and drink wine together in the Holy Eucharist, we feed our hearts and souls and minds on the humanity of Jesus, and revitalize our lives by drinking his life into our bloodstream. And we do this together, not as solitary individuals. The humanity of Jesus is present in the humanity of the congregation, and the human ways in which we relate to one another. The life of God flows through us, when we have a lively fellowship, and allow God's love to pass through us in service to our neighbours. We set aside the Thursday after Trinity Sunday to honour this remarkable sacrament, in which so much happens to change us, our character, our relationship to God and our relationships to each other.

### Suggested hymns

*Let all mortal flesh keep silence; My God, and is thy table spread; Sweet Sacrament divine; The heavenly Word, proceeding forth.*

## St Barnabas the Apostle   11 June

**Barnabas the Martyr**   Job 29:11–16 Like one who comforts; Ps. 112 Generous; Acts 11:19–30 Barnabas encourages Saul (*if the Acts reading is used instead of the Old Testament reading, the New Testament reading is* Gal. 2:1–10 Barnabas and me); John 15:12–17 Love one another

> '[Jesus said,] "This is my commandment, that you love one another as I have loved you. No one has greater love than this, to lay down one's life for one's friends."' John 15:12–13

### Famagusta

In North Cyprus, which at present is the Turkish part of that divided island, on the east coast stands the city traditionally known as Famagusta – I won't try to pronounce the modern Turkish name. Shakespeare set his tragedy of *Othello* in Famagusta, and a tower in the charming citadel near the harbour is called Othello's Tower. Famagusta was established when the Christian population evacuated another city, six miles to the north, following the Arab invasion of Cyprus in AD 647. I must be careful how I pronounce the name of the other city, because it's spelt exactly the same as the spicy sausages known as sa*l*amis. But the stress comes on the first syllable, so that the city was called *Sal*amis. There are extensive remains today of the city of *Sal*amis, standing beside the sea, and those who've been there say the air's filled with the sound of the waves. In this city, it was claimed, the Apostle Barnabas was martyred and buried. His alleged tomb is in the crypt of a small chapel about a hundred yards from the remains of the fifth-century monastery of St Barnabas.

## The Acts of Barnabas

The story of the life and death of the apostle are in a document called *The Acts of Barnabas*. This is supposed to be written by Barnabas's nephew John Mark. Most scholars now think that it's a fifth-century document, written to claim that the church in Cyprus was independent because it was founded by an apostle. But these old documents often contain traditions dating from several centuries earlier. Whether it's true or not, the story it tells is an edifying one. Here are a few short quotations:

> Having gone into Salamis, we came to the synagogue near the place called Biblia; and when we had gone into it, Barnabas, having unrolled the Gospel which he had received from Matthew his fellow-labourer, began to teach the Jews.

(At this point the author mentions a magician called Bar-Jesus, who, according to the Acts of the Apostles, had opposed Paul and Barnabas on their visit to Cyprus.)

> And Bar-Jesus, having arrived after two days, after not a few Jews had been instructed, was enraged, and brought together all the multitude of the Jews; and they, having laid hold of Barnabas . . . took [him] by night, and bound him with a rope by the neck; and having dragged him to the hippodrome from the synagogue, and having gone out of the city, standing round him, they burned him with fire, so that even his bones became dust.

The author goes on to describe how he stole the ashes of St Barnabas from his persecutors, and buried them in a cave.

## The Encourager

Barnabas the Apostle was nicknamed the Son of Consolation, which is best translated as 'the Encourager'. He encouraged others all through his life, and his death was an encouragement, also. Jesus told his followers to 'love one another, as I have loved you'. Barnabas loved his fellow Christians by his words, in which he reassured them that they were doing the task that Jesus had called them to. He encouraged them also by his example, when he gave generously towards the costs of the Church's work. Barnabas loved his non-Christian neighbours also, by proclaiming the love of God shown by the self-sacrifice of Jesus. His preaching was effective, and many of his fellow Jews became Christians through his words. But the example of the way he died was the greatest encouragement of all. Jesus had warned his followers that they'd be hated and persecuted, so they knew exactly what they were letting themselves in for. That included willingness to die for what they believed in, after the example of Jesus on the cross. Jesus said, 'No one has greater love than this, to lay down one's life for one's friends.' Barnabas, like all the other Christian martyrs, loved his neighbours in the best possible way. His martyrdom showed the depth of his faith that the death of the Christian is followed by a glorious resurrection into eternal life. After seeing that, what doubter could fail to be convinced? If the legend of his martyrdom is true, Barnabas continued his ministry of encouragement right up until the end. And even if it isn't, the Apostle can be an example and an inspiration to us today, with his willingness to share his faith with his neighbours, whatever the cost.

### Suggested hymns

*A new commandment I give unto you; Brother, sister, let me serve you; Lord, it belongs not to my care; Take my life, and let it be.*

# The Birth of St John the Baptist    24 June

**Death Row**    Isa. 40:1–11 A voice in the wilderness; Ps. 85:7–13 Salvation is at hand; Acts 13:14b–26 A baptism of repentance; *or* Gal. 3:23–29 The law our schoolmaster; Luke 1:57–66, 80 Birth of the Baptist

*'And you, child, will be called the prophet of the Most High; for you will go before the Lord to prepare his ways, to give knowledge of salvation to his people by the forgiveness of their sins.'*
*Luke 1:76–77*

## Death row

A group of prisoners was in a jail in Singapore. They were members of criminal gangs, and had committed murder and other terrible crimes. In that place at that time, these were punishable by the death penalty. They had been through all the appeals procedures, and failed to have their convictions overturned. So now they knew that before long they would all die. Most people would say that for prisoners on death row there's no hope. In a worldly sense, that's true. If they turned to the choice of religions locally, there was no hope to be had there either. Hinduism and Buddhism believe in *karma*; any sins you've committed in this life will result in your being reborn in a lower state, to suffer for them in your next incarnation. Chinese traditional religion has a theme park in Singapore, in which concrete models depict the sufferings of the wicked in the chambers of hell. Islam promises paradise to those who have submitted to the will of Allah throughout their lives, but sinners are condemned eternally to the fires of hell.

## A minister

Then a Methodist minister came to visit them in prison. He came day after day to death row, and read to them from the Christian Gospels. Patiently he showed how Jesus had welcomed sinners, and promised that, for all who repented, their sins would be forgiven. He explained that God has created us so that we should live with him in eternity, and although God doesn't want us to sin, he's provided a way in which we can avoid punishment for our sins, by putting our trust in Jesus. The minister showed how the death of Jesus was a sacrifice leading to the forgiveness of sins. He pointed out where John the Baptist had described Jesus as the Lamb of God who takes away the sin of the world. John the Baptist had appeared in the wilderness, proclaiming a baptism of repentance for the remission of sins, a message which Jesus had continued to preach to his disciples. When he was born, John's father had predicted that he would 'go before the Lord to prepare his ways, to give knowledge of salvation to his people by the forgiveness of their sins'.

## Baptism

This was a message the condemned men on death row had never heard before. None of the other religions had taught them about a God who welcomes sinners and forgives them. So they repented of their sins, and asked the minister to baptize them. They received the baptism of repentance which John had taught, with the addition of putting their faith in John's cousin Jesus. Now they regained hope. They accepted calmly that their bodies would shortly die, because they knew that their souls would survive, washed clean of sin by their baptism, to live for ever with Jesus in heaven.

## A letter

So the prisoners asked the Methodist minister who'd brought them the good news to write a letter for them, and they all signed it. They asked the minister to have copies made, and give them to all their former friends, and any strangers who would be willing to read it. In the letter, the prisoners on death row stated publicly that they had repented for the wicked things they'd done, and been baptized. They described the joy and peace in their hearts as they awaited their execution. And they invited and pleaded with their friends to do the same. Jesus is the Saviour of the world, they said, Chinese, Indians, Malays, Europeans. Others might not have sinned in the way they had, but all have sinned, and God's forgiveness is offered to all. A month later they were all dead, and the minister described the peaceful smiles on their faces as these wicked, but forgiven, men went to their execution.

## John's message

This sermon isn't about John the Baptist, whose birth we commemorate today; it's about John's message, the baptism of repentance for the remission of sins. Until John came, everybody believed that you could only wheedle forgiveness out of God by bribing him with endless sacrifices. John proclaimed a God who wants to forgive us as soon as we repent, and that we can demonstrate that repentance, and receive that forgiveness, through baptism. Thank God for that.

### Suggested hymns

*And can it be that I should gain?*; *On Jordan's bank the Baptist's cry*; *The great forerunner of the morn*; *Ye that know the Lord is gracious.*

## SS Peter and Paul, Apostles  29 June

**Institutions**   Zech. 4:1–6a, 10b–14 Two anointed ones; Ps. 125 Stand fast for ever; Acts 12:1–11 Peter released from prison (*if the Acts reading is used instead of the Old Testament reading, the New Testament reading is* 2 Tim. 4:6–8, 17–18 Poured out); Matt. 16:13–19 Peter recognizes the Messiah; *or for Peter alone*: Ezek. 3:22–27 Preaching to his own; Ps. 125; Acts 12:1–11 (*if the Acts reading is used instead of the Old Testament reading, the New Testament reading is* 1 Peter 2:19–25 Suffering for God); Matt. 16:13–19

> '*Jesus answered him, "Blessed are you, Simon son of Jonah! . . . I tell you, you are Peter, and on this rock I will build my church."*' Matthew 16:17–18

### Groucho Marx

Groucho Marx famously remarked, 'They say that marriage is a fine institution. But who wants to live in an institution?' People have said much the same about the Christian Church. It's a fine idea, but the trouble is that it's become institutionalized.

### Jesus

So let's look at what the Bible says about the Church. Jesus said, 'You are Peter, and on this rock I will build my Church.' It's the only time Jesus mentions the word 'Church' in the Gospels, so people who don't like the Roman Catholic Church are driven to ever more desperate measures in the attempt to prove that it doesn't mean what it seems to mean. But whatever you believe about that, there's no denying that Jesus meant his followers to continue his work after he died, and in particular to proclaim the gospel and witness to his resurrection. He intended them to take this message around the world, to every nation, and baptize believers into some sort of community, of which 'the Twelve', including Peter, were to be the original leaders.

## Paul

St Paul wasn't one of the original twelve apostles, but he claimed as much right as they had to be an apostle, a travelling missionary, founding new churches and appointing leaders to care for them. He addressed his letters to 'the church in' such and such a city. Sometimes he mentions the church which meets in somebody's house. But he also refers to the whole worldwide Church as a single body, which mustn't be divided.

## Meaning?

So on St Peter and St Paul's day, we're bound to ask what they meant when they referred to the Church. There were certainly no church buildings at that time. It's doubtful whether they had thought far enough ahead to envisage the Church as a worldwide institution under a central control. Rather, they thought of small gatherings of Christians, meeting together in a private house once a week for the Eucharist, which was a sort of family meal. But these house churches were all conscious that they were only a part of a larger whole. When they received a letter from another congregation, they organized mutual care and support, to show their fellowship. They'd obey the instructions of the apostle who first preached the gospel to them, but often only after long persuading, and sometimes vigorous argument, and mainly out of affection for the missionary who was their founder.

## Institutions

But every gathering of people who intend to do something together needs some sort of leadership. The bigger the fellowship becomes, the stronger the leaders have to be, to keep it together and guide it to work co-operatively. Before long, it's become an institution, with all the faults that institutions have. The members squabble, and the leaders, who are just as sinful as everybody else, start taking ego trips. To prevent this, lists of rules are drawn up, and a constitution and committees. This is true of any institution, and it's true of the Church. It's hard to see how it could possibly be otherwise. The saints themselves were far from perfect sinless human beings, and although St Paul addresses his letter to 'the saints in Corinth', it's clear they had many failings. Yet the Christian Church, with all its faults, is the only tool God has for doing his work in the world today. If there'd been no Church, the Good News of God's love wouldn't have been taken to new nations, and wouldn't have been passed down from generation to generation. Without the Church, many hungry people wouldn't have been fed, and many sick people wouldn't have been healed. There wouldn't be the widespread understanding, that there is today, that God expects certain standards of behaviour from us, however far short we fall in putting them into practice. So we must love the Church our mother, in spite of her imperfections as an institution, and be grateful to Saints Peter and Paul for getting the whole show on the road in the first place.

### Suggested hymns

*The Church's one Foundation; The Church of God a kingdom is; Thou art the Christ, O Lord; We sing the glorious conquest.*


## St Thomas the Apostle   3 July
**The Limits of Science**   Hab. 2:1–4 The righteous live by faith; Ps. 31:1–6 I trust in the Lord; Eph. 2:19–22 The foundation of the apostles; John 20:24–29 Doubting Thomas is convinced

> *'Thomas said to them, "Unless I see the mark of the nails in his hands, and put my finger in the mark of the nails and my hand in his side, I will not believe."' John 20:25*


### Evidence

Doubting Thomas declared that he wouldn't believe until he had some evidence. In this he is the patron saint of all scientists, who hold that it's mere superstition to believe anything unless there's some evidence for it. But Thomas was willing to join the other disciples and look for evidence. He knew that Jesus had been dead, and then he saw him alive again, and greeted him as 'My Lord and my God'. When you think of it, that's not a conclusion that could be reached by a set of logical deductions from measurable observations. The fact that Jesus was alive wasn't a proof of the existence of God. But it was enough for Thomas, because he trusted Jesus, and he trusted those who told him about Jesus, and he trusted his own instinct about the evidence which was staring him in the face. Jesus said, 'Blessed are those who have not seen, and yet have believed.' When you add together the beauty of the universe around us, the number of intelligent people who've believed, and all the other arguments for the existence of God, then, although they're not proofs, they do add up to a strong probability, and that's enough to bring many intelligent people to faith.

## The Limits of Science

In 1987, Sir Peter Medawar wrote a book called *The Limits of Science*. He won the Nobel Prize in 1960 for his work on immunology, and was well known for his writings on scientific method. He claimed to be a rationalist, but he argued that there are limits to the scope of science. Scientific investigation's superb when it demonstrates that DNA has the shape of a double helix. But the bigger questions – such as 'What's life all about?' – these, said Professor Medawar, are 'questions that science cannot answer, and that no conceivable advance in science could empower it to answer'. But you can't dismiss the fundamental questions about human existence, he wrote, 'as "non-questions", or "pseudo-questions" such as only simpletons ask, and only charlatans profess to be able to answer'. In saying this, he continued, he wasn't criticizing science, only calibrating its capacities.

## Freedom to believe

This analysis by such a distinguished scientist leaves other scientists free to decide their religious beliefs, or lack of belief, in their own way, without claiming that they are being either scientific or non-scientific. There's an enormous variety of beliefs among scientists, and many of the most eminent among them believe strongly in God. Recently Owen Gingerich, an astronomer at Harvard University, wrote a book with the title *God's Universe*. Dr Francis Collins, the director of the Human Genome Project, wrote another called *The Language of God*. Nobody could accuse these distinguished scientists of muddled thinking, but they're both convinced that it's quite rational to believe in God. Religious people must take seriously what science says, within its own limitations; but in return scientists must allow that religious discourse is a legitimate and reasonable way of looking at the world. Yet nobody can talk about a proof for their view of the world, whether it's a Christian view or one of atheism. We can only ask which view offers the best explanation of things. And as there's no clear understanding of how we could decide which of two explanations is better than the other, scientists and non-scientists will have to make their own decisions on purely personal grounds.

## Christianity

Christians are well aware that they can't prove the existence of God. But atheists and believers alike all base their lives on certain fundamental beliefs that they know they can never prove, but nevertheless hold to be important enough to act upon. Christians argue that their world-view offers a magnificent way of making sense of our lives. But they will respect the views presented by sceptics. C. S. Lewis wrote, 'I believe in Christianity as I believe that the Sun has risen – not only because I see it, but because by it, I see everything else.'

## Believing Thomas

So St Thomas is significant for all of us, scientists and non-scientists, in forming our view of the world. He emphasizes that we shouldn't jump to conclusions without any evidence to support them. But neither should we wait until we have absolute proof, or otherwise we would wait till our dying day. And then it might be too late.

### *Suggested hymns*

*Firmly I believe and truly; Light's glittering morn (Part 3); Lord of beauty, thine the splendour; O Lord my God, when I in awesome wonder (How great thou art).*

## St Mary Magdalene   22 July
### God Knows You by Name   S. of Sol. 3:1–4 Seeking and finding; Ps. 42:1–10 As deer long for water; 2 Cor. 5:14–17 A new creation; John 20:1–2, 11–18 Go and tell

*'Jesus said to her, "Mary!" She turned and said to him in Hebrew, "Rabbouni!" (which means Teacher).' John 20:16*

### Forgetting names

The famous Dr Spooner, inventor of the Spoonerism, once said to a friend, 'I remember your name perfectly, but I can't for the life of me think of your face.' And Sir Thomas Beecham, the conductor, saw a woman at a prestigious reception whom he recognized; so he fished around trying to remember her name. 'Are you well?' he asked. 'Yes thank you,' was the reply. 'And the family?' 'Yes, they're fine.' 'And your husband, is he well?' 'Yes, very well, thank you.' Getting more desperate, Sir Thomas asked, 'And is he still in the same line of business?' The gentle reply was, 'Yes, he's still king.'

### Liking to be remembered

We all hate it if somebody forgets our name, though we may try to cover it up, as the Queen did, to save the other person embarrassment. But we feel that the implication is that we're not important enough to remember, which is very insulting. Conversely, we're delighted if somebody remembers our name, when we didn't really believe they would. Particularly if somebody important knows enough about you to get your name right. Or imagine a situation where you're groping about in the dark, maybe because the fuses have blown, and you hear a noise or feel a limb, and with a muffled scream you yelp, 'John, is that you?' If the answer comes back calling you by your name, it's a great relief. Calling somebody by their name gives a sense of security, dignity and value.

### Mary Magdalene

Mary Magdalene knew this when she met Jesus in the garden after his resurrection. She knew he was dead, because she'd seen his plainly dead body laid in the tomb. Yet she'd returned to find the guard and the seal were gone, and the heavy stone had been rolled back. She clung to the vain hope that perhaps the gardener had moved the body somewhere else to stop the mourners treading on the flowers. The figure of a man appeared behind her, and half-turning round, her eyes blinded by the tears, she didn't recognize him. 'Woman, why are you weeping?' he asked. 'Who are you looking for?' 'Woman,' he called her. Just what you'd expect of a gardener. You don't get respect from anyone these days, she thought. Supposing him to be the gardener, she said to him, 'Sir, if you've removed the body, tell me where you've laid him, and I'll find a good place for it.' Then, we read, Jesus said to her, 'Mary!' *Now* she recognized him, when he called her by name. He knew her. It must be Jesus. He wasn't dead, after all. She didn't understand, but because he used her name, she believed. Now she turned fully round and called him by the dialect name for a teacher, what she'd always called him, '*Rabbouni!*'

## On first-name terms

Jesus called his disciples, men and women alike, his friends. He knew them personally, he was on first-name terms with them all. Jesus knows your name too. Listen, I'll repeat that: Jesus knows *your* name too. It was given you when you were baptized in his house. He knows all about you, your hopes, your fears, your laughter and your tears. Jesus knows you better than you know yourself. This is nothing to be afraid of, for Jesus knows you with love. He calls you by your name, when you pray to him, as tenderly as he said the word 'Mary' in the garden. Isn't that amazing? It's better than being recognized by a VIP; better than the dignity of being named by somebody you haven't seen for a while. It means that you're the personal friend of the Son of God. On first-name terms with the Saviour of the world. Prayer's no longer a chore that has to be got through; prayer's the wonderful experience of chatting with someone who knows you by name, something you'll want to do as often as you can. Jesus treats you with respect, so you'll want to treat everyone else with respect, and especially other friends of Jesus. You'll never be afraid again, not even of death. Mary Magdalene learnt that. Death will be simply like going to sleep, and when you wake up again, Jesus will be there, waiting for you, and he'll call you by your name. Because he loves you; always has, and always will; you're absolutely unique and special to Jesus. Remember that!

*As water to the thirsty; Good Joseph had a garden; Great God, your love has called us here; Thine be the glory.*

## St James the Apostle  25 July
*(See page 199.)*

## The Transfiguration of Our Lord  6 August
**The Son of Man**  Dan. 7:9–10, 13–14 The Son of Man;
Ps. 97 Clouds are around him; 2 Peter 1:16–19 We saw; Luke
9:28–36 The transfiguration

> *'I saw in the night visions, and, behold, one like the Son of man came with the clouds of heaven, and came to the Ancient of days.' Daniel 7:13 (King James Version)*

### Son of . . .

It's considered very insulting by some people to call someone a 'son of a bitch'. And yet Franklin D. Roosevelt, the President of the United States of America, said of President Somoza of Nicaragua, 'He may be a son of a bitch, but he's *our* son of a bitch.' It's a peculiar way of calling somebody a dog, but perhaps people feel that phrases beginning 'son of . . .' are an indication of character, so that this epithet implies a bitchy sort of person. If so, this is a throw-back to the Hebrew language, which is deficient in adjectives. So a Jerusalemite woman's a 'daughter of Jerusalem'; a destructive man's a 'son of destruction'; and stormy characters are 'sons of thunder'. In Hebrew, there's no simple way to distinguish between a divine figure and a human person, so you have to call them respectively a 'son of God' and a 'son of man'. In the Hebrew Scriptures, God addresses Ezekiel as 'Son of man'; modern versions of the Bible translate it as 'mortal man'. The phrase was used to show the prophet what an honour it was that a mere human being should be spoken to by God, and used as his messenger.

## Daniel

In the book of Daniel, Daniel has a vision of hideous animals, each of which symbolizes one of the terrifying empires which occupied the land of Israel. Contrasted with these is the figure who represents Israel itself, the Chosen People. This is a purely human figure; though to show that it is a symbol, it is described as 'looking like a human being' – literally 'one like a son of man'. That's how it appears in the King James Version of the Bible. Modern versions translate it as 'one like a human being, coming with the clouds of heaven to [God]'.

## Transfiguration

So at the transfiguration, the disciples saw Jesus covered by a cloud. God was in the cloud, and said of Jesus, 'This is my Son.' God uses the same words about the king in Psalm 2: 'You are my son, this day have I begotten you.' The disciples must have been wondering what the connection was between the Davidic king, the Divine Son, and the Son of Man in Daniel coming to God surrounded by clouds. The phrase 'Son of Man' was developed to represent Israel in other Hebrew books – books which are not in our Bible, but were written before the time of Jesus, so he probably knew them. Here the Son of Man represents the Messiah, who takes on an almost supernatural character.

## Jesus

Jesus often used the term 'Son of Man' to refer to himself. Not surprisingly, many books have been written trying to unravel what he meant by this. Was he being humble, and saying 'I'm only a human being like you'? Or, especially when he told the High Priest, 'You will see the Son of Man coming on the clouds', was he claiming to be the divine Messiah, representative of God, come to earth to save his people?

## Both and

My guess is that it's not so much a case of 'either or' as of 'both and'. Perhaps Jesus was being deliberately ambiguous, to make his hearers wonder and think. The same ambiguity lies at the heart of the appearance of Jesus surrounded by clouds at the transfiguration: Jesus is both the utterly human being they'd known as their friend, and at the same time the divine Son of God, sent to rescue his people. We have to live with this ambiguity, and understand the paradox that Jesus was both utterly human and completely divine at the same time. Not 'either or', but 'both and'.

## Christology

There are plenty of hints at this in the pages of the New Testament. Jesus said, 'I and my Father are one', but the Letter to Hebrews says he was 'tempted in all things as we are, only without sin'. Yet it's this duality which saves us. Because Jesus is human, we can know him and talk to him as our friend. Because he's divine, he has the power to represent God his Father, to forgive sins and to heal the sick. The transfiguration was a spiritual experience which the disciples had, to show them, and us too, that we can pray to Jesus in perfect confidence. Jesus understands and sympathizes, because he's human like us; and he has power to answer our prayers and to save us, because he's the Son of God.

### Suggested hymns

*A man there lived in Galilee; Lord, the light of your love is shining; The Son of God proclaim; 'Tis good, Lord, to be here.*

## The Blessed Virgin Mary   15 August
(*See page 213.*)

## St Bartholomew the Apostle   24 August
**A God with a Mission**   Isa. 43:8–13 My witnesses; Ps. 145: 1–7 Speak of your wondrous acts; Acts 5:12–16 The apostles heal (*if the Acts reading is used instead of the Old Testament reading, the New Testament reading is* 1 Cor. 4:9–15 The shame of the apostles); Luke 22:24–30 Judging the twelve tribes

> '[Jesus said to the Twelve,] "I confer on you, just as my Father has conferred on me, a kingdom, so that you may eat and drink at my table in my kingdom, and you will sit on thrones judging the twelve tribes of Israel."' Luke 22:29–30

## A growing kingdom

At the Last Supper, the apostles, Bartholomew among them, were squabbling over which of them was the most important. Jesus tried to teach them that the only sort of greatness that counts with God is the question of who shows the greatest love in serving other people. It's a lesson that many Christians still haven't learnt. The temptation to show off's always there in the background, and the warning which Jesus gave against pride's always timely. Yet Jesus did promise the Twelve, Bartholomew among them, a kingdom and thrones. That sounds cosy. They might be tempted, as we all are, to say, 'Now we've arrived; all we have to do is to sit back and enjoy it.' But that would be to ignore what Jesus had already told them about the nature of the kingdom of God. In most of the parables of the kingdom, the emphasis is on growth. The kingdom's like a mustard seed, like a seed growing secretly in a field, like yeast fermenting in a lump of dough, like new wine fermenting fit to burst the old containers. There's nothing cosy about a position in a growing kingdom like that; as Lewis Carroll's Red Queen said, 'It takes all the running you can do, to keep in the same place.'

## Church growth

The reason the kingdom's growing so fast, as Jesus describes it, is that it's God's kingdom, and God's beavering away at the heart of it. The kingdom of God is wherever God's acknowledged as king. More and more people every day are learning to crown God as the king of their life. As each generation dies out, new converts must be made to replace them. Then, conversion's not the end but the beginning of the growth phase: when you call yourself a Christian, you discover that new areas of your life have continually to be placed under God's sovereignty. One of these areas is the task of spreading the good news of the kingdom, and drawing more fish into the net of the kingdom of God. Each of us has a part to play in this – are you growing in your understanding of your own role in it?

## A Church with a mission

The fact is, we're all members of a Church with a mission. The mission of the Church today's the same as it always was. That is, to bring every individual life, and every area of human activity, completely under God's kingly rule. As far as you're concerned, it'll involve being unembarrassed to explain to your friends the reasons why you go to church, and what God has done for you in answer to your prayer. You'll need to be involved in the life of your village or your city, of the nation, and concern for the planet, and if that means politics, you can't shrug it off as though politics doesn't matter to God – it does! The Church mustn't take sides in party politics; but every Christian should recognize that involvement in political debate and action is an inevitable part of loving our neighbours and seeking their well-being.

## A God with a mission

David Urquhart, the Bishop of Birmingham, has said, 'We're not a Church with a mission, serving God; we're a Church serving a God with a mission.' That's a thought which takes a little wrestling with, but I think what he meant was that the numerical growth of the Church, the spiritual growth of its members, and claiming the whole of human life for God, isn't a sort of optional extra for those who feel that way inclined. It's the task of each one of us, just because we've each heard God's call to be part of a Church in which God's active. We don't have to labour on our own; just co-operate with God in his struggle to make his kingdom come on earth, as it is in heaven.

## The insignificant

That applies to you, even if you think you're completely insignificant. We know hardly anything about St Bartholomew, other than his name; you can't get more insignificant than that! Yet he was given a place within the kingdom of God, not to loll back on his throne, but to show greatness in serving others, and co-operating in the mission of God to the whole world.

### Suggested hymns

*God is working his purpose out; Jesus, where'er thy people meet; Seek ye first the kingdom of God; The Church of God a kingdom is.*

# Holy Cross Day    14 September

**Empress Helena**    Num. 21:4–9 The bronze serpent; Ps. 22:23–28 All the earth shall turn to the Lord; Phil. 2:6–11 Obedient to death on the cross; John 3:13–17 God so loved the world

*'All the ends of the earth shall remember and turn to the Lord; and all the families of the nations shall bow before him.' Psalm 22:27 (Common Worship)*

## Constantine

Constantine was in charge of the Roman army in York in AD 306, and in his early thirties, when his father, the Emperor Constantius, died. The soldiers all hailed Constantine as the next emperor but, although he was the oldest son, there were altogether six men all claiming to be the emperor. According to Constantine's biographer, Bishop Eusebius, he marched the army from Britain to Rome to challenge his rivals. To enter the city he had to cross the Milvian Bridge, where the army of his rival Maxentius was drawn up for battle. The night before the battle, Constantine, who was not yet a Christian, had a vision, during which he saw the Christian cross shining in the sky, and heard the words, 'In this sign you shall conquer.' From then on, he reverenced the crucified Christ and encouraged the growth of Christianity. That's one version of the story. In another, he saw the Greek letters Chi-Ro – Chi with a hard 'c' as in Mackie – the first two letters of the word Christ. That's why we see them, looking like X P, in so many churches. To describe this as the moment of Constantine's conversion to Christianity is probably going too far; he wasn't baptized until he lay dying 25 years later. But he seems to have regarded Christianity as the only religion which could unite his divided empire. All other gods were associated with one particular race, who claimed that their god favoured them above all other nations. But Jesus said, 'I tell you, many will come from east and west and will eat with Abraham and Isaac and Jacob in the kingdom of heaven.' St Paul had struggled to unite Jew and Gentile in one faith under the cross of Christ. So Constantine saw that the religion of the crucified Messiah was the only one which could build the whole world into a single family. He called all the Christian bishops together for the Council of Nicaea, to draw up the Nicene Creed, so that all Christians could agree what they believed.

## Helena

Constantine's mother was the Empress Helena; when he became emperor, he made her Empress Dowager. She was already a Christian, and 14 years later, she made a pilgrimage to the Holy Land, spending her wealth on helping the poor and building churches on sites associated with the life of Jesus. When the Romans destroyed Jerusalem, a temple to Venus had been built over the hill of Calvary, to prevent Christians from worshipping there. That, of course, identified the site of the crucifixion for all time. Constantine had the temple taken down and the Church of the Holy Sepulchre erected to protect the tomb of Jesus. It's said that Helena had a dream, in which she was commanded to have her workmen dig out an old well nearby. At the bottom they found the wooden cross on which Jesus had hung. Pieces of the true cross were taken all over the world and reverenced; they're mostly quite small, and could all possibly have come from one cross; but whether that was the actual cross on which Jesus died is a question which faith alone can decide.

## Holy Cross Day

Today is Holy Cross Day. In the calendar at the front of the Book of Common Prayer, people are sometimes surprised to find a day called 'The Invention of the Cross'. This is, of course, old English for the *discovery* of the cross, and commemorated the finding of the true cross in Jerusalem by the Empress Helena. Today's a modern amalgamation of that day with several others on which the cross was commemorated, to give us another chance to step back and think again about how much we owe to Jesus for dying on the cross. It's difficult for us in the twenty-first century to get inside the minds of people like Constantine and his mother, and those who told their stories, who lived so long ago. In his novel *The Go-Between*, L. P. Hartley wrote, 'The past is a foreign country: they do things differently there.' Yet we're all human beings, whatever country or age we live in, with similar feelings and needs. We're not entirely different, or we couldn't communicate – we're not exactly the same, or we'd have nothing to say. But if we use our imaginations to think what it was like to be them, we can understand that we all need to be reassured of God's love, and the holy cross is the visible sign of that love for all to see.

## St Matthew, Apostle and Evangelist    21 September

**Riches**    Prov. 3:13–18 Wisdom more precious than jewels; Ps. 119:65–72 Better than gold; 2 Cor. 4:1–6 The open statement of the truth; Matt. 9:9–13 The call of Matthew

> *'The law of your mouth is dearer to me than a hoard of gold and silver.' Psalm 119:72 (Common Worship)*

### Taxes

'Death and taxes and childbirth,' says one of the characters in *Gone with the Wind*. 'There's never any convenient time for any of them!' That's because they're all potentially painful experiences. In principle we know taxation's a perfectly fair system. But still, when it comes to parting with our hard-earned money, none of us enjoys it. So tax-collectors may be perfectly charming people; but in their professional character nobody likes them. St Matthew, according to the Gospel which bears his name, was a tax-collector; when Jesus called him, he was sitting in the customs post, collecting revenue from everybody who passed along the road. In those days, you bought at auction the right to collect taxes in a particular place, and then kept for yourself all you could rake in. So the tax-collectors became very rich, and very unpopular.

### Levi

The other Gospels call him Levi; Matthew was probably a nick-name: it means 'gift of God'. You can imagine some young relative asking him, 'Where did you get all your money from, Uncle Levi?' To which the cunning rogue would reply with a wink, 'The gift of God, my boy, the gift of God!' But Jesus passed along that road a number of times, with his followers, and Levi summed him up quickly: an honest man, who'd no money at all, but seemed far happier than those who had. Then to his astonishment, he saw Jesus coming across to his customs booth. Jesus stopped outside and spoke to Matthew, quietly but challengingly. Just two words, but they'd change the tax-collector's life for ever: 'Follow me!' St Luke's Gospel tells us that 'he got up, left everything, and followed him'.

## Left everything

He left everything. He left the customs house, never to return. He left his cosy job with a secure income. He left the money which he'd collected that day, and he left the hoard which he kept securely locked up in a safe place in his house. He left his house, and his luxurious lifestyle, and his ample meals. He left his friends, after throwing one last party for them, to which he invited Jesus. Zacchaeus, the chief tax-collector in Jericho, said to Jesus, 'Look, half of my possessions I'll give to the poor, and if I've cheated anyone, I'll pay him four times what I took from him.' I doubt whether Levi was any less generous. Jesus told one young man to give away everything he had; that was an extreme case, because the young man loved his money very much, but Jesus knew what people are like. Jesus probably challenged Matthew enough to ensure he made a firm break in the golden chains which bound him to the old way of life. There can be no compromise for the followers of Jesus: love God, or love money; nobody can love them both. That doesn't mean every Christian has to live the life of a penniless preacher like Matthew; but money can no longer be your priority. It's a means to an end, not an end in itself.

## Get a life

We sometimes say to someone whose days are the boring repetition of a dull routine, 'Oh, go out and get a life!' Levi-Matthew left everything, but he got a life. He got a life of excitement, following Jesus heaven knows where. He got a life of self-respect, knowing that he was being useful to others. He got a life of purpose, sharing the good news with all he met, first by speaking it, and later by writing it down in his Gospel. And although he'd left his money behind, he got a life of real wealth. Jesus said:

Do not store up for yourselves treasures on earth, where moth and rust consume and where thieves break in and steal; but store up for yourselves treasures in heaven, where neither moth nor rust consumes and where thieves do not break in and steal. For where your treasure is, there your heart will be also.

344

Matthew exchanged his worldly wealth, which would run out one day, for a heavenly treasure which would last for eternity. He got a life – an eternal life, which truly is 'the gift of God'. Jesus warned us that we must calculate the cost of discipleship. There are some things which every Christian has to be ready to give up, if only the dream of inexhaustible riches. But it's worth it if, like Matthew, we receive in exchange for what we've left behind, the priceless gift of eternal life, which is 'dearer . . . than a hoard of gold and silver'.

### Suggested hymns

*He sat to watch o'er customs paid; Jesus calls us – o'er the tumult; Take my life, and let it be; There's a wideness in God's mercy.*

# St Michael and All Angels   29 September
**Heavenly Worship**   Genesis 28:10–17 Jacob's ladder; Psalm 103:19–22 Bless the Lord, you angels; Revelation 12:7–12 Michael fought the dragon; John 1:47–51 Angels descending on the Son of Man (*or if the Revelation reading is used instead of the Old Testament reading, the New Testament reading is* Hebrews 1:5–14 Higher than the angels)

'Bless the Lord, you angels of his.' Psalm 103:20

### Brother Corncrake

In a certain monastery they'd worked very hard at the quality of their singing, until it was the most beautiful music of any monastery in that region. Except that there was one old monk, and no matter how hard he tried to sing in tune, the other monks said he had a voice like a corncrake. One night at Vespers the monks looked up, and in the rafters there stood a multitude of angels, listening to their worship with wrapt attention. 'How wonderful,' said the monks to each other as they came out of chapel. 'Our singing's so beautiful that even the angels want to come and listen. But what are we going to do about Brother Corncrake?' They decided to send him at once to their daughter house in the next valley. The next evening there were no angels to listen to the music in the mother house: they'd all moved to the daughter house, because what they were listening to was not the music, but the beauty of the old monk's prayers!

## Music for God

The point of the story is that we should always offer our best to God, but it's the intention to do our best that matters, not some critic's abstract standard of excellence. Jesus told us not to bury our talents. If God's given us a talent, it's a sin not to use it in his service. We're to love God with all our heart and mind and soul and strength, and that surely means we're to offer him the highest level of musical performance that we can. Many Christians have been brought to God by music: the beauty of the cathedral choir, the hearty singing in the chapel, have made them want to come again. Then, having come to listen to the music, they heard the gospel, gave their hearts to Jesus, and stayed to pray. In a church with a fine choir, there are parts of the service when their role is to perform their best, and the rest of the congregation are to silently offer it to God. In a church with only a tiny congregation, it may be everyone's job to sing as loud as they can, to make a cheerful noise for the Lord. There are many different ways of worshipping. The unmusical must be careful not to spoil the service for those with a musical ear. The musical must do their best in the solo sections to make the worship as heavenly as they can, and at other times give everyone a chance to play their part to the best of their ability. Many people get a great deal of enjoyment out of church music, and God's pleased about that. But it must be done with consideration for others, and consciously offered to God, by a silent prayer before or after we sing.

## Caught up into heaven

A deputation from Prince Vladimir of Russia was sent to Byzantium in AD 988 to choose which religion Russia should follow. They went into the St Sophia church, and were so overcome by the beauty of the building, the icons and the singing, that they reported unanimously that Russia *must* become Christian, because at Christian worship they felt as though they'd been transported to heaven. Others have felt the same – and so we should, for the Bible tells us that heaven is full of worship. The worship of people who've 'died and gone to heaven' is surrounded by that of spiritual beings that the Bible calls angels. Harps and wings and haloes are only words to help us imagine the invisible world, but we must never doubt that there is an invisible world, and it's full of praise to Almighty God.

## Be encouraged

Be encouraged by this. If you've sung your Orlando Gibbons anthem better than ever before, don't be disappointed that there were so few people in church to hear it. If you've sung your contemporary worship song with great enthusiasm but not a great deal of skill, don't worry. Offer both of them to Jesus, and ask him to blend them with the worship of the angels. The angels will note the sincerity of your intention, and offer your worship up with theirs to God, for whom it was intended. Then your little offering will become a part of the music of the world, which – from the blackbird singing on the bough to the angels' Hallelujah chorus – is heard with pleasure by God, and accepted as his creation's offering of love and beauty, which is what he made us for.

### Suggested hymns

*Angel voices, ever singing; Hark! hark, my soul! angelic songs are swelling; Stars of the morning, so gloriously bright; Ye holy angels bright.*

## St Luke the Evangelist   18 October
**Do Not Fear!**   Isa. 35:3–6 Healing in the new age; *or* Acts 16:6–12a The Macedonian call; Ps. 147:1–7 God heals the broken-hearted; 2 Tim. 4:5–17 Only Luke is with me; Luke 10:1–9 Sending out the seventy

> *'Say to those who are of a fearful heart, "Be strong, do not fear! Here is your God."' Isaiah 35:4*

### An epitaph

An epitaph was composed by the eighteenth-century poet James Thomson:

Here lies a man who never lived,
Yet still from death was flying;
Who, if not sick was never well;
And died – for fear of dying!

Fear can kill you. Or at the very least, it can cripple and disable a person who is always afraid. The emotion appears to have evolved in animals to prepare them physically, in a dangerous situation, for either fight or flight. Yet, in humans, it can have the opposite effect. President F. D. Roosevelt, in his inaugural address, said, 'The only thing we have to fear is fear itself – nameless, unreasoning, unjustified terror that paralyses needed efforts to convert retreat into advance.' To be unafraid of danger is stupid; but whereas a coward is someone who gives in to fear, courage is being afraid, but conquering one's fear and behaving bravely in spite of it.

## Healing fear

The crippling effect of fear can cause psychological illness. So medical doctors, psychotherapists and spiritual healers must be ready to address the fears of their patients. St Luke, the beloved physician, reports that the healing ministry of Jesus started in Nazareth. There, he preached in the synagogue, beginning with a quotation from Isaiah:

> The Spirit of the Lord is upon me, because he has anointed me to bring good news to the poor. He has sent me to proclaim release to the captives and recovery of sight to the blind, to let the oppressed go free, to proclaim the year of the Lord's favour.

In another passage, Isaiah describes the task of healing, in the new age which begins with the coming of the Messiah, like this:

> Strengthen the weak hands, and make firm the feeble knees. Say to those who are of a fearful heart, 'Be strong, do not fear! Here is your God. He will come with vengeance, with terrible recompense. He will come and save you.' Then the eyes of the blind shall be opened, and the ears of the deaf unstopped; then the lame shall leap like a deer, and the tongue of the speechless sing for joy.

Fear prevents us seeing situations as they really are; fear stops us walking in the way of love; fear deafens us to the message of God's love; struck dumb by fear, we cannot share this good news with others.

## Replacing fear by hope

The Bible promises that the coming of the Messiah will bring healing by driving out fear. Sadly, some Christians have turned the fear of God, which in the Bible means awe and respect, into cringing terror before a cruel dictator. They teach fear of death, fear of judgement and fear of hell. Ours was never meant to be a religion of fear, but one of love, for Jesus promised that 'Perfect love casts out fear.' If you have faith in Jesus, you'll trust him to defend you against all the things you're frightened of. Some bad things will continue to happen to you, but the Bible's promised that nothing will be more than you can bear – God will give, with the testing time, the spiritual strength to see you through. Remember Isaiah: 'Say to those who are of a fearful heart, "Be strong, do not fear! Here is your God".'

## Fear of death

So what of the man in my opening parody, who 'died – for fear of dying'? Why are we so afraid of death? It's something that comes to all of us sometime. Probably fear of death arises from fear of the unknown. That's only natural. But for the Christian, death's *not* unknown, because Jesus has been that way before us, and come back to tell us there's nothing to fear. Death becomes much less frightening when you think of it as the gateway to life. When we die, we shall meet again those we love who've gone before. And we shall also, at last, be able to meet Jesus face to face, whom we love, and who loves us. Then pain, disease and fear will be no more. As we celebrate St Luke the healer, let's hear the voice of Jesus ringing in our ears: 'Do not be afraid.'

## *Suggested hymns*

*Make way, make way for Christ the King; Fear not, rejoice and be glad; For all the saints, who from their labours rest; God's Spirit is in my heart.*

## SS Simon and Jude, Apostles   28 October

**Zealot Terrorists**   Isa. 28:14–16 A foundation stone; Ps. 119:89–96 I am yours, save me; Eph. 2:19–22 The foundation of the apostles; John 15:17–27 You have been with me

> 'When they had entered the city, they went to the room upstairs where they were staying, Peter, and John, and James, and Andrew, Philip and Thomas, Bartholomew and Matthew, James son of Alphaeus, and Simon the Zealot, and Judas son of James.' Acts 1:13

### Saint who?

Today we celebrate St Simon and St Jude. Do I hear you asking, 'Saint who? Never 'eard of them!' You're right; we know less about them than almost any others among the twelve apostles. Yet it's on these twelve that the Bible tells us the Church is built. In the list of apostles in the Acts of the Apostles, Simon and Jude come last: 'Simon the Zealot, and Judas son of James'. St John's Gospel merely dismisses Jude as 'Judas (not Iscariot)'. That's nearly as insulting as the talented novelist who's always introduced as 'Kate Mosse – no, not the supermodel'! But the other semi-anonymous apostle whom we honour today is given a very revealing one-word description: he was 'Simon the Zealot'. Did I hear somebody ask, 'Simon the what?' Oh, come on now! Everybody knows what a Zealot is. Don't you? Then I'll tell you.

### Zealots

Isaiah wrote that the zeal of God led him to destroy the enemies of his people: 'O LORD . . . let them see your zeal for your people, and be ashamed. Let the fire for your adversaries consume them.' When the Jews were occupied by the Greek armies of Alexander the Great's successors, a revolt was led by Judas Maccabeus and his family, who 'burned with zeal' for God's covenant. In the second book of Maccabees, one of the extremist rebels, who plotted against the quisling government, is described as 'a *zealot* for the laws'. That means that he was very zealous, very enthusiastic, about obeying God's commandment not to worship foreign gods, and getting others to do so, even if it incurred the wrath of their Greek rulers. Zeal became an instrument of rebellion, killing the enemy on behalf of God. In AD 6, Judas the Galilean raised a revolt, protesting against the tax-raising census of Quirinius. The Jewish historian Josephus says that's the first time the word 'Zealot' was used of Jewish rebels. In AD 66, another rebellion broke out against the occupying Romans. The murderous wing of the Zealots were called the 'Sicarii', or 'dagger-men', because they mingled among the crowds with their daggers hidden beneath their robes, and stabbed Roman soldiers in the back, before vanishing back into the throng. They also killed Jews who were suspected of being collaborators. The Zealots occupied Jerusalem in 66, and weren't driven out till the Romans destroyed the city and the Temple in AD 70.

## Terrorists

So those were the Zealots. In case you're beginning to recognize a familiar pattern, more than one modern historian has described the Zealots as 'the earliest forerunners of modern terrorism'. The terrorist, as his name implies, isn't interested so much in how many people he kills, as in spreading fear and terror among the rest of the population. If terrorists can make the rulers so alarmed that they clamp down violently on a whole people, and the people so terrified that they join the rebels in the revolt, then their objects will have been achieved. Terror's far more effective than a conventional war. So resisting terror by violent means only assists their cause. The only resistance that works is to remove the grievances on which they feed, and refuse to be frightened.

## Simon the terrorist

So one of the apostles whom we honour today was Simon the terrorist, was he? Surely not, for Jesus refused the way of armed insurrection, and wouldn't have accepted a violent man among his closest followers. Perhaps zealotry hadn't yet become violent; or perhaps Simon had dabbled in it, and then seen how wrong it was, and seen the light. In that case, he should be described as Simon the 'ex-terrorist', Simon the reformed Zealot. It's encouraging that Jesus was prepared to admit men with a murky past like that among his apostles, provided they'd renounced their violent ways. Very many of us in this church today have done things in the past we're ashamed of, but Jesus still welcomes us, and promises to make something of us.

## Foundations

The apostles were the foundation of the Church, but they weren't (in inverted commas) 'saints'. They were a mixed bunch, much like you and me and everybody else. And if Jesus can found his Church on people like Simon and Jude, known respectively as 'the ex-terrorist' and 'not the famous one', then there's hope for ordinary folk like you and me too.

### Suggested hymns

*Captains of the saintly band; God works in a mysterious way; Judge eternal, throned in splendour; O God of earth and altar.*

## All Saints' Day   1 November

*(If 31 October is not kept as All Saints' Sunday, the readings on page 263 are used on 1 November. If those are used on the Sunday, the following are the readings on 1 November.)*

**Beatitudes**   Isa. 56:3–8 My house for all people; *or* 2 Esd. 2:42–48 Crowned by the Son of God; Ps. 33:1–5 Rejoice, you righteous; Heb. 12:18–24 Come to Zion; Matt. 5:1–12 The Beatitudes

> *'When Jesus saw the crowds, he went up the mountain; and after he sat down, his disciples came to him. Then he began to speak, and taught them, saying: "Blessed are the poor in spirit, for theirs is the kingdom of heaven."' Matthew 5:1–3*

### What's a saint?

What's a saint? In Cardinal Newman's poem *The Dream of Gerontius*, set to music by Elgar, a crowd of demons is supposed to be mocking the Christian soul, while the soul's being carried by the angel to meet God. 'What's a saint?' they ask in derision, and give their own answer: 'A bundle of bones which fools adore when life is o'er.' A schoolboy defined a saint as 'a dead Roman Catholic'. When Pope John Paul the Second canonized more saints than all his predecessors put together, some Catholics joked that the day was coming when every dead Roman Catholic would be made a saint. But in fact the Vatican demands proof of two healing miracles caused by prayers addressed to the dead person before they'll begin the process of canonization. Many Protestants are doubtful about the Pope's ability to declare that such and such a Christian has been promoted from purgatory to heaven, and their ability to answer prayers. There's also scepticism as to whether some of the saints who used to be reverenced ever existed.

## We need heroes and heroines

Yet everybody still needs heroes and heroines. There are Christians whose life we want to copy, or at least try to. They weren't perfect in every respect, but they led lives of heroic sacrifice. Without waiting for official canonization, popular acclaim says that she or he lived a saintly life. 'I wish I could be like her (or him),' we sigh. And because of their example, we try a little harder to live a good life. This includes those we call the saints, but many others as well.

## Holy ones

Yet the Bible nowhere calls any individual a saint. The word we translate as 'saint' means 'holy'. A famous book by Rudolf Otto defined holiness as the sense of awe we feel in the presence of a power greater than ourselves – the mystery which attracts us, but also makes us afraid. A 'holy place' came to mean somewhere set aside for worship. 'Holy robes', 'holy vessels' and 'holy people' were set apart for sacred use. So, surprisingly, St Paul writes to 'the saints who live in Corinth', and goes on to rebuke them for sins we haven't even thought of! They'd been set aside by God to serve him, says St Paul; they *are* saints, now they must become holy in their lives. This doesn't mean goody-goody – a holy life is a life full of love.

## Called to be saints

So you and I are all saints – God's chosen us for his service, so we're holy people. Now we're 'called to be saints', we must grow into people who are able to serve him. So once again we ask, 'What's a saint?' What are people supposed to be like, if they've been chosen by God to serve him? What sort of people are we supposed to be growing into? The answer to these questions is given in the eight Beatitudes at the opening of the Sermon on the Mount. You and I should be aiming to become:

1 Poor in spirit. That means contended with just a few possessions.
2 Mournful about all the evil in the world.
3 Meek, not proud.
4 Hungering for righteous behaviour, in ourselves and in the
world.
5 Merciful and forgiving.
6 Pure in heart, single-minded.
7 We're supposed to be peacemakers.
8 And lastly, we should be so much better than the average that we
attract persecution.

Those are the blessed; those are the saints; that's what we're called
to be like.

### The communion of saints

So the saints were quite ordinary people, called like us to an extra-
ordinary commitment to God's service. We're surrounded by the
communion of saints: a great crowd of witnesses, rooting for us and
cheering us on – we're never alone. We can look forward to joining
them in eternity. All Saints' Day reminds us that, through the mercy
of God, we shall all be saints together in heaven. How wonderful
that will be!

### *Suggested hymns*

*Blest are the pure in heart; For all the saints who from their labours
rest; Give us the wings of faith to rise; Rejoice in God's saints,
today and all days.*

## Commemoration of the Faithful Departed
## (All Souls' Day)   2 November
**Unchanging Love**   Lam. 3:17–26, 31–33 New every
morning; *or* Wisd. 3:1–9 Souls of the righteous; Ps. 23 The
Lord is my shepherd *or* 27:1–6, 16–17 He shall hide me; Rom.
5:5–11 Christ died for us; *or* 1 Peter 1:3–9 Salvation ready to
be revealed; John 5:19–25 The dead will hear his voice; *or* John
6:37–40 I will raise them up

*'[Jesus said,] "Very truly, I tell you, the hour is coming, and is now here, when the dead will hear the voice of the Son of God, and those who hear will live."' John 5:25*

## You've changed

Her husband had been away on a long journey. When he came home again, his wife greeted him with kisses and tears, and then they told each other what had been happening during the time they'd been apart. The conversation wandered over many subjects, they had so much to talk about. Then suddenly the wife stopped short. 'You've changed,' she said accusingly. 'I feel as though I don't know you any more.' Her husband tried to reassure her. 'Yes, certainly,' he said, 'there are some things about me which have changed since you last saw me; that was bound to happen. But inside of me, deep down, I'm the same man I've always been: the man who loves you, and whom you love.' A few more kisses and tears, and she accepted the truth: though the outward part of us changes all the time, love is unchanging.

## Death

So think of someone you've known for a very long time: your parent, wife, child or best friend. Your relationship's gone through many phases, and had its ups and downs; there've been many vicissitudes, and both of you've changed over the years. Yet, underneath, your unchanging love's survived. Now, you won't thank me for saying this, but everyone dies sometime. If we believe in the promises of Jesus, we shouldn't feel sorry for the person who's died, because a great change has come over them, they've been forgiven, and welcomed into the glorious world of heaven, where all sorrows are forgotten. The one who's left here on earth, however, deserves our deepest sympathy, because they're bereft of the visible fellowship of someone they've loved. No more kisses, no more cuddles, for the time being. So as you think of those you love, you're bound to ask yourself, who would you prefer should die first? Would it be better for them if you died and left them, or if they died first and you had to endure the loneliness? Neither situation's ideal, but unless you're both killed in the same accident, one or other of you is bound to get to heaven first. That's why we need All Souls' Day.

## All Souls

All Souls' Day proclaims that love is unchanging. Remember the husband and wife who'd been apart for a while, that I told you about? Their circumstances had changed, but their love continued as strong as ever. If that's true in life, shouldn't it be true of death also? When somebody dies whom you love, they change outwardly: they have a glorious resurrection body, instead of the weak and perishable body you knew them in. But as St Paul said, that's just like a change of clothes: inside we remain the same. So shouldn't our relationships with each other continue and deepen, despite our temporary separation? 'Many waters cannot quench love,' says the Bible's great love song; not even the deep waters of death.

## Talking to them

Sometimes a bereaved person will confess, 'I think I must be going mad. I catch myself still talking to him [or her] as though they were still here.' We have to reassure them that there's nothing wrong with that at all; it's perfectly natural and right. At the Reformation, Protestants were so alarmed that people in the Middle Ages were praying to the saints more than they spoke to God, that they seemed to suggest that it was altogether wrong to talk to the dead. But if what I've said about unchanging love has any truth in it, then continuing to speak to your loved ones who've died is not only natural, it's a duty. Pray for them; tell them what you've been doing, and tell them that you still love them, and always will, just as you always have. Tell them that you're looking forward to being together again when the right moment comes. The deceased, as we call them when we're being formal, will be talking to you, too, though you won't hear them with your ears. In your heart, though, you'll know that deep down, nothing's changed. Love is unchanging, even after death.

### Suggested hymns

*Give rest, O Christ (Russian Contakion); He wants/lacks not friends that hath thy love; Lead, kindly light; Lord, it belongs not to my care.*

# Saints and Martyrs of (our own nation)

## 8 November

**My Native Land**   Isa. 61:4–9 Build up the ancient ruins; *or* Ecclus. 44:1–15 Let us now praise famous men; Ps. 15 Who may dwell in your tabernacle?; Rev. 19:5–10 A great multitude invited; John 17:18–23 To be with me to see my glory

> *'Then I heard what seemed to be the voice of a great multitude, like the sound of many waters and like the sound of mighty thunderpeals, crying out, "Hallelujah! For the Lord our God the Almighty reigns. Let us rejoice and exult and give him the glory, for the marriage of the Lamb has come, and his bride has made herself ready; to her it has been granted to be clothed with fine linen, bright and pure" – for the fine linen is the righteous deeds of the saints.' Revelation 19:6–7*

### Sir Walter Scott

The poetry of Sir Walter Scott's not as popular today as once it was. Nor is the spirit of national pride, which he celebrated in words from his 'Lay of the last minstrel':

> Breathes there the man, with soul so dead
> Who never to himself hath said,
>    This is my own, my native land!
> Whose heart hath ne'er within him burn'd,
> As home his footsteps he hath turn'd
>    From wandering on a foreign strand!

The poet celebrates the feeling that there's somewhere where we belong, somewhere that we can call 'home'. It doesn't need to be a mighty nation; it doesn't need to be perfect in its behaviour, or world-famous in its scenery; people who were born there will love that landscape because it's their own, and to them, it'll have the most beautiful countryside and monuments in the world.

### Natives

Sir Walter was writing about Scotland, but different people have applied those words to other parts of the British Isles, and to many countries around the globe. Because they love their homeland, in spite of its failings, they try to make it better, "'til we have built Jerusalem in England's green and pleasant land'. They'll be proud to call themselves natives; they refer to 'my native heath', and joke about 'the Return of the Native'. Yet from being a word of pride, the term 'native' curiously turned to one of contempt for those who were native to other places than our own: 'The natives are friendly' or 'The natives are restless tonight'. This double standard was parodied in *1066 and All That*, when the authors wrote that 'The Roman Conquest was, however, a *Good Thing*, since the Britons were only natives at the time.' That was before we heard of 'African Americans' or 'British Asians' – people who may have lived in a country more generations than some of their neighbours, but who retain a duality of affection, both for their adopted country and the one their ancestors hailed from.

## National pride

So what's the source of national pride? Often it arises naturally when you've lived in a place for a while. But it can be engendered by learning about the heroes and heroines of the past. Discovering the stories of people who lived here before us can give us an affection for the place for which they struggled and died. That's why in some countries, the day a week after All Saints' Day is celebrated as the commemoration of 'The Saints of our own Land'. To hear their life-story can be an inspiration; to read about them can fill our hearts with pride. That's not to say that they were perfect, nor that the causes for which they fought were always just. At the Reformation, there were heroic preachers and martyrs on both sides of the Catholic–Protestant divide. We probably haven't even yet reached the point at which we shall be able to celebrate, at one and the same time, the blessings which colonial pioneers brought to the countries where they settled, and the heroism of their subjects who fought against oppression. But ours is not to judge. Enough that they're part of our history, and have made our nation, and us, what we are.

## Honour

So let's honour our national saints for the good they did, and forgive them for their errors, knowing that none of us is perfect. Every year we can think about the famous ones, and discover a few more obscure ones, to deepen our love for the place where we live. We can use them as an example for us to follow. A deep and abiding love for our country will make us more eager to serve our fellow-countrymen and women, and make our nation proud of what we, too, in our small way, have done for our native land, when our turn comes to join the saints in glory.

## Suggested hymns

*God, whose city's sure foundation; He wants/lacks not friends that hath thy love; Lord, while for all mankind we pray; Rejoice in God's saints, today and all days.*

# Saint Andrew the Apostle   30 November
**Galilee**   Isaiah 52:7–10 The messenger who announces peace; Psalm 19:1–6 The heavens declare God's glory; Romans 10:12–18 God's messengers reconcile Jew and Greek; Matthew 4:18–22 The call of the fishermen

> *'As [Jesus] walked by the Sea of Galilee, he saw two brothers, Simon, who is called Peter, and Andrew his brother, casting a net into the sea – for they were fishermen.' Matthew 4:18*

## Sabbath rest by Galilee

A parish group were enjoying a pilgrimage in the Holy Land. They had survived the bustle of Jerusalem and the commercialism of Bethlehem. When they complained that it wasn't like the Holy Land they had seen in their Sunday-school picture books, their vicar told them that, in the time of Jesus, the traders concentrated on making money, and there was a soldier on every street. For the second part of the pilgrimage, however, they moved to Tiberias on the shore of Lake Galilee, and were struck by the contrast. They climbed the hill where Jesus preached the Sermon on the Mount, and admired the lilies of the field. They crossed the lake in a boat and ate a meal of St Peter's fish. 'This,' they said to each other, 'this is the real Holy Land as we imagined it.' On the Sunday morning they sat on the beach for an informal service of breaking of bread. Then they sang 'Dear Lord and Father of mankind', with the lines,

> O Sabbath rest by Galilee,
> O calm of hills above,

Where Jesus knelt to share with thee
The silence of eternity,
Interpreted by love.

Most of the group were in tears.

## Harp Lake

Although the Gospels grandly call it the Sea of Galilee, Lake Galilee's only nine miles long and five miles wide. The River Jordan flows into it in the north and out again in the south, so it's a freshwater lake, with many fish. If you climb the hills to east or west and look down on it, its shape resembles that of a harp, so its old name was Harp Lake, or Chinnereth in Hebrew. At other times it was called after the name of one of the towns on its shore, Lake Genessareth or Lake Tiberias. Galilee's the name of the region, and means 'a circle'.

## Galilee of the Gentiles

It's always been a fertile area. The Israelites settled mainly in the hills, while the Canaanites farmed the rich agricultural valleys at least until the time of King David. It was the first part of Israelite territory to be conquered by the Assyrian invaders. Because so many different races of non-Jewish inhabitants settled there, Isaiah called it 'Land of Zebulun, land of Naphtali, on the Way of the Sea, across the Jordan, Galilee of the Gentiles'. Multiracial Galilee didn't adopt the Jewish religion again until six hundred years later, in 103 BC. By that time, many of them had adopted the Greek way of life, like most of the Middle East.

## Bethsaida

Andrew had a Greek name; his brother Simon's name was Jewish. They settled in Capernaum, on the lakeshore west of where the River Jordan enters the lake; but they were born in Bethsaida Julias, east of the river mouth, in the area called the Ten Towns, or Decapolis.

## The Way of the Sea

A great highway ran along the shoreline here. No, it wasn't a motorway covered in tarmac, but the dust and stones were trodden by the feet of hundreds of merchants and camels who daily passed to and fro. They travelled between the port of Alexandria, on the River Nile in Egypt, and Damascus, the gateway to the east. The fishermen of Galilee weren't provincial rustics; they lived on a great trade route, spoke several languages for business purposes, and exported barrels full of salt fish to be sold in the market in Rome.

## Fishing

Andrew and Simon Peter were fishermen, owning their own boat. Fish were caught by trawling, by the casting net, by a net hanging from floats on the surface, or by rod and line. You could describe these two as businessmen in a small way, and it was a real sacrifice when they gave away their capital to follow Jesus.

## A cosmopolitan faith

So when we commemorate St Andrew, Peter or any other of the Twelve, we should think of Galilee where they came from, as did Jesus of Nazareth. The 'sabbath rest by Galilee' may have been a necessary time of calm, which prepared them for the struggle of living as a disciple. We all need periods of peace and reflection. But their cosmopolitan background was also important, enabling them to carry the Christian faith of inter-racial tolerance and reconciliation all the way across the Roman Empire.

### Suggested hymns

*Dear Lord and Father of mankind; I danced in the morning; Jesus calls us, o'er the tumult; Will you come and follow me?*

# Sermon for Harvest Festival

**Ethical Eating**   Deut. 26:1–11 First fruits; Ps. 100 Enter his gates with thanks; Phil. 4:4–9 Rejoice! *or* Rev. 14:14–18 The harvest of the wicked; John 6:25–35 Work for the food that lasts

> *'For the Lord is gracious; his steadfast love is everlasting, and his faithfulness endures from generation to generation.' Psalm 100:4 (Common Worship)*

## Harvest celebrations

It was the Reverend R. S. Hawker, the eccentric vicar of Morwenstow in Cornwall, who introduced the Harvest Festival, as we know it, there in 1843. It's an opportunity to decorate the church with flowers, fruit and vegetables; some churches display a sheaf of wheat. We sing with gusto the harvest hymns. The popularity of Harvest Festival spread like wildfire, so a mere twenty years later the Church of England issued a form of service. Even in city parishes where few of the congregation had ever seen wheat growing, Harvest became an essential landmark in the Church's year; from 1928 the prayer books in several countries included a special Collect, Epistle and Gospel. In the USA, the equivalent celebration's Thanksgiving Day, on the fourth Thursday in November, commemorating the first harvest gathered by the Pilgrim Fathers in 1621; in Canada, Thanksgiving Day's the second Monday in October.

## Giving thanks

We gather in church at Harvest time to thank God for giving growth to the crops which yield us our food. We acknowledge our total dependence on God's mercy, without which we'd starve. Even those who aren't yet certain whether or not they believe in God come to Harvest Festival because they feel deep down that we're not entirely self-reliant. The problem comes when we have a poor harvest. Why's God not giving us this year what he gave us before? Is he punishing us for something? And what about the people who are starving in Africa and Asia; is God less merciful to them than he is to us? While acknowledging God's part in the harvest, we need to look again at our own responsibility.

## Changing agriculture

For the pattern of harvest is changing, and we must do something about it. When Harvest Festival first became popular, most of the population lived in the country. Now the agricultural labour force has shrunk to less than less than 1 per cent of the British population; many people in cities have no idea how their food is grown. Agricultural machinery today's designed for prairies, so that more than 80 per cent of Britain's ancient hedgerows have been torn down. Hence most of the wild birds and wildflowers, and country people too, have deserted the countryside. Heavy machines compact the soil, making it less fertile, and contributing to flash floods in some places. The industrializing of agriculture in the developed world has also impoverished peasant farmers in the developing nations, by driving down food prices so that they can hardly make a living. Moreover the battery hens and animals which seldom see the daylight suffer because of our insistence on food which is cheap and plentiful. You and I could do something about this, if we wanted.

## Global warming

Another problem that our eating habits are contributing to is global warming. Not long ago we all ate simple foods grown near to where we lived. So much of our food is now flown in from exotic places that the carbon footprint's destroying the environment. We sing psalms at harvest time to God whose 'steadfast love . . . endures from generation to generation'. If God loves the next generation, how dare we change his creation into a place where our children won't find enough to eat?

## What to do

Yet these changes are within our control. At harvest time, we should resolve to look more carefully at the labels on the food we buy. Why buy imported food when it could be grown locally? Why buy from factory farms when we could get better produce from a small farmer? How many animals have suffered to provide the meat and eggs on our table? How dare we buy cheap food, when paying a little more for fair-trade produce would keep dozens of people, who are needier than we are, above starvation level? Otherwise, our shopping and eating habits could lead to poor harvests for future generations, however bountiful God tries to be.

## A moral issue

Food's a profoundly moral issue, and has always been at the heart of our religion. In thanking God for the bread and wine used in our worship, we hold a weekly harvest festival, and remember our interconnectedness with nature. God's been very generous to us. We need to look at the ways in which we help him or hinder him as he tries to be equally generous to others.

### All-age worship

*Make sticky labels to put on the harvest produce, with 'Grown within 50 miles'; 'Fairly traded'; 'No animals suffered to produce this', or symbols which younger children can draw.*

### Suggested hymns

*Above the moon, earth rises; Fear not, rejoice and be glad; We plough the fields and scatter; You shall go out with joy.*

## Sermon for a Wedding
### The Wedding Ring    Mark 10:2–9

> '[Jesus said,] "From the beginning of creation, 'God made them male and female.' 'For this reason a man shall leave his father and mother and be joined to his wife, and the two shall become one flesh.' So they are no longer two, but one flesh. Therefore what God has joined together, let no one separate."' Mark 10:6–9

### Jesus's teaching

Those words from St Mark's Gospel are quite difficult to apply in the modern world. The principle that Jesus laid down is clear: marriage is meant to be for life. But first you have to remember that those words were spoken by Jesus, who was a Jew, two thousand years ago in Israel. Under the Jewish law, a wife couldn't divorce her husband. But a husband could very easily divorce his wife: all he had to do was call two witnesses to hear him say, 'She burnt my lunch! I divorce her!' Then she was out on her ear. There was no social security; she'd either starve, or suffer 'a fate worse than death', as people used to say. So Jesus was protecting women when he said those words, emphasizing the permanence of the marriage vows.

## Today

How, then, do we apply them to the totally different society of today? The first thing to say is that Jesus wouldn't want anyone who's been divorced to go round with a burden of guilt. The past is past, then was then, and now is now. If anyone feels that they've been less than perfectly loving in their life, they should confess it to Jesus, and he'll forgive you, and then you can forget it. The important thing is to build for the future, for your own future, and for the future of your former family, and of any new family you may have formed.

## People marrying

But the couple who are marrying today don't want to hear about divorce at their wedding service, and quite rightly so. They intend their marriage to be a lifelong relationship, and the vows they take today are meant to be for ever. Which is exactly the point that Jesus made. There are many people here today who'll tell you that it's possible to remain happily married to the same partner all your life. Possible, but not easy! A couple recently celebrated their eightieth wedding anniversary, the first couple to have ever done so – they were both over 100, of course. They were asked the inevitable question, 'What's the secret of staying happily married for so long?' They said, 'We can answer that in two words: "Yes, dear"!'

## The secret

Yes, it's a joke, but it enshrines an important truth. The secret of happy marriage is willingness to give way. You can't be happy together if either expects always to have their own way. There has to be give and take; and that doesn't mean 'You give and I take'! A lasting marriage depends on both partners being equally willing to make sacrifices. Their life's priority must become making the other happy. Human nature being what it is, selfishness can easily slip in unnoticed, and then neither of you is contented. So lifelong marriage takes hard work, and constant vigilance over your own words and deeds. But you know that already.

### The wedding ring

In fact, you've declared your intention of staying together by the symbol of the wedding ring. A ring has no beginning and no end, it just goes on and on. So it's a symbol of eternity. The wedding ring's usually made of gold, which is a precious metal. So it says that your love is very precious to you. You're not going to let anyone else come between you, nor are you going to allow your own selfishness to wreck a happy relationship of equality and mutual self-sacrifice. Your vows are meant to last for ever. If there are difficulties, you intend to seek help and counselling; you won't lightly take the first step towards ending the relationship, so long as there's any hope of making a go of it.

### God's help

Isn't that making impossible demands on a couple? Yes, if it was left to them to do on their own, it would be. But the ring's a symbol of eternity, so it's also a symbol of God. Jesus said that God has joined you together; so God will help you stay together. He'll open your eyes to your own sinfulness, and then forgive your mistakes as soon as you confess them. God loves you; so God will pour his love into the hearts of each of you until it overflows in love for each other. 'The family that prays together stays together', because if you make God the centre of your relationship, God's love will be the glue that stops you falling apart, now and into eternity.

### *Suggested hymns*

*Jesus, Lord, we pray, be our guest today; Love divine, all loves excelling; Morning has broken; Thine forever, God of love.*

## Sermon for a Baptism or Christening
### We are Being Transformed

> *'All of us . . . are being transformed into the same image from one degree of glory to another.' 2 Corinthians 3:18*

### A railway carriage

An absent-minded vicar was reading his newspaper in a railway carriage as it drew into a station. As they stopped at the platform,

the train manager said loudly over the loudspeakers, 'All change!'
Startled from his meditations, the vicar looked up at the other
passengers and said, 'Yes, they do, don't they?' His fellow travellers
were astonished at what seemed a completely illogical remark. But
to the vicar it made perfect sense. He'd just been reading about the
constant changes in national politics and world affairs which the
newspapers report. Which led him to think about some of the people who attended his church, and how they'd grown and matured
in the years he'd known them. Above all, he recognized that we're
all changing.

## All change

Perhaps you hadn't noticed that. Did you think that you're the
same person today that you were a few years ago? It would be
very disappointing if you were. I hope you've learnt lessons from
your mistakes, and have been changed into a better person than
you were then. Sometimes the changes are so slow that you hardly
notice them. But everybody, without exception, is changing all the
time. As the train manager said, 'All change!'

## Transformed

St Paul wrote to his friends in the Greek city of Corinth that 'All
of us are being transformed.' He may have been thinking about
how the disciples saw Jesus transfigured on the mountain top. They
realized that Jesus was what we're meant to be. Jesus is our pattern
of love and unselfishness. In that way, he is the image of God his
Father, who's got 'Unselfish Love' written all through him, like
Blackpool rock! God created all of us to be unselfish and loving,
like Jesus was, only we haven't got there yet. God's still working on
us, changing us every day until we become what he wants us to be.
It's a process, and a slow one. God hasn't finished with us yet. He's
working away on us, scrubbing away the dirt and grime which are
covering up our inner beauty, and he won't finish transforming us
till we're ready to live with him for ever in heaven.

## The transformation scene

When the Bible says we're being transformed, it sounds like the
Transformation Scene at a pantomime, where the pumpkin's magi-
cally transformed into a coach, and the white mice into horses. And

it really is magic, when you think about it, that you and I should be changed into perfect human beings fit to live with God. The process lasts a lifetime, and it begins at baptism.

## Washing

When a small boy comes indoors from playing outside, he has a good scrub, and we say he's been transformed into a civilized human being at last. God gave us baptism as a ritual symbol of washing us clean, but the cleansing process lasts all our life long. Naturally it begins with the parents teaching their child to talk and to think. Godparents are chosen to help the parents to bring the child up as a Christian. They promise to teach their godchild about Jesus, teach them to pray, and to be loving and kind. They promise to pray for the child, bring the children with them to church and Sunday school, and eventually encourage them to take for themselves the promises that we've made on their behalf, at a confirmation service. The congregation promise to support you in this, so that all of us together help God in the transformation of this baby into the sort of person God wishes.

## From glory to glory

Maybe you think the baby's perfect already, and you don't want any changes. Yes, I agree, there's something glorious about being a baby. But just imagine the potential. With your help, God can transform this baby into a glorious toddler, and then a glorious teenager and a glorious adult. That doesn't mean that anyone has to fit into a mould; God rejoices that we're all different. Perfection only comes many years from now, when God finally changes the adult human being into a person fit for heaven. Then all the dirt and grime of sin will finally be washed away, revealing the image of God which has been growing in this child of God ever since their baptism. Remember what St Paul said: 'All of us . . . are being transformed into the same image from one degree of glory to another.'

## Suggested hymns

*Awake, my soul, and with the sun; From glory to glory advancing; O Jesus, I have promised; Wind, wind, blow on me.*

# Sermon for a Funeral or Memorial Service
## How to Grieve   John 11:17–27

*'Jesus wept.' John 11:35*

### Everybody's different

'Jesus wept.' It's the shortest verse in the Bible; and it teaches us the important lesson that grief in bereavement is normal. Well, of course it is. But how often have you heard people say, either 'Don't cry, dear,' or else, 'You really ought to let yourself go more.' The fact is, everybody grieves in their own way, and everybody's different.

### Friends of Jesus

You've only to look at the friends of Jesus in the story I've just read from the Gospel of John. Jesus had three friends in the village of Bethany; he often stayed in their house when he was visiting Jerusalem. Then Lazarus died, and his two sisters were plunged into grief. But Martha and Mary were as different as chalk from cheese. On another occasion when Jesus was eating a meal at their house, Martha complained that she was left to do all the housework while Mary sat listening to Jesus. Jesus wasn't unsympathetic to Martha, but he tried to help her sympathize with her sister, and respect the differences between them. When Lazarus died, Jesus didn't arrive until the funeral was over. As soon as she heard he was on his way, Martha didn't even wait for him to reach their house, but stormed out to meet him on the road.

### Anger

There, in full view of everybody, she gave Jesus a telling off. She was very angry with him. 'If you'd been here,' she shouted, 'my brother wouldn't have died!' Well, at least that showed a remarkable faith; she believed that Jesus, who'd healed so many people, could have healed whatever sickness it was that killed Lazarus. So why didn't he? She felt exactly as many people do, when they pray for someone who's sick, and the patient dies. Doesn't Jesus answer prayers? Jesus said to her, 'Your brother will rise again.' 'Yes,' grumbled Martha, 'but not until Judgement Day, at the end of the world.' Jesus tried to show her that life after death isn't limited by time considerations, because eternity's one great timeless 'now'. Jesus said to Martha, '*I am* the resurrection and the life. Those who believe in me, even though they die, will live, and everyone who lives and believes in me will never die.' It's perfectly natural to be angry when you lose somebody you love. But the anger's usually directed against the wrong target. People get angry with the doctors, or the government, or the person who's died, or themselves. The one they should be angry with is God. God's big enough to accept your anger, without loving you any the less because you swear at him.

## Tears

After Martha'd finished with Jesus, she returned to their home in Bethany and told her sister that Jesus was asking for her. Mary went out to meet Jesus; she wasn't angry, like her sister Martha; she was in floods of tears. 'When Jesus saw her weeping,' says the Gospel, 'and the Jews who came with her also weeping, he was greatly disturbed in spirit and deeply moved.' Tears are also a natural response to the deep emotions that come with bereavement. But they come at different stages of the grief process. For some, like Mary, heartbreak's an immediate reaction. Nobody who hasn't experienced it can understand how some souls are torn apart by the loss of one they love. Saying 'Don't cry' is a waste of time; if someone needs to cry they can't help themselves. But for others, tears won't come when they're bidden. Later, sometimes much later, a sudden memory of the one they love will set them off. That too is healthy: you can't bottle up your emotions for ever; but different people express them in different ways.

## Jesus

Just look at Jesus. He was full of faith and trust in our heavenly Father, and hope for life after death. 'I am the resurrection and the life,' he said. 'Those who believe in me, even though they die, will live, and everyone who lives and believes in me will never die.' To someone with a deep faith, death isn't an end, but the beginning of a new and better life. For the person who dies it's not a tragedy but a blessing. It's for the people who are left behind that we should weep. And 'Jesus wept'. For Martha and Mary, not for Lazarus. Even for those who believe in heaven, tears are a natural response to feelings too deep for words.

## Funerals

Funerals are a time when we gather to comfort and support each other; sometimes to renew relationships which had been allowed to grow a bit rusty. But you mustn't try to fit others into your own mould. God's made us all different, and we praise him by rejoicing in the diversity of human nature, and the unique way each person responds to grief.

### Suggested hymns

*Jesus lives! Thy terrors now; Soon and very soon; The Lord's my Shepherd, I'll not want; Thine be the glory, risen, conquering Son.*

# Scripture Index to Sermon Texts

| | ch | v | page | | ch | v | page |
|---|---|---|---|---|---|---|---|
| Gen. | 2 | 8 | 60 | Daniel | 7 | 13 | 336 |
| | 9 | 1 | 163 | Joel | 3 | 14 | 4 |
| | 24 | 15 | 173 | Micah | 4 | 3 | 275 |
| | 41 | 15–16 | 194 | Zeph. | 3 | 14 | 319 |
| | 50 | 9–11 | 203 | | 3 | 15 | 142 |
| Ex. | 33 | 11 | 153 | Zeph. | 3 | 19 | 11 |
| Num. | 9 | 15 | 53 | Matt. | 1 | 19 | 306 |
| 1 Sam. | 8 | 18 | 280 | | 1 | 23 | 18 |
| Ezra | 1 | 2 | 237 | | 4 | 18 | 359 |
| Neh. | 8 | 18, 17 | 256 | | 5 | 1–3 | 352 |
| Ps. | 16 | 5 | 301 | | 6 | 30 | 63 |
| | 22 | 27 | 341 | | 10 | 16 | 303 |
| | 24 | 7 | 298 | | 16 | 17–18 | 329 |
| | 29 | 1 | 158 | | 22 | 42 | 260 |
| | 46 | 10 | 43 | | 28 | 20 | 144 |
| | 69 | 10 | 103 | Mark | 4 | 33–34 | 168 |
| | 72 | 11 | 291 | | 6 | 1–5 | 178 |
| | 77 | 11 | 189 | | 6 | 17 | 183 |
| | 96 | 1 | 21 | | 10 | 6–9 | 364 |
| | 98 | 1 | 272 | | 13 | 13 | 132 |
| | 100 | 4 | 362 | | 16 | 3–4 | 137 |
| | 103 | 20 | 345 | Luke | 1 | 14–15 | 9 |
| | 118 | 17 | 115 | | 1 | 37 | 308 |
| | 119 | 72 | 343 | | 1 | 53 | 16 |
| Isa. | 1 | 18 | 265 | | 1 | 76–77 | 327 |
| | 11 | 10 | 208 | | 1 | 78–79 | 13 |
| | 30 | 21 | 218 | | 1 | 79 | 6 |
| | 35 | 4 | 347 | | 2 | 8 | 24 |
| | 38 | 19 | 127 | | 2 | 14 | 51 |
| | 53 | 5 | 110 | | 2 | 21 | 289 |
| | 58 | 6 | 71 | | 3 | 15 | 41 |
| | 65 | 17 | 29 | | 4 | 1–2 | 74 |
| Jer. | 31 | 15 | 286 | | 7 | 15–16 | 161 |
| Ezek. | 44 | 4 | 56 | | 8 | 29 | 171 |

| | ch | v | page | | ch | v | page |
|---|---|---|---|---|---|---|---|
| | 9 | 28 | 66 | | 16 | 13–15 | 156 |
| | 10 | 38–39 | 191 | | 17 | 20 | 294 |
| | 11 | 9–10 | 196 | | 17 | 20–21 | 146 |
| | 12 | 20 | 201 | | 20 | 16 | 334 |
| | 12 | 51 | 210 | | 20 | 25 | 331 |
| | 13 | 1–2 | 84 | | 20 | 27 | 118 |
| | 13 | 34 | 79 | | 20 | 29 | 120 |
| | 14 | 11 | 220 | | 21 | 11 | 125 |
| | 14 | 31–32 | 82 | | 21 | 25 | 34 |
| | 15 | 3–4 | 230 | Acts | 1 | 13 | 350 |
| Luke | 15 | 18–19 | 90 | | 1 | 16–18 | 315 |
| | 16 | 31 | 239 | Acts | 2 | 1–4 | 151 |
| | 17 | 6 | 244 | | 7 | 48 | 58 |
| | 17 | 14 | 248 | | 7 | 56 | 284 |
| | 18 | 9 | 77 | | 9 | 18 | 296 |
| | 20 | 38 | 267 | | 12 | 1–2 | 199 |
| | 22 | 1–2 | 98 | Rom. | 8 | 39 | 270 |
| | 22 | 29–30 | 338 | 1 Cor. | 11 | 23–24 | 108 |
| | 22 | 42 | 101 | 2 Cor. | 3 | 18 | 366 |
| | 23 | 42 | 277 | Gal. | 2 | 16 | 166 |
| | 24 | 5 | 113 | | 4 | 4–5 | 213 |
| | 24 | 35 | 122 | | 5 | 22–23 | 176 |
| John | 1 | 14 | 26 | | 6 | 14 | 181 |
| | 1 | 29 | 87 | Eph. | 1 | 7–8 | 36 |
| | 2 | 11 | 46 | | 1 | 17–18 | 263 |
| | 3 | 29 | 222 | | 4 | 12–13 | 148 |
| | 5 | 6 | 139 | | 4 | 14–16 | 48 |
| | 5 | 25 | 354 | Col. | 1 | 7 | 187 |
| | 5 | 39–40 | 227 | | 3 | 12 | 93 |
| | 6 | 54 | 322 | | 3 | 16 | 31 |
| | 6 | 63 | 232 | 1 Tim. | 2 | 1–2 | 234 |
| | 8 | 32 | 241 | 2 Tim. | 3 | 15–16 | 253 |
| | 9 | 7 | 246 | | 4 | 7–8 | 258 |
| | 10 | 30 | 130 | Philemon | | 15–16 | 225 |
| | 11 | 35 | 369 | Heb. | 9 | 22 | 106 |
| | 12 | 2 | 96 | | 11 | 8 | 206 |
| | 12 | 32 | 68 | | 12 | 22, 24 | 215 |
| | 13 | 34–35 | 134 | 1 John | 4 | 11 | 38 |
| | 14 | 8–9 | 313 | Rev. | 6 | 2 | 1 |
| | 15 | 12–13 | 324 | | 12 | 7 | 310 |
| | 15 | 14 | 251 | | 19 | 6–7 | 357 |

# Subject Index

Entries in *italics* are sermon titles

*153 fish* 125
Abraham 141, 174–5, 206, 240
ACTS of prayer 198
Addiction 72, 140, 232
*Advertising Jesus* 70
*Aelred* 251–3
*Afterlife* 202, 239, 263–4
*AIDS* 3, 11–13
*Any dream will do* 194–6
Apocryphal Gospels 35
Army-ants 219
Artist, God as 64–5
Ascension 70, 142, 144–5
Assumption of the Virgin
    Mary 213
Atheists 54, 121, 234, 275, 333
Augustine of Hippo, St 56, 96, 156

*Banknote* 322
Baptism 41, 328, 366
*Barnabas the martyr* 324
Beatific vision 45
*Beatitudes* 352
*Believe and you'll achieve* 244
*Benedictus* 7, 13
Bereavement 142–3, 369–70
*Best Man* 222
Bethesda 140
Bible 32–5, 61, 228–31, 254
Blind 212, 247–8, 297
*Blood* 99, 106, 217, 265–7, 323
*Boasting* 181
Bodmer, Prof. Sir Walter 301
Boundaries 256–7
Bride of Christ 224

British Library 34
Buddhism 135, 211, 327

Cambodia 135
Carbon emissions 3, 17, 164
Carols 22
Celebrities 153
Cellophane® 48, 51–3
*Celtic Fringe* 301
*Charles, King and Martyr* 280
Children 9–10, 256, 286–8, 318
Chinese evangelist 289
Choral rehearsal 158
Church unity 126, 130, 147, 294
Churchgoing 53, 58, 60, 273
Clapham Sect 226
*Clearly displayed* 51
Climate change 3
Colossians 33
Compass 206
*Compostella* 199
Computer, God as a 191
Conscience 101, 207, 281
Constantine, Emperor 341
*Contemplation* 43
*Contemporary language* 267
*Contempt* 77
Corncrake 345
Cost of Discipleship 83, 345
Covenant 216–7, 237–8, 255
Creation 29, 54, 61, 64, 363
*Cuckolded?* 306
Cultures 293, 304–5

Daniel 255, 285, 337
*David's Son* 260

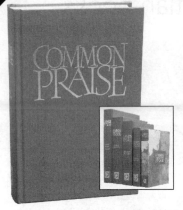

Death 84, 143, 179, 262, 287, 355
Death row 327
Deliver us 79
Dividing families 210
Do not fear! 347
Do you want to change? 139
Does religion cause wars? 275
Down to earth 28, 67, 179

Easter eggs 116
Ecology 163
Einstein, Albert 264, 309
Elgar, Sir Edward 158, 319, 352
Elijah 67, 161–3
Emotions 103, 124, 272–4, 370
Empress Helena 341
Ensign for the nations 208
Environment 62, 164, 219, 363
Ephesians 37, 49, 149
Epidemic 3, 11
Eternal life 129, 264
Ethical eating 363
Every-member ministry 187
Existence of God 54, 332–3
Ezra 237, 257

Facing our inner demons 171
Failure is success 179
Fair trade 3, 227, 363
Faith 118, 120–3, 130, 157
Faith is the compass 206
Faith transcends knowledge 156
Family 211
Famine 3, 18
Fatherhood of God 80
Fear 242, 347
Feed, force, fascinate them 75
Fiction 26, 169, 230–1, 311
Filled with expectation 41
Filling the hungry 16
Fire in the farmyard 79
First-fruits of God's harvest 151
Forgive us 90
Forgiveness 3, 92
Four horsemen 1, 7
Friends of God 44, 183, 251, 369
Fruit of the Spirit 176, 270

Galatians 166
Galilee 359
Garden of Eden 4, 29, 60
Generosity 84, 125, 201
Gentiles 210, 293, 360
Gethsemane 76, 97, 101
Give and take 365
Give unto the Lord 158
Global warming 3, 17, 164, 363
God is in your midst 142
God knows you by name 334
God speaks face to face 153
God the storyteller 230
God with a mission 338
God's will 85, 96, 207, 281
Grace 38, 168, 198, 257, 273
Grief 287–8, 369
Guilt 52, 106, 111, 168, 226

Hallowed be thy name 289
Hawker, Revd R. S. 362
Heavenly worship 345, 238
Heavens opened 285
Hellfire 240
Herod Mob 183
His glory is his love 56
Holy Spirit 75, 142, 151–5, 176
Honouring mothers 213
Hope 42, 218, 349
How to grieve 369
How to hug 196
How to pray 196
Human biodiversity 191
Humble goodness 220
Hymns xviii

I finished the race 258
I nearly died 127
Immigrants 226
Inner clothing 94
Institutions 329
Interpreting Scripture 229, 241
Is it true, kind, necessary? 49

Jesus and Elijah 161
Jesus 18, 255
Judas Iscariot 98, 315

375

Judgement 2–3
Judging others 78

King loved a peasant girl 26
King, Martin Luther 25
Kingdom of God 10, 47, 85, 147, 339
*Kings bow down* 291

*Lamb of God* 87
Law 166, 177, 181, 211, 228, 238, 256
Lazarus 97, 129, 240, 369
*Lead us not* 74
*Leap of faith* 118
*Learning from nature* 63
Left everything 344
Legion 172
*Lepers* 248
Letters of St John 39
Light-bulb jokes 139
*Limits of science* 331
Lord's Prayer 73, 74, 80, 85, 90, 96, 290
Lost sheep 230
*Love and acceptance* 134
Love 94, 68, 134
*Love of God in Christ* 270

Maccabees 111, 283, 350
Magnificat 16, 273, 319
Martha and Mary 97, 191, 369
Martyrs 68, 280, 283, 284, 326, 358
*Maturity* 148
*Mediator* 215
Meditation 44
*Memory* 189
Messiah 41, 209, 261–2, 292
Miracles 46, 137, 162
*Miserable or happy Lent?* 71
Missionaries 131, 133, 248, 304
Motherhood of God 64, 80
Mothers 56, 93, 213
*Mountain-top experiences* 66
Moving mountains 245
Music 272, 345

*Music Makers* 319
*My native land* 357
*Myths and heroes* 310

Name 289, 334
National pride 357
*New life* 115
*New-found happiness* 21
*No indispensable man* 313
*Nothing's impossible* 308

Oberammergau 106
*Odessa* 122
One flesh 130
*One, holy, catholic* 130
*Open the gates* 298

Parables 91, 169, 230
Paradise 62, 278
Paralysed man 139
*Party clothes* 93
*Passion* 103
*Passover Plot* 98
*Paul's priorities* 296
Peace 6, 62, 275
*People like us* 24
Perseverance 133
Pharisee 77, 147, 247, 261
*Politics and prayer* 234
Pontius Pilate 85, 100, 106
*Pool which means 'sent'* 246
*Power of music* 272
Prayer 43, 59, 73, 96, 155, 197, 234
Prempeh 277
Profumo, John 36
Progressive revelation 276
Prophets 29, 285
Punishment 12, 186, 256
*Pyrrhic victory* 82

Racism 238
*Reality* 284
Reason 26, 104–5, 114, 124, 156–7, 207, 273
*Rebecca* 173
Reconciliation 91–2, 293
*Recreation* 29

*Redemption* 36
*Rejoicing in the law* 256
Relationships 118, 265
Repentance 41, 91, 267, 328
Resurrection 20, 113, 137, 162, 240, 334, 370
Retirement benefits 259
*Riches* 343
*Rigoletto* 110
Romans, Paul's Letter to 270

*Sacrament meeting all needs* 108
Sacrifice 87, 111
Sadducees 268
Saints 131, 312
*Sat-nav* 218
Science 114, 308, 331
*Search the Scriptures* 227
*Secularism* 120
Seek and you will find 115, 116
Self 73, 111, 171, 232, 242
Sermon on the Mount 310
Servant Songs 111
*Signs* 46
Sin 86, 135, 147, 243
*Sins as scarlet* 265
*Slavery* 38, 225
Social justice 16, 264
*Son of Man* 336
Spiritual gifts 94, 176
*Splendid funeral* 203
*St Nicholas* 9
*Staying-power* 132
Stewardship 202
Stilling the storm 159
Stories 168, 230
Substitutes 110
*Suffering and sin* 84
Suffering 297
*Suicide* 315

Tax-collector 77, 147, 343
Telephone helplines 318
Temple 59, 238
Temptation 74, 172, 182

Ten Commandments 228
Terrorism 3, 7, 350
*That the world may believe* 146
*That they may be one* 294
Tolerance 78, 193, 361
*Too many books* 34
*Transcendence* 53
*Truly human* 26
Truth 91, 275, 278
*Truth will make you free* 241
*Truthfulness* 48

*Unchanging love* 354
*Unseen presence* 144

Valentine, St 68
*Valley of Decision* 4
Value 322
*Virtuous circle* 38
Vladimir, Prince of Russia 346
*Vulnerability* 178

War 2, 6
*Way of peace* 6
*We are being transformed* 366
Wedding banquet 46, 52
*Wedding ring* 364
Wesley, John 124, 202
*Whatever next?* 263
*When children die* 286
*When I am lifted up* 68
*When you are king* 277
*Who moved the stone?* 137
*Who was Jesus?* 18
*Why go to church?* 58
*Why seek the living among the dead?* 113
Wilberforce, William 226
*Without loss of life* 303
*Word of Christ* 31
*Word of God* 253

*You can't reason with them* 232

Zeal for your house 103
*Zealot terrorists* 8, 350

# Author Index

ACTON, Lord John, 'Power tends to corrupt' 235
ANON., *The Acts of Barnabas* 325
ANON., 'An epistle is the wife of an apostle' 39
ANON., 'As I am loved, so shall I love' 39
ANON., 'The family that prays together' 366
ANON., *The Golden Legend* 311
ANON., 'I want to be a Christian inna my heart' 177
ANON., *No indispensable man* 313
ANON., 'A pig in a poke' 51
ANON., *Teamwork* 188
ANON., 'Were you there when they crucified my Lord?' 114
ARMSTRONG, Sir Robert 'Economical with the truth' 50
AUSTEN, Jane, *Emma* 216

BALDWIN, Stanley, 'Birds, wild flowers, and Prime Ministers' 235
BENCHLEY, Richard, 'A man died laughing' 127
BENCHLEY, Richard, 'Opera is where a guy gets stabbed' 127
BLAKE, William, 'Jerusalem' 88, 105
BLAKE, William, 'The Lamb' 88
BLAKE, William, 'The Tiger' 88
BOOK OF COMMON PRAYER, The Invention of the Cross 342
BUNYAN, John, 'And especially my poor blind child' 212

CARROLL, Lewis, 'It takes all the running' 339
CARROLL, Lewis, 'Six impossible things' 157
CARROLL, Lewis, The passion flower 104
CHURCHILL, Sir Winston, 'To become a politician' 234
CLARKE, Arthur C., '. . . impossible, he is very probably wrong' 308
CLEESE, John, 'Loving your neighbour . . . is impossible' 310
COLLINS, Dr Francis, *The Language of God* 333
CONGREVE, William, *The Mourning Bride* 272
COUNSELL, Michael, 'Human biodiversity' 193
COWPER, William, 'There is a fountain filled with blood' 107
CRASHAW, Richard, 'The conscious water . . . blushed' 48
CRASHAW, Richard, 'Hymn of the Nativity' 95
CURÉ D'ARS, 'I looks at God' 43

DARION, Joe, *Man of La Mancha*, 'Dream the impossible dream' 310
DARWIN, Charles, 'The survival of the fittest' 128
DAWKINS, Prof. Richard *The God Delusion* 83, 275
DESCARTES, Réné, 'I think, therefore I am' 190
DICKENS, Charles, *David Copperfield* 281
DIDACHE, 'As this broken bread . . .' 115
DIX, Dom Gregory, *The Shape of the Liturgy* 108
DOSTOYEVSKY, Fyodor, *The Brothers Karamazov* 287
DURANT, William James, 'That a few simple men . . .' 35

EINSTEIN, Albert, General theory of relativity 264, 309

FLETCHER, Andrew, 'Let me but make the songs of a nation' 273

GELDOF, Bob, 'Do they know it's Christmas?' 16
GINGERICH, Owen, *God's Universe* 332

HALLACK, Cecily, 'The Divine Office of the Kitchen' 332
HAMMERSTEIN, Oscar II, *The Sound of Music* 66
HARDY, Thomas, *The Return of the Native* 358
HARTLEY, L. P., *The Go-Between* 342
HERBERT, George, 'I looks at God' 43
HICK, John, *Evil and the God of Love* 287
HOBBES, Thomas, 'Nasty, brutish and short' 61
HOMER, *The Odyssey* 74
HUGO, Victor, 'Music expresses that which cannot be said' 272

INCHFAWN, Fay, 'The Divine Office of the kitchen' 192

JAMES I, 'Dr Donne's verses' 54
JOHN OF THE CROSS, 'The dark night of the soul' 45
JOHNSON, Dr Samuel, 'Triumph of hope over experience' 42

KELVIN, Lord William, 'Heavier-than-air flying machines are
    impossible' 308
KEN, Thomas, 'Awake, my soul, and with the sun' 37
KIERKEGAARD, Søren, 'The king who loved a peasant girl' 26

LAMARTINE, Alphonse de, 'Liberty! What crimes . . .' 242
LERNER, Alan Jay, *My Fair Lady* 31
LEWIS, C. S., *Christianity* 333
LOVELACE, Richard, 'To Lucasta, going to the wars' 212

MARX, Groucho, 'Marriage is a fine institution' 329
MEDAWAR, Sir Peter, *The Limits of Science* 332
MITCHELL, Margaret, *Gone with the Wind* 343
MONTEFIORE, Rt Revd Hugh, *The Probability of God* 157
MOORE, Clement Clarke, 'The night before Christmas' 9
MORRISON, Frank, *Who Moved the Stone?* 137

NEWMAN, Cardinal John Henry, *The Dream of Gerontius* 352
NEWTON, Sir Isaac, *De Motu Corporum* 308

O'SHAUGHNESSY, Arthur, *The Music Makers* 319
OTTO, Rudolf, *The Idea of the Holy* 353

POPE, Alexander, 'Blessed is the man who expects nothing' 41

RICE, Grantland, 'Only the brave' 260
RICE, Tim, *Joseph and his Amazing Technicolor™ Dreamcoat* 194
ROOSEVELT, President Franklin D., 'He may be a son of a bitch
  . . .' 336
ROOSEVELT, President Franklin D., 'The only thing we have to fear is
  fear' 348
ROOT, George F., 'The battle cry of freedom' 208
RYMAN, Geoff, *The King's Last Song* 135

SACKS, Sir Jonathan, The sat-nav 218
SCHONFIELD, Hugh, *The Passover Plot* 99
SCOTT, Sir Walter, 'The lay of the last minstrel' 357
SEARS, Edmund H., 'It came upon the midnight clear' 63
SELLAR, W. C., and R. J. Yeatman, *1066 and All That* 358
SHACKLETON, Sir Ernest Henry, *The Presence* 144
SHAKESPEARE, William, *Macbeth* 106, 265
SHAKESPEARE, William, *Othello* 324
SOUTH, Dr Robert, 'Snore so loud you will wake the King' 291
SPOONER, Dr William, 'I remember your name . . .' 334

TENNYSON, Alfred, 'Nature red in tooth and claw' 64
TERESA of Avila, St, 'Help me to pray spontaneously' 44
THOMSON, James, 'Here lies a man who never lived' 347
TOLKIEN, J. R. R., *Leaf, by Niggle* 314
TREVOR, William, *Death in Jerusalem* 213
TROLLOPE, Anthony, 'People wishing to be high, must hold their
  monarch high' 291
TUTU, Archbishop Desmond, 'Forgiveness does not mean condoning' 91

URQUHART, Rt Revd David, 'A God with a mission' 340

WESLEY, John, 'Heart strangely warmed' 124
WHITE, T. H., *The Once and Future King* 161
WHITTIER, John Greenleaf, 'Dear Lord and Father of mankind' 359
WILCOX, Ella Wheeler, 'Laugh, and the world laughs with you' 41
WILDE, Oscar, *The Importance of Being Earnest* 49
WILLIAMS, Isaac, 'Be thou my guardian and my guide' 173
WORDSWORTH, Christopher, 'Songs of thankfulness and praise' 52

# Notes

# Notes

# Notes

## Notes

## Notes

# Notes

# Notes

# Notes